MONTGOMERY
as Military Commander

MONTGOMERY

as Military Commander

Ronald Lewin

STEIN AND DAY/*Publishers*/New York

First published in the United States of America in 1971
by Stein and Day/*Publishers*
Copyright © 1971 by Ronald Lewin
Library of Congress Catalog Card No. 77-163496
All rights reserved
Printed in Great Britain
Stein and Day/*Publishers*/7 East 48 Street, New York, N.Y. 10017
ISBN 0-8128-1426-6

Contents

For
a great master-at-arms
Basil Liddell Hart
'the captain who taught generals'

Illustrations

Maps

Acknowledgments

Lord Montgomery kindly consented to talk to me without imposing any conditions with regard to what I might write about him: for this typical courtesy I am deeply grateful.

For conversations, criticism and encouragement I owe many debts: in particular to the late Maj.-Gen. D. R. Bateman, Maj.-Gen. Raymond Briggs, Professor Guy Chapman, the late Gen. Sir Miles Dempsey, Maj.-Gen. Sir Charles Dunphie, Dr Hugh L'Etang, Lieut.-Gen. Sir Geoffrey Evans, Gen. Sir Richard Gale, Frank Gillard, Professor Michael Howard, Lieut.-Gen. Sir William Jackson, Captain Sir Basil Liddell Hart (who shortly before his death was giving to this book his meticulous attention – my special debt to him will be evident from my dedication), Alex Lumsden, Maj. Kenneth Macksey, Brig. C. J. C. Molony, Gen. Sir Richard O'Connor, Brig. Michael Roberts, Col. David Rooke, Marshal of the Royal Air Force Sir John Slessor, Brig. John Stephenson, John Terraine, and Brig. E. T. Williams.

A critical study involves the statement of a point of view. The point of view I present here is entirely my own and does not necessarily associate those who have helped me reach it.

R.L.

The publisher and author are grateful for permission to quote from the following works in copyright: Field Marshal the Viscount Montgomery of Alamein, *Memoirs*, William Collins Sons & Co. Ltd; Chester Wilmot, *The Struggle for Europe*, William Collins Sons & Co. Ltd; Lieutenant General Sir Brian Horrocks, *A Full Life*, William Collins Sons & Co. Ltd; Keith Douglas, *Alamein to Zem Zem*, Faber & Faber Ltd; Siegfried Sassoon, lines from his poem *Song-books of the War*, G. T. Sassoon Esq. and Faber & Faber Ltd; L. F. Ellis, *Victory in the West*, H. M. Stationery Office; *Alamein and the Desert War*, Sphere Books Ltd, in association with *The Sunday Times*.

The publishers and author would also like to thank the Imperial War Museum for all the photographs used in this book and Hutchinson & Co. Ltd for permission to use the maps 'Medenine' and 'The Mareth Line' from K. J. Macksey, *The Crucible of Power*.

Foreword

The first volume in this series was about Napoleon. Montgomery is comparable with Napoleon – with Churchill, with Roosevelt, with Stalin – in so far as the attitudes of those who had to deal with him are polarised in an extreme way, and the emotional intensity reflected in these attitudes has an unusual passion. The military historian's duty is to understand and interpret these passions and polarisations, but not to be affected by them. As a psychiatrist must not become personally involved in the problems of his patients, so the historian must remain clinical and detached. Montgomery presents a special problem for the analyst, because his nature and his record have caused men to become so emotionally committed that what they have felt or written about him has tended to be coloured by an excessive prejudice – whether hostile or favourable. And so, like a Member of Parliament speaking in the House of Commons about a matter of particular private concern, I must 'declare my interest' in writing this book. I served under Montgomery as a regimental officer from the Nile to the Baltic, and I know personally many of the men who have denigrated or applauded him. But, so far as possible, I have sought to discard my own interests, to consider coolly the hot expressions of opinion by those who have taken sides about Montgomery, and to assess him as a military commander in the spirit of von Ranke's dictum that one should write history '*wie es eigentlich gewesen*'. Of course this is an ideal. Still, it is hardly a waste of time to seek to understand a very remarkable British commander by trying to establish 'what actually happened'.

In Montgomery's case polarisations of attitude are especially perplexing, because they occur not only between himself and soldiers and politicians of other nations but also within the military and political hierarchy of his own country: and not only among those who shared active service with him, but also between contemporaries who admire him and younger, post-war historians who have adopted a virulently critical stance. Haig, alive or dead, was exposed to a similar bifurcation of critical regard; there were, and are, those who will always see him as mainly white or mainly black. MacArthur's critics and defenders also diverge like bigots. Such intense and extreme variation in reactions to an individual commander cannot be simply ascribed to a detached, intellectual evaluation of his professional performance: its roots must lie in personal response. Any study of Montgomery as commander must therefore start with an interpretation of Montgomery as a man.

R.L.

The Standing Civil War

'. . . his mind and personality emerge most clearly from his
public acts. His interest was so much concentrated on politics and
government, his private life was so restricted and simple, that he is
revealed most convincingly and fully in his work. . . . If a close
attention to his circumstances, therefore, is needed in order to
help to explain him, it is equally desirable in order not to explain
him away.'

John Ehrman, *The Younger Pitt*

'Modern opinion assigns increasing importance to the influences of early
years on the formation of character. Certainly the whole life of John Churchill
bore the imprint of his youth. That impenetrable reserve under graceful and
courteous manners; that iron parsimony and personal frugality, never relaxed
in the blaze of fortune and abundance; that hatred of waste and improvidence
in all their forms. . . .' Winston Churchill, writing about his ancestor Marlborough with (in view of his own youth) a deep knowledge of what he was
talking about, might well have been adumbrating an analysis of the career
of the most applauded British general of his own lifetime, Bernard Law
Montgomery. It is a curious but not necessarily significant fact that of those
few British commanders who have achieved supreme distinction three of the
most outstanding, Marlborough, Wellington and Montgomery, were unhappy or at least uncertain in their childhood. The fact is not necessarily
significant simply because we do not and cannot know enough that is definite
about the childhood of all the great commanders of history to be able to
correlate military skill and a mismanagement of their early years. But this we
do know. Marlborough's childhood was confused. Wellington's father Lord
Mornington died when he was twelve, and he was brought up by an icy
mother whose final verdict on her son was that he was 'food for powder and
nothing more'. In Montgomery's case the record is more ample and exact
simply because he has himself reviewed his own upbringing with a frankness
so innocent, it might be said, that he has offered to the world a psychologist's
case-history: but with a knowledge of what he has done which may be either
profound or simple-minded, yet is certainly aware. Those who have talked to
him during his latter years will recall his habit of harking back to his boyhood,

B

his family relationships, his unhappiness, and will not forget his perennial quest for the answer to, as he puts it, 'What makes me tick?'

Montgomery's problem was his mother. She was Maud, the daughter of the Victorian Dean Farrar whose *Eric, or Little by Little* was a best-seller and is unreadable now, and whose *Life of Christ* had its successful day. At the age of sixteen she married her father's thirty-four-year-old curate, Henry Montgomery—in Westminster Abbey on 28 July 1881. The future Field Marshal was their fourth child, born on 17 November 1887: and in 1889 they departed to the far side of the globe for Tasmania, where Henry Montgomery became Bishop of Van Diemen's Land.

Montgomery himself quotes Churchill on Marlborough in the second paragraph of his *Memoirs*: 'The stern compression of circumstances, the twinges of adversity, the spur of slights and taunts in early years, are needed to evoke that ruthless fixity of purpose and tenacious mother-wit without which great actions are seldom accomplished.' Montgomery then continues, 'certainly I can say that my own childhood was unhappy'. And this unhappiness he ascribes wholly to his mother—his father, a gentle saint, he worshipped. He generously admits that she had to administer a large household on slender means: but what appears to have been lacking is love. It does not perhaps matter in such a situation if the love is actually there, or latent or absent: what is evident from Montgomery's own account is that he *felt* the lack, felt a sense of perpetual harassment . . . 'go and find out what Bernard is doing and tell him to stop it'. This sense of being outlawed persisted to his eighties, as something keen, real and unforgettable: a sense, too, that it offered a challenge to see whether he could get away with doing the forbidden—if not, he accepted that he must take the ensuing punishment.

It would be inexcusable to embroider these delicate matters too elaborately. Nevertheless, a number of the traits Montgomery manifested as a commander of men in action appear to derive from the circumstances of his childhood. He was trained in austerity. Something of an Ishmaelite, he developed at an early age not only the habit of self-reliance but also the urge to 'try it on'. A deeper analysis might suggest that a deficiency in his temperament, due to this early starvation but happily fulfilled during the period of his marriage, was also met in war by his habit of surrounding himself with a selected group of able but young liaison officers—'the family'. There was something masochistic, too, in the dutiful acceptance of punishment if a misdeed was discovered. Alan Brooke recorded in his Diary during the winter of 39/40 in France that, after Montgomery had got into a scrape and been admonished, 'his reactions to all I said to him on that day were admirable. He thanked me for telling him where he had failed, told me that he knew he was apt to do foolish things and hoped I would always help him in a similar way in the future. What more could I have asked for?' Indeed the relationship between Montgomery and Alan Brooke could well be probed more extensively, for their correspondence, while Alan Brooke was Montgomery's Corps Commander in France and later when he was Chief of the Imperial General Staff, suggests that Montgomery had found here the sure safe substitute for a father he lost in 1932.

There was another famous commander—an Irishman, too—who also endured a mother: T. E. Lawrence. Writing to Bernard Shaw's wife he once said: 'I have a terror of her knowing anything about my feelings or convictions, or way of life. If she knew they would be damaged; violated; no longer mine.' Lawrence described this relationship between himself and his mother as 'the standing civil war'. In a couple of mordant sentences he also said 'it isn't right to cry out to your children for love. They are prevented by the walls of time and function from loving their parents.' Lawrence and Montgomery each spent a lifetime dissecting what their early years had meant to them: but each in his lifetime also achieved *la gloire* and self-consciously revelled in it . . . backing always into the limelight. Why was this?

In a perceptive article in the *American Journal of Psychiatry** Professor John E. Mack makes the profound observation, in an analysis of T. E. Lawrence, that 'as a schoolboy, he later wrote, he dreamed of leading a national movement, and his childhood readings were dominated by medieval heroic romances. Lawrence's struggle for heroism, to give value to the Arab cause, to turn a beleaguered struggle into a glorious triumph may be regarded psychologically as a displacement—an attempt to redeem his fallen self-regard. . . .' Anyone seeking to fathom Montgomery's motivation might well ponder those sentences. They could explain why, after Alamein, his nature was transformed. 'To turn a beleaguered struggle into a glorious triumph may be regarded psychologically as a displacement—an attempt to redeem his fallen self-regard . . .', i.e. to compensate for the humiliations of his childhood.

Montgomery's case was, of course, wholly different from that of Lawrence: there was no question, for example, of a vague feeling, developing into a certainty, that he was illegitimate. But the comparison is instructive in that we have here two men of military distinction both of whose mothers, for entirely different reasons, sought to dominate them during their formative years. The drives within the sub-conscious which lead to a quest for power and achievement are obscure: but insecurity about one's mother appears to be one, and in Montgomery's case one of which he was very much aware. It cannot be discounted.

* February 1969. John E. Mack is Assistant Professor of Psychiatry at the Harvard Medical School, Harvard University.

Out of this crucible of pain there certainly emerged a character. One of its aspects was a capacity for decision. When in *The Path to Leadership* Montgomery wrote about Gustavus Adolphus he was surely defining his own principles of action: 'he was ruthless in weeding out inefficient generals and promoting younger officers; he considered that merit was more likely to win battles than seniority. He ensured that the morale and loyalty of his soldiers did not have to stand undue strains from inferior equipment, hunger, or lack of pay.' The independence of attitude Montgomery's childhood instilled goes far to explain the fact that he is a classic case of the soldier whose mind is strong enough to grasp and maintain the view that 'there are only two answers to most military problems. One of them is wrong.'

Indeed, he elevated simplification of the complicated into a high art. I have talked to many senior officers (not, by any means, all his admirers) and over and over again the point was stressed by his comrades-in-arms that he had a particular gift for reducing an abstruse military problem to the basic and communicable essentials. This is no mean ability in a representative of a type often considered inarticulate and unsophisticated. There *is* a sophistication in simplification—if it entails a reduction of muddle to clear and comprehensible truths. Montgomery was good at this: and his childhood conflicts undoubtedly contributed to his skill. They gave him assurance . . . what Dr. Johnson called 'the first requisite to great undertakings'.

His origins also brought him, as a soldier, another inestimable endowment: he was Irish. In fact the Montgomerys came from Falaise in Normandy in 1066—where in 1945 Montgomery was suitably to destroy the Germans in the battle of the Falaise Gap: and it was in the French village of Sainte Foy de Montgomery that his opponent, Rommel, was to be removed from action by a British fighter plane on 17 July 1944. By the seventeenth century the Montgomery *famille* was establishing itself in Northern Ireland, and in 1773 the successful Londonderry merchant Samuel Montgomery acquired 1,000 acres on the banks of Lough Foyle and created there a home called New Park. Here lay the roots of Montgomery's life. His grandfather Robert, indeed, sought his fortune in India, did well as a Lieutenant-Governor of a province during the Mutiny, and was awarded a Knighthood. And it was at Cawnpore that the future Bishop of Tasmania, Montgomery's father, was born. One of his remarks might well apply to his son. 'I think I may say,' he once observed, 'I was brought up on almost undiluted hell-fire. On the whole such diet has done me immense good.'

Still, the roots were Irish: and this is a reminder of the extraordinary and quite disproportionate contribution made by the people of Ireland to the history of the British Army: not only a matter of famous regiments—the Connaught Rangers, the Inniskillings, the Royal Irish Fusiliers, the Ulster

Rifles and so on, but also by outstanding senior officers who, with family connections in Ireland, have distinguished themselves in service with the regular forces of the British Crown. The list is enormous: but to mention names like those of Alexander, French, Gough, Allenby—not to speak of Wellington—is enough. In this great succession Montgomery was a worthy heir.

Such being the roots, it is essential for an understanding of Montgomery's mentality to know about their transplantation.

There was a gentleman in Abilene, Kansas (a tough town on the cattle trails), called James Butler Hickock, who was appointed Marshal because he was known to have killed forty-three men before his appointment: (he then finished off fifty-seven in the course of it). He was shot in the back after a poker game in 1876, 'only fourteen years', said Alastair Cooke in a broadcast at the time of the death of Montgomery's great coeval, 'before the birth in Denison, Texas, of Dwight David Eisenhower, whose family moved him, when he was a small boy, to Abilene'. Cooke made the sensible point that here was a youth, born and bred in that atmosphere of extreme violence which the American West particularly tended to produce, who emerged 'a generous and sunny soldier, and an incorruptible leader of all manner of men on two continents'. But it should not be thought that of these two leading Allied Commanders in the Second World War Eisenhower was the only one who, in his earlier years, was a frontiersman. Montgomery spent a childhood in Tasmania which, no less than Abilene (Kansas), was by no means remote from the rigours of the outpost. The countryside was convenient and compatible: but recent memories must still have been alive for Montgomery . . . of convicts, and expelled men: Ishmaelites, in whose class his mother had included him. In Tasmania she held him on a very tight rein.

Then, in 1897, his father was called back to London for a Lambeth Conference. In 1901 this disturbance occurred again when Henry Montgomery was asked finally to return to England to supervise the Society for the Propagation of the Gospel in London. To-and-fro and to-and-fro can rarely be good for a young child: what Montgomery carried away from his experience were two qualities which would remain with him through the rest of his life. One was an uncorrupted innocence. This may be a surprising thought to those who have digested Montgomery's doctrine that a commander must be something of a cad—as indeed he must: decisions must be made, decisions sometimes seeming deplorable. But the boy aged nine whose photograph appears in his *Memoirs* was neither a cad nor corrupt. This was an innocent being who, when he was transferred to St. Paul's School (the same buildings in which he effectively planned, from the High Master's study, the invasion of Normandy in 1944), arrived as the son of a saint and a difficult mother. But the qualities of innocence and indeed sweetness of character which came with him to St. Paul's were matched by other and less agreeable characteristics. In his time Montgomery has been ruthless, merciless and unforgiving. This was forecast. Contemporaries at school are sufficiently objective to be able to declare that the Emperor lacks clothes: this they did in the case of Montgomery. He was known as Monkey. 'To hunt this animal' (a St. Paul's journal read) 'is a dangerous undertaking. It runs strongly and hard, straight at you, and never falters, . . . it is advisable that none hunt the monkey.'

The monkey proceeded to Sandhurst in the same spirit in which it had survived St. Paul's—there was a sense of braggadocio: and though Montgomery performed adequately as a cadet, he certainly did not do brilliantly and had some narrow escapes through acts of pure folly. There followed a problem: what regiment to join? The Montgomerys had no means. A stylish regiment (which in pre-1914 days meant the possession of a private income) was out of the question. Montgomery had hoped to make the Indian Army. But in passing out at Sandhurst he came 36th in the list, too low to ensure, or at least make possible, a place in an Indian regiment. 'I was bitterly disappointed,' he says in his *Memoirs*. He opted, alternatively, for the Royal Warwickshire Regiment, a sound and inexpensive county regiment, by whom he was accepted and which he has certainly honoured by his membership—as the Regiment has recognised: he is now its Colonel. He joined the 1st Battalion, at Peshawar on the North-West Frontier of India, in December 1908.

The first distinction he provided for the Regiment was when it went to France as part of the British Expeditionary Force in 1914. In October of that year his battalion put in an attack on a German position. As a young officer Montgomery was in the lead, in an assault on a village called Meteren. During the advance he found himself confronted by an armed German. 'An immediate decision was clearly vital. I hurled myself through the air at the German and kicked him as hard as I could in the lower part of the stomach; the blow was well aimed at a tender spot. I had read much about the value of surprise in war. There is no doubt that the German was surprised and it must have seemed to him a new form of war; he fell to the ground in great pain and I took my first prisoner!' The judgement of Montgomery's contemporaries at St. Paul's was undoubtedly accurate. But during the day's action Montgomery was so severely wounded that a grave was dug for him. His recovery is self-evident: the important fact is that he recovered to accept the award of the DSO—a considerable distinction for a junior officer.

This decoration was earned by Montgomery's general conduct during that day in the first battle of Ypres when with his platoon he captured the village of Meteren by a bayonet charge. But he had displayed his quality as early as 25 August when, two days after leaving England, the Warwicks were plunged into the battle of Le Cateau with disastrous results, and Montgomery left his retreating troops to return and help to bring in a wounded Company Commander. It was not surprising, therefore, that when he got back to hospital in England he found himself a Captain, or that when he was discharged in January 1915 he became, within a month, a brigade-major. He was 27. Montgomery puts the matter with a deceptive modesty: 'I had time for reflection in hospital and came to the conclusion that the old adage was probably correct: the pen was mightier than the sword. I joined the staff.' The modesty is deceptive because on the next page of his *Memoirs* he observes: 'I went through the whole war on the Western Front, except during the period I was in England after being wounded' . . . a period when he helped to train one of the newly formed volunteer divisions.

In fact he was back in France by 1916 as a brigade-major in the 35th Division. Thereafter he rose steadily up the hierarchical ladder—G.S.O.2 to the 33rd Division in 1917; G.S.O.2 to 9 Corps later in the year; G.S.O.1 to the 47th London Division in 1918: on Armistice Day Lieut.-Colonel B. L. Montgomery DSO was still only in his thirtieth year.

With the Army of the Rhine he moved forward to Cologne, and Guy Chapman* has a significant story to tell about this period. Chapman had served on the Western Front since 1915 as an officer in a Fusilier battalion. He was a true veteran. His battalion was now lying near Cologne, in poor shape—a recently departed C.O. of marked inability, and a mixture of old sweats, dreaming of demobilisation, and virgin young drafts. Chapman was Second-in-Command. 'One day', he told me, 'a tough little chap called Montgomery arrived to take command. All we knew was that he'd been wounded and came from the Staff. But,' said Chapman, 'he gripped the battalion immediately. He smartened it up with drills and exercises, and gave the men something to interest them with games and competitions and so on. He was rather like a keen scoutmaster.' Montgomery made himself personally responsible for all training. And it worked. 'But,' said Chapman mournfully, 'for two months I had to sit next to this fellow at dinner, and conversation was impossible: he could only talk about the Army.'

Relief, however, came rapidly. In January 1920 Montgomery reported to the Staff College, Camberley. He had missed a nomination for the first post-war course (being a young officer entirely without strings to pull) and it appeared that he had missed the second. But it is typical of Montgomery's

* Professor G. P. Chapman, OBE, MC, author *inter alia* of *Vain Glory*, the best anthology of writing about the First World War, and *A Passionate Prodigality*, an account of his own experiences on the Western Front which must rank among the best half dozen of its kind.

iron will that, having decided the career of a professional soldier was his *métier* and a Staff College initiation essential, he tackled in person the Commander-in-Chief of the British Army of Occupation in Germany, Sir William Robertson, and successfully persuaded him to obtain a nomination.

What Montgomery did during the First World War is less important than what the War did to him. These were his salad days: but they were also his Road to Damascus. Many officers as young as he were as gallant, and many were even as efficient. But what distinguishes the *bon officier ordinaire*, those who 'are but soldiers for the working day', from the steady, dedicated professionalism of the considerable commander is the capacity of the latter to reflect on past experience, to analyse it, to discard what is obsolete and to generate fresh, constructive ideas. Most of Montgomery's contemporaries were only too happy, in 1919, to forget the last few years as speedily as possible, and even happier was the greater proportion of those remaining in the higher ranks of the peacetime regular army not to think about what had happened, but to get back to 'real soldiering'. That magnificently flexible instrument which Haig had handled so triumphantly during the last victorious months of 1918 quite suddenly became hidebound.

Not so Montgomery. It cannot be too clearly understood that the military philosophy which he put into practice between 1939 and 1945 was formulated as a result of what he observed between 1914 and 1918, and of his subsequent brooding about what had gone wrong and what could be put right. The bases, the major premises of that philosophy, were already established by the time he went up to the Staff College, and thereafter were hardly modified. And they were certainly not 'the staff solution'. Critics of Montgomery's operations in Africa and Europe have an easy way of writing him off as a conservative 'First World War' general. But this is to overlook the fact that the Montgomery who emerged in 1919 was, in terms of the attitudes of the current military Establishment, a rebel, a radical, an uncomfortable man to have about the place, a man with *ideas*. Alan Moorehead makes this point well in his biography, when describing Montgomery's attitude at the Staff College. 'To him and a group of the young veterans who had been in France the curriculum was "all nonsense", entirely out of date, and unrealistic. Montgomery in particular was regarded by the authorities as quarrelsome and argumentative, "a bit of a Bolshevik". He appeared to think he knew better than his instructors or anyone else. The course was of one year. Montgomery and his friends went through it jeering, deriding, arguing— and passed.' And this would be Montgomery's *persona* in the years to come —unorthodox, wilful, originative, imaginative, sometimes wrong-headed, but never conventional or acquiescent.

He might easily have emerged a cynic. Indeed he has said and can say things which imply a deep bitterness of spirit about his first war. As late as June 1969, for example, he remarked in a radio interview that 'I would have said myself that Haig had a complete disregard for human life'. Two factors, I suspect, preserved him: his unshakable religious convictions and his total commitment to his trade. There was so much to do, so much to reform, that the main trend of his mind was positive. Perhaps, too, his years on the staff protected him from the neuroses of the regimental soldier. Somehow, at any rate, he retained a core of tranquillity and a mental balance which, in another war, would prove to be inestimable possessions.

Carnage due to incompetent planning, and low morale due both to unnecessary slaughter and to absenteeism from the Front on the part of senior officers, were the aspects of the '14-'18 war which affected him most profoundly. He was determined that the British soldier should never suffer another Passchendaele. No battle should be launched until calculation and careful preparation (and by that Montgomery would mean *intelligent* preparation) had ensured success.* His soldiers in Africa and Europe sensed this: one of the main reasons for Montgomery's remarkable hold over his troops was their subconscious feeling that they would never be sent into a forlorn and ill-prepared assault such as occurred so many times in the First World War. They never felt themselves to be mere sheep for the slaughter. Nobody in Montgomery's armies ever cried 'Baa' as did the French battalions trudging up to the death-trap of Verdun. A case like that at Enfidaville in Tunisia in April 1944 (see p. 137), when Montgomery sent the 56th Division, just arrived after a 3,200 mile journey from Iraq, straight and quite unnecessarily into an attack on a German position, strongly emplaced among the hills, which had just repelled the expert New Zealanders—the result was inevitably disastrous—was so extraordinary an aberration from his general principles that historians are puzzled to account for it. Of course it is true that as the Second World War advanced Montgomery was master of a diminishing asset. The infantry available to him from the British Commonwealth were declining in numbers. As early as Alamein (see p. 73) Montgomery's battle tactics were influenced by this factor. After Normandy the situation was even more acute—my own Division, the 59th Staffordshire, was then broken up to provide reinforcements for other infantry divisions, and many field and anti-aircraft gunners were turned into footsloggers. Husbandry of his infantry resources—the *sine qua non* of any commander—was therefore at all times a matter of common prudence for Montgomery: and he was a prudent man. But to leave it at that would be ungenerous: it would be to overlook a pure

* It is significant that, writing of '14-'18 in *A History of Warfare* (Collins, 1968), Montgomery observes, 'I would name Sir John Monash as the best general on the western front in Europe', since this Australian was outstanding not only for his originality but also for the thoroughness with which he worked out in advance every minute detail of a forthcoming operation.

vein of compassion implanted in him amid the Flanders mud. 'The frightful casualties appalled me.'

Competent planning, Montgomery thought, could only derive from a continuous, concentrated and self-abnegatory examination not merely of the principles but also of the practices of war. 'By the time the 1914–1918 war was over it had become very clear to me that the profession of arms was a life-study.' All else must take second place: austerity must accompany dedication. It is a monk's view of a way of life. Hitler might sit beneath a portrait of Frederick the Great in the gloomy concrete womb of his head-quarters at Rastenburg; he might pore over his letters and remind himself how his hero saved Prussia from a converging coalition: but what Hitler got from his obsession was 'military qualities don't show themselves in an exercise on a sand model. In the last analysis, they show themselves in the capacity to hold on, in perseverance and determination. That's the decisive factor in any victory.'* Far from feeding on such windy generalisations, Montgomery's merit was that, while he steadily trained himself to 'think big', he never, as it were, ignored the sand model. Thus in the Second World War his battles were always prefabricated down to the smallest detail. He was, in fact, a better disciple of Frederick the Great than the Führer, for like Frederick he spent the middle years of his life in an unremitting search, by reading, thinking and exercising, for a mastery of all aspects of his profession right down to the *minutiae*, for the highest possible level of personal competence.

And of competence in others. It was this urge which, surprisingly, con-verted so withdrawn a character into so brilliant a teacher. The prophet came in from the wilderness, and the people hearkened. Between the wars Mont-gomery spent no less than six years in this role. In 1926 he went back to the Staff College for three years as an instructor (Alan Brooke being one of his colleagues, and Oliver Leese and John Harding—both to rise later to great heights under his command—among his pupils). In 1934, again, he was posted as Chief Instructor to the Staff College at Quetta. Among the many officers I have talked to who either served beside him or sat at his feet during these years I have found no one who (whatever his other reservations) had anything but unstinted praise for Montgomery's skill in imparting informa-tion and inspiring enthusiasm.† If, as I believe, the British Army in 1939 contained a far greater leavening of properly educated officers than it did in

---

* Walter Warlimont, *Inside Hitler's Headquarters, 1939–1945*, Weidenfeld and Nicolson, 1964.

† This is a characteristic example. 'In our small world he was no less of a controversial figure than he has since become in the world at large. . . . The principles he gave us and the basis of his doctrine remained constant throughout the changing conditions and developments of war. . . . I remember most vividly one day in 1936 when he impressed on us that war would be delayed only until Germany considered herself sufficiently re-armed and made clear that it was our duty to prepare ourselves for it.' General Sir Dudley Ward, GCB, KBE, DSO, in *The First Fifty Years of The Staff College, Quetta* (Quetta, Pakistan, 1942).

1914, Montgomery is certainly among the foremost of those to whom credit is due. Brigadier Essame has caught his methods perfectly: 'He could describe a complex situation with amazing lucidity and sum up a long exercise without the use of a single note. He looked straight into the eyes of the audience when he spoke. He had a remarkable flair for picking out the essence of a problem, and for indicating its solution with startling clarity. It was almost impossible to misunderstand his meaning, however unpalatable it might be. In argument he was formidable and ruthless: quick as a ferret to detect faulty reasoning or half-truths (some said "and about as lovable").' Anyone who attended one of Montgomery's famous wartime lectures, in a cinema in Kent, it might be, or a theatre in Tripoli . . . no smoking, no coughing! . . . will recognise the accuracy of this description. You might disagree with what he was saying, but by God you caught his drift!

Moreover, Montgomery's proselytism and quest for perfection were not confined to the classroom: indeed, they largely explain another curious facet of this complicated character—his perennial kindness towards the young officer, and his concern both for the education of those prepared to seek knowledge (in an Army which, certainly between the wars, tended to sniff at the studious) and for the advancement of those showing promise and potential. This trait soon became manifest. Before he went to Camberley in 1926 he held two posts which gave him the right scope for this unusual talent. In 1923 he went up to Yorkshire, to the 49th West Riding Division, and there he not only initiated weekly lectures (by himself) on tactics, but went so far as to help young officers with their studies during the evening. One of these aspirants was Francis de Guingand, who later, as Chief of Staff to Montgomery throughout his great campaigns, achieved, with his master, one of the classic combinations of military history. In *Operation Victory* de Guingand gives a lively account of Montgomery's far-sighted but self-denying behaviour at this time, and of the surprise and gratitude of the fortunate subalterns who chanced on such a mentor. 'He can have had little sleep during this period,' de Guingand observes. And then Montgomery was returned, after eleven years' absence, to his old regiment, the Warwicks, in the rank of Company Commander. The situation was full of possibilities. A hardened warrior and military intellectual was not the most likely candidate for acceptance in a mess from which some might think he had ratted for too long. And Guy Chapman's recollections of those weeks at Cologne do not suggest the kind of 'clubbable' man whose bonhomie might ease the situation. Still, a distinguished senior officer who was a member of the regiment at the time told me, when I asked him what he particularly remembered, that it was Montgomery's kindness and helpfulness towards the younger officers which most impressed him . . . an impression which has remained indelible after so many years. The truth is that for his seniors (except Alan Brooke) Montgomery usually felt either contempt or indifference: but the young were the seed-bed of the future, and it was essential that they should be properly prepared for a place in that New Model Army of his dreams.

Montgomery's ideas about morale, as clear-cut as all his concepts, can equally be seen to stem from the days of the Somme and Passchendaele. What nauseated him about these years was the extinction of the individual personality. The Higher Command, he saw, had come to visualise a division as a sort of undifferentiated block of flesh to be propelled forward behind a screen of metal. The human being as such was ceasing to count. The infantry Montgomery served as a staff officer—'my war experience led me to believe that the staff must be servants of the troops'—seemed to be progressively regarded, in the words of the poet Wilfred Owen, as

> *Men, gaps for filling :*
> *Losses who might have fought*
> *Longer ; but no one bothers.*

He was haunted by the recurrent order (quoted by him half a century later in *A History of Warfare*) which used to insist, day after day, that an attack would be maintained *regardless of losses*.

Montgomery reversed this attitude. When he published his *Memoirs* in 1958 he wrote: 'Unlike steel, an army is a most sensitive instrument and can easily become damaged; its basic ingredient is men and, to handle an army well, it is essential to understand human nature. Bottled up in men are great emotional forces which have got to be given an outlet in a way which is positive and constructive, and which warms the heart and excites the imagination. If the approach to the human factor is cold and impersonal, then you achieve nothing.' This was, in essence, no more than a re-statement of the basic truth he had grasped 40 years previously. In any unit, whether it be a platoon or an Army Group, the individual soldier must feel that he matters as an individual, that his superiors care about him as an individual, and that he knows clearly what he has to do and why. As a young man Montgomery seized on these principles which, when written down, look like banal platitudes but which so many officers, senior as well as junior, have failed to understand. With the passing of the years he developed techniques for applying them so that, when he took over the Eighth Army, he transformed it into perhaps the best-informed, the most self-assured and the most buoyant of all the Allied formations. He evolved a knack of seeming to address each man as a person. By his own confession, it is clear that many of his characteristic creeds and methods were based on a study of Napoleon. After the young Corsican's famous Italian campaigns of 1796 and 1797 General Desaix observed: 'he has never seen a regiment which he has not persuaded that he considered it the best in the Army'. This was an art which Montgomery gradually perfected, once he had seen the need for it—gradually, for it certainly did not come to him without effort. It had to be carefully and consciously developed until he attained what Liddell Hart once said Marlborough possessed—'the power of commanding affection while communicating energy'.

For what I have called the absenteeism of the Higher Command Montgomery had nothing but contempt. Though his own fighting days ended in 1914, the nature of his staff work brought him much closer to the mud of the trenches than to the gilded châteaux of G.H.Q. He is blunt about it. 'There was little contact between the generals and the soldiers. . . . I never once saw the British Commander-in-Chief, neither Haig nor French, and only twice did I see an Army Commander. The higher staff were out of touch with the regimental officers and with the troops.' Considered simply in relation to the building of morale, Montgomery saw that this was fatal. When he in due course became an Army Commander, therefore, it was habitual for him to let his troops see him as much as possible, and it was commonplace to spot the red bands of his generals right up in the front line. Indeed, neither in the Eighth Army nor in Europe did there open a 'credibility gap' such as existed so painfully between front and base in '14–'18. For this closing of the ranks Montgomery was, of course, certainly not wholly responsible: it was a widespread phenomenon. But by his inter-war preaching and his wartime practice he powerfully assisted the trend, and in so doing remained faithful to an insight of his youth.

Apart from his service as an instructor, and a brief phase when he was working on a new Infantry Training Manual for the War Office, Montgomery spent from 1918 to 1939 in direct contact with troops, and the variety of his experience was such that when war again broke out there can have been few regular officers with so wide and so intimate a knowledge of their function. Some of this experience, moreover, was truly operational. After Montgomery passed out from the Staff College, for example, he was sent, again as a brigade-major, to the 17th Infantry Brigade at Cork. It was the blackest depth of the Sein Féin rebellion, 'a murder campaign', as Alan Moorehead puts it, 'through the damp back streets of the towns'. The Cork Brigade contained no less than nine battalions, and Montgomery's responsibilities were large. But at least for a Protestant from the North there was no stress of loyalty, and he tackled the unsavoury problems of security and repression in an essentially clinical spirit. It was a military job to be done. In Montgomery's career the main significance of this episode is that it provided an invaluable realistic background for a man who in 1938 would find himself responsible for the military control of one half of an insurgent Palestine.

Montgomery's code of conduct is simple and strong: like all his statements of principle it looks jejune until you ask how you yourself would apply it. It is a throwback to Napoleon's declaration that he wanted lucky generals: implicit in which is the thought that a general who, granted luck, cannot exploit it is useless. The Montgomery doctrine reads: 'At certain moments in life an opportunity is presented to each one of us; some of us are not aware of the full significance of what has happened, and the moment is lost. Others, alert and enthusiastic, seize the opportunity with both hands and turn it to good advantage; these have ambition, as every man who is worth his salt should have. . . .' Montgomery had ambition; and the various appointments he undertook between the wars gave him opportunities to prove it. Some have already been noted: all of the others he turned, quite properly, to his advantage. He was certainly alert and enthusiastic.

After Ireland, for example, he did a short term with 3 Division at Plymouth. (A man of coincidence, Montgomery was later to command a brigade in this division and ultimately to lead the whole division to France in 1939.) His brigadier was a man after Montgomery's heart; the name was Hollond. They spoke the same language. Under Hollond Montgomery learned the essential lesson in humility which he himself has defined: 'that the discipline demanded in the soldier must become loyalty in the officer'. Hollond appreciated Montgomery's capacity and gave him a very free hand. Alan Moorehead comments: 'While the General planned and encouraged, his Brigade-Major, Montgomery, jumped into the actual control as his executive officer. It was Montgomery who issued the orders, Montgomery who was always on the telephone at headquarters, Montgomery who hurried about in a whirl of new training schemes and projects.' This was a marvellous practical preliminary to his years as an instructor at the Staff College. 'Inside his mind it was the first tentative beginning of a new theory of the training of troops for the next inevitable war.'

After his Staff College service Montgomery again returned to his Regiment, in the salubrious setting of Woking. But once again the opportunity came his way and the exploitation occurred. He was appointed, in 1930, Secretary of a committee which had the task of re-writing the Army's manual on Infantry Training. 'Get into the team and then run it' was a Montgomery maxim. As secretary he extended his functions, and wrote the manual in his own terms. His committee exploded, as did the War Office, but 'I could not accept many of their amendments to my doctrine of infantry war. We went through the manual, chapter by chapter. I then recommended that the committee should disband and that I should complete the book in my own time; this was agreed. I produced the final draft, omitting all the amendments the committee had put forward. The book when published was considered excellent,* especially by its author.' Many years of experience as a regular officer had taught Montgomery the lesson enunciated by his brother-in-law, that brilliant pioneer of armoured warfare General Hobart, that 'the secret of success in the Army is to be sufficiently insubordinate'.

That he did in fact acquire a brother-in-law astonished all who knew him. In his Yorkshire days with the 49th Division Montgomery used to lay down the dogma that 'marriage is not a good thing for officers. You cannot be both a soldier and a husband.' And indeed, if one accepts the dedicatory attitude towards the military profession which Montgomery avowedly adopted, one should not be surprised. A Jesuit must be a bachelor. (Many a disconsolate officer had cause to remember this when, in the days after Dunkirk, Montgomery ordered a *diaspora* of military wives from the threatened fringe of South-East England.) And yet, in his typical way, the man who trampled over so many Army traditions turned traitor on himself. He married.

To write about this aspect of his life is difficult but essential. Montgomery is a very shrouded character in spite of so much that he has made explicit about himself. How much more did Alamein matter in the development of his character than his marriage? How different a person might he ultimately have become had his wife shared his life for longer? Unanswerable questions —to which Montgomery has written his personal reply when he describes 'something much more important than my military career, the ten short years of my married life'. What is certain is that, after an acquaintance of two years, he married in 1927 the widow (with two sons) of an officer who had died at Gallipoli: Betty Carver. She too died, from poison following, apparently, an insect bite, in October 1937. In the decade she spent with him she humanised Montgomery in many ways, steadily abolishing the temperamental after-effects of his childhood. But then—death. For long this sudden and shattering experience made Montgomery's life a void: and those who are critical of his performance as a commander must, in charity, consider how far his innermost being was permanently scarred by this traumatic event. Field Marshals, too, are human. Certainly Montgomery's own account of his wife's illness and end is so vivid and so moving that quotation is almost unbearable—the reader must be referred to the *Memoirs*, for one cannot summarise the breaking of a heart.

And yet it must be observed that in his marriage, as in his military career, Montgomery displayed a remarkable gift for blending the incompatible. It

---

* Excellent or not, it illustrated an important and permanent weakness. Neither in it, nor earlier nor later, was Montgomery strong on the concept of 'exploitation'. This limitation of vision had an important bearing on his conduct of the pursuit after Alamein (see Chapters 5 and 6) and at times in N.W. Europe. For a fuller discussion of this central point, see *The Liddell Hart Memoirs*, Vol. 1, pp. 55, 56).

was improbable that his Calvinistic soul would match, in Africa and later, the bland delight in life's good things of Freddie de Guingand. It was unlikely that a civilised youngster like John Poston (see p. 45) would serve him with devotion both as A.D.C. and, afterwards and until his death in action, as Liaison Officer. It was even more improbable that he would find complete fulfilment with a wife who was an artist, who had Chelsea affiliations, who was the antithesis of most of what her husband worshipped or even under-stood. But it worked: all the evidence indicates that they very happily agreed to differ and were contented in their difference. Montgomery ran the house and his wife ran her own life, wherever duty might call them, but, in so doing, softened her husband by a sympathetic toleration of his idiosyncrasies—some of which undoubtedly remained unusual. When, for example, Montgomery in the 'thirties was commanding a battalion in Palestine and Sir Richard O'Connor held a similar command in Egypt, O'Connor went up to stay with them. 'His wife was alive then, and I was amused at the ritual that went on after breakfast. His staff (domestic) was drawn up in line and he gave detailed orders to them all about every subject, including food, and his wife took no part!' This was pure Monty. He protected his wife, throughout the decade of their happiness, from the trivia of a household because he understood her calibre and her qualities; there was a Staff answer to problems of menus and dusting, and he could apply it. Why trouble her? For her husband, therefore, Betty's death involved an absolute 'dark night of the soul', and brought him nearer to a moral and mental collapse than any of the battles or controversies he endured in either war. 'I went back to my house in Portsmouth, which was to have been our home; I remained there alone for many days and would see no one. I was utterly defeated. . . . I seemed to be surrounded by utter darkness; all the spirit was knocked out of me.' But after a few weeks 'I began to live again'; and it is worth noting that Montgomery had before him an example of fortitude in the man he so much admired, Alan Brooke, who survived a similar and indeed more dreadful ordeal. Just after Montgomery first met him, in 1926, Alan Brooke and his first wife were in an appalling motor accident. Both arrived in hospital unconscious, and Alan Brooke came round to find his wife dead in the bed beside him. Left with two children, he also found his way out of the Slough of Despond, to become the pivot of British military power in the Second World War.

At least Betty had the happiness and satisfaction of sharing with her husband what was, for him, a Golden Age. Between 1927 and 1937 Mont-gomery became more and more evidently destined for the higher echelons of command, his natural habitat. After the stimulating years at the Staff College, and his unconventional success with the Training Manual, he put his foot in 1930 on the first rung of that ladder of promotion which can lead

straight to the top—a rung, indeed, which is for many officers their ultimate objective: Lieut.-Colonel B. L. Montgomery was given command of a battalion of his own Regiment, the Warwickshires, then stationed, amid fairly peaceful circumstances, in Palestine. There the worst was yet to come. This one battalion was the whole country's garrison.

In his biography Alan Moorehead makes much of the impact of the Holy Land on a God-fearing officer. 'Like his predecessor, Gordon of Khartoum, the Colonel was sometimes seen walking among the sights of Jerusalem and Bethlehem with his Bible and his guide books.' He allies this with the growing influence of father on son in religious matters. And indeed, in the letters the old Bishop (with not long to live) despatched to his son there were many ringing words of exhortation. 'Place your faith in God . . . whatever you do place God first in your life,' and so on. But the essential thing to note in a broad study of Montgomery as a commander is that throughout the whole of his life, in peace and in war (and even after his wife's death), he preserved, as an unshakeable conviction, a simple and unquestioning faith in the Christian religion. The simplicity made the statement of it sometimes embarrassing. In his Messages to his troops the word God seemed to appear as frequently as it does in the last lines of Robert Browning's poems! Not surprisingly, there were ribald reactions. The more one heard of 'The Lord mighty in battle' the more one was reminded of what Gladstone once noted in his diary: 'I feel when speaking on any religious question I am always at bottom seeking to glorify myself.' The reiteration of such appeals to the Almighty also recalled the fact that a count of the number of generals who have fervently believed that God was on *their* side would produce a figure of astronomical proportions. But all this is beside the point. When Churchill called Montgomery a 'Cromwellian figure' he was correct. He was indeed one of the Protector's plain russet-coated captains, 'such men as had the fear of God before them and as made some conscience of what they did'. When Montgomery referred to God he meant, quite simply, what he said. And if in his armies there was many a doubting Thomas, there was also many a disciple.

An observant student of Montgomery's writings about himself or his campaigns will note that while on some matters the Field Marshal is capable at times of breath-taking frankness, on others he is almost painstakingly dumb. This apparent secretiveness over events about which he is rightly or wrongly sensitive is a childish trait: for truth will out. His *Memoirs*, for example, skip in a few banal sentences over those three years from 1931 to 1934 when his battalion acted as the garrison of Alexandria and trained in the nearby desert. Yet for several reasons this was a critically formative phase in his progress. Then why the silence?

Montgomery with his son David, 1941

The reason, I suspect, is that particularly during the early days of its garrison duty Montgomery ran his battalion as if Alexandria was a city lying somewhere between Sodom and Gomorrah. Certainly in the early 'thirties that age-old siren offered every possible temptation to both officer and man. Conscious of this, and with a harsh self-righteousness, Montgomery used too firm a grip—and used it tactlessly. *Trop de Zèle*! He paid for it by a crop of rumours that he was unpopular with his men and—a sure sign of an unhappy unit—by too much indiscipline and consequently too many punishments. The 'keen scoutmaster' went too far. Fortunately the Commander-in-Chief, Egypt, Sir John Burnett-Stuart, was not only one of the outstanding soldiers of his day but also a wise man, and Montgomery's brigadier, 'Tim' Pile, who revealed the highest qualities in his wartime command of the anti-aircraft defences of Great Britain, was of similar calibre. Together they stoically (though not always silently) tolerated unorthodoxies, inadequacies, and major and minor contretemps which would certainly have led to the sacking of a man less evidently valuable than Montgomery. Stories about this period, whether malicious or true, are still in circulation, and no doubt Montgomery feels that it would be better if all were now forgotten. Unfortunately for him, he has wounded too many feelings in the course of his life for that to be likely.

Yet the 'stories' are only half the story. There was a credit side. These years were part of Montgomery's learning process. By going too far he discovered the hard way that compromise can gain more, as a rule, than arrogance: and that, though in the 'twenties he had believed and taught that it is the individual soldier who matters, in practice it is fatally easy for a commander to lose the confidence of his troops.

In the end his men took his measure. The real test of a soldier is not whether he can mount a spotless guard or keep out of the brothels, but how he operates in the field. Burnett-Stuart and Pile held frequent exercises to try out their battalions and commanding officers; in these it was observed that the Warwickshires had a habit of performing exceptionally well, while Montgomery, so spiky a character in cantonments, seemed to change his nature even though the battle might be only a make-believe. Bolshie battalions don't shine on exercises. And in the end, in fact, all was well. 'Definitely above the average of his rank and should attain high rank in the Army,' reported Pile when in 1934 the Warwickshires were transferred to India. 'He can only fail to do so if a certain high-handedness, which occasionally overtakes him, becomes too pronounced. . . . He has fertile and original thoughts which he expresses in the most inimitable way. *He is really popular with his men whom he regards and treats as if they were his children.*' (Author's italics.) There were further benefits. The future victor at Alamein was given his first taste of the tactical requirements of desert warfare—and of one in particular, the night attack. Liddell Hart has written in his *Memoirs* that ' "Monty" was at first sceptical about the practicability of night action, especially on a large scale, and inclined to argue that it would lead to hazardous and perhaps disastrous confusion—a view that he had expressed in mutual discussion when I was writing the post-war *Infantry Training* in 1920, and again when he was writing the next but one edition of that manual ten years later.' But Pile was an ardent believer in the development of 'night sense' and used many devices to make his troops feel at home in the darkness of a vacant desert. He ordered a dubious Montgomery to 'get on with it'. With the aid of de Guingand (also serving in Egypt) Montgomery 'got on with it' with a vengeance . . . the tale is vividly told in de Guingand's *Operation Victory* . . . and by using the night attack on exercise they achieved a shattering victory over their opponent. Always amenable to success, Montgomery adopted the method as part of his military philosophy, and applied it during the Second World War so frequently, and usually so effectively, that it became his trademark. British and German soldiers alike knew what was meant by 'a Montgomery moon'.

So it was, therefore, that when in the spring of 1934 the 1st Battalion of the Royal Warwickshires moved to Poona, and a few months later Montgomery was translated to the Staff College, Quetta (as Chief Instructor with the rank of full Colonel), he had a rich and recent experience of men and manoeuvre to support the theories of warfare which he now proceeded to preach with animating fervour. Coincidence occurred again, for by chance de Guingand turned up and (with the future casting its shadow) Montgomery was able to aid him in securing a nomination to the Staff College—observing, typically, 'I am not used to backing the wrong horse when it comes to asking favours of people in high places; it would result only in one's own undoing!'

'At certain moments in life an opportunity is presented to each one of us.' Montgomery's undoubtedly was his promotion in the summer of 1937 to command of the 9th Infantry Brigade, stationed at Portsmouth. For the 9th Brigade was in the 3rd Division, and the 3rd Division was in Southern Command, and the General Officer Commanding Southern Command was Archibald Wavell, eminent among that small group of senior soldiers who, during the 'thirties, had been striving to effect a revolution in the Army's methods of training, the nature of its equipment, the quality of its higher ranks, and its political support. They sought for an army capable of fighting a modern war: and in the event of such a war, incidentally, the troops of Southern Command were ear-marked to form the Second Corps in any British Expeditionary Force despatched overseas. Thus in 1937 Montgomery found himself in an important position under a key man at a critical point in time.

All turned to dust and ashes. During their marriage his wife had always 'followed the drum'; he and she, in consequence, had never known the delights of a home they could think of as truly theirs. Now they were allotted their own domain—Ravelin House at Portsmouth, a substantial setting for a brigadier—and enthusiastically started to share the novel experience of furnishing and decoration. Then Betty died: and Montgomery was left, with his young son, to enter into occupation of a ghost-haunted shell.

It took some time, as has been seen, for Montgomery to recover his equilibrium—almost, his sanity. But an innate toughness and resilience gradually reasserted themselves, and by 1938 the 9th Brigade began to fizz. Montgomery had learned much during and after those stormy days in Alexandria. He is himself quite frank about this. 'I had received many rebuffs and there is no doubt they were good for me; they kept me from kicking over the traces too often and saved me from becoming too over-bearing.' He trained his brigade hard—mostly under his own supervision—but there are no echoes of murmuring in the ranks. Indeed, his men soon proved outstanding in such manoeuvres as were held. These were (on the eve of a European war) small beer. Wavell himself noted that 'there were no manoeuvres on any scale during this period and I had no practice in the art of command in the field'—a bitter reflection by a man who might at any time have to lead a whole Corps into action. Still, in July 1938, there was one relatively large scheme which Wavell was able to observe, an invasion exercise in which troops carried in the cruiser *Southampton* and a number of destroyers were then embarked in small boats and landed near Dartmouth. 'That it was held at all,' writes Wavell's biographer, John Connell, 'was due to the energy and imagination of the officer commanding 9th Infantry Brigade at Portsmouth, Brigadier Bernard Montgomery, and the willing help of the naval Commander-in-Chief at Portsmouth, Admiral of the Fleet Lord Cork and Orrery.' Naturally it was a shambles.* Wavell described it as a pitiful assessment of our complete neglect of landing operations. 'There was *one* so-called landing craft,' he noted, 'an experimental one made many years before and dug out of some scrap-heap for this exercise, in which I rather think it sank. For the rest the troops landed in open row-boats as they had done for the last 200 years and more.' But Montgomery was undaunted. When Wavell landed he greeted him, 'bubbling with enthusiasm', to explain

---

* But nevertheless a historic and prophetic event. The I.S.T.D.C. (Inter-Services Training and Development Centre), which was to pioneer many of the essential techniques for successful Combined Operations, had just been formed. The first task of its skeleton staff was to attend this exercise. In a sense, therefore, this was a first step towards D.-Day: so it is appropriate that not only Montgomery was present, but also the future Sir Frederick Morgan who was to supervise the draft plan for the Normandy landings. Morgan noted that in this exercise 9 Brigade staff used 30,000 sheets of foolscap paper!

how the exercise had run. 'I see,' said Wavell: and proceeded to his car which then proceeded into a dung-heap. 'Strange fellow, Montgomery,' Wavell observed on a later occasion. 'One of the most capable officers we have, but for some reason not popular with senior officers.'

Of course events like the famous case of the Clarence Football Ground at Portsmouth—government property used by the army—did not help to increase Montgomery's popularity. On his own initiative he let it for £1,500, for use during a Bank Holiday Fair, to raise money for his Brigade Welfare Fund. Whitehall inevitably screamed when the news percolated, and this was certainly one of those occasions when, as Montgomery would put it, he was 'dickey on the perch'. Still, he survived, and later in the year his brigade was selected to carry out secret gas trials on Salisbury Plain. Wavell's subsequent report says more than his previous grunt. 'Brigadier Montgomery is one of the clearest brains we have in the higher ranks, an excellent trainer of troops and an enthusiast in all he does. His work this year in the gas trials was of a very high order.' From one who never used words lightly this was praise indeed, and it was not surprising, therefore, that in October Montgomery was promoted Major-General and given the toughest assignment that had yet come his way—to take over military command of the northern half of Palestine, and to form the various scattered units there into the 8th Division. More coincidence: for the division which was to control the south was to be commanded by Richard O'Connor.

Since Montgomery was in Palestine in 1931, able to garrison the whole country with a single battalion, conditions had dangerously deteriorated. The fixed quota system, whereby an annual entry of Jewish immigrants was permitted within a limit set by the British, itself infuriated the Palestinian Arabs, who visualised a flood of aliens seeping over what they held to be their native lands. But Hitler made the atmosphere electric. As Nazism came out into the open, an alternative system of illegal entry grew up. Profiteers cashed in on the misery of the European Jew, and shiploads (at a price) of refugees from death or the concentration camp sought out the Promised Land, evading British naval patrols and welcomed by Jewish reception committees. By the winter of 1938–1939, when Montgomery was operating, something akin to war was in progress. Travel within an armed convoy had become necessary; sabotage of essential services was frequent; a curfew was imposed and ignored; there were secret assemblages of arms, and illicit conspiracies. In a sense it was worse than those days when Montgomery had helped to combat the Irish Rebellion, for this time the British were no man's friend.

He tackled the problem in characteristic fashion—rather in the way that he would play his hand during the Ardennes battle (see p. 243). First came the process of 'tidying up'. His area had previously been covered by a single brigade. Now, under his divisional H.Q. at Haifa, there were three. He divided the whole territory up into blocks, and appointed a separate commander for each of these sectors. He got a proper intelligence system working. He improved the feeble co-operation with the police. By these and other means he began to feel a sense of 'balance'. Now was the time for counterattack. Centres of disaffection would be surrounded at night, without warning: whole stocks of arms would be suddenly impounded, or suspects arrested. The wrongdoer was punished with justice, but without compassion. As the months passed Montgomery clamped the countryside in a vice, and by the spring of 1939 the worst dangers had passed.

And now, for Montgomery, good luck was followed by bad—it seemed to be an emerging pattern. The commander of the 3rd Division (called, oddly enough, General Bernard) was appointed Governor of Bermuda, and the question of his successor arose. Montgomery in Palestine was informed that he had been selected to take up the post in due course, and he was overjoyed. A war was coming—he could see that—and what better than to command one of the best divisions in the country, the old 'Iron' Division of World War One, a division he knew well, and one that was bound to be in the forefront of the British Army ? Little did he know the circumstances of his choice. Wavell, as head of Southern Command, was naturally involved, and his description indicates how much he had come to appreciate Montgomery's military virtues during the relatively brief period when he saw him at work as a brigadier. 'When I was asked at the selection board whom I wanted to succeed Bernard in the 3rd Division, I replied at once—"Monty". There was something like a sigh of relief from the other Army Commanders and instant acquiescence. Monty's name had come up several times before in front of the selection board; everyone always agreed that he ought to be promoted, but every other commander who had a vacancy for a major-general had always excellent reasons for finding someone else more suitable than Monty. I never had any doubts about his ability and also I liked him and was not afraid of his independent ideas and ways, which I could control.'

Montgomery was scheduled to take over his division in August, but in May he became desperately ill. A patch appeared on his lung. He failed to respond to treatment. The residual effects of his 1914 wound did not help, and tuberculosis was suspected. Medical facilities in Palestine were inadequate, his condition got steadily worse, and fears even arose that he might die. He was flown down to the Canal, almost too weak to move, and was carried by stretcher on to a liner making for England: but there seemed little hope. Yet for the second time Montgomery returned like Lazarus. He had maintained a curious, subconscious sense that if only he could get back to England he would recover: and he was right. The man who was carried aboard at Port Said walked off the ship at Tilbury. He rapidly obtained a clean bill of health, took some sick leave, and then called at the War Office to ask when he could take up his new command. He got a dusty answer. Mobilisation was impending, and 'on mobilisation all appointments made previously automatically lapsed'. There appeared to be nothing for him but to be sunk in a pool of generals awaiting jobs. However, the tenacity which Montgomery showed in fighting for a nomination to the Staff College re-asserted itself. For ten days running he persistently badgered the War Office (no doubt pre-occupied with many other matters) with arguments to prove that he was *the* man they needed: on 28 August Major-General B. L. Mont-gomery DSO took command of the 3rd Division—just in time to watch it go into full mobilisation for the war which began on 3 September. Montgomery hardly had time to inspect his troops before they were on their way to France.

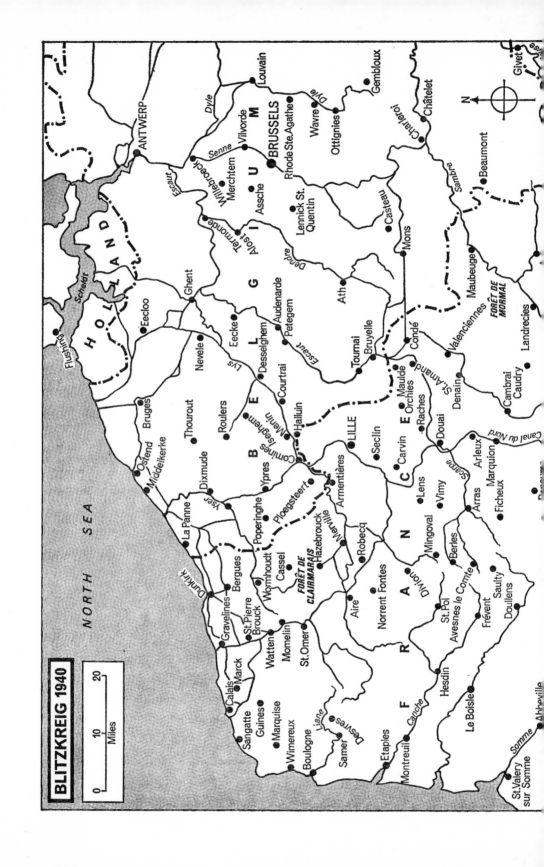

2

Dunkirk to Cairo

'This is a time to try men of force and vision and not to be exclusively confined to those who are judged thoroughly safe by conventional standards.'

Winston Churchill, *19 October 1940*

'Thou hast given him his heart's desire: and hast not denied him the request of his lips.'

Psalms, XXI.2

Before Montgomery went to war in August 1914 he proceeded, on the third day of mobilisation and according to Standing Orders, to the battalion armourer's, where his sword was solemnly sharpened. Now he had to handle a weapon of infinitely greater strength and bite. But even a crack division like the 3rd was incapable of achieving its full potential—largely through lack of the proper equipment. In October Hore-Belisha, the Secretary of State for War, made the astonishing and mendacious declaration in the House of Commons that 'our army is as well if not better equipped than any similar army'. To which Montgomery and his colleagues reacted in the spirit of the favourite phrase of that great soldier of '14–'18, Field Marshal Sir William Robertson: 'I've 'eard different.' The officers of the Expeditionary Force knew the truth. For Montgomery, the quintessence of the professional soldier, soaked in the history of the military failures of the past, the predicament seemed grave.

'In September 1939,' he recalled in his *Memoirs*, 'the British Army was totally unfit to fight a first class war on the continent of Europe. . . . The Field Army had an inadequate signals system, no administrative backing, and no organisation for high command; all these had to be improvised on mobilisation. The transport was inadequate and was completed on mobilisation by vehicles requisitioned from civilian firms. . . . The anti-tank equipment of my division consisted of 2-pounder guns. The infantry armament against tanks was the ·8-inch rifle. Some small one-pounder guns on little hand-carts were hurriedly bought from the French and a few were given to each infantry battalion. Apart from these, a proportion of the 25-pounders of my Divisional Artillery was supposed to be used in an anti-tank rôle, firing solid shot. . . . There was somewhere in France, under G.H.Q., one Army Tank Brigade.

For myself, I never saw any of its tanks during the winter or during the active operations in May. And we were the nation which had invented the tank and were the first to use it in battle, in 1916.'

The British had undertaken to assemble two corps in France by the thirty-third day after mobilisation, and they kept their word. As early as 27 September 152,031 army and 9,392 air force personnel, together with some 24,000 vehicles, 36,000 tons of ammunition, 25,000 tons of fuel and many other miscellaneous supplies had been transported across the Channel without the loss of a single life. In the Expeditionary Force's deployment, the 3rd Division took its place in the line under 2 Corps (now commanded by Lieut.-Gen. Alan Brooke—Wavell having departed to the Middle East Command). The other corps, the 1st, was commanded by Sir John Dill. The general area of the British concentration was eastwards of Lille.

Here they dug in. During the harsh winter months of 1939/1940 the tasks facing them were, in fact, training and self-protection. Anti-tank obstacles, pill-boxes, trenches and wire entanglements all had to be prepared, for though there were many, perhaps the majority, who both in the army and in Parliament* decried the notion that Hitler might soon attack, it had at least to be assumed by those who would have to face his Panzers that he *might* attack. And the assumption was in fact correct. Various intelligence indications suggested during October that something was brewing, and on the 29th Brooke and Dill tried, unsuccessfully, to arouse their Commander-in-Chief, Lord Gort VC, to the gravity of the situation. Yet that very day Hitler was instructing his own Commander-in-Chief that Operation YELLOW, the invasion of the Low Countries, would start on 12 November. It is true that the shocking weather of that winter persuaded Hitler to postpone the attack from day to day, but on 10 January he gave the go-ahead for the 17th. It was only the chance capture in Belgium of a German plane which had been compelled to force-land, and with it papers which contained the complete details of Operation YELLOW, that persuaded Hitler to put his invasion temporarily on ice. Thus in spite of the optimists Montgomery and his fellow generals were in very real danger of having to face a German onslaught while their defences were still rudimentary, and while the B.E.F. was only about half the size to which it had swelled when the real blow fell in May.

Yet for the percipient, and those 'in the know', the very place and nature of the B.E.F.'s preparations produced a numbing sense of insecurity. Alan Brooke wrote in his diary on 28 November: 'I feel that we are unlikely ever to defend the front we have spent so much thought and work in preparing.

---

* On 16 February 1940 the Secretary of State for War, in a conversation with Alan Brooke, 'expressed the view that he thought it very doubtful whether the Germans would attack on the western front this year'.

How can we avoid being drawn forward into Belgium?' And how could they? Just over a week earlier, on 17 November, the Supreme War Council in Paris had concluded: 'given the importance of holding the German forces as far east as possible, it is essential to make every endeavour to hold the line Meuse-Antwerp in the event of a German invasion of Belgium'. To save Brussels and Antwerp and the line of the Meuse involved, for the British, an abandonment of all they had achieved in the way of defences and a helter-skelter dash of some 60 miles to the line of the River Dyle, which, running due south from Antwerp, is linked by a gap of not many miles with the Meuse at Namur. It is a matter of history that this is the fate which befell the B.E.F. in the following May.

But pessimism was not a word in Montgomery's vocabulary. His personal duty was quite clear to him—he must bring his division to the highest pitch in what was obviously the short time available. Pre-eminent as a trainer of troops, he exercised all his talents and worked his men hard—an investment which was to pay large dividends for him and them when the battle began. Throughout the whole period, indeed, from 3 Division's arrival in France to its evacuation at Dunkirk, Montgomery's performance as a divisional commander was exemplary. In later and wider areas of responsibility the quality of his generalship will be debated eternally: but only a bigot could fault him for the way he prepared 3 Division for action and led it in the face of an overwhelming opposition.

Of this 'phoney war' period Alan Moorehead writes: 'For the first time on the field of war he was able to put into practice his theory of personal command. All details were handed over to the staff; the General himself spent most of his day with the men and commanders along the line. He seized every chance to show himself, to meet the soldiers and impress on them that he was their leader. When senior commanders called on the division no staff officers accompanied them on their inspections; Montgomery himself took them round. He had a remarkable knowledge of every corner of his command. It became a joke to try and ask him questions which he could not answer.' But if he felt confidence in himself and his men, Montgomery was less certain about his allies. It was the practice to send British brigades in rotation to serve with the French on the Saar front, where, in the face of the German positions before the Siegfried Line, there was at least a minimal appearance of active warfare. Montgomery visited one of his brigades down there in January, had a look at the French, and returned so seriously alarmed that he made a report to his Corps Commander. But Brooke had preceded him: he needed no persuasion.

It is typical of the atmosphere of this twilight period that the only time Montgomery (self-confessedly born to trouble as the sparks fly upward) was really in difficulty was as a result of a letter he wrote to his subordinate officers giving them very explicit guidance about how to cope with the problem of venereal disease among their soldiers. This was prevalent and increasing. But the letter came into the hands of the senior chaplains at G.H.Q., and then—if the metaphor is appropriate—all Hell broke loose. The Adjutant-General informed the General Officer Commanding 2 Corps that the C.-in-C. required the withdrawal of the offensive document. But Brooke stood firm and extricated his General. 'I never ceased to thank Heaven that I saved Monty at this danger point in his career.' Idiotic though the fracas may now seem, it is symptomatic of the low intellectual temperature prevailing at G.H.Q. at this time that the man who led victorious British armies from Egypt to Germany might have been sacked and sent home for trying to protect his division from the pox.

This was the period, in fact, when Brooke (long though he had known Montgomery), began to single him out in his mind as a senior officer of quite exceptional promise. Brooke was proud of his Corps, and was indefatigable in studying and assessing its units. He observed Montgomery, in his own words, improving every day as he began to find his feet as a Divisional Commander, and the conduct of some of Montgomery's exercises was, to Brooke, an eye-opener. What was now required was the final and absolute test of action.

This came on 10 May, when at 3 a.m. the Germans invaded Holland and Belgium. As Brooke had so long ago foreseen, the B.E.F. immediately galloped eastwards. 2 Corps moved up to the Dyle with Montgomery's division in the van and the 4th and 50th Divisions in his rear. The forward move of 3 Division went like clockwork; so much so that, when they arrived in the dark during the night of the 10th, they found the 10th Belgian Division still occupying the front which had been allocated to them. Brooke, up with the Division next day, took immediate action 'at the highest level' (i.e. with the King of the Belgians), to obtain a readjustment of the line. But when he later called on Montgomery he discovered that the latter had already achieved an accommodation. 'This episode is typical of Monty's resourcefulness; something had to be done, the Germans might arrive at any moment, and he certainly found a solution to settle the matter. I think I remember saying to him, "Poor Belgian Commander, how little he knows the viper he is harbouring in his breast!" '

Each day brought its evil tidings—Rotterdam bombed, the Dutch asking for an armistice, the German armour pouring over the bridges of the Meuse, the Belgians in retreat over the Albert Canal, the French armies on the British right collapsing. The 3rd Division could only watch and wait. It was a nerve-racking phase: but Montgomery, at least, was unperturbed. Indeed it was now that he evolved his notorious routine of touring his front during the day, returning to his H.Q. about tea time, seeing his staff and issuing orders, taking dinner and then retiring to bed with strict instructions that he must NOT be disturbed except in a crisis. R. W. Thompson once coined a phrase which in this context is most apt. 'Montgomery,' he writes,* 'had the knack of creating oases of serenity around himself.' There are many witnesses to this charismatic gift. When, for example, Goronwy Rees, a brilliant Fellow of All Souls, Oxford, was posted to Montgomery's staff in those later days when he was in charge of South-Eastern Command, Rees approached his first interview with a natural trepidation. But he later remembered 'that air of calm and peace which he carried with him was so strong that after a moment my panic and alarm began to die away: it was something which one felt to be almost incongruous in a soldier'. At a higher level, I recall how Sir Miles Dempsey told me that, when he was commanding Second Army in Normandy, he never failed, at bad moments, to be re-invigorated by a visit to Montgomery, and that the Field Marshal, with his cheerful smile and his confident air, had a way of turning apparent difficulties into phantoms. The habit of the undisturbed night and the daily routine were, in fact, no more than particular aspects of something which by now was deeply rooted in Montgomery's nature. He was sure of himself.

It must have been during the night of 14 or 15 May that a staff officer, obviously unaware of the sanctity of Montgomery's couch, roused him to report that the Germans had entered Louvain. Montgomery, true to form, replied, 'Go away and don't bother me. Tell the brigadier in Louvain to turn them out.' Which was done. On the 14th and 15th the 3rd Division tasted blood for the first time as the Germans shelled, attacked and penetrated across the Dyle and into Louvain, only to be thrown back by fierce counter-attacks in which the Grenadier Guards and Royal Ulster Rifles were prominent. Nothing shook the 3rd: it only withdrew in the end because of the exposure of its southern flank. Sir Brian Horrocks, then a Lieut.-Colonel commanding the 2nd Middlesex (the divisional machine-gun battalion), used in those days to mark up a rough map, taking his information from the divisional intelligence map, so that as he went round his platoons he could show it to them and keep them in the picture. Each time he called at Divisional H.Q. the situation portrayed on the master-map looked more and more disquieting. 3 Division had the appearance of a rock past which a tide-race was pouring with ever-increasing energy.

Horrocks had a strange career in this battle. At 7 a.m. on invasion day, 10 May, he was at the Staff College, Camberley. That evening he was in France and on the 13th took over his machine-gun battalion. With it he per-

* R. W. Thompson, *The Montgomery Legend*, Allen and Unwin, p. 75.

formed the many maid-of-all-work tasks which are a machine-gunner's lot:
and then, in the last stages of the battle, he was given a brigade. The
enthusiastic Lieut.-Colonel whose command lasted 17 days before he was
promoted, and who was ultimately to become an enthusiastic Lieut.-General,
captured exactly the qualities which made Montgomery (whom until then
Horrocks had never met) so superb a man of war. In his autobiography
A Full Life Horrocks remembered that:

'A divisional machine-gun officer is a general dog's-body who gets all sorts
of jobs thrust on his shoulders. I was detailed to carry out reconnaissances,
act as commander of flank guards, rearguards, and often had to slip off with
my battalion to build up the defensive framework of the next position before
the arrival of the division.

'Orders for all these tasks were given me by Monty himself, so I was in a
unique position to watch him at work during this testing period. It was a
remarkable performance. I remember once sitting packed into a room lit only
by a few candles, and with a most inadequate map at my disposal—during
the final stages of the withdrawal the supply of maps, down to battalion level,
at any rate, completely failed, and at one stage I had to rely on a fly-blown
railway map which I had removed from the wall of a small wayside station.

'Monty was about to issue orders, and I wondered desperately how on
earth I could possibly grasp the complicated rôle which had been allotted to
my battalion. I needn't have worried. With the minimum of words he made
the whole plan clear to us all.'

At last the tide raced so far past 2 Corps that retreat was unavoidable. By
the 17th, 3 Division was west of Brussels, and the city's canal bridges had
been blown. On the 18th Brooke's sister Corps, the 1st, was showing signs
of moving sluggishly, thanks largely to the weariness and confusion of an
elderly Corps Commander. To reduce his burden Brooke took over from
him one of his divisions, the 1st, commanded by Major-General Harold
Alexander. And so it was that the triumvirate which was to steer Britain to
victory in Africa (Brooke as C.I.G.S., Alexander as Commander-in-Chief
Middle East, and Montgomery as the Commander of the Eighth Army), were
now banded together* in a situation which by any rational standards was
hopeless. Indeed, by the 19th a conference at G.H.Q. was already discussing
the merits of a scheme for a perimeter defence of Dunkirk, through whose
port personnel, less all stores and equipment, might be evacuated. Nor was
this discussion premature, for by the evening the 2nd German Panzer Division was at Abbeville, the 1st at Amiens, and other units were sweeping

---

* Alan Brooke frankly confessed that it was the appreciation of the two generals which he made
during 'those critical days' which resulted in their African appointments. See his interesting note
in Arthur Bryant, *The Turn of the Tide*, Collins, pp. 107, 108.

north-eastwards towards Montreuil and Etaples. The Channel coast was in the enemy's grasp, and the B.E.F. was already, in effect, surrounded. The much-quoted counter-attack by British armour which drove into the German flank at Arras on the 21st (much-quoted largely because it is almost the only one the British have to quote!), was too frail and disorganised to achieve any immediate effect—though in the longer term its psychological effect on Hitler and his commanders was out of all proportion to its weight. It is not surprising, therefore, that on the 23rd Brooke was noting in his diary, 'nothing but a miracle can save the B.E.F. now'.

2 Corps was at last established in the defensive line to which it had devoted a winter's preparation; but it was to abandon within days what had taken months of hard labour to create. Montgomery was as alert as ever—indeed, he remained fresh right down to the beaches as a result, in part, of his systematic daily regimen. He looked after his men carefully—in the most significant way, by looking after their food. He had beef 'on the hoof' in the form of his private herds of cattle. He set up butcheries and bakeries. He raided an abandoned ammunition train. He was, in fact, living up to that famous definition of the qualities of the ideal infantryman which Wavell enunciated in his classic lecture at the Staff College in 1932, on 'The Training of the Army for War': these included the skills of a successful poacher and cat-burglar. But all this was only a preliminary to more deadly business.

If the B.E.F. was to escape it must continue to be encircled by an unbroken protective ring. The perimeter, as it solidified, was exposed to two major threats—one from the German armoured columns closing in from the west, the other from von Bock's Army Group thrusting against the Belgians from the east. The first threat was averted by Hitler himself, when he ordered Guderian's tanks to stand fast. The second deeply affected Brooke and his Corps.

On the night of 27/28 May there came the moment of truth. The Belgian collapse was now complete: King Leopold's capitulation occurred at midnight. For Brooke, holding with his Corps the line Roubaix-Halluin-the Ypres/Comines canal, this meant that a gap now yawned between his left flank and the French *Division Lourde Motorisée* in the north. Yet this line was the sole bastion between von Bock's masses and the chaos within the British perimeter. A breakthrough here might have produced a disaster infinitely greater than Rommel's capture of Tobruk and its contents. But the line held. During the day 5 Division under General Franklyn came under tremendous pressure, but maintained an intact front. It was the *gap* that caused Brooke the greatest concern. He therefore ordered Montgomery to disengage his division, now out on a limb at Roubaix, and move it to block the hole.

This was a daunting instruction: it impelled Montgomery to carry out a march which, in terms of sheer military *expertise*, was as perfect a piece of work as any of his later and larger achievements. He was required to execute what is notoriously one of the most difficult manoeuvres in war—a flank march past the front of attack. During a single night he had to extricate his division from its positions in front of Roubaix, get it into transport, transfer it (in the dark, and by minor roads), some 25 miles to the north, and have it entrenched by dawn, ready to receive a predictable drive by the Germans aimed at smashing across the river Yser and cutting the road to Dunkirk. The move, moreover, had to take place only a few thousand yards behind the precarious line of 5 Division, which could conceivably crack at any moment. Brooke spent most of the night uneasily watching Montgomery's progress, but there was no need for alarm. 'The 3rd Division', Brooke noted, 'through constant practice had become most proficient at this method of movement.' Montgomery might have aroused, in peacetime, the suspicion or even contempt of certain officers in the British Army, and elicited from others a pitying smile, but the fact remains that in 1940 there were very few Major-Generals who could have undertaken this manoeuvre so confidently or executed it so impeccably. 'It was with a feeling of intense relief that I found Monty in position,' wrote Brooke in his *Papers* as a comment on an entry in his diary which he made at the time. This read: 'Found he had, as usual, accomplished almost the impossible.'

From now on the day's work consisted of fending off the Germans and gradually falling back on Dunkirk and the beaches. As the Navy and the 'little ships' went steadily ahead with evacuation, in spite of the Luftwaffe, the size of the B.E.F. was reduced, and in proportion to its reduction the most senior officers were ordered back to England, peremptorily and against their will. The system made sense, for tomorrow's war was still to fight: but it was anguish for a passionate and highly-strung man like Brooke to have to abandon his cherished Corps. Nevertheless, the order came, and during the evening of the 30th he sailed for home. Before leaving, however, he had had to make appropriate dispositions. 'I had no hesitation in selecting Monty to succeed me . . .' though Montgomery was the junior of his three Major-Generals. Montgomery was succeeded at 3 Division by Brigadier Kenneth Anderson who, by a strange coincidence, was later to command First Army in N.W. Africa while Montgomery was commanding the Eighth. Horrocks succeeded Anderson. In so doing, he was witness to a moving spectacle. '. . . I was summoned to 3rd Div. H.Q. As I approached I saw two figures standing on the sand-dunes. I recognised our Corps Commander, General Brooke, and my divisional commander, General Montgomery. The former was under considerable emotional strain. His shoulders were bowed and it looked as though he were weeping. Monty was patting him on the back. They then shook hands and General Brooke walked slowly to his car and drove away.' It is not to be sentimental to suspect that this moment on the sands played its part in later years when, as C.I.G.S., Brooke was to support Montgomery so staunchly.

As a Corps Commander Montgomery had already attended, that afternoon, Gort's final conference at his H.Q. on the Dunkirk sea-front. Gort read out to his subordinates the Government's telegram which contained its instructions for the last phase of the evacuation. The gist was that a Corps Commander must be nominated by Gort (before he himself withdrew) to supervise this phase, and according to Montgomery the man selected was Lieut.-General M. G. H. Barker, who commanded 1 Corps. (This was to be the last Corps to go.) After the conference, however, Montgomery addressed Gort in private, and did what for a brand new Corps Commander and a very junior Major-General was a remarkable thing. He questioned his superior's judgement in this vital matter. He said Barker was not now in a fit state for the final command, in which poise and clarity of mind would be essential. Alexander, whose 1 Division was back in 1 Corps, was the man with these qualifications. 'I knew Gort very well; so I spoke very plainly and insisted that this was the right course to take.'*

Gort was not a great man. As a senior commander in the field he had grave limitations. But he was a good, steadfast man of honour, and when he saw where the path of duty lay he would follow it unflinchingly. He could see clearly—for a limited distance. During the May retreat he saw just far enough—saw that a French defeat was inevitable, and that his personal obligation to his country was to return to it as much of the B.E.F. as possible. When Montgomery made his proposal, therefore, Gort did not strike an attitude, talk about impertinence, or stand on his dignity: he accepted it, for Montgomery had convinced him that his sacred trust could be placed the more safely in Alexander's hands. So Barker went back to England and Alexander remained in supreme charge of a dwindling command. There can be little doubt that to Montgomery's act of intelligent effrontery a good many men owe, if not their lives, then at least salvation from years in a German prison camp.

2 Corps came out during the night of 31 May. Montgomery himself disembarked at Dover on the morning of 1 June. Alexander, having coolly disposed of the remnants, arrived two days later. His account of his departure from Dunkirk, in his *Memoirs*, is a classic and characteristic essay in understatement: 'On the last night I toured the beaches with Admiral Bill Tennant

---

* It is amusing to note that in a conversation with Liddell Hart in November 1937 Gort remarked that Montgomery was 'only good at minor tactics'!

D

in a small naval craft, to make sure that no one was left behind. Having satisfied myself that the whole of the rearguard had got safely away, I boarded a destroyer at the mole—which, incidentally, was receiving attention from spasmodic German machine-gun fire.'

In England it was still not clear that something irrecoverable had happened. When Brooke called at the War Office on 2 June to see the C.I.G.S., now Sir John Dill, and to ask what was now required of him, he was told, 'Return to France to form a new B.E.F.' 'As I look back at the war,' Brooke wrote, 'this was certainly one of my blackest moments.' He knew from first-hand observation and experience that the French were finished, and that they would drag down into the abyss with them whatever scratch force he might be able to pull together. Still, orders were orders. He was offered two Scottish Territorial divisions, 51 Highland (which was still in France, having avoided the Dunkirk débâcle because it was operating with the French further south) and 52 Lowland, as well as the fragments of the only Armoured Division, 1 Canadian Division and sundry bits and pieces. Brooke also asked for 3 Division. Dill demurred, Brooke pressed, and finally it was agreed that after re-equipping the Division should be sent back across the Channel. The fact was that in Britain at that moment there was only enough transport and other essentials to refit a single division. It was therefore a high compliment that the 3rd, after the drubbing it had taken, should have been accepted by the C.I.G.S. to go to the head of what, after Dunkirk, was a hungry queue.

This conversation at the War Office directly affected Montgomery. It went, of course, just as he would have wished it to go had he been present, for at his own request he had been allowed to retire from command of a Corps and return to his old post at the head of the 'Iron' Division. Now there was a chance of further action. As the days passed the 3rd Division reformed down in Somerset, made up its lost equipment, and by mid-June was ready to go. But there was nowhere to go to: on 17 June came the French capitulation.

All priorities were now altered. Britain stood alone, and invasion appeared to be imminent. Montgomery's division was therefore switched immediately to one of the most vulnerable areas—the coastal region round Brighton—and set about preparing the defences which were sadly lacking. But Montgomery was dissatisfied with his rôle. He had the only fully equipped division in England, a division adept at movement—as it had superbly demonstrated in the face of the enemy—yet here he was in a static situation, watching his men dig holes in seaside gardens and picket Brighton pier; drawing, as it were, a thin red line a few yards beyond highwater-mark. Further inland, according to the current anti-invasion plan, so-called Stop Lines and anti-tank ditches were being dug (to be manned by whom?), and it might be said that the general principle governing the overall scheme after the fall of France was one of linear defence.

Montgomery thought this was nonsense. He wanted his division to be pulled back further inland and provided with transport, so that he could act as a mobile reserve capable of launching a quick counter-attack to seal off and abolish any force which might make a successful landing, and thus prevent the establishment of bridgeheads—the great danger—through which German follow-up divisions might pour. (It is interesting to note that this was precisely the method Rommel had in mind as he planned the defences of Western Europe in 1944.) Such operations required practice if they were to be effective: 3 Division must have the necessary equipment. The opportunity, which Montgomery was quick to exploit, came when the Prime Minister took a look at his division on 2 July. Though Montgomery had been close to him at least once, at a Victory Parade in 1919, he had not yet actually met Churchill. He stage-managed the inspection successfully, and was invited to dine with the Prime Minister and his entourage in Brighton that evening. Here Montgomery expounded his theories—meat and drink to a Prime Minister who, in those dark days, was seeking everywhere for signs of an aggressive spirit to match his own. Montgomery's theme was 'Why was I left immobile? There were thousands of buses in England: let them give me some. . . .' Churchill was impressed, and the division got its transport. This was doubtless due to a magisterial minute dictated by the Prime Minister next day (with a characteristic Churchillian sting in its tail).

(Action this Day)

Prime Minister to Secretary of State for War　　　　　　　　3.VII.40

　　I was disturbed to find the 3rd Division spread along thirty miles of coast, instead of being, as I had imagined, held back concentrated in reserve, ready to move against any serious head of invasion. But much more astonishing was the fact that the infantry of this division, which is otherwise fully mobile, are not provided with the buses necessary to move them to the point of action. This provision of buses, waiting always ready and close at hand, is essential to all mobile units, and to none more than the 3rd Division while spread about the coast.

　　I heard the same complaint from Portsmouth that the troops there had not got their transport ready and close at hand. Considering the great masses of transport, both buses and lorries, which there are in this country, and the large numbers of drivers brought back from the B.E.F., it should be possible to remedy these deficiencies at once. I hope, at any rate, that the G.O.C. 3rd Division will be told today to take up, as he would like to do, the large number of buses which are even now plying for pleasure traffic up and down the sea front at Brighton.

Montgomery's tactical thinking was certainly correct, as was proved in one assault landing after another in the latter stages of the war. But attitudes were to change. On 19 July Brooke was summoned to see Anthony Eden, now Secretary of State for War in the Churchill administration, and was told that Ironside was to be put out to grass, with a peerage and a promotion to Field Marshal, and that Brooke was to replace him as Commander-in-Chief, Home Forces. Four days later he was touring Eastern Command, which then ran from Sussex to the Wash. He first noticed the absurdity of a Command so massive that it was beyond one man's power to control it properly, especially as it was split down the middle by the Thames. He soon put that right, by dividing it into two Commands of which the southern, S.E. Command, would ultimately become Montgomery's domain. But he also noted, in words which Montgomery might have used to Churchill at Brighton a few days earlier: 'To my mind our defence should be of a far more mobile and offensive nature. I visualised a light line of defence along the beaches, to hamper and delay landings to the maximum, and in rear highly mobile forces trained to immediate aggressive action intended to concentrate and attack any landings before they had time to become too well established.'

This, independently arrived at, was the basis of Montgomery's military philosophy throughout his 'English' period, which it is best to think of as a whole—i.e., the period from June 1940 to 10 August 1942, when he departed for Egypt. He became a Corps Commander again in July 1940, taking over 5 Corps (roughly Hampshire and Dorset); in April 1941 he moved to 12 Corps (which guarded the particularly endangered Kentish coast); and in December 1941 he took over the South Eastern Command which Brooke had created, within whose bounds—Kent, Surrey and Sussex—lay most of the areas that might tempt an invader. It was, as near as possible, an operational command. But during these two years, it might be said, the only things that changed were the number of troops under his orders and the number of stories in circulation about him. He himself sees a certain unity in this phase of his career. What bound it together was the fact that his notions about how to train troops and how to employ them in battle were now fixed, and were applied consistently to the formations under his command, whatever their size. 'So,' he writes, 'the ideas and the doctrine of war, and training for war, which began as far west as Dorset, gradually spread along the south of England to the mouth of the Thames.' Montgomery may have paid but little attention to Liddell Hart's famous concept of the 'expanding torrent' in relation to armoured warfare, but he clearly accepted the notion of an expanding torrent of ideas—*his* ideas.

Montgomery was always his own worst enemy. 'That intensely compacted hank of steel wire,' as Bernard Shaw called him, contained a number of flawed strands. Warm and considerate towards those of whom he approved, he could be icy in his contemptuous disregard of those he rejected. In certain cases this behaviour was so flagrant that it caused, and still causes, even men of good will towards him to qualify their admiration. His treatment of Auchinleck is a painful example. Throughout the war, and afterwards, Montgomery's conduct in respect of 'the Auk' was unpardonable. What happened in Africa in the course of his taking over the Eighth Army is described in the next chapter. But the trouble started at least as early as 1940. When Montgomery took over 5 Corps he succeeded Auchinleck who, himself taking over Southern Command, became Montgomery's immediate superior. A note he made in his recollections suggests that he was not wholly enchanted by his successor. 'I used to go and listen in to his lectures—no coughing, no smoking, runs before breakfast—all very inspiring and made me feel a bit inadequate. But I doubt if runs before breakfast really produce battle winners, of necessity.' All Montgomery has to say about this period in his *Memoirs* is, 'I cannot recall that we ever agreed on anything.' But there is more to it than that.

On 15 August Auchinleck wrote to Montgomery a long and a stern letter. In it he pointed out that Montgomery had badly over-stepped the mark by calling at the War Office and discussing with the Adjutant-General in person the question of the transference from his Corps to other formations of personnel with B.E.F. experience. 'I am quite aware that it is a common practice in the Army for officers of all ranks to visit the War Office, but in this case it appears that you interviewed the Adjutant-General on a matter which directly concerns my Headquarters, in that they had issued orders for certain transfers to take place. I do not consider this is the proper manner in which this, or any other matters of this nature, should be handled. . . .' Auchinleck also pointed out, firmly, that he disapproved of Montgomery's having issued a memorandum 'thereby indicating to your subordinates that you had gone over the head of my Headquarters to deal with the problem direct with the War Office'. Montgomery, however, was unabashed. On 19 October Auchinleck had to write him another letter. This was because Montgomery had again been dealing directly with the Adjutant-General's office, in an attempt to get particular officers posted to his Corps from other units in Southern Command. 'I want you to realise that this procedure, however justifiable it may seem to you, is likely to cause extreme annoyance to the commanders of the formations and units concerned, more particularly where, in their opinion, your selections do not tally with their ideas as to who is the best man in the unit concerned for the job for which you want him.' This time Auchinleck also sent to the Adjutant-General a diplomatic complaint.

The poacher-cum-cat-burglar had been caught *in flagrante delicto*. But Montgomery was far too experienced a soldier not to have realised the impropriety of his actions. In each instance he had succumbed to the old urge to 'try it on' which had damaged him in the past and would damage him in the future. His misdemeanours were so glaring, and so certain to be detected, that one gets the feeling that he was going out of his way to openly flout Auchinleck's authority. Why?

5 Corps was trained by Montgomery to be an all-weather formation '. . . in rain, snow, ice, mud, fair weather or foul, at any hour of the day or night—we must be able to do our stuff better than the Germans'. He tested his troops on the fail-safe principle. Officers at any level, whether regimental or staff, got their congé if they cracked under the strain. Wives were expelled from the invasion coast (though there were ways of circumventing this instruction: one officer, on Montgomery's staff, informed his landlady that because of his master's ruling his wife, coming down to stay with him that weekend, must be known as 'Miss Smith'. It happened that her real name *was* Miss Smith!) He was now in a position to apply the ideas which he and Brooke shared about coastal defence. A thin screen held the beaches: inland lay the counter-attack groups, mobile and unrestricted by obligations to man the conventional Stop Lines which were still in preparation in other parts of the country. Everyone was expected to be continually on the alert.

In this matter Montgomery was once hoist by his own petard. Michael Calvert (later to win the DSO as a column commander with Wingate's Chindits) and Peter Fleming (who had as varied a war as most), in 1940 had the task of making Kent and Sussex as unpleasant a region as possible in the event of the Germans achieving a successful landing. (The full story is told in Peter Fleming, *Invasion 1940*, Rupert Hart-Davis.) One of their incidental tasks was to test the security arrangements of other units in the danger area. They were ordered to tackle in this way the H.Q. of what Michael Calvert in his own book, *Fighting Mad*, describes as 'a promising young general named Montgomery'. Aware of his reputation, they knew they had a tough nut to crack. They decided, therefore, to employ the principle of the double bluff. In the local pubs they talked largely about how they were planning to blow up with gelignite the flower pots along the terrace in front of Montgomery's H.Q. The message got through, and Montgomery's guardians reasonably assumed that this was a cover story for another line of attack. On a moonless night the pair slipped past the look-outs, planted their explosives in the pots (with time-fuses attached), fastened a booby trap to the leg of the sleeping officer of the watch, and successfully retired. Next morning they reported to Montgomery, who greeted them triumphantly. At that moment the time-fuses worked, and outside the window there occurred a series of explosions. Montgomery stood them a drink.

When he transferred to South Eastern Command Montgomery stuck to the same methods. Horrocks, now commanding 44 (Home Counties) Division in Kent, says that the impact of Montgomery's arrival was 'as though atomic bombs were exploding all over this rural corner of Britain'. Irrespective of age or rank, every officer in the command was ordered to carry out two cross-country runs weekly. Those who said they would die were told they might as well die. Ralph Arnold, who had been A.D.C. to Ironside when he was C.I.G.S., was now serving as an Intelligence Officer in the H.Q. of South Eastern Command at Reigate. He recalls how all officers on the staff under 45 had to parade weekly in full marching order, carrying rifles and ammunition, and run, *as a formed body*, for ten miles cross country. But these important gentlemen were coddled. Behind the procession there would travel the Major-General Administration in his staff car, then the Director of Medical Services, then two Military Policemen on motorcycles, and then an ambulance. Thus the failures could be noted* and the casualties rescued. In all this apparent madness there was, of course, a method. I happened to be in 44 Division at the time, as an officer in a Field Regiment whose guns were dug into pits, ready to fire on the beaches. In spite of manoeuvres, it was a sluggish way of life, and though we loathed it the imposed exercise shook away the cobwebs. At the bottom of Montgomery's thinking, in fact, was the realisation of an important truth, which is that in certain respects the worst place in which to train to defend your own country is your own country.

Perhaps the most controversial event with which Montgomery was connected during his tenure of South Eastern Command was the assault on Dieppe. Much of the odium has stuck to his name. There are Canadians who—pardonably—lay the catastrophe at his door. Montgomery has not helped matters by the terse and inaccurate account he provides in his *Memoirs*. An impartial examination of the facts suggests that he bears a certain responsibility for what occurred, but that if accusations of delinquency are to be made there are a good many others who should first face the firing line.

During the early months of 1942 the Chiefs of Staff, Combined Operations (under Lord Mountbatten), the Americans and, not least, the Prime Minister spent much time considering whether either or both of two daring projects could be made viable: they were named ROUNDUP and SLEDGEHAMMER. The former was the code-name for a full-scale return to the Continent: the second covered contingent plans for a smaller sortie into France if Russia got into extreme difficulties or, *per contra*, the Germans showed signs of collapse. By April SLEDGEHAMMER was seen to be impracticable in the immediate

---

* Under the Army Act physical failure (except drunkenness, V.D., self-inflicted wounds, etc.) is not an offence. But there are ways of making the 'punishment' fit the 'crime'.

future, though ROUNDUP was retained as a prospect for April 1943. By July SLEDGEHAMMER was defunct, ROUNDUP was receding from view, and attention was now diverted towards an Anglo-American entry into N.W. Africa, under Eisenhower's command, which was given a code-name TORCH.

Without an understanding of this background it is difficult to see the Dieppe raid in a proper perspective. It was bred 'by despair upon impossibility'. In all the discussions of SLEDGEHAMMER and ROUNDUP it was universally agreed that one essential factor in any successful return to Europe would be the early capture of a good port, in working order, which could be over-run before the enemy could destroy its installations. As the major projects died or disappeared into the distance, it was felt to be even more necessary, during 1942, to attempt some sort of trial across the Channel in order to discover pragmatically what was entailed in the capture of a port. A careful study of alternatives indicated Dieppe as the best bet—unlike some other candidates, it was within fighter range, and it contained a reasonable collection of 'military objectives', a radar station, an airfield, and sundry batteries of artillery, besides its harbour and shipping.

A draft plan, offering alternatives, was evolved by Combined Ops. H.Q., and after consideration a final scheme was selected which was approved by the Chiefs of Staff, on 13 May. Only then was it decided to appoint Force Commanders and, since the assault was to be made by Canadians, and the Canadian Corps was in South Eastern Command, Montgomery was appropriately nominated to represent the Commander-in-Chief, Home Forces.

This is where he enters on the scene, and this is where his partial responsibility begins. For on 5 June there was a meeting of the Force Commanders at which the crucial question was discussed of whether heavy bombers should, as had been intended, be used in advance to soften up the Dieppe defences. Air Vice-Marshal Leigh-Mallory for the R.A.F. and Major-General Roberts for the Canadians both opposed the proposal, which was dropped. (The post-mortem on the Dieppe raid suggested that this was a mistake, and the lesson was not forgotten in the planning of D-Day.) Now in his *Memoirs* Montgomery states quite flatly, in regard to 'the elimination of any preliminary bombing of the defences from the air', that he would not have agreed to such elimination. However, in his history of Combined Operations, *The Watery Maze*, the distinguished soldier and writer Brigadier Sir Bernard Fergusson (whose book is strongly founded on the relevant documents), observes that 'far from not agreeing with the change, he was in the chair at the meeting where the decision was taken; and he is not on record in the minutes as having demurred'! This appears to be one of those not infrequent occasions when Montgomery has had a convenient lapse of memory—as some shut off a hearing aid to exclude a disagreeable noise.

Furthermore, Jacques Mordal, the French historian who has specialised in the study of the Second World War, points out in his book on Dieppe that it was Montgomery who, as was proper, tackled General McNaughton, commanding 1 Canadian Army, and General Crerar, commanding 1 Canadian Corps, and obtained their agreement that the Dieppe operation should be carried out by 2 Canadian Division under Major-General Roberts, on the grounds that a mixed Anglo-Canadian force would render difficult the essential unity of command. Mordal also notes that on 1 July, just before the first abortive attempt, Montgomery reported that in his opinion, 'the operation afforded reasonable prospects of success, provided the weather was fine, an average possibility, and provided the Royal Navy landed the troops at the hour prescribed and at the correct spot'.

It can be argued, therefore, that directly or indirectly Montgomery bore some responsibility for the plan for the first attempt, Operation RUTTER: but when this was cancelled, because of adverse weather conditions, he wrote immediately to General Paget, Commander-in-Chief Home Forces, to advise that a raid on Dieppe should be put off 'for all time'. He was convinced that, owing to the delays and the many troops involved, security must have been irretrievably broken. 'At least,' he said, 'if they want to do something on the Continent, let them choose another target than Dieppe.' On 10 August he left for Egypt. On 19 August the bloody battle for Dieppe finally took place.

Weighing the evidence as impartially as possible I cannot feel that Montgomery should carry a large burden of guilt over Dieppe—not, I am sure, that he does. If his advice had been followed, the raid would never have taken place. And even the question of the use of heavy bombers, eliminated with his connivance from the first plan, can be argued two ways. For might not a Caen or a Cassino have been created? What, it might be asked, is the point of trying to land tanks if you have just blocked the streets in front of them?

When Montgomery received the news of Dieppe during the night of 19 August he was entertaining Churchill at the H.Q. of Eighth Army, in his capacity as Commander. The transitional stages from the 12th Corps at Reigate to this desert eminence had been complicated, but swift in sequence. The *proximate* cause, as the philosophers say, was a decision by Brooke in early July that he must visit Cairo and, as C.I.G.S., take the opportunity of examining on the spot the situation in Gibraltar, Malta, and the Persia/Iraq area, ending up with a private consultation with Wavell, the Commander-in-Chief in India, about the defence of the Indo-Burmese frontier. All this made sense. As to the Eighth Army Brooke noted that 'it was quite clear that there was something radically wrong, but not easy to judge what this something was, or how wrong it was. . . . The crisis had now come and it was essential that I should go out and see what was wrong. But for this I wanted to be alone.' It was not to be. On 15 July, seizing a favourable moment, Brooke obtained Churchill's permission for the journey. On 30 July, however, the day before his departure, he and the Chiefs of Staff Committee were surprised to be suddenly informed that the Prime Minister had decided to go too. And so it was that under the code-name BRACELET Churchill's expeditionary force assembled in Cairo early in August to settle the fate of the Eighth Army. The Prime Minister, after following a circuitous route, arrived on the 3rd, preceded by Brooke who had travelled more directly.

The *final* cause of the whole affair was the simple fact that, as Sir Arthur Bryant puts it, 'In the one theatre of war where it had been actively engaged since the débâcle of Singapore and Burma, it' (the Army) 'had lost the bulk of its armour and been driven back for four hundred miles, with the result that the Nile Delta and the Canal were in imminent danger. . . .' For both national and personal reasons, therefore, the man who was not only Prime Minister but also self-appointed Minister of Defence required a *victory*—a victory as soon as possible, a dramatic victory, a victory self-evidently decisive. Auchinleck's defeat of Rommel in the First Battle of Alamein in July had not been seen in this light. Neither Parliament, nor the nation, nor, in particular, the Prime Minister had grasped its profound significance. In spite of the kind things he was later to say about Auchinleck, it is doubtful whether Churchill ever did.

On the evening of the 3rd Brooke was summoned by Churchill and held in discussion till 1.30 a.m. All revolved round the point that Auchinleck could no longer perform the dual function of C.-in-C. Middle East and Commander, Eighth Army—the rôle he had assumed when he took over control from Ritchie on the afternoon of 25 June. Brooke naturally agreed with this proposition, but the crux was, who should now command the Army? Churchill argued the case for Gott, the old desert hand now commanding 13 Corps. Brooke argued that he was worn out. Churchill countered by offering Brooke the command. This, Brooke recalled, 'gave rise to the most desperate longings'. However, next morning he was early at work with Auchinleck and later in the day found him agreeable to the suggestion that Montgomery should be sent to Eighth Army. Brooke did not think the combination would work, but he wanted Montgomery so much that he was prepared to contemplate shifting Auchinleck, if necessary.

The next day the scene is the desert. After starting at 5.45 a.m. the Prime Minister, Brooke and their satellites visited H.Q. Eighth Army, having been introduced en route to a number of subordinate commanders. 'We were given breakfast,' Churchill acidly observed, 'in a cage full of flies and high military personages.' It was, of course, a Battle Headquarters. Churchill had not entered such an establishment in the field for a long time, and was excessive in his irritation at the discomfort: certainly the visit did Auchinleck's cause no good—and it does, in fact, seem that he overdid the austerity.

After breakfast Churchill had something of an altercation in the Operations caravan with Auchinleck and his right hand man, Dorman-Smith. It was the usual business; 'Attack, attack.' Discouraged by the soldiers' arguments in favour of delay, Churchill left in a black mood, ordering Gott, whom he had just met for the first time, to drive him to his aeroplane. During the journey Gott significantly said he was tired, and spoke of a long leave in England. That afternoon Brooke went down to 13 Corps H.Q. for further talk with Gott, and found that his doubts were confirmed. Gott said he had used up most of his own ideas and that what was required was new blood.

The next day, 6 August, brought a change of front. While Brooke was dressing 'and practically naked' Churchill burst in on him with the news that his thoughts were taking firm shape. After breakfast a conversation revealed that the Prime Minister proposed to split the Middle East Command, making a Persia/Iraq Command that would be offered to Auchinleck and a Near East Command which he wanted Brooke to take, with Montgomery at Eighth Army. Brooke, to his honour, refused because, though an operational command was very dear to him, he thought that he had now some skill in managing the Prime Minister and therefore could serve his country better if he continued that arduous task. During the day, however, the situation altered (possibly due to the influence of Smuts on Churchill). Brooke was summoned to the British Embassy where, sitting with Smuts, Churchill showed him a telegram which was to go off to Attlee, the Deputy Prime Minister and, in Churchill's absence, the chairman of the Cabinet. Apart from proposing the division of the Middle East Command, the main items of interest were the recommendations of Alexander for the Middle East, Gott for Eighth Army, and Montgomery for TORCH, the invasion of N.W. Africa. Brooke agreed to the proposed formulae, though he retained misgivings about Gott. 'I may have been weak; in any case Fate took the matter in its hands within twenty-four hours of our decision.'

The War Cabinet met, agreed the various appointments, but raised certain queries about the plan for two new commands. Churchill replied and then, on the afternoon of the 7th, departed to visit the 51st Highland Division, which had just arrived. But Fate now intervened. Gott was flying down the Burg el Arab/Heliopolis route, which was considered 100 per cent safe—so much so that no escort was provided for Churchill when he used it. But a German fighter which had been driven from on high came across the lumbering transport plane in which Gott was travelling, and shot it down. Gott was killed. The news came to Churchill and Brooke that evening, and he, Smuts and Churchill discussed and argued until it was finally decided that Montgomery should succeed Gott. Brooke also spoke on the telephone to Auchinleck (still unaware of his dismissal) who agreed with the decision. A telegram was despatched.

> *Prime Minister to Deputy Prime Minister*   7 August 1942
>   C.I.G.S. decisively recommends Montgomery for Eighth Army. Smuts and I feel this post must be filled at once. Pray send him by special plane at earliest moment. Advise me when he will arrive.

The reply containing the War Cabinet's approval arrived in the early hours of the next morning. All that remained was for Colonel Ian Jacob to take up to Auchinleck a personal letter from Churchill relieving him of both the Commands he had been administering.

There can be no doubt that Fate was kinder to the British people than Churchill during this crucial conference. All the evidence, starting with Gott's own words, indicates that he was the wrong man for the job. Following Lord Moran's thesis that every man has a certain stock of courage which, in battle, can be gradually expended until there is nothing left in the bank, so one might say that each man has a similar stock of vitality. By August 1942 Gott had been in the desert since before the war. He was one of the true 'desert rats', and he was greatly loved by officers and men. 'Strafer' Gott was a name to conjure with. Nevertheless, his stock of vitality had run out. Jacob soon appreciated this as he talked around Cairo. Brooke saw it clearly. It seems likely that at least some of those who pressed Gott's claims were actuated by affection and memories of his past, rather than by an appreciation of his recent performances and his future potential, for his recent conduct of his Corps had been less than masterly. There were signs, indeed, that his judgement was slipping. He had, for example, recently sacked one of the most fearless men in the British Army, 'Pete' Rees, from the command of 10 Indian Division in terms which implied something like cowardice. (In Burma, as Field Marshal Slim would affirm, Rees rose to great heights as a divisional commander; there was nothing craven about the captor of Mandalay.) In sum, Churchill was misguided: but it was tragic that it required the death of a very gallant soldier to rectify his error.

Montgomery was of course unaware that the king-makers were at work. At the beginning of August he was up in Scotland, having travelled in the special train of the C.-in-C. Home Forces to watch a major exercise. The War Office got on to him by telephone and told him that Alexander, commander-designate for the British First Army which was to take part in TORCH, was now to go to the Middle East and Montgomery was to succeed him. He would proceed south and start work on planning immediately. However, his morning shave next day was interrupted by another call from the War Office, informing him that he was to take over the Eighth Army. He left England on the 10th and reached Cairo early on the 12th.

The transference within 24 hours from First to Eighth Army was the greatest stroke of luck in Montgomery's career. With the latter he was able to win at Alamein a dramatic victory and defeat a famous enemy, watched by the vigilant eye of the Prime Minister and the press of the world. After Alamein Montgomery's star was bright. But, to adapt a phrase of Rommel's, there were no laurels to be earned in TORCH. Nothing that Montgomery could have done would have altered the fact that, in the early stages at least, the British component was much smaller than the American, that Eisenhower rather than his Army Commanders was the focus of attention, and that the build-up of German forces probably precluded a snap victory before the winter closed down the fronts. In other words, TORCH was an operation in which, for a variety of reasons, it was impossible to win within days a world-wide reputation. Of course Montgomery would have conducted the campaign more 'tidily' than did his successor, Kenneth Anderson, though whether liaison with the Americans would have run more smoothly is a matter of doubt. All this is academic, except the undeniable fact that in the latter part of 1942 the Western Desert was the place for a man who wanted to make a reputation.

On the morning of his arrival Montgomery called on Auchinleck. (The course of their conversation is discussed in the next chapter.) He also found an A.D.C., John Poston, a young officer in the 11th Hussars who had served with Gott. 'I could not have made a better choice. We trod the path together from Alamein to the Elbe, fighting our way through ten countries. I was completely devoted to him. He was killed in Germany in the last week of the war.' Next morning another essential appointment was made. Montgomery's old friend was now serving as Brigadier General Staff—Freddie de Guingand. En route to Eighth Army H.Q. Montgomery met de Guingand at the cross-roads outside Alexandria where the Cairo road turns left and begins to follow the coast. As the pair drove along Montgomery quietly sized up the present Freddie, bearing in mind the high opinion he had formed of him as a young officer. De Guingand in turn put Montgomery in the picture: and it is some-times suggested that it was this conversation which fixed in Montgomery's head the false notion that Auchinleck was bent on further retreat. This I doubt: there was plenty of other evidence about for Montgomery to mis-interpret if he so wished. Be that as it may, he decided that de Guingand was his man.

The temporary commander of Eighth Army was Major-General Ramsden, who had served under Montgomery as a battalion commander in Palestine.

Cross-questioning him, Montgomery found 'an air of uncertainty about everything in the operational line'. He was staggered, also, to find that this H.Q. and that of the Desert Air Force were widely separated. Moreover, though Montgomery was no sybarite, it was one of his doctrines that commanders and staffs should enjoy reasonable comfort—if only for efficiency's sake. He was as shocked as Churchill by the prevailing squalor. He therefore dismissed Ramsden back to his Corps, and, without consulting G.H.Q. in Cairo, assumed command of the Eighth Army as from 1400 hrs. that day, 13 August, two days before he was entitled to do so. 'This was disobedience, but there was no come-back'; it was certainly an act probably without parallel in the annals of the British Army. But was it necessary? Nothing significant was stirring along the front. Rommel, indeed, was in no condition to mount anything more than local attacks. Granted that Montgomery was eager to energise the army and to start preparations along his own lines for that defeat of Rommel about which he was already determined, there still seems something gratuitously offensive in his usurpation of power. The old British principle of not kicking a man when he is down applies. Auchinleck had been cruelly treated, in view of what he had achieved, and with the slightest empathy on Montgomery's part he might at least have been allowed to terminate his office in a proper and orderly fashion. But Montgomery was not the make of man to allow a beaten but gallant opponent to march out from his post with colours flying. Not even those who think much of Montgomery's military attributes would condone his treatment of Auchinleck on this August day: it besmirches what should have been a day of triumph.

For triumph it was. In spite of professional jealousies, private griefs and personal follies Montgomery had won through to the finest position that can come the way of a professional soldier—the command of an army in action with the enemy. That night, he wrote: 'I'm afraid that it was with an insubordinate smile that I fell asleep: I was issuing orders to an Army which someone else reckoned he commanded!' He had been given his heart's desire.

3

Alam Halfa: The Model Battle

'Every great operation of war is unique. What is wanted is a
profound appreciation of the actual event.'

Winston Churchill, *Marlborough*

Ensconced in command of the Eighth Army, Montgomery now started to
tackle four main tasks which, as he saw it, required immediate attention. The
first was to impose his image on his army and renew its confidence in both
itself and its officers—at the top. The second was to review the command
structure and cut out the dead wood which, he suspected, was omnipresent.
Thirdly, he must create a system of control congenial to his own temperament and philosophy of battle. Finally, there was Rommel. For Montgomery
as for Auchinleck the question was not so much whether Rommel would
attack as where, and when. The battle whose imminence was taken for
granted, the first to be fought under his direction, must be won: and won
decisively.

There is an apocryphal story which relates that on D-Day Montgomery and
Admiral Ramsay crossed the Channel to find out how things were going on in
Normandy. As they disembarked both fell into the sea. Ramsay could not
swim. They were hooked out, and Ramsay said, 'For Christ sake don't tell
the Navy I can't swim.' 'All right,' replied Montgomery. 'So long as you
don't tell the Army I can't walk on the water.' Like most apocryphal stories,
this one contains a grain of truth. Montgomery believed and believes passionately that if troops are to give of their best they must have an absolute
faith in the man who is putting them into battle. This is a deeply considered
creed. It goes back to the autumn of 1914 when he found himself on his way
to France with the B.E.F., leader of a platoon of 30 Warwickshires—experienced soldiers in the main—and realised for the first time what it is like to be
weighed up by men under one's command. What they wanted to know, he
sensed, was whether this chap could be trusted: not, would he cosset them?
They were going to war and their lives might be in his hands. Would he
care for those lives *efficiently*?

Since then Montgomery's belief has always been that a commander must
stand or fall by his competence, a competence recognised and ultimately

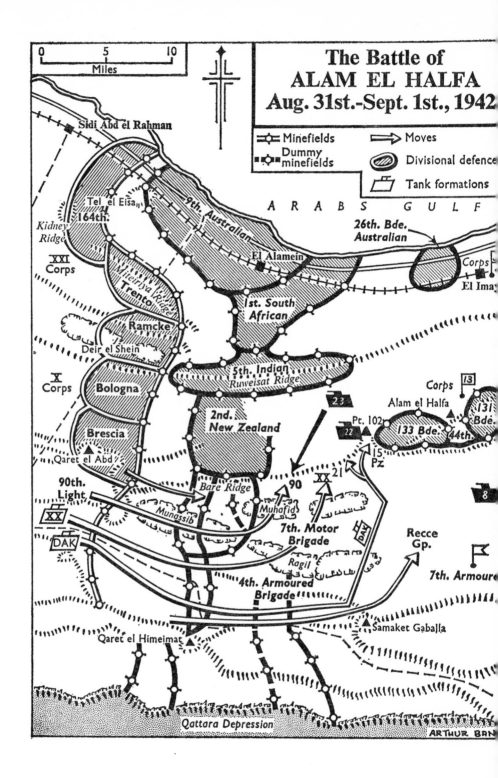

The Battle of
ALAM EL HALFA
Aug. 31st.-Sept. 1st., 1942

Minefields — Moves
Dummy minefields — Divisional defence
Tank formations

Sidi Abd el Rahman

Tel el Eisa
164th.
9th. Australian
Kidney Ridge
XXI Corps
Mteirya Ridge
Trento
El Alamein
26th. Bde. Australian
Corps
El Ima
A R A B S   G U L F

Ramcke
Deir el Shein
1st. South African
X Corps
Bologna
5th. Indian
Ruweisat Ridge
Corps
Alam el Halfa
13
131 Bde.
Pt. 102
133 Bde.
22
44th.
2nd. New Zealand
23
Brescia
Qaret el Abd
15 Pz

90th. Light
DAK
Bare Ridge
Munassib
90
Muhafid
21
DAK
8
7th. Motor Brigade
Ragil
Recce Gp.
4th. Armoured Brigade
7th. Armoure
Qaret el Himeimat
Samaket Gaballa

Qattara Depression

ARTHUR BANKS

0   5   10
Miles

taken for granted by his troops. But in 1942 he was also aware that his desert army was made up of a very different stamp of man from those regulars and reservists he led to France in 1914. Now he was responsible for a mass of individuals most of whom had a relatively high degree of education—who were capable of thinking for themselves. They would want to see what this unknown newcomer from England was like, and to take his measure. He must show himself to them, get among them and let them see his face and hear his words (understanding, of course, that nothing would carry more conviction than a manifest victory). With this creed and these considerations in mind he set about visiting as many units as possible during the early days of his office.

But his spirit went before him. At 6.30 p.m. on the 13th, after his return from that fateful first trip into the desert which had provided him with a Chief of Staff, caused him to take over an Army prematurely, and enabled him to assess the generals of his two Corps, 13 and 30, he addressed the staff of Eighth Army H.Q. outside his caravan in the cool of the evening. 'I introduced myself to them and said I wanted to see them and explain things. Certain orders had already been issued which they knew about, and more would follow. The order "no withdrawal" involved a complete change of policy and they must understand what that policy was, because they would have to do the detailed staff work involved. If we were to fight where we stood the defences must have depth; all transport must be sent back to rear areas; ammunition, water, rations, etc., must be stored in the forward areas. We needed more troops in the Eighth Army in order to make the "no withdrawal" order a possibility. There were plenty of troops back in the Delta, preparing the defence of that area; but the defence of the cities of Egypt must be fought out *here* at Alamein. . . .' The significance of addresses and orders such as these soon filtered round the front; and perhaps rumour did as much for Montgomery as his physical presence. But is not one of the arts of a leader the propagation of those rumours which best suit his cause?

Next there was what he felt to be the dead wood. Pruning and replacement was effected speedily and clinically. Montgomery was a believer in the principle enunciated by Eisenhower to Patton when handing over to him 2nd U.S. Corps: 'you must not retain for one instant any man in a responsible position where you have become doubtful of his ability to do the job. . . . This matter frequently calls for more courage than any other thing you will have to do, but I expect you to be perfectly cold-blooded about it.' Montgomery had the courage, and the sang froid. Corbett and Dorman-Smith had gone – to be followed by others – Dorman-Smith, a brilliant soldier who was subsequently treated with grave injustice, but a man who was his own worst enemy, earning the self-inflicted reputation of being 'too clever by half'. Ramsden went. Renton of 7 Armoured went—in due course, having

E

made the mistake, on his first meeting with his Army Commander, of observing that when the coming attack occurred there was only one question to be decided: who would loose the armour against Rommel? When told that 'it would not be loosed and we would let Rommel bump into it for a change' he made what, in dealing with Montgomery, was a further egregious error: he argued the toss . . . and after Alam Halfa was succeeded by John Harding. As a future substitute for the chief of intelligence Montgomery noted a young Oxford don, E. T. Williams, an intuition brilliantly justified by Williams' subsequent career as Montgomery's main intelligence officer until the end in Germany. Then there was the C.O. who told Montgomery that his second-in-command was responsible for the training in his unit; when Montgomery was informed by the second-in-command that his C.O. was responsible for training, that was the end of that C.O.! And the chief gunner was unseated. To back his punch at Alamein Montgomery wanted to use his artillery, as he put it to me, 'like an 800 gun battery', capable of switching *en masse* from target to target as required. He felt that his gunner couldn't comprehend this form of concentrated fire and had a mind fixed in terms of artillery used in small packets here and there, as in the older desert days.

By these and other moves Montgomery hacked out what he diagnosed as dead wood, introducing fertile growth either by promotion or by introduction from England, whence he summoned Oliver Leese to take over 30 Corps in the north, Horrocks to command 13 Corps in the south, and Brigadier Kirkman, 'whom I regarded as the best artilleryman in the British Army', as his Brigadier, Royal Artillery. He would also have brought out Miles Dempsey to direct the new armoured corps he envisaged, but Alexander persuaded him that three new Corps Commanders were one too many: so against his better judgement he settled for Lumsden, an old desert hand who had commanded 1 Armoured Division. All this was not mere aimless butchery. The record shows that, broadly speaking, Montgomery was a shrewd selector of subordinates—indeed it may be doubted whether, after they were run in, there was a better staff in any army in World War Two than that which served Montgomery. The difference between him and his predecessors lay in his single-minded capacity for ruthlessness when the occasion demanded. On his third day in the desert he looked up his old acquaintance from the First World War, Bernard Freyberg (G.O.C. 2 New Zealand Division). They took a short walk over the sand together, alone. Montgomery outlined his policies. Freyberg said, sardonically, 'What you have to be out here is "a nice chap".' But this was not Montgomery's code.

The effect on Eighth Army of the self-advertisement—and the sackings—was widespread and salutary. Montgomery was and is often criticised for the former, and sometimes for the latter. But it was the medicine the Army needed and was justified in the result. A raw new arrival, I sensed the change in atmosphere, in the indefinable 'feel', immediately. But the most convincing testimony comes from one not disposed to respect for generals, 'Popski'— Lieut.-Colonel Vladimir Peniakoff, DSO, MC, who founded his famous Private Army for long range penetration behind the enemy lines. In his autobiography 'Popski' says: 'In Groppi's I met McMasters, a former C.S.M. of mine in the Libyan Arab Force, and now R.S.M. of a Hussars Regiment, a hard-boiled regular of fifteen years' service, a man who naturally, and rightly, assumed that he and his fellow sergeant majors *were* the British Army, and who entertained an affectionate contempt for all officers.' McMasters graphically described a visit by Montgomery to his regiment and ended, 'Talked to the officers, then to the N.C.O.s. He told us everything: what his plan was for the battle, what he wanted the regiment to do, what he wanted *me* to do. And we will do it, Sir. What a man!' 'Popski' commented: 'A general who has the courage to sack brigadiers from Army Staff and who knows how to evoke enthusiastic devotion in the hearts of regular sergeant majors will, I thought, have no difficulty in defeating Rommel—or even in winning the war.'

The key to Montgomery's new system of control was found during that journey westwards from the cross-roads outside Alexandria on 13 August, when after assessing him keenly he decided to make de Guingand his Chief of Staff. He soon implemented this decision. He told the rest of his staff at the meeting outside his caravan that evening that every order issued by de Guingand must be accepted as coming direct from the Army Commander and obeyed *without demur*.* To de Guingand Montgomery remitted an exceptional authority. He made the point again next morning when an officer awoke him with a situation report, on the grounds that Auchinleck was always roused to read the dawn SITREP. Montgomery replied that he was not Auchinleck and that if anything was wrong he would be informed by the Chief of Staff. Once again his intuition proved to be correct, for the marriage of these two personalities, so diametrically opposed in most other respects, stood firm until the end of the war. Indeed de Guingand—as will be seen— was able to extricate his master from more than one entanglement in which Montgomery had been snared by folly, misjudgement or insensitivity.

De Guingand's appointment derived from Montgomery's perennial search for clarity and simplicity. He believed, in effect, that every problem has a heart and that if you can penetrate to the very heart the resolution of the problem will present no difficulty. He sought always to probe to the essence

---

* Montgomery preserved, however, the orthodox right of the Senior Administrative Staff Officer and the Heads of Services to have direct access to the Commander.

of a matter, with a mind like a lasar beam. Having found the essence, he could then define it to himself and so to others in crisp, brief and unusually simple terms. This in part accounts for the apparent banality of his addresses and messages to his troops. In these he was summarising the results of his mental voyages of discovery: but he rarely communicated the inward agonies of the voyage. His concern was always to transmit certainty. Once he had found the answer to his satisfaction, all shadow of doubt dropped away. This also accounts in part for his stoical capacity to see a battle through to the end without flagging or failing. Buoyed by an inner certainty, he maintained the slogging match at Alamein because he *knew* he must beat Rommel *there*, and that if he could beat Rommel there the rest, he said (bearing in mind the TORCH landings at the other end of the Mediterranean), 'would be a piece of cake'. A similar iron conviction enabled him to persist with his Master Plan in Normandy without regard for the cynics, the dubious or the critical.

But it was an axiom with him that clarity and simplicity cannot be achieved by a mind muddled with a plethora of minor detail. His only experience of an Army Commander in action had been his observation of Gort, C.-in-C. of the B.E.F. in France in 1940—Field Marshal the Viscount Gort VC of whom Alan Brooke wrote despairingly in his diary 'unfortunately his brain was geared to details the whole time. He wandered about scratching the barks of the trees and you could never get him to come out and look at the wood as a whole.' It was in whole woods that Montgomery was mainly interested, and he therefore provided himself with a Chief of Staff even though it was a post disapproved of by the War Office. 'How could I co-ordinate all the staff work of the desert campaign? That is what all the others had done and it had led them to lose sight of the essentials. . . .' An enormous burden was thus thrown on de Guingand, and indeed his health broke down more than once. But the system worked.

It also made possible a second innovation, whereby Montgomery operated in the field from a small Tactical H.Q. established well forward of his Main H.Q., the domain of de Guingand where all detailed planning, administration, etc. were executed. At his Tac. H.Q. Montgomery maintained a minimal staff, signals and cypher personnel, and his liaison officers. His principle was to place his Tac. H.Q. on a level with the H.Q. of the formation next to him in the military hierarchy. Thus as Army Commander his Tac. H.Q. would be on the level with those of his Corps Commanders: as an Army Group Commander he would lie level with the headquarters of his armies. This not only freed him from the distraction of a Main H.Q., as busy as a beehive; it also enabled him to keep in close touch with the generals actually fighting the battle. As to that, when he had issued an instruction to a subordinate, e.g. a Corps Commander, he would always try to make a call one further down the line (in this case to a divisional H.Q.) to see how the instruction was being implemented. Montgomery was not a leader from the front line,* like Rommel: but there can be no dispute about his awareness of the capacities and performance of his generals, brigadiers and even colonels, or of the idiosyncracies of his divisions. 'It is essential to understand that all men are different. The miners from Durham and Newcastle, the men from the Midlands, the Cockneys, the farmers from the West Country, the Scot, the Welshman—all are different. Some men are good at night; others prefer to fight in daylight. Some are best at the fluid and mobile battle; others are more temperamentally adapted to the solid killing match in close country. Therefore all *divisions* are different.'

There now remained Rommel. But before considering his attack at Alam Halfa and the counter-measures successfully applied by Montgomery, it is necessary to pause and dispose of a subject which has engendered long and often bitter controversy, namely the nature of the plans for the future which Auchinleck and his staff had in mind when he handed over the Eighth Army to Montgomery.

No one knows exactly what Auchinleck said to Montgomery on that morning of 12 August when he took Montgomery into his map-room and locked the door, having given orders that they were not to be disturbed. In the account which he gave in his *Memoirs* Montgomery stated that Auchinleck's plan of operations was primarily to preserve the Eighth Army 'in being' and that retreat on the Delta appeared to be the intention if Rommel attacked in strength. He goes into no further detail. But in other places he has stated quite categorically that he took over no specific plans. The allegation that a withdrawal to the Nile was the consideration uppermost in Auchinleck's mind, made in the first edition of Montgomery's *Memoirs*, was effectively challenged by both Auchinleck and Dorman-Smith, his Deputy Chief of General Staff, and Montgomery had to amend it. In the arguments more heat than light has been generated. I can only summarise the situation as I see it myself.

The key text in the controversy is a long memorandum entitled *Appreciation of the Situation in the Western Desert* prepared by Dorman-Smith for Auchinleck under the date-line *El Alamein, 14.45 hours, 27 July 1942*. The whole document is printed as Appendix One in John Connell's *Auchinleck*. The immediately relevant passages occur in para. 18, *Tactical Technique and Future Organisation*. 'B. Eighth Army may have to meet an enemy's sortie developing into manoeuvre by the southern flank from his firm front on the

---

* Not that he shirked the front line. There is abundant evidence to show that he would enter the forward zone when necessary—on reconnaissance in a mobile battle, for example—and that a number of narrow escapes failed to disturb his equanimity.

general line Bab el Qattara-Taqa Plateau. We must therefore organise and train a strong mobile wing, based on 7th Armoured Division. . . . C. Eventually we will have to renew the offensive and this will probably mean a break through the enemy positions about El Alamein. The newly arrived infantry divisions and the armoured divisions must be trained for this and for pursuit.' Dorman-Smith also appreciated that neither side would be likely to attack successfully during August. By mid-September Eighth Army could be reinforced by two armoured and two infantry divisions. 'This may give us a superiority sufficient to justify a direct attack on what may be by then a strongly organised front.'

There can be no doubt that Auchinleck endorsed this paper with its aggressive intent. There can be no doubt that the character of the man, and his conduct of the July battles when he fought Rommel to a standstill, was aggressive. There can also be no doubt that Montgomery is convinced that he took over no plan and indeed de Guingand in his *Generals at War*, reviewing the controversy, says explicitly that when he first met Montgomery and mentioned the various alternative schemes that were being hatched Montgomery said 'Burn the lot.' 'To the best of my knowledge,' he adds, 'he never examined any plans or appreciations that existed at the time.'

The answer appears to me to be clear. Montgomery certainly did Auchinleck an injustice by implying that he was craven, as he also did him an injustice by never paying adequate tribute to Auchinleck's fighting defence in July, and his troops and their predecessors a grave wrong by denying them the Africa Star. This is what rankles most sourly. For the rest, the dispute seems to be terminological and to revolve around what is meant by the word 'plan'. Put briefly, I am convinced that Auchinleck had an *intention* (as Alexander subsequently recognised in his *Despatch*) to give Rommel a bloody nose at Alam Halfa and then attack him at El Alamein; I am equally convinced that when Montgomery took over nothing existed by way of the elaborated operational scheme which we normally understand to be a 'plan'. And finally, I am convinced that if Auchinleck *had* fought Alam Halfa and Alamein he would not, in spite of his enormous merits, have done so as effectively as did Montgomery. I will revert to this point after describing the battle which began among the minefields at the southern extremity of the Alamein Line during the night of 30/31 August.

But, it might be asked, why did this battle ever happen? On a purely rational calculation it would seem that for Rommel, situated as he was, the wiser course would have been to effect a 'Hindenburg Line' type of withdrawal to some suitably defensible position many miles westward, thus abbreviating his dangerously extended lines of communication, and placing him in closer juxtaposition to his bases. The rational arguments are strong.

Rommel wished to avoid what he called 'mechanised static warfare' because he realised that in this 'the good points of the British soldier, his tenacity, for instance, would have the maximum effect': yet he saw the northern and central sectors of the British front rapidly solidifying into a series of inter-connected boxes flanked on the south by extensive minefields—just the setting for British tenacity. A calculated withdrawal would have nullified these elaborate preparations, whereas he himself was desperately short of men and material: his divisions 16,000 under strength, his transport composed as to 85 per cent of captured vehicles lacking spares, his fighting equipment 210 tanks and 175 troop-carriers under establishment, his ammunition scanty, the quality of his rations deplorable. At the same time a revived Malta enabled air and seaborne strikes on the Italian convoy routes to increase markedly the rate of sinking, while *Luftwaffe* squadrons had been switched from the Mediterranean to the Russian front. Thus Rommel's fuel stocks were already low, and replenishment was uncertain. For this reason, too, withdrawal towards his bases would have been beneficial.

But Montgomery was right to assume that Rommel would attack, for whatever the *rationale* in favour of withdrawal it was, in practice, impossible. Hitler alone was a sufficient bar—the Hitler who refused to accept Rommel's recommendation for a withdrawal from Alamein, the Hitler who, in the last stages of the Tunisian battle, held back his permission for the salvaging of his seasoned troops until the very day of the Axis surrender. Moreover, in August the grand strategic scheme of the Germans still looked viable—that great pincer movement whereby the armies in Russia were to press down through Asia Minor, link up with an advancing Afrika Korps and penetrate to the rich oil zones and the Indian Ocean. Throughout August the drive through southern Russia continued: Maikop fell on 9 August, Piatigorsk on the 10th, Mosdok on the 25th, Novorossisk on 6 September. It would have been an unpalatable confession of defeat for Rommel to pull back his portion of the pincer while the German surge to the Caucasus was still proceeding so favourably.

Furthermore, he was now a sick as well as a tired man. The High Command had been informed by his medical adviser that he was suffering from gastric and nasal disorders, and a poor circulation. He was unfit for command, and indeed proposed that he should be replaced by Guderian—though this was refused. Neither before nor during Alam Halfa, in fact, was Rommel at his best, whereas his opponent was buoyant, eager and self-assured, working on the principle that 'what I now needed was a battle which would be fought in accordance with my ideas and not those of former desert commanders'. It was in a mood of desperation and despondency that Rommel made his final fling.

The ideas Montgomery brought to bear in his defensive scheme included important innovations. It has been seen how he dealt cursorily with Renton of 7 Armoured when the latter proposed that the armour should be 'let loose': but Montgomery went further. He gave strict instructions to Horrocks, Commander of 30 Corps, that he was not to allow his tanks to get engaged in close conflict, for already Montgomery was looking ahead (on his principle that one should always be planning the next battle) to Alamein where he would want 7 Armoured as a complement to his new panzer corps. And so, hoisting Rommel with his own petard, he devised a trap for the Afrika Korps such as the British had so far failed to contrive. Taking the refused southern flank of the New Zealand box (see map on p. 48) as a corner-stone, he filled in the gap between it and the Alam Halfa ridge with 22 Armoured Brigade, whose tanks were to dig in in hull-down positions. On the Halfa ridge he placed two brigades of the newly arrived 44 Division which had been rushed up from the Delta as a result of Montgomery's urgent plea to Alexander. Behind 22 Armoured lay 23 Armoured Brigade in reserve. Thus the northern rim of the trap was firm. South of the Halfa ridge lay 8 Armoured Brigade in a lay-back position, while the mobile units of 7 Armoured Division had a skirmishing rôle in protection of the minefields and the open flank to the south.

By these means Rommel was stymied whatever approach he adopted. If he moved due east he would be held up by 8 Armoured while 22 Armoured and the artillery of two divisions pounded him from his left. If, after penetrating the minefields, he made a left hook it would be in the direction of the hull-down 22 Armoured with 8 Armoured poised on his right. Whichever way he moved, he must stick: and when he stuck the Desert Air Force was ready to smash him with relays of planes flying in close order and dropping what Rommel was to call 'bomb carpets'.

So much for the air and the armour. Additionally, the artillery was to be used in a far more concentrated fashion than had previously been customary —a preliminary exercise for Alamein. Dorman-Smith had already, according to de Guingand, been critical of 'the lack of real concentration of the artillery'. But Montgomery not only saw the need, he enforced it. ('Renown awaits the Commander who first in this war restores Artillery to its prime importance upon the battlefield, from which it has been ousted by heavily armoured tanks.' Churchill, as Minister of Defence, 7 October 1941.) It was indeed part of his luck at Alam Halfa—that luck which had brought him to command via Gott's unexpected death at a time when men and munitions were flowing in unparalleled abundance and his opponent was straitened, sick and down-cast—that this was a period when careful and continual experimenting in England with the use of wireless for the simultaneous direction of the fire of large groups of artillery was beginning to bear fruit—a technique in which, until the end of the war, the British would always be ahead of the Germans. Still, when Napoleon asked for lucky generals he was also demanding men who could put their luck to good use!

The days immediately before the battle were characterised by a sense of poise. This is most marked in the memoirs of Sir Howard Kippenberger, the New Zealand Official Historian who at this time was commanding the 5th New Zealand Brigade—a severe, dedicated soldier and a man made sceptical and wary by his experiences as a battalion commander in Greece, Crete and earlier days in the desert. Yet Kippenberger wrote: 'The whole plan for the battle was thoroughly explained to us and I liked it more than that for any action I had taken part in. More pleasing even that the plan itself was the ready, balanced feeling we all had; and that feeling undoubtedly came down from Army Headquarters. It was the first and typical Montgomery battle. All our preparatory moves were made unhurriedly and in plenty of time, and we were completely ready when the blow fell.' Horrocks even held two exercises: and I well remember as a young officer awaiting his first action the curious sense of incongruity in practising it all beforehand. But one of Horrocks' brigadiers told him that when he wanted to know what was going to happen next in the course of the battle he looked up the exercise!

There was no sense of poise in Rommel's mind. General Bayerlein recalls that he said to his medical adviser: 'Professor, the decision I have taken to attack today is the hardest I have ever taken. Either the army in Russia succeeds in getting through to Grozny and we in Africa manage to reach the Suez Canal, or. . . .' The Canal was indeed the ultimate target. There exists a map drawn by Rommel's own hand which shows that 21 Panzer was to mask Alexandria while 15 Panzer and 90 Light made for Cairo; then 15 Panzer would take Suez while 20 Italian Corps secured the Nile valley. In view of his fuel shortage this reveals a lack of proportion—no doubt due to Rommel's illness—which was also evident in his battle-plan. This imposed on the Afrika Korps the task of breaching the minefields and then advancing, in the dark, some 30 miles in seven hours over unreconnoitred territory. 'Things,' Rommel said, 'were then to move fast. The decisive battle was on no account to become static.'

Yet this is precisely what happened, and it may fairly be said that Rommel lost Alam Halfa in the first few hours. In fact the Desert Air Force was already out at dusk on 30 August, bombing his laagers with Wellingtons. As the Afrika Korps sought to clear a breach through the minefields they found them to be more extensive and elaborate than had been anticipated, and the first gap was not cleared until 0430 on the 31st. At 0800 Rommel was told that progress was still very slow. He had already lost General von Bismarck of 21 Panzer, blown up on a mine, and the commander of Afrika Korps,

Nehring, was incapacitated by a wound. Bayerlein took over, and he and Rommel decided to continue with the attack.

They thus committed a grave error and played straight into Montgomery's hands. They should have gone into reverse immediately. Alternatively, a rapid thrust eastwards during the night might just conceivably have had an effect, but now their columns had hardly made headway through the mine-fields, while Eighth Army and the Desert Air Force were fully alerted, the tanks were in their battle stations and waiting (22 Armoured Brigade even had aiming posts out in front of them) and the artillery was standing ready. The soft going of the depressions was consuming precious fuel; and Rommel therefore took a middle course and ordered his armour to make the predicted left wheel to the north, so pointing it straight at the hull-down tanks of 22 Armoured Brigade.

'Hull-down' is actually a misnomer. The tanks were American Grants whose 75mm. gun was slung so low that to fire it the tank commander had to move forward and expose virtually the whole body of his machine. This technical weakness produced the only *moment critique* for the British, whose tension is vividly recreated in the running commentary by Brigadier Roberts (of 22 Armoured) as quoted in Liddell Hart's *The Tanks*.

> Now I can see the enemy myself through my glasses. They are coming straight up the line of the telegraph posts which lead in front of our position. There is some firing by their leading tanks, presumably at our light squadrons, so I instruct these squadrons to come back—but to take it wide so as not to give our position away.
>
> On they come, a most impressive array. . . . It is fascinating to watch them, as one might watch a snake curl up ready to strike. But there is something unusual too; some of the leading tanks are Mk IVs, and Mk IVs have in the past always had short-barrelled 75mm. guns used for close support work and firing H.E. only, consequently they are not usually in front. But these Mk IVs have a very long gun on them; in fact it looks like the devil of a gun. This must be the long-barrelled stepped-up 75mm. the 'Intelligence' people have been talking about.
>
> And now they all turn left and face us and begin to advance slowly. The greatest concentration seems to be opposite the C.L.Y. and the anti-tank guns of the Rifle Brigade. (87 German tanks were counted at this time opposite this part of the front.) I warn all units over the air not to fire until the enemy are within 1,000 yards; it can't be long now and then in a few seconds the tanks of the C.L.Y. open fire and the battle is on. Once one is in the middle of a battle time is difficult to judge, but it seems only a few minutes before nearly all the tanks of the Grant squadron of the C.L.Y. were on fire. The new German 75mm. is taking heavy toll. The enemy tanks have halted and they have their own casualties, but the situation is serious; there is a complete hole in our defence. I hurriedly warn the Greys that they must move at all speed from their defensive positions and plug the gap. Meanwhile the enemy tanks are edging forward

again and they have got close to the Rifle Brigade's anti-tank guns, who have held their fire marvellously to a few hundred yards. When they open up they inflict heavy casualties on the enemy, but through sheer weight of numbers some guns are overrun. The S.O.S. artillery fire is called for; it comes down almost at once right on top of the enemy tanks. This, together with the casualties they have received, checks them. But where are the Greys? 'Come on the Greys,' I shout over the wireless. 'Get out your whips.' But there is no sign of them at the moment coming over the ridge and there is at least another half-hour's daylight left.

Meanwhile some of the enemy have started to work round our left flank and the 5th R.T.R. are in action. . . .

And now in the centre the enemy is edging forward again. The artillery is the only thing I have available to stop them, so we bring down all we can, and again they are halted. And then the Greys come over the crest from the north; they have not really been long, but it has seemed an age. I describe the situation to them over the air as they come in sight of the battlefield and charge down the hill; they are quite clear as to the hole they have to plug and they go straight in.

The situation was actually less serious than it appeared to be, for that morning, when it was appreciated that the whole of the Afrika Korps was committed, Horrocks asked Montgomery's permission to take the reserve 23 Armoured Brigade under his command. This granted, the Brigade with its Valentines moved forward to man the reverse slope behind 22 Armoured. There was thus a good defence in depth. In any case Rommel, oppressed by his shortage of fuel (of 5,000 tons promised him by 3 September, 2,600 were sunk and 1,500 remained in Italy), called off his armour in the late afternoon, and all that night the Afrika Korps lay dormant under the flares and bombs of the R.A.F. and the shells of the artillery of 13 Corps. Next morning Montgomery, realising that there was now no likelihood of an eastward thrust by Rommel, started to concentrate his armour. But it was hardly necessary. There were desultory attacks during the day, but nothing as powerful as that on the 31st. At 0640 15 Panzer made a short stab at the Halfa ridge, there were two more small localised efforts at 0705 and 0830, and during this period there was also a sharp engagement with 8 Armoured Brigade as it endeavoured to move westwards into concentration with 22 and 23 Armoured. But Horrocks, mindful of his instructions, pulled 8 Armoured back after a few tanks had been lost.

During the afternoon Montgomery made two preparatory gestures in expectation of the victory which was now certain. He ordered planning to begin 'for a counter-stroke which would give us the initiative' and also alerted 10 Corps H.Q. to stand by ready to 'command a pursuit force . . . to be prepared to push through to Daba with all reserves available'. This latter instruction is baffling and presumably can have been no more than a form of insurance, since neither before, during nor after the battle did Montgomery betray any intention to pursue: on the contrary. The first instruction, for a 'counter-stroke', which envisaged a southward attack by the New Zealanders on the night of 3/4 September, is equally perplexing—as will appear when this abortive enterprise is described.

Rommel now had only one day's supply of fuel available, and on 2 September he began the first stage of a withdrawal, increasing the tempo on the 3rd. Montgomery resisted all requests to 'let the armour loose' (which makes his instructions to 10 Corps H.Q. read very strangely), and indeed he forbade Horrocks to attempt to follow up and take the high ground of Himeimat, saying that he wanted Rommel to retain observation from there so that he could take note of the various devices of deception which he intended to employ in preparation for the great battle ahead. By 7 September the Afrika Korps was safely established amid and behind the old British minefield, and Montgomery called the battle off.

Rommel's retreat was not in the least affected by the 'counter-stroke' Montgomery set in motion during the night of 3/4 September. Indeed, to judge from his *Papers*, he seems to have been scarcely aware of it. 'All attacks against our flank made by other formations, especially the New Zealanders, were too weak to make any penetration and were easily beaten off.' They were certainly weak, and their weakness emphasises a weakness in Montgomery's generalship. He was supreme at initiating and mounting a battle, but it is instructive to observe how often his battles ended with a *diminuendo*— Alamein, El Hamma, Akarit, Falaise, Arnhem. A pattern seems to emerge which suggests that in spite of his enormous will-power some inhibition prevented him from garnering the fruits of his initial victories in the spirit of Haig's message to his troops in August 1918, 'risks which a month ago would have been criminal to incur ought now to be incurred as a duty'.

He describes the object of his counter-stroke in *El Alamein to the River Sangro*: 'I decided to thin out in 30 Corps sector in the north so as to provide reserves, and to order 13 Corps to prepare to close the gap in our minefields through which the enemy attack had come. The operation would be developed southwards from the New Zealand sector, and proceed methodically and by easy stages.' Methodically and by easy stages! This was a curious way of tackling a vicious retreating Afrika Korps whose withdrawal had started on the 2nd and had been fully observed on the 3rd. It was surely the moment for a crash action: or nothing. What happened was something half-hearted. Two New Zealand brigades with, sandwiched between them, the totally inexperienced 132 Brigade from 44 Division, and two squadrons of tanks, one each from 46 and 50 R.T.R., went in by night into the Munassib Depression. The result of this attempt to 'start closing the door behind

Rommel's forces' was a shambles. It was an attack by an *ad hoc* amalgam.

The experienced New Zealanders, especially the Maoris, made some progress during the night but had to pull back next morning because 50 R.T.R. lost direction and its squadron leader ran on to mines, and suffered casualties —11 tanks in all. 132 Brigade was decimated. In spite of warnings from the New Zealanders, who knew better, they brought their soft transport forward very much too soon, lorries went up in flames illuminating the scene for the enemy artillery, digging was difficult in the hard ground, and an extreme confusion followed. That night the Brigade suffered 700 casualties, an enormous proportion of the 1,700 odd which represented the total casualties of Eighth Army during the whole of the battle. (The Germans lost some 2,900, and 49 tanks and armoured cars as against the British loss of 67 tanks: but the British were masters of the field and 13 of the Grants could be repaired.)

It is sometimes argued that in the latter stages of Alam Halfa Montgomery lost a supreme opportunity for finishing off the Afrika Korps. But there are several countervailing factors. The first, of course, is psychological. Montgomery needed a clean-cut victory in his first battle, and this plus his innate caution made him avoid risks. He was not going to let his armour rush pell mell on to one of Rommel's famous anti-tank screens as had so often happened in the old days. His chief argument is that he did not consider the state of his Army's training adequate. 132 Brigade's débâcle is a case in point: but it should also be remembered that in his July memorandum Dorman-Smith had observed that 'none of the formations in Eighth Army is now sufficiently well trained for offensive operations. The Army badly needs either a reinforcement of well trained formations or a quiet period in which to train'; and that Auchinleck himself at the end of July had signalled to London that he could not foresee the possibility of offensive operations by his Army until mid-September, having in mind the need for considerable re-organisation and indoctrination with new ideas. Montgomery was determined to smash the Axis forces at Alamein, but he was prepared to wait for a certainty rather than to go off at half-cock.

An analysis of Montgomery's conduct of the battle indicates why he succeeded where Auchinleck (or Gott) might have failed. There can be little doubt that his tight control of his armour during the battle and his disposition of the tanks before it were both beneficial and a breakaway from the British desert tradition. His appreciation of the need to command the sky (learned by bitter experience in France in 1940) had produced better co-operation between the Desert Air Force and the Army, and at Alam Halfa the air effort was exemplary. His use of massed guns as a complement to heavy bombing of a trapped enemy was also novel. Let Auchinleck have all credit for having assessed the possibilities of the Alam Halfa area as a defensive position: it still remains true that Montgomery's actual operations bear all the impress of a keen, fresh mind, and that the Eighth Army had perhaps never before fought with such cool certitude.

Certainly Montgomery, aided by Tedder and Coningham, taught Rommel a lesson at Alam Halfa which stayed with him to the end of his days and had an important bearing in 1944 on his attitude towards the defence of Normandy. It is this, as recorded in his *Papers*: 'anyone who has to fight, even with the most modern weapons, against an enemy in complete control of the air fights like a savage against modern European troops, under the same handicaps and with the same chances of success.'

4

Alamein

'Victory was simply impossible under the terms on which we entered the battle.'

Field Marshal Rommel

'Of course a victorious battle makes amends for much delay.'
Churchill to Alexander, *23 September 1942*

The day after Alan Brooke heard that Rommel had been defeated at Alam Halfa he noted in his diary 'my next trouble will now be to stop Winston from fussing Alex and Monty and egging them on to attack before they are ready': and he was right. But Montgomery ensured a victory by first defeating his Prime Minister and thus obtaining the time necessary for his preparations. He tells the story in his own inimitable way.

I had promised the Eighth Army on arrival that I would not launch our offensive till we were ready. I could not be ready until October. Full moon was the 24th October. I said I would attack on the night of 23rd October, and notified Alexander accordingly. The come-back from Whitehall was immediate. Alexander received a signal from the Prime Minister to the effect that the attack must be in September, so as to synchronise with certain Russian offensives and with Allied landings which were to take place early in November at the western end of the north African coast (Operation TORCH). Alexander came to see me to discuss the reply to be sent. I said that our preparations could not be completed in time for a September offensive, and an attack then would fail: if we waited until October, I guaranteed complete success. In my view it would be madness to attack in September. Was I to do so? Alexander backed me up whole-heartedly as he always did, and the reply was sent on the lines I wanted. I had told Alexander privately that, in view of my promise to the soldiers, I refused to attack before October; if a September attack was ordered by White-hall, they would have to get someone else to do it.* My stock was rather high after Alam Halfa! We heard no more about a September attack.

'Of course,' Montgomery said to me when we were discussing this episode, 'it was blackmail.' Blackmail which Wavell and Auchinleck would perhaps have done well to attempt!

Churchill had good reasons for being in a high state of tension at this

---

* But *c.f.* Montgomery, *The Path To Leadership*, p. 47. 'The question of "resignation" does not arise in wartime.' He is referring to Wavell.

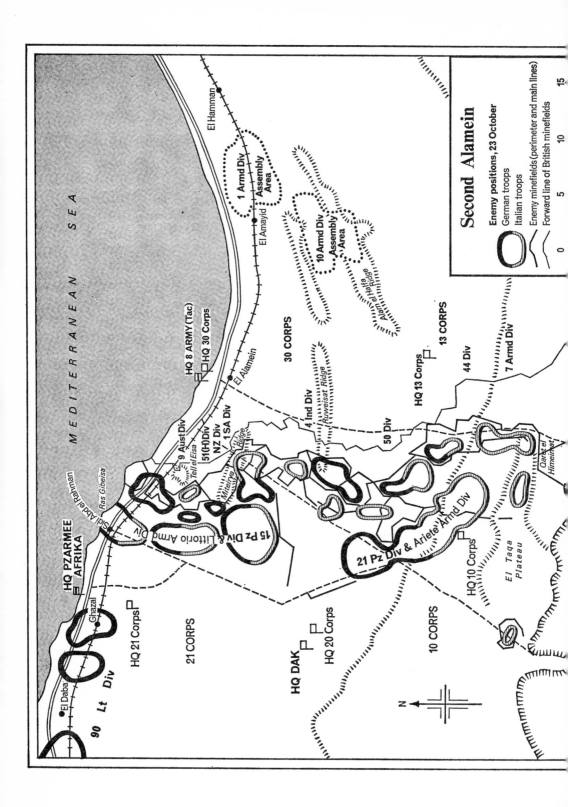

Second Alamein

Enemy positions, 23 October
German troops
Italian troops
Enemy minefields (perimeter and main lines)
Forward line of British minefields

0   5   10   15

MEDITERRANEAN SEA

El Hamman

1 Armd Div Assembly Area

El Amayid

10 Armd Div Assembly Area

Alam el Halfa Ridge

HQ 8 ARMY (Tac)
HQ 30 Corps

30 CORPS

El Alamein

9 Aust Div
51(H)Div
NZ Div
1 SA Div
Tell el Eisa
Miteiriya Ridge

4 Ind Div
Ruweisat Ridge

50 Div

HQ 13 Corps

13 CORPS

44 Div

7 Armd Div

Qaret el Himeimat

HQ PZARMEE AFRIKA

Sidi Abd el Rahman
Ras Gibeisa

Ghazal

HQ 21 Corps

21 CORPS

15 Pz Div & Littorio Armd Div

21 Pz Div & Ariete Armd Div

HQ 10 Corps

El Taqa Plateau

90 Lt Div

El Daba

HQ DAK
HQ 20 Corps

10 CORPS

N

time—so overwrought that he interrupted the only brief holiday Alan Brooke had taken that year to bring him to the telephone à propos Alexander's latest signal. ' "You have not seen it! Do you mean to say you are out of touch with the strategic situation?" I replied, "I told you I was going grouse shooting today, and I have not yet solved how I am to remain in touch with the strategic situation whilst in a grouse-butt." ' But Churchill was not mollified, and a wretched Contact Officer had to ride through the night on a motorcycle from Whitehall to Darlington with a copy of the signal for the C.I.G.S. The reasons for the Prime Minister's agitation were not merely personal—not merely because in the summer he had had to fend off a Vote of Censure in the House of Commons or because the Lord Privy Seal, Sir Stafford Cripps, was dissatisfied with the organisation for the higher planning of the war and was now threatening to resign. Churchill was also oppressed by grave national considerations. It was not simply a matter of the Russian offensives and the impending TORCH. The staunch support of the President of the United States was now endangered by a Congressional election. And Malta was in dire peril. Brooke estimated that its resources could only hold out until mid-October and that its very survival depended on Montgomery's coming offensive or on TORCH. 'If neither succeed God knows how we shall keep Malta alive.' On 14 September Hitler ordered a fresh attempt by the *Luftwaffe* to eliminate the island, and this, beginning on 11 October, was sustained for ten days on a scale of 200/300 planes per day. Though some 100 Axis planes were destroyed for the loss of 30 Spitfires, re-fuelling became so difficult that one of the special, fast minelayers had to be used for the purpose. The long-term solution was obvious: Eighth Army must press so far westwards along the African shore that the R.A.F. could work from airfields which would enable it to regain control over the Mediterranean. This in effect meant establishing the Desert Air Force on the Martuba group of airfields near Derna, and also to the south of Benghazi.

These factors account not only for Churchill's frenetic concern—a concern which on 23 September clouded his imagination with the thought that Rommel might be 'fortifying a belt twenty miles deep by forty miles broad'! —but also for the cautious manner in which Montgomery stage-managed the battle. The fact was that not only his own interest, but also the nation's, demanded nothing less than a decisive and manifest victory. He could not afford a stalemate: still less a defeat. When Rommel in 1944 wrote the chapter in his *Papers* entitled 'Alamein in retrospect' he observed that 'the British based their planning on the principle of exact calculation'. This describes Montgomery's method precisely. By a nice estimate as to how far he might profit from a liberal use of his material superiority and a careful manipulation of his human resources he broke Rommel's line in 12 days, captured 30,000

F

prisoners including nine generals, shattered the Italian Army and routed the Afrika Korps. And thus by early November the Prime Minister, so lately despondent, was in a mood to set the church bells ringing.

Montgomery began his preparations for Alamein on the first day he arrived in Egypt. After seeing Auchinleck he visited Alexander and put to him a plan for 'a reserve corps for Eighth Army, strong in armour, similar to Rommel's'. This was not required for the defensive battle he saw looming: it was to be the hammer in a subsequent attack. Alexander approved, but as he still had no executive authority Montgomery went to the Deputy Chief of the General Staff, Major-General John Harding (a former pupil of Montgomery at the Staff College) and asked whether such a corps was feasible. By 6 p.m. that evening Harding had formulated a scheme for 10 Corps, to consist of 1, 8 and 10 Armoured Divisions and the New Zealand Division. By the 15th Montgomery was thinking hard about Alamein, so that when the Prime Minister visited him on the 19th he was able to put him in the picture. His refusal to let Horrocks recapture Himeimat at the end of Alam Halfa indicated how, already, the basic idea for the battle had taken a firm shape in his mind. (Indeed after Alam Halfa Montgomery possessed the great strength Rommel lacked—the certainty that he must and moreover could attack.) His victory over Rommel at Alam Halfa caused an upsurge of confidence in his Army, and now he himself could proceed with confidence to work out the manifold details of his next offensive. Yet though these details, (operational and administrative), were extremely complicated the main course of the actual battle, and its preliminaries, are relatively simple and were well summarised by Alexander in the signal he sent to Churchill when all was over, on 9 November.

> This great battle can be divided into four stages: the grouping and concentration of our forces for battle and deception methods employed, which gained for us surprise, that battle-winning factor. The break-in attack—that great concentration of force of all arms which punched a hole deep into his defences, and by its disruption created artificial flanks whch gave us further opportunities for exploitation. The thrust now here, now there, which drew off his forces and made him use up his reserves in stopping holes and repeated counter-attacks. The final thrust, which disrupted his last remaining line of defence and broke a way through—through which poured our armoured and mobile formations.

The shaping of the battle-plan, and its implementation, were Montgomery's responsibility. 'I always kept Alexander fully informed; he never commented in detail on my plans or suggested any of his own;* he trusted me and my staff absolutely.' There was a vast amount to be done in the rear to

---

* Like many of Montgomery's later statements, this reads like an exaggeration designed to emphasise his independence: but the main battle was undoubtedly his.

provide the infrastructure for the fighting—there was also Whitehall to be handled—and it was in these fields that Alexander made his special contribution, while giving Montgomery his head. This, Montgomery observed in his essay on Lord Alanbrooke in *The Path to Leadership*, is what is most congenial to him. 'I like to be told by my boss what he wants me to do, and then to be left alone to do it.'

There were actually two plans for Alamein, each named LIGHTFOOT: but both were framed from the same assumption—that since Rommel's line ran from the sea some 45 miles down to the edge of the impassable Qattara depression there was no possibility of turning an open flank. Thus, since Rommel must inevitably be expecting an attack, the only possibility of surprise was to delude him as to the date and the area of the Eighth Army's *Schwerpunkt*. This was attempted by the 'deception methods' to which Alexander referred, and by staging a secondary offensive, by 13 Corps, down in the south.

Montgomery's cover plan, devised and developed during August and September, was the most elaborate yet evolved in the desert campaigns. It was handled as an Army operation under the code name BERTRAM. First there was the problem of camouflaging the huge forward dumps of ammunition and other battle stores. Next, tank and vehicle movement was disguised by the use of dummies which gradually habituated the enemy to large concentrations in what were, operationally, the right places. At night soft vehicles of the assault divisions replaced soft vehicles already *in situ*, and special dummies called 'sunshields' or 'cannibals' were waiting to provide shelter for guns and tanks as they took up their stations. As early as a month before D-Day slit trenches were dug for the assaulting infantry to lie up during the daylight hours of 23 October, and these were so camouflaged as to become an accepted part of the landscape, while to emphasise the likelihood of the main thrust coming in the south a false water-pipe-line was laid steadily (with bogus pumping stations, waterpoints and reservoirs), at a daily rate which suggested completion not before early November. In addition, since the projected 8 Armoured Division was incomplete, its armour was detached from it, and the divisional signal section was used to simulate wireless traffic which also suggested a main effort in the south. Care was taken in the marking of new tracks, and to complete the picture lower echelons of officers were only informed about what was to happen by careful stages between 28 September and 21 October, on a decreasing scale of seniority. On the latter day other ranks were also informed, and all leave and city visits were stopped. The effect of these measures was that Rommel later recorded that 'the 23rd October passed just like any other day on the Alamein front—until the evening'.

So far as was practicable, Montgomery solved the tricky problems of training and regrouping simultaneously. The need for the former was forcibly emphasised by another disastrous operation by the raw 44 Division, whose 131 Brigade made a second attack on the Munassib depression during the night of 29 September. One battalion sustained heavy casualties. The reason was, once again, inexperience leading to a flaunting of the rules of the desert. Patrolling was inadequate, much of the supporting gunfire was wasted because correct information about the enemy's positions was lacking, and the brigade had not yet learned to cope with the difficulties of a long approach march in darkness over featureless ground. Thus two brigades of this division had already been shaken by failure and losses: the third, 133, was now removed to provide a lorried infantry brigade for 10 Corps and had, at the same time, to discover what it meant to be desert-worthy and to master the novel techniques required for infantry in an armoured division. The 44th Reconnaissance Battalion and carrier platoons were also detached for an unfamiliar rôle, that of a minefield-clearance task force. Thus, few divisions can have had a more inauspicious launching into battle than the 44th.

The other new infantry division was 51 Highland, which had better luck. Based on the Halfa ridge, where it had relieved 44 Div. which in turn had released 2 New Zealand Division for rest and exercises on the coast, 51 Highland had its own training area where it carried out several rehearsals, and at the same time attached its units brigade by brigade to the Australians in the north, so allowing the latter to pull out a brigade per week for intensive exercises. In 7 Armoured, 4 Light Armoured Brigade had an operational function until 18 October and was unable to train at all, but 22 Armoured Brigade was less committed and carried out three exercises. In 10 Corps the difficulty of training was further bedevilled by the gradual and tardy arrival of new equipment. The 300 Shermans which Roosevelt had generously provided after the fall of Tobruk had indeed arrived in the Delta in September; but in some cases they were slow to reach units. 8 Armoured Brigade, for example, did not receive the first 15 of the 33 Shermans due to it until 17 October and the residue arrived only on the eve of the battle . . . short of necessary accessories. In the case of 9 Armoured Brigade, it may be noted that when it made its desperate attack in SUPERCHARGE (see p. 90) in one of its squadrons the squadron-leader's tank was the only one in which the compass worked.

In view of the nature of Rommel's defences the most important aspect of the training programme was that devoted to the minefield-clearance units. This was organised under the supervision of the Chief Engineer of Eighth Army, Brigadier Kisch, a brilliant officer later to be killed. He selected for the purpose a remarkable man, Major Peter Moore, commanding the 3rd (Cheshire) Field Squadron R.E., of whom it was written that:

One morning shortly before the battle he found some of his sappers lying down on the Ruweisat Ridge, returning fire from a German machine gun post. They had just cleared a gap through a minefield. . . . But why, Moore demanded, hadn't the machine gun been cleared? He removed the pins from two hand grenades and ordered a sapper to drive him straight at it. On the way the jeep hit a mine; Moore was sent flying through the air, presumed killed.

He came back a few minutes later, carrying his wounded driver. The machine gun wasn't yet stilled, but when he was blown up Moore kept his fingers on the levers of the two bombs, landed and wedged them under the rear wheels of the jeep. They would kill the Germans who came out to salvage it.

Kisch assembled the views of his senior officers about the clearing of mines and gave them to Moore with this instruction: 'I am sure that there should be a drill for this, just as there is a drill for loading and firing field guns. Go away and come back in a week's time with your recommendations. When you have worked out a drill and I have approved it, you will form the Eighth Army School of Mine Clearance.' Under Moore and later a New Zealander, Major Currie, this school evolved a drill and trained 56 separate groups before 23 October.

Mechanical aids were also produced to help the sappers in their lonely and dangerous task. Two dozen Matilda tanks were converted into flails which, as they moved forward, could beat the ground ahead by whirling chains on a rotating shaft. Unfortunately they were cumbrous in action and the flailing threw up dense clouds of dust which caused over-heating. These 'Scorpions', as they were called, were therefore used mainly by 7 Armoured in its southern feint, where in practice they did little good. But it was a valuable test under field conditions of an instrument which, developed to a greater degree of efficiency in England, would play a useful part on D-Day in Normandy and during the following months. Of more immediate value were the 500 odd mine detectors issued to the three corps which, in so far as their numbers allowed, made detection swifter and therefore safer than the traditional method of prodding by hand. The scale of the sappers' effort is indicated by the fact that 120 miles of marking tape and 88,775 lamps were issued for their gapping operations.

The reward for this strenuous programme of rehearsal which Montgomery forced forward was the professional comment of his opponent. Reflecting on the battle, Rommel noted the expertise with which lanes were cleared through the minefields and with which tanks and infantry then advanced. 'Particular skill,' he wrote, 'was shown in carrying out this manoeuvre at night and a great deal of hard training must have been done before the offensive.' Indeed Rommel mentions the generally high state of training of his opponents a number of times, and in this he was not being merely self-justificatory. It was the master acknowledging the master.

But it was Rommel who also remarked that 'the battle is fought and decided by the Quartermasters before the shooting begins'. Montgomery's forward administrative arrangements and the support he received from the base areas were such that during the 12 days of Alamein his field artillery fired over a million rounds, an average of 102 rounds per gun per day, while the daily rates for his mediums were even higher. In this as in all other respects Montgomery was amply furnished. The relative figures for the strength of the British and Axis forces tend to vary in different accounts, but those given in the British *Official History* may be assumed to be reliable. They are:

	British	*Axis*
Armoured cars	435	192
Tanks (other than light)	1,029	496
Guns (field and medium)	908	500 approx.
Anti-tank guns	1,451 (849 6-pdr.)	850 approx. (86 88mm., 300 Italian)
Fighting troops	195,000	50,000 German 54,000 Italian

The figures for equipment exclude reserves, in which Montgomery also was superior. In the base workshops and depots, for example, over 1,000 further tanks were available. Thus in human and material resources Montgomery was the stronger by an average factor of something like two to one. And of course he had the enormous advantage of short and uninterrupted lines of communication.

But in spite of this preponderance in men and metal, Eighth Army faced a formidable task. Montgomery is often accused of having fought at Alamein a 'set-piece', First-World-War-type of battle. The fact is that Rommel's dispositions made this inevitable. For the first time in the desert the aggressor had to seek to penetrate a *continuous* line of defensive fortifications. These varied in depth from two and a half to four and a half miles. Along most of their line, and particularly in the north and north/centre where Montgomery would attempt to break through, there were two roughly parallel belts of mines separated by a gap which was suitably nick-named 'The Devil's Garden', an area scattered with every form of underground explosive. Rommel describes how 'vast numbers of captured British bombs and shells were built into the defence, arranged in some cases for electrical detonation'. (He also mentions that dogs were employed as sentries!) The southern sector of this intricate system was based on the two British fields, *January* and *February*, which he had been allowed to retain after Alam Halfa, backed by a rudimentary set of defences running from Bab el Qattara to the upland of El Taqa.

This general scheme was strengthened by judicious arrangements for each of its segments. Only one company per battalion was placed in the *Gefechts- vorposten* or battle outposts which ran in some depth along the rim of the eastern minefields: the main bodies were held well back in the *Hauptkampf- feld*, the chief zone of defence which lay behind the western fields. Strips of mines were also laid between the two fields in such a manner as to form 'boxes' which would provide flank protection for the forward units. The actual extent of all this minelaying is known, for in a report two days before the battle began Rommel's Chief Engineer stated that over 445,000 mines had been used—an impressive total even though only three per cent or some 14,000 were anti-personnel. A further difficulty for the British arose from the fact that even persistent patrolling could only provide exact information about the skirts of the minefields facing them: for the rest they had to rely on air photographs. In addition the artillery and heavier anti-tank guns were held well back, in or beyond the main defensive zone. By all these methods Rommel hoped that the first shock of the British attack, which he knew would be powerfully supported by gunfire, might be absorbed before the *Hauptkampffeld* was reached or breached. The more effective thrusts could then be swiftly sealed off by convergent blows from the flanks and the front. His nightmare was that a clean hole might be punched through which the mass of British armour might pour, for he knew that his shortage of fuel denied him the possibility of prolonged mobile action.

This was one reason for his placing 21 Panzer and Ariete behind the southern and 15 Panzer and Littorio behind the northern portion of the line. Wherever a breakthrough looked possible, he hoped to be able to move tanks to block it without too much expenditure of petrol. But there was another consideration. In the case of his infantry, also, he placed an Italian unit beside a German, envisaging that by this alternation of the stronger and the weaker he would always have a German group close at hand to move wherever the British thrusts were proving effective. Unfortunately for Rommel this policy of 'plugging the gap' by piecemeal reinforcement was, as will be seen, precisely the one which Montgomery wished him to adopt. Even more un- fortunately, Rommel was not even in Africa when the battle began. His health had so deteriorated that on 23 September he left Derna for Germany, having handed over on the 19th to General Stumme, a panzer officer who had commanded a corps on the Russian front but was a tyro in the desert. Bayerlein has, however, made it absolutely clear (in a footnote in the *Rommel Papers*) that it was Rommel and not Stumme who was responsible for the layout of the Axis defences, and in particular for the separation of his armoured divisions.

In his first LIGHTFOOT plan Montgomery aimed at splitting these defences and then compelling his opponent to fight a tank battle. 'The main attack,' he says, 'would be made by 30 Corps (Leese) in the north and here I planned to punch two corridors through the enemy defences and minefields. 10 Corps (Lumsden) would then pass through these corridors and would position itself on important ground astride the enemy supply routes; Rommel's armour would have to attack it, and would, I hoped, be destroyed in the process. . . . I planned to attack neither on my left flank nor on my right flank, but somewhere right of centre.' Stumme, incidentally, expected the chief thrust to come against the centre of the line, but he retained his reserves, 90 Light and Trieste, in the coastal area where Rommel had left them.

When Montgomery said that he did not intend to attack on his left flank he was not, of course, overlooking his intention to mount a feint ancillary to the main assault of 30 Corps further north, by 13 Corps on the *January* and *February* minefields in the south. This had two objectives. It was to be sufficiently threatening to prevent a switch of Axis troops (and particularly armour), to the northern front in the early stages of the conflict, and if successful it was to open a gap through which light mobile forces could slip to harry the enemy's rear. But Montgomery laid down firmly that the corps was not to suffer heavy casualties and he was specially concerned that 7 Armoured should be kept in good trim for exploitation when the main breakthrough occurred. Suddenly, however, on 6 October this first LIGHTFOOT plan was abandoned.

Montgomery began to feel that he was asking too much of his Army. Training was indeed proceeding as fast as possible, but it was not fast enough, especially among the armoured units, to ensure the clean swift breakthrough and superiority in the tank Armageddon which LIGHTFOOT demanded. He quite rightly points out that since its formation Eighth Army had suffered 80,000 casualties, and since CRUSADER there had been very little time for training. So he produced a plan based on entirely different principles. 'It had been generally accepted that the plan in a modern battle should aim first at destroying the enemy's armour, and that once this had been accomplished, the unarmoured portion of his army would be dealt with readily. I decided to reverse this concept and to destroy first the unarmoured formations. While doing this I would hold off the armoured divisions, which would be tackled subsequently.' In a broad sense it might be said that he proposed to enlarge on Rommel's tactics in the Cauldron area during Gazala. He would push forward a screen of tanks to block the western exits of the gaps through the enemy minefield, methodically wipe out the infantry in the Axis defensive zone by what he called a 'crumbling' process, and so compel the enemy to come to him. Rommel could not stand by and see his infantry destroyed, and thus Montgomery hoped that he would stimulate urgent but desperate counter-attacks by panzers put in piecemeal. 'The "crumbling" operation would be carefully organised from a series of firm bases and would be within the capabilities of my troops'—on the principle, as Rommel observed, of exact calculation. The early establishment of an armoured screen was obviously crucial in this conception, and Montgomery determined to push 10 Corps into and through the gaps even before he knew they were clear: he went further, and laid down that if by the morning of D + 1 the sappers and infantry had not completed the necessary lanes, his armoured divisions must fight their own way out into the open. Churchill was not far out in his brooding concern over the coming battle when he signalled to Alexander on 23 September, even before the plan had been changed, that 'the tank was originally invented to clear a way for the infantry in the teeth of machine-gun fire. Now it is the infantry who will have to clear a way for the tanks, and it seems to me it will be a very hard one now that fire-power is so greatly increased.' And so it was to be.

Lumsden and his divisional commanders certainly felt about Montgomery's plan that there was a strong possibility that the infantry might be held up, and that to execute the order for their armour to fight its way out of the minefields might lead to disaster. Their doubts affected Freyberg, commanding the New Zealanders, Morshead commanding the Australians and Pienaar commanding the South Africans. These three, individually responsible as they were to their respective Dominions, communicated to 30 Corps' commander, Leese, their joint lack of confidence in the armour's capacity to carry out its task. Leese informed Montgomery. And de Guingand, coming from a conference at 10 Corps, also expressed to the Army Commander his doubts about Lumsden's resolution. But Montgomery would have nothing to do with what he called 'belly-aching'. Quibbling about orders had been a bad tradition in the desert, especially among the armour. Montgomery would not stand for soviets among his subordinates, believing with John Milton that 'most voices ought not to prevail where main matters are in question . . . there being in number little virtue'. He had issued an instruction and 'I was determined to see that it was carried out to the letter'.

My own view is that, in the event, Montgomery was justified in remaining adamant and imposing his will on his subordinates, as he was to do later at a turning-point of the battle, in the early hours of the 25th.* Moreover, his was the overall responsibility, and while, on the one hand, he was anticipating that the 'break-in' would be followed by a 'dog-fight' lasting at least a week, on the other he knew that he was not over-rich in infantry. For the Dominion divisions, in particular, reinforcements were running low. Thus he could not

---

* I argue the case for Montgomery in full knowledge that well-informed critics have subsequently and sometimes reasonably, but not, I think, convincingly, disputed his judgement.

afford to squander his infantry in the early phase of the battle, and the armour must play its part. He *could* afford to lose tanks—if not tank crews. But he is unjust, in his memoirs, to use the words 'infirmity of purpose' of 'certain senior commanders', by whom he obviously means Lumsden and Gatehouse (commanding 10 Armoured Division). Nobody could impugn the record of either for lack of courage or battle-experience. In Lumsden's case, Montgomery's attitude was certainly affected by a mutual antipathy—the temperament and tradition of the two men were poles apart: Montgomery was also genuinely suspicious of Lumsden's capacity to drive on an armoured corps with an iron will, because Lumsden was by training an armoured car officer. 'Armoured car officers,' Montgomery observed to me, 'don't fight unless they have to. Their job is to observe and get away.' But there is something deeper. When I discussed this issue with Major-General Raymond Briggs, commander of 1 Armoured (the other division in Lumsden's corps), he pointed to the fundamental difference in training, philosophy, and indoctrination between an Armoured Brigade, accustomed to mobility, freedom and space, and an Army Tank Brigade habituated to the idea of 'getting the infantry on to the objective'. At Alamein, Montgomery was in effect proposing to use cavalry as battering-rams; it is therefore wholly understandable that Lumsden and Gatehouse should have been repelled by the idea of what seemed to them a sacrifice of their tanks and crews in a rôle for which they were not properly prepared. Still, at the time they accepted their orders. Perhaps the matter may be summed up by an apothegm of Admiral Mahan; 'when to clarity of vision is allied the will and the capacity to bring into effect what is seen to be required, the ill-disposed speak of ruthlessness while those well-disposed refer to firmness of decision'.

On the eve of the battle Montgomery issued a personal message to his Army which, because it was the first—there would be many more!—gave fresh confidence to troops whose morale was already high. He then held a press conference on the morning of the 23rd, moved up to his tactical headquarters, read a book and went to bed early. De Guingand has described the unconcealed excitement at Tac. H.Q. (which was set up on the coast near to the H.Q. of 10 and 30 Corps) as the watches ticked forward to zero hour. Coningham of the Desert Air Force was there—he had a caravan permanently available for him, a significant change from the apartheid of Army and Air in earlier days. The evening situation report which Stumme sent to the Army High Command read 'Enemy situation unchanged': but on the main 30 Corps front there opened up at 2140 hrs. the greatest bombardment seen or heard since the First World War. Major-General Francis Tuker, whose 4 Indian Division down at Ruweisat had at this stage a subordinate rôle, has described it unforgettably:

There was no roar of cannon, at least none that we heard as the sound came through the muffling sands below Ruweisat—none even from our divisional guns hard by. Wide to the north and south played the swift flickering lightning flashes, dead white, as if giants danced a Khuttack war dance whirling their swords about their heads under the moon. And the sound, too, it fluttered all around and above us. Many a time have I been in a bombardment, my own and the enemy's, and never have I listened to so seemingly gentle a noise of guns. When I say fluttered, I mean fluttered like a thousand moths—no other.

For fifteen minutes the fire continued, in the form of a neutralisation programme directed at the enemy batteries whose positions had been fixed with particular care. 408 25-pdrs. and 48 medium guns were engaging an estimated 200 field, 40 medium and 14 heavy guns, on which concentrations fell at a minimum rate of 10 to 1, rising at times to 22 to 1. The British mediums alone got off 1,800 rounds. In the south 13 Corps fired a gentler programme which started at 2125 and also stopped at 2155. Then along the the whole front there was silence for five minutes. At 2200 precisely the artillery of both corps opened up again, this time on the enemy's forward posts: it was zero hour, and the assaulting infantry began their approach march, aided by searchlights in the sky and tracer pumped out on fixed lines by light anti-aircraft guns. 'The battle which is now about to begin,' Montgomery had said in his personal message, 'will be one of the decisive battles of history. It will be the turning point of the war. The eyes of the whole world will be on us, watching anxiously which way the battle will swing.' Certainly the eyes of the allies were watching. Alexander sent off a pre-arranged code word.

C.-in-C. to Prime Minister and C.I.G.S.　　　　　　　　　　　　　　23 Oct 42
　　　　Zip!
Former Naval Person to President Roosevelt　　　　　　　　　　　23 Oct 42
　　The battle in Egypt began tonight at 8 p.m. London time. The whole force of the Army will be engaged. I will keep you informed. A victory there will be most useful to our main enterprise. All the Shermans and self-propelled guns which you gave me on that dark Tobruk morning will play their part.

Three main objectives lay ahead of the four infantry divisions of 30 Corps as they moved off in line abreast on a front which, six miles in width at first, would gradually fan outwards to an extent of eight miles. The first, called 'Oxalic', ran along the western or reverse slope of Miteirya Ridge, then swung north-west to the rim of Kidney 'Ridge', known to the Germans as Hill 28 (though in fact the ring contour on the maps represented a slight depression), and then turned due north. The LIGHTFOOT plan assumed its occupation by 0310 hrs. next morning. Next came 'Pierson', a line running due south-east from the western lip of Kidney Ridge, to be held at dawn by three armoured brigades. Finally there was 'Skinflint', an area due west of 'Pierson' which roughly overlay the Rahman track to the south of Tell el Aqqaqir. This was the goal of the armour. (See map on p. 64.) In the north 9 Australian Division with 51 Highland on their left were to gain the 'Oxalic' objective down to Miteirya Ridge. The Ridge itself was to be over-run by 2 New Zealand Division flanked by 1 South African Division. A corridor for 1 Armoured was to be cleared through the Highland Division's front right up to Kidney Ridge, and a second corridor was to be made through the New Zealanders' territory, for 10 Armoured Division, terminating beyond the reverse slope of the northern section of Miteirya Ridge. Initially the infantry divisions were responsible for clearing mines, but thereafter each armoured division had to make safe its own routes, using their minefield task forces to cut four narrow lanes per division. Each lane would only be a few yards wide at first, but the aim was to broaden them as soon as possible. The night's work by no means fulfilled these intentions: far from reaching 'Pierson', the armour had not yet struggled beyond 'Oxalic'.

At first all went well. It was not until the early hours of the 24th that the enemy's defensive fire became menacing—for several reasons. Montgomery's neutralisation and counter-battery programme and the subsequent barrage had played havoc with the heavy weapons of the enemy infantry, and evidently put many guns out of action. Moreover, Rommel noted that 'our communication network was soon smashed by this drumfire', with the result that Stumme was unable to form a picture of what was happening. The damage and confusion was increased by the 125 tons of bombs dropped by Wellingtons on the gun areas, and by other specially equipped Wellingtons which flew overhead jamming the Axis wireless traffic. Stumme was also concerned about his shortage of ammunition and, according to Rommel, withheld permission for his artillery to put down defensive fire during the early stage of the assault. Thus the British and Dominion troops were, in the main, able to make good headway through the outpost line. With three of the divisions there moved a regiment of Valentine tanks from 23 Armoured Brigade, while the New Zealanders had a whole brigade, the 9th, to assist them. These were 'to be used as necessary in order to ensure the capture of the bridgehead at all costs'.

But seizure of a bridgehead was prevented by a number of factors which, to a greater or lesser degree, affected both 30 and 10 Corps. As the night wore on the enemy's resistance stiffened, more and more weapons being brought to bear on the men, vehicles and armour groping among the minefields. And, apart from the difficulties of clearing gaps through the more formal fields, groups of scattered mines caused great delay and many casualties. The terrain was featureless, great clouds of dust and smoke limited visibility, and as the

advance proceeded more and more unsubdued enemy positions were encountered. A part of the story of the adventures of Major Moore's squadron of
sappers (with whom the C.R.E., Lieut.-Colonel McMeekan, was travelling)
vividly illustrates what was happening all the way from Tell el Eisa to
Miteirya:

A few sappers seemed to be utterly alone in a fearful noise as the barrage
began and the New Zealanders started forward. McMeekan found the noise
'soothing'. Dust hadn't blotted out the moon yet. There was a No Man's Land
of perhaps a mile before the first belt of mines and the 3rd squadron gapping
parties walked to within 500 yards of the garden, their sandbagged pilot vehicle
driven by Sapper Bill Shaw. Then they waited for the blue light signal from the
reconnaissance officer. They had no infantry protection. 'We felt rather lonely
and naked,' said Moore afterwards. As they reached the fringe of the minefield,
machine guns were turned to them and a few shells fell. The pilot vehicle blew
up and provided a splendid target for about ten minutes.
   The advance was twenty minutes late and McMeekan found that his communications were valueless: telephone wires were broken by the shelling and
wireless was scarcely better. Moore's men worked at first without serious
interference, then a heavy machine gun put in a word on their left. Lt. John
Van Grutten, a former undergraduate, was sent to silence it. He did.

   Bromley Hotchkiss, when he joined the squadron, felt 'a bit of an outsider'.
Now he was a corporal. In the gapping of the first belt of mines all his section
had been shot away, killed or wounded. He moved the thousand yards to the
next field by himself and marked his section's gap. A lorry bringing M.P.s,
wire and marker posts had failed to arrive. Hotchkiss found some wire and
scrounged posts from the New Zealanders ahead. Then he hung the regulation
lamps (green on the safe side of the gap) crouching down below the machine
gun tracers, reaching up to the posts like a monkey. The first he knew of his
Military Medal was an item in the *Birkenhead News*, sent by his mother.

   At the next minefield 3rd squadron were in the very jaws of the assault. The
floor was thick with New Zealand and German dead and with anxious casualties.
Here, too, was a more elaborate sowing of mines, Italian Red Devils, booby
traps, wires inviting the feet. Moore went crawling to find a deviation and
almost had his hands on an S mine's horns. . . . The tanks were to use the gap
at 4 a.m. By 3, Moore's sappers were actually in front of the infantry. Bottle
gap had been prepared on schedule and Col. McMeekan, his eardrum shattered
by a shell's blast, was trying to get the delayed Hat gap open. He was now
almost totally deaf and had to give up the driving of his jeep after he failed to
hear a Maori sentry's challenge. When another party of Maoris yelled at him
McMeekan got out of his jeep and found a trip wire tangled on the back axle.

The picture available for Montgomery on the morning of the 24th, therefore, was roughly as follows. On the right 26 Australian Brigade, in the centre

most of the New Zealand Division, with 154 Brigade of the Highlanders beside them, and on the far left 3 South African Brigade were more or less on 'Oxalic'. But the other Australian brigade, two from the Highland Division and one South African were still short of the objective. 23 and 9 Armoured Brigade had not established a bridgehead, and by dawn the minefield task force of 1 Armoured had only cleared one through lane, in the Australian sector, while none of the four lanes cleared by 10 Armoured Division reached beyond the crest of Miteirya Ridge.

The news Montgomery received from 13 Corps in the south was no more reassuring. 7 Armoured Division supported by 131 Brigade of 44 Division were supposed, starting like 30 Corps at 2200 hrs. on the 23rd, to breach both the *January* and *February* minefields and form a bridgehead with a view to further exploitation to the west, while 1 Free French Brigade was to take the elevation called Naqb Rala at the western foot of Himeimat. Everything went wrong. The flailing Scorpions broke down or were knocked out, and at a cost of 200 casualties in 22 Armoured Brigade and 180 in a single battalion of 131 Brigade the whole force, by daylight, was crammed along both sides of *January* with *February* still unbreached. The French had even worse fortune. Soft going hampered the advance, anti-tank guns were not got forward, the German Kiel group (guarding Stumme's right flank) put in a counter-attack at 0730 with captured British tanks, and the upshot was that the two battalions of the Foreign Legion lost their Colonel and all their vehicles for practically no gain of ground. At 13 Corps Horrocks was reduced to considering whether he would now try to break through *February* or simply 'crumble' between the two fields.

His general situation became gradually clear to Montgomery, and some time after 0900 hrs. he issued fresh orders for the 24th. But in fact, had he known it, there was one ray of light: his chief opponent, Stumme, was dead, while Rommel was still taking his cure at Semmering in the Austrian mountains.

At dawn on the 24th Stumme had been so much in the dark that he decided to make a forward reconnaissance. He said he was only going up to 90 Light, in its reserve position, but in fact he strayed to the front and it appears that Australians fired on his vehicle, killing his companion. The driver turned and tried to get away, travelling at full speed while Stumme hung on to the outside of his car. He seems to have had a heart attack and to have fallen off without his driver noticing. (Stumme suffered from high blood pressure.) In consequence Rommel was ordered by Hitler in the early hours of the 25th to return to Africa, and he was back in his desert headquarters that evening. But by then much had happened.

Montgomery's chief instructions for the 24th were for the northern corridor to be properly cleared and for the New Zealand Division to exploit southwards from 'Oxalic' and the Miteirya Ridge. Freyberg had already been active, having told Leese at 0700 that all was set for 'a supreme effort for 10 Armoured Division to pass through'. But its movement was sluggish and Freyberg therefore had to rely on 9 Armoured Brigade. The latter, however, could make no ground beyond the crest of the Ridge and sustained heavy casualties in the attempt. At midday Montgomery held a conference at Freyberg's headquarters, and there ordered that during the coming night Gatehouse's 10 Armoured Division, supported by the whole of 30 Corps' artillery, should force their way beyond the New Zealand line and out into the open. This order Montgomery emphasised by a call to Lumsden's Chief of Staff, in which he reiterated that the armour *must* press on to 'Pierson' to provide protection for an advance by the New Zealanders, and that he was prepared to accept casualties. It is clear that during the 24th Montgomery was full of doubts about the aggressiveness of his armoured commanders, and indeed in his memoirs he states bluntly that 'the 10th Corps Commander was not displaying the drive and determination so necessary when things begin to go wrong and there was a general lack of offensive eagerness in the armoured divisions of the corps. *This was not the sort of battle they were used to.*' (Author's italics: see p. 74.) This is not wholly fair. During the day the Highland Division and 1 Armoured fought hard to clear the northern corridor in spite of heavy tank losses, and by dusk the armour was almost up to Kidney Ridge. In the southern sector Gatehouse was quite reasonably dubious about thrusting his armour in daylight over the top of Miteirya in the face of tank and anti-tank guns. An outflanking move to the right of the Ridge was foiled by the minefields.

The greatest damage during the day was achieved from the air, and it must be remembered as a continual background to the fighting that the steady softening-up carried out by the Desert Air Force reached a climax in its unremitting tactical support of Eighth Army throughout the battle. On the 24th, for example, some 1,000 sorties were flown, mainly in direct support of the army. Cannon Hurricanes knocked out the Kiel group who had routed the Free French; the tank assemblies of 15 Panzer and Littorio were harassed by a shuttle-service of light bombers and fighter bombers; enemy landing fields were attacked, and a protective air-umbrella covered the British front.

As night fell preparations were in hand for a forward move by 10 Armoured, with 24 Armoured Brigade on the right and 8 Brigade on the left, their left flank being guarded by 9 Brigade which was now reduced to two regiments of tanks. Freyberg's earlier fears were renewed, and he was soon reporting to his Corps Commander that 10 Armoured was not 'properly set up for the attack'. Checking with Lumsden, Leese found him uncertain about the viability of the operation: and as things went, these doubts certainly seemed justified. The minefields on the ridge were deeper than had been expected, and there was much shelling and much confusion, increased by a false report of an enemy attack on 24 Brigade's front and the fact that the exit from one of 8 Brigade's lanes was an enemy-made gap covered by defensive fire. To make confusion worse confounded, at 2200 hrs. bombs from enemy aircraft hit the Sherwood Rangers of 8 Armoured. The tanks were crowded like sardines in a tin. Petrol and ammunition lorries went up in flames, making a splendid target for the enemy's guns. The British barrage was advancing steadily away from the halted armour, which had to disperse to avoid further casualties from the shelling. In consequence Custance, the Brigade's commander, proposed to Gatehouse early on the 25th that his attack should be called off and Gatehouse made the same recommendation to Lumsden, who passed it on with his own approval to de Guingand.

There then occurred what Montgomery calls 'the real crisis in the battle' and de Guingand 'the first stepping stone'. The Army Commander was asleep, and his standing orders about being woken up were strict. Montgomery explained his principles clearly in a pamphlet on *High Command in War* which he issued in 1945; 'The wise commander will see very few papers or letters; he will refuse to sit up late at night conducting the business of his army; he will be well advised to withdraw to his tent or caravan after dinner at night and have time for quiet thought and reflection. It is vital that he should keep mentally fresh.' This way of life suited Montgomery's temperament and method of command, though whether it is generally applicable may be questioned. General Sir Richard O'Connor is certainly 'a wise commander'; but in a discussion of this episode, though he agreed with the line Montgomery was about to take, he also observed to me 'in war most things happen at night!'

De Guingand, as he describes in *Operation Victory*, realised that a crisis was at hand and summoned Leese and Lumsden to a conference with Montgomery at 0330: he then woke Montgomery up and told him what he had done. (Montgomery once said to me that it was typical of de Guingand's staunch qualities as a Chief of Staff that he issued the summons *before* waking him up.) The situation, quite simply, was that though the Staffordshire Yeomanry were now through one of the gaps on 8 Armoured Brigade's front, Gatehouse was deeply concerned about what might happen at dawn when such armour as had struggled free might find itself on the exposed western slope of Miteirya, ready to be picked off one by one. He wanted to retire to the relative safety of the eastern slope. Montgomery made it crystal clear to Lumsden, and by telephone to Gatehouse, that his plan must be followed through and that a withdrawal was out of the question. All his doubts about

4 *North Africa: Leclerc arrives (second from right)*

5 *North Africa: Montgomery confers with General Spaatz, U.S.A.A.F.,
Air Vice Marshal Broadhurst and Air Chief Marshal Tedder*

Lumsden were now confirmed (he would ease Lumsden out of his command when Eighth Army reached Benghazi), and he now held Lumsden back and made it plain to him that if he or Gatehouse were not in favour of continuing the push, he would find others who were.

In my study of Rommel I wrote: 'This was a turning point in the battle of Alamein and for the British Army during the Second World War. For better or worse, the "cavalry concept" died that night: the "old desert hands" had to swallow their resentment and their anguish because their tanks would no longer have a free rôle but would, thereafter, usually be units in organised actions involving all arms. Montgomery started a process which the Germans had long ago brought into being: the armour began to be part of the army.' In a few days' time, indeed, 9 Armoured Brigade would be going into action in SUPERCHARGE prepared to accept 100 per cent casualties without demur. In fact it is difficult to think of any major occasion after this when armoured commanders indulged in the sort of 'belly-aching' argument about their orders which had marred Eighth Army's operations at Gazala in May/ June 1942.

Though Montgomery's energising conference was, from his point of view, obviously necessary, the situation on 10 Armoured's front soon improved temporarily, for by dawn two regiments of 24th Brigade had extricated them-selves free from the minefield, the third lying back in reserve. And by the time Gatehouse was able to pass down Lumsden's post-conference orders to Custance, 8 Armoured had got two regiments beyond the ridge and the third was moving up through the corridor. But their reception was such that by 0700 all three were back under the cover of the ridge, while on their left 9 Armoured and the New Zealand Cavalry were having an uncomfortable time, sitting in the open in front of enemy tanks and guns some 1,000 yards away—a fair justification for the armoured commanders' doubts!

After a visit from Alexander, Montgomery again conferred with his two Corps Commanders at the New Zealand H.Q., and then began to embark on the first of those thrusts 'now here, now there' which Alexander was to report to Churchill. He had come to the conclusion that further pressure by the New Zealanders to the south would be too expensive, and therefore switched his thrust-line northwards, instructing 9 Australian Division to start 'crumbling'. It was now evident that it was only on his northern front that he could hope for success, because in the south the second attack by 13 Corps on the *February* minefield during the night of the 24th/25th had failed; and, in effect, after a further abortive attempt by a brigade of 50 Division to break into Munassib, the whole of Montgomery's southern wing settled down on the defensive.

During the night of the 25th/26th 9 Australian made a neat and impressive attack which brought them closer to the coast road and greatly improved observation for themselves and the artillery. But little important progress was made by the armoured divisions or the Highlanders, and the dynamism of Eighth Army's offensive was steadily diminishing. Moreover, though this was not known to Montgomery, Stumme was dead and Rommel was back in command—a change which, as might be expected, soon increased the weight and energy of Axis counter-attacks.

Several factors contributed to the deep concern about the state of the battle which Montgomery has never fully admitted he felt, but which drove him to spend 26 October in a quiet review of his position. On 29 October Alan Brooke, describing in his diary a moment of great tension and anxiousness, ended by writing: 'It was fortunate that on that day I had not yet received a letter from Monty which arrived a few days later telling me what his feelings were at this juncture of the battle.' Those feelings can be imagined. The phrase 'surgical callousness' has been used to describe Montgomery's attitude about casualties at this point, but a simple mathematical calculation could have indicated to him that the rate of attrition of his infantry was dangerously high. Between the 23rd and dawn on the 26th the New Zealand Division had lost some 1,000 in killed, missing and wounded; the South Africans 600; the Australians 1,000; the Highland Division 2,000. The total for the whole army was estimated at 6,140. And though the equivalent losses of the Germans and Italians were grossly over-assessed, the concrete evidence in terms of prisoners was so far trivial—628 German and 1,534 Italian. British tanks put out of action were less significant—about 300, of which 10 Corps alone had 93 under repair. (It is almost impossible to establish a true figure for British tank *losses* during this battle, since at any point in time it would be necessary to know how many had been recovered from a front line which the British chiefly controlled, how many were undergoing local repair, how many had been sent further back, and so on. But an indication is given in a signal from Alexander to Churchill on 1 November, reporting the latest estimate, which ends 'Recovery of wounded tanks is getting on well. During first six days 213 tanks were recovered. Of these only sixteen were condemned as unrepairable.') In any case Montgomery still had some 900 runners. It was the infantry that mattered. The fighting spearhead of an infantry division is a surprisingly small proportion of the whole, and the casualties had largely been fighting men.* Montgomery had virtually no infantry reserves, his divisions all being

---

* 'The average infantry battalion would cross the start line with 20 officers and 400 men: a further 130 or thereabouts would join them on the final objective, bringing supporting weapons, wireless and the like. About 250 men of the battalion would take no part in the active fighting. If the 420 of the original attacking force fell to 300, the battalion became incapable of carrying out a further serious attack until reinforcements had been received, absorbed and trained. In armoured regiments the number who went into battle was even smaller. With the full complement of tanks the tank crews of a regiment numbered less than 200.' Michael Carver, *El Alamein*, Batsford.

in the line, and in particular replacements for the New Zealand and South African Divisions were very few. Montgomery had also to face the brute fact that on the 26th, for all his expenditure of men and metal, he was still far from attaining the objectives he had set for the 24th. It is not surprising, therefore, that he observes in *El Alamein to the River Sangro*, 'I spent the day in detailed consideration of the situation.'

But for Rommel, too, there was much to consider and much to cause concern. His first situation report to Hitler on the evening of the 25th was pessimistic. His armoured losses—more important to him than to Montgomery in view of the lack of reserves—had been relatively heavy: nor had he equivalent facilities for repair. 127 Axis tanks dead meant that now he could only call on 221 of the less valuable Italian and 148 German: 15 Panzer was down to 40. And the shortage of fuel appalled him. Stopping at Rome on his way back to Africa he had been told that only three issues of petrol remained in the African theatre. (This was approximately sufficient for three days' fighting.) Quick replenishment of his stocks was vital: but on the 26th 3,000 tons went down at sea in the *Proserpina*, and another 1,000, together with 1,000 tons of ammunition, when *Tergestea* was sunk at Tobruk. During his first night at the front he snatched a few hours' sleep, but when he got back to his command post at 0500 hrs. he heard of continuous assaults under a heavy artillery barrage, in some places 'as many as five hundred rounds for every one of ours'. And Hill 28, or Kidney Ridge, was said to have been taken. He watched a counter-attack by 15 Panzer, Littorio and a battalion of Bersaglieri and was oppressed to note the powerful response of the British guns and aircraft and the small results achieved by his troops. Here, he thought, was the focus: the British were seeking to drive north west from Kidney Ridge towards the coast between Sidi Abd el Rahman and Daba. He therefore pulled 90 Light forward from its reserve position and placed Trieste in a long-stop rôle east of Daba, and that evening, knowing well that the tanks could not return if further trouble arose on his right, he ordered 21 Panzer to march north. But he was already desperate. 'At the same time I reported to the Führer's H.Q. that we would lose the battle unless there was an immediate improvement in the supply situation. Judging by previous experience, there was little hope of this happening.'

Montgomery, however, emerged from his brooding with a clear mind and a definite plan of action. At midday on the 26th he issued a first set of orders. The Highland Division was to carry on mopping up within the limits of the first objectives. The Australians were to prepare for a second attack to the north on the night of the 28th. Meanwhile 30 Corps would otherwise make no major effort except to aid 1 Armoured to make progress beyond Kidney Ridge. 7 Armoured was to keep quiet. But his long-term decision was of far greater importance. He had made up his mind to carry out his favourite manoeuvre and create a substantial reserve, by re-grouping his forces, with which to effect a strong and final blow. In the evening he called a conference to settle how this should be done.

The object of the re-shuffle was to enable him to send an augmented New Zealand Division through the German defences along the coast, i.e. somewhat to the right of the original northern corridor, and thus create a hole through which 10 Armoured Division could pour. He named this operation SUPERCHARGE. As a first step, he made it possible to pull out the New Zealand Division into a rest area by side-stepping to the right the South Africans, and 4 Indian Division who had so far not been closely engaged. 7 Armoured, also, was later given a warning order to be prepared to move north (the H.Q. of 21 Panzer having been located, by radio direction finding, opposite Kidney Ridge on the morning of the 27th). In the meantime 10 Armoured proceeded to try to 'make progress'.

The attack this division mounted during the night of the 26th/27th aimed at the seizure of two defended localities each about a mile from Kidney Ridge. One, to the north west, was named 'Woodcock'; the other, south west of the Ridge, had the code-name 'Snipe'. Aided by the artillery of both 30 and 10 Corps, two battalions of 7 Motor Brigade were to capture these during the night and at dawn 2 Armoured Brigade was to advance past 'Woodcock' and 24 Armoured Brigade past 'Snipe'. As so often at Alamein, the operation failed to proceed according to plan, but it led to one of the most gallant actions of the whole battle and another mauling of Rommel's armour. The details of the story are long and fascinating . . . it is vividly narrated in Brigadier Lucas Phillips' *Alamein* . . .; in brief, what happened was that the battalion of the 2nd/6oth failed to take 'Woodcock' but a portion of 2 Rifle Brigade under their Colonel, Victor Turner, managed after various misadventures to get through to the 'Snipe' area in the darkness and dig in their 13 6-pdr. anti-tank guns and the 66-pdrs. of 76 Anti-tank Regiment which had accompanied them.

From dawn till dusk on the 27th this little force held out against a succession of fierce assaults by German and Italian armour. It was virtually on its own, for 24 Armoured Brigade was unable to make sufficient headway to relieve it and their gunner Forward Observation Officer had disappeared into the night, so Turner was without contact with the artillery on which he might have called. The heaviest attack came in about four o'clock in the afternoon, when Rommel made a massive thrust against the British line, having assembled 21 and 15 Panzer, Littorio and part of Ariete to deal with the Kidney Ridge positions while 90 Light tackled the Australians. The Rifle Brigade shared in the decisive repulse of these attacks, which went in under

Rommel's eye. Next day the latter wrote to his wife, 'the enemy's superiority is terrific and our resources are very small. Whether I would survive a defeat lies in God's hands. The lot of the vanquished is heavy.' But there was nothing despondent about the Rifle Brigade who, in spite of many casualties and a badly wounded Colonel, towed out that evening their one remaining gun in triumph. Their achievement was carefully investigated by an official committee of inquiry, which established that they had knocked out 22 German and 10 Italian tanks. Colonel Turner very appropriately was awarded the Victoria Cross.

The feeling in London and Cairo, reflected by some subsequent critics, that during this phase of the battle Montgomery was 'dragging his feet' is scarcely justified by the facts, disappointing though it was that the anticipated breakthrough had not yet occurred. The British *Official History* sums up the latest developments as follows: 'the two days' fighting from 26 to 28 October shows how reverses can occur locally during a battle which is nevertheless being steadily won. For the enemy had suffered losses he could not afford: the fit tanks in the D.A.K. fell from 148 to 77, and the Littorio lost 27. The change from attack to defence had favoured the British. . . .' Rommel's policy of battering against a front thick with an abundance of tanks and anti-tank guns and powerfully supported by a superior weight of artillery had, when analysed, proved to be self-destructive. He himself knew that it was a policy of the second-best. Ideally, he would have wished to pull his armour far back, forming a new line on to which—as in the past—he could have drawn the British tanks and savaged them before the guns of 10 and 30 Corps were able to move forward and find new positions in the mine-cluttered area of the main battlefield. Yet even that, he saw as he reflected retrospectively, would have been no more than an operation to gain time. 'In the absence of their massive artillery support, a British attack at Fuka against a line similarly constructed to that at El Alamein would have met with a bloody rebuff. They would have been forced to bring up their artillery, and this would have meant moving all their installations forward. Thus we would have been given a reprieve during which many things could have happened. The Nebelwerfer regiment might have come across, we might indeed have actually received our 'Tigers'—at the very least, somebody might have done something to improve the supply situation. Even so, it is still very doubtful whether we could have held out in the African theatre any longer than we did.' For, over-riding all else, there was his permanent shortage of fuel. On the evening of the 28th a Wellington torpedoed the tanker *Luisiano* off Greece, and 1,459 tons of petrol were sunk, and on 1 November an air attack on a convoy disposed of the *Tripolino*, with its petrol and ammunition, and another ship, the *Ostia*. Even the desperate measure of flying in fuel from Crete was hampered by attacks on the Junkers 52 transports working from Maleme.

In any case, on the 28th Montgomery put in train his new plan which, very soon, would lead to the decisive victory he and the allies required. At 0800 he gave his instructions to Leese and Lumsden. The Kidney Ridge area was to go on the defensive; 1 Armoured Division was to come out of the line and reorganise; and at midday Freyberg was told that after the Australians had gained more ground in the north his New Zealand Division, now rested, would force its way down the coast. This was a venture Freyberg would not, and indeed could not, have undertaken alone, so he was to be buttressed by a sequence of infantry brigades and once again to have under command 9 Armoured Brigade, which would have first priority on tank replacements. The same evening 7 Armoured was ordered north, leaving behind 4 Light Armoured Brigade but bringing with it 131 Infantry Brigade from 44 Division. Thus a substantial reserve group would be established for the knock-out blow: and that night the Australians took the first step by eating further into the core of the German salient which ran from a point north west of Tell el Eisa to the coast.

The news that divisions were coming out of the line soon reached Cairo and London, and caused great alarm. Alan Brooke vividly describes Churchill's reactions on the morning of the 29th. 'What, he asked, was *my* Monty doing now, allowing the battle to peter out. (Monty was always my Monty when he was out of favour.) He had done nothing now for the last three days, and now he was withdrawing troops from the front. Why had he told us that he would be through in seven days if all he intended to do was to fight a half-hearted battle?' A Chiefs of Staff meeting was summoned for 1230, where Alan Brooke had to defend Montgomery against the strictures of Churchill and other members of the Cabinet. Alan Brooke's defence had little effect until Smuts gave the C.I.G.S. his unqualified support. Nevertheless, in his heart even Alan Brooke had doubts. 'On returning to my office I paced up and down, suffering from a desperate feeling of loneliness.'

It was not by luck, but by performance, that Montgomery could at times like this rely on the backing of a C.I.G.S. who was worried about what he might achieve. In the Dunkirk days, and earlier and after, Alan Brooke had taken Montgomery's measure. At Alamein, therefore, Montgomery could rely on a confidence in himself on the part of his professional superior—and also on a strategic appreciation on the latter's part of the value of the Middle East—which Wavell, for example, never could fall back on in the case of his own superior, the C.I.G.S. Sir John Dill. Alan Brooke never failed to support his commander-in-the-field as Dill failed to support Wavell in his memorandum to the Prime Minister, of 6 May 1941 (*written shortly after Rommel's successful first offensive in Africa*), in which he declared: 'The probability of invasion may seem to have receded for the moment, but German land and air forces could be concentrated for invasion within six to eight weeks of their release from the Balkan theatre. In my view it would be unjustifiable, during the next three months, to risk sending away from this country more than an adequate maintenance reserve for the tanks already in or on the way to the Middle East. Even this, at a wastage of 10 per cent per month, will involve the monthly dispatch of about fifty tanks.' The ability of a field-commander to think that his operations seem credible to his military superior at the political seat of power is a strong reinforcement which Montgomery in Africa usually possessed and Rommel (and Wavell) normally lacked.

But once again, as he had done in the past and was to do so often in the future, Montgomery created a misunderstanding and a loss of confidence in his capacity by thinking and acting merely on 'the military necessity'. He lacked the empathy or intuition which might have enabled him to foresee and take precautions against the effect on others of his unexplained actions. It is very unlikely that he had the least idea that what he saw as a perfectly logical military operation would present itself in a very different light to his anxious superiors in London.

He was soon to learn. On the morning of the 29th, Alexander, Casey (the Minister of State in Cairo), and Alexander's Chief of Staff, Major-General McCreery, called at his H.Q., and 'it was fairly clear to me that there had been consternation in Whitehall'. De Guingand remembers that Casey asked him if a signal should not be sent off to the Prime Minister to prepare him for a reverse, and that he replied, 'If you send that signal I will see that you are hounded out of political life!' But after Montgomery had explained his intentions his visitors went away comforted, and reassuring signals were sent off to London by both Casey and Alexander. Then Tedder appeared. The Air Force was also extremely anxious about Montgomery's apparent sloth, fearing that the promised advance would happen too late for them to grasp the air-fields which would enable Malta (and *its* airfields) to be saved. He was shown the SUPERCHARGE plan, but felt it was not sufficiently ambitious. Tedder argued his case eloquently, but 'the only response I got was, "It's a slogging match." All I could do was to shrug my shoulders and say, "Well, it's your battle." From the map caravan we walked down together a few yards to the mess tent where Montgomery and I had a very quick lunch. We were just finishing the meal when Montgomery said, "There is some fresh intelligence regarding Rommel's dispositions. This means a change." '

The intelligence was of the first importance: one of the units engaged by the Australians during their attack the previous night had been identified as Battle Group 155 of 90 Light. This indicated that the whole of Rommel's best formations were now committed in the northern sector, with the obvious aim of blocking an attack down the coast towards Sidi Abd el Rahman—and that Rommel now had no reserves of German troops left. Before the battle began Williams had pointed out to Montgomery, by what the Field Marshal calls 'a brilliant analysis', that German and Italian units were 'corsetted' . . . that is to say, placed in alternation (see p. 71), and that if the two could be separated there should be no problem in breaking through a purely Italian front. What Williams had recommended now appeared to have happened, and he and de Guingand advised (as had McCreery that morning) that the thrust-line for SUPERCHARGE should be orientated further to the south, so that the New Zealand attack would hit the point of division between the Germans and the Italians. Montgomery immediately changed his plan, and decided that during the night of the 30th/31st the Australians should make a third attack, in considerable strength, towards the sea, but that during the following night SUPERCHARGE should be directed at the junction-point of the Axis armies, with its main weight falling on the Italians.

This shift of direction caught Rommel off balance. He had correctly appreciated the intention of SUPERCHARGE ONE and made the appropriate dispositions. But they were now in the wrong place. The Australians did their job well. In a highly complicated attack, stubbornly resisted, they failed indeed to break right through to the sea but gained positions astride both the road and the railway, captured 500 prisoners, won a VC, and managed to hold their ground against the several vicious counter-attacks Rommel launched against them. The stage for SUPERCHARGE was set, but Montgomery deferred Zero hour for another 24 hours because of what he called the 'stage management problems' involved. This was due to Freyberg, who was impressed by the weariness of the infantry, the need for reconnaissance, and the difficulty of fitting together the different units involved and their supporting arms. The scheme was for him to have two infantry brigades, 151 and 152, each supported by a regiment of Valentines, to help his own division forward. Behind them 9 Armoured Brigade, now reinforced to a level of 79 Shermans and Grants and 53 Crusaders, was to move up, pass through the infantry objective and seize ground beyond Tell el Aqqaqir and the Rahman track, making a barrier behind which 1 Armoured Division could form up before dawn, ready to undertake what was expected to be a final, decisive armoured battle. Accepting Freyberg's arguments, at 0630 hrs. on the 31st Montgomery shifted zero hour for SUPERCHARGE to 0105 hrs. on 2 November.

When considering the work of the British armour in SUPERCHARGE, the breakthrough and the subsequent pursuit, it is important to remember that by this time a considerable number of the tanks involved were replacements, and that these were often unsatisfactory, either because they arrived at the last minute or were delivered without essential parts. The sort of thing that happened is described by the poet Keith Douglas (later killed in Normandy), whose *Alamein to Zem Zem* provides a brilliant first-hand account of the battle. At the time of which he is writing, his regiment was waiting to advance with 1 Armoured Division in the dark early hours of 2 November.

'The new tanks, long despaired of, were arriving. During the next hour came four of them. This necessitated a complete revision of the composition of troops and the provision of crews for the new tanks, whose skeleton delivery crews returned to their delivery point. N.C.O.'s acting as gunners were promoted to tank commanders. Changing tanks about meant hasty unstrapping of kit, redistribution of rations, particularly the canteen stuff, and a frenzied search for more maps, which had to be marked. All this in darkness.

'The arrival of the new tanks utterly altered the geography of the area. Having grown used to recognizing each tank by its distance from the next and by the direction in which it faced, a man sent from one side of the area to the other in the dark had to contend with the sudden apparition of tanks where none had been before. This caused immense confusion. The wirelesses in the new tanks had to be checked and netted on the regimental frequency. One of the tanks allotted to me had a wireless out of order. A spare part had to be found and fitted: at first the wireless mechanic shut himself in the turret and worked with the light on: but this was soon forbidden because light streamed out through cracks between the two halves of the turret-top. After that he worked by touch. The new tanks were deficient in ammunition, petrol, oil, water and internal fittings. They had no tommy-guns in them, no bivouac tents strapped along their sides. Their tracks wanted tightening. Their machine-guns were half hidden in a paste of dust and oil, in which they would have to stay, since to strip them in the dark would only result in the loss of all the essential small parts. The delivery of these tanks at this hour and in this state was nothing in the least unusual: it would not be too much to say it was typical.'

Such are the realities of war . . . realities which tend to be forgotten by Prime Ministers in their Cabinet Offices and post-war commentators without battle experience, as they study the arrows on their maps.

When SUPERCHARGE started on the 2nd the infantry performed their task in exemplary fashion. Both 151 and 152 Brigades got on to their objectives by the allotted time, while on the right and left flanks the 28th Maori Battalion and 133 Lorried Infantry Brigade had taken positions enabling them to set up a flank guard. Now it was the turn of 9 Armoured Brigade, whose rôle was certainly unenviable. It was known that along the Rahman track and around Tell el Aqqaqir the Germans had strong anti-tank defences, well dug in. At his conference before the attack Freyberg had said: 'We all realise that for

armour to attack a wall of guns sounds like another Balaclava; it is properly
an infantry job. But there are no more infantry available, so our armour must
do it.' John Currie, commanding 9 Armoured, observed that this might
involve 50 per cent losses. Freyberg replied, 'It may well be more than that.
The Army Commander has said he is prepared to accept 100 per cent.' The
Brigade's 11 mile approach march was a discouraging overture. Replacement tanks had inefficient equipment, the dust-clouds as they churned up the
corridor made visibility difficult, shelling caused casualties to tanks and men,
one unit lost direction and had to turn and catch up, and as a result only 94
tanks out of the Brigade's three regiments were available at its zero hour,
which at Currie's request had been postponed by half an hour to 0615. This
postponement, though unavoidable, was critical, since it gave the enemy a
bonus of 30 minutes during which the light was steadily improving.

But, unlike the charge at Balaclava, the suicidal attack by 9 Armoured
Brigade was by no means a disaster. On paper its casualties look appalling:
70 out of 94 tanks out of action (though many were recovered); 230 officers
and men killed or wounded by the end of the day; and the gun-line on the
Rahman track still unbroken. But in that line the Brigade had destroyed 35
guns—a satisfactory *quid pro quo* at this stage of the battle—and such tanks
as survived were able to hold on long enough to allow 2 and 8 Armoured
Brigades of 1 Armoured Division to crawl out of the corridor and deploy.
Both brigades were also halted: but again the relative loss to the Afrika
Korps was the greater and the more menacing. 1 Armoured was reduced by
14 tanks killed and 40 damaged or broken down—which in view of Keith
Douglas' evidence is not surprising. The Afrika Korps, on the other hand,
lost another 70 of its few remaining panzers during the day. And though
Montgomery had cause for chagrin in that his ambitious SUPERCHARGE plan
had not proved to be the final answer, what he could not know was that at
0815 General von Thoma, commander of the Afrika Korps, told Rommel
that his front was only just holding and that if the British continued to attack
a breakthrough was inevitable. If the essence of a victory is the moral defeat
of one's opponent, then by SUPERCHARGE Montgomery had already achieved
one, for after reviewing his situation Rommel decided that his only possible
course of action was to retreat to the tenuous reserve position at Fuka. Even
this offered little hope, and his situation report to O.K.W. stated 'in these
circumstances we must therefore expect the gradual destruction of the Army'.

All that Montgomery now had to do was to finish off the 'set-piece battle'
and organise a pursuit. He was aided by Hitler, who on the 3rd sent the
following disastrous signal:

To Field Marshal Rommel
    It is with trusting confidence in your leadership and the courage of the

German-Italian troops under your command that the German people and I are following the heroic struggle in Egypt. In the situation in which you find yourself there can be no other thought but to stand fast, yield not a yard of room and throw every gun and every man into the battle. Considerable air force reinforcements are being sent to C.-in-C. South. The Duce and Comando Supremo are also making the utmost efforts to send you the means to continue the fight. Your enemy, despite his superiority, must also be at the end of his strength. It would not be the first time in history that a strong will has triumphed over bigger battalions. As to your troops, you can show them no other road than that to victory or death.

Adolf Hitler

The effect of this signal on Rommel was traumatic. 'A kind of apathy took hold of us as we issued orders for all existing positions to be held on instructions from the highest authority.' There were now only 30 tanks left in the Afrika Korps. Von Thoma, when Rommel passed on to him Hitler's message, said in so many words that it was impossible for him to 'yield not a yard of room'. British armoured car squadrons had already slipped through to harass the open flank in the south. The instructions Rommel had given for the withdrawal of the footslogging Italian infantry and the fighting withdrawal of his mobile formations were already being implemented. It was difficult to put them into reverse. Rommel did his best, but the Desert Air Force was out in strength over the battle zone and the routes of retirement, and during the night of 3/4 November two hard punches by the Indian and Highland Divisions finished the matter. More armoured cars swept forward into open country, and the heavier armour began its more stately advance. By the 12th day, as he had predicted, Montgomery had driven Rommel into retreat.

It would be superfluous to comment on the courage and self-sacrifice displayed by the men on both sides in this conflict. I prefer a coda in a lower key. It is provided by General Horrocks, who after the battle took the trouble to visit General Morshead, Commander of 9 Australian Division which, in the estimation of those who took part in the battle, was the lynch-pin. Horrocks visited Morshead to congratulate him on the performance of his division. Morshead replied, simply, 'Thank you, General. The boys were interested.'

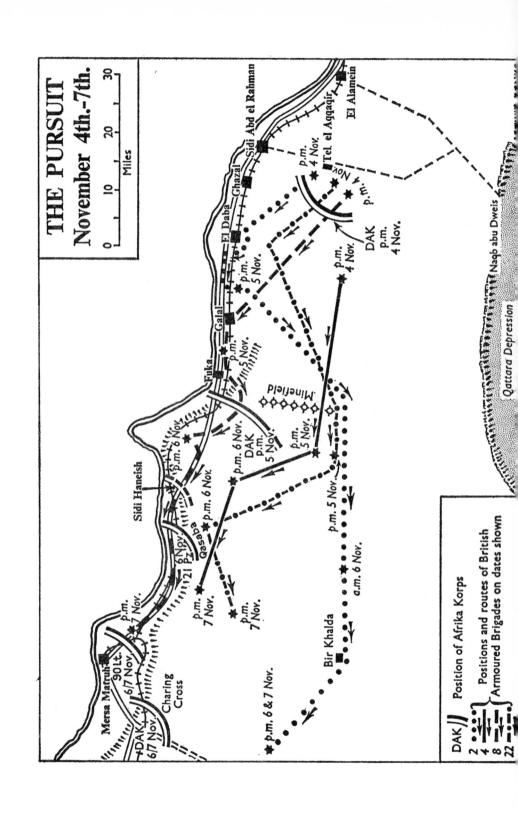

THE PURSUIT
November 4th.–7th.

Miles
0   10   20   30

El Alamein
Tel. el Aqqaqir
Sidi Abd el Rahman
Sidi Abd el Rahman
Ghazal
El Daba
Galal
Fuka
Qattara Depression
Naqb abu Dweis

p.m. 4 Nov.
4 Nov.
DAK p.m. 4 Nov.
p.m. 4 Nov.
DAK p.m. 4 Nov.

p.m. 5 Nov.
Minefield
p.m. 5 Nov.
p.m. 5 Nov.
p.m. 5 Nov.
p.m. 6 Nov.
DAK p.m. 6 Nov.

Sidi Haneish
p.m. 6 Nov.
21 Pz.
6 Nov.
Qaseba p.m. 6 Nov.

p.m. 7 Nov.
p.m. 7 Nov.
p.m. 7 Nov.

Mersa Matruh
90 Lt.
p.m. 7 Nov.
6/7 Nov.
DAK 6/7 Nov.
Charing Cross

Bir Khalda
a.m. 6 Nov.
p.m. 6 & 7 Nov.

DAK Position of Afrika Korps
2
4   Positions and routes of British
8   Armoured Brigades on dates shown
22

5

To the African shores

Yearly we've ridden the Djebel Stakes,
Yearly fought back on our course,
Yearly we've made the same silly mistakes,
Over-ridden a failing horse,
At a fence too stiff for his strength to leap,
With a rotten take-off, unfirm, too steep,
Heavily breasted the top of the bank,
Pawed, gasped and struggled, then hopelessly sank,
Shocked, hurt and surprised at the toss we took—
Rolling back adown the ditch at Tobruk.
Major General Sir Francis Tuket *The Djebel Stakes*

'A commander's despatches may claim a victory; the historian, reading in a critical spirit, will ask: "if it was a victory, why was it not followed up in this or that way?"'
R. G. Collingwood, *The Idea of History*

Montgomery's vision of the aftermath of Alamein was that of the men who landed on the beaches of Normandy on D-Day, 6 June 1944. 'The troops who had specially prepared and trained for the invasion had been so long keyed-up for this great assault that they were unable (and were perhaps understandably unwilling to try) to project their thoughts beyond it.'* In other words, Montgomery was so wholly absorbed by the paramount necessity of defeating Rommel on the *battlefield*, of stage-managing the 'break-in', the 'dog-fight' and the 'break-out', that (to judge from what happened), he failed to devote enough attention and foresight to the problems that would face him on the battle's morrow. It is significant that neither in the 'Orders About Morale' which he issued on 14 September, nor in the 'Orders About Leadership' of 6 October, nor in the rough notes for his final address to senior officers about LIGHTFOOT which he delivered on 19 and 20 October, nor in his Personal Message to Eighth Army of the 23†

---

* Bellfield and Essame, *The Battle for Normandy*, Batsford, p. 56. The Germans suffered from a similar myopia during the Spring 1940, when planning SICHELSCHNITT. It was not until March that Guderian was *first* asked about the crossing of the Meuse—and that by Hitler—'And then what are you going to do?' 'Most of the energy that O.K.H. had lavished upon SICHELSCHNITT had been absorbed in planning the actual breakthrough, but little on its immediate aftermath.' Alistair Horne, *To Lose a Battle*, p. 142.
† All these are reproduced in Montgomery's *Memoirs*.

is there any reference to what might follow the set-piece battle other than vague remarks about 'general "clearing-up" operations', and 'together we will hit the enemy for "six", right out of Africa'. In fact, before and during the follow-up, the commander who subsequently wrote, 'I hold the view that the leader must know what he himself wants. He must see his objective clearly and then strive to attain it; he must let everyone else know what he wants and what are the basic fundamentals of his policy. He must in fact give firm guidance and a clear lead', notably failed in these particulars. The muddles, the improvisations, the break-down of supplies, the sense of everything being 'too little and too late', the sequence of minor miscarriages such as afflict any army whose commander's touch is unsure—all these, beginning on 4 November, contrast strangely with the far-sighted and meticulous preparations which led to the success of the twelve-day battle. And yet, as Liddell Hart comments in his edition of *The Rommel Papers*, 'the most crucial stage of the pursuit was during the day and night of the 4th. During that period, escape looked hardly possible.' Indeed, it is not too much to say that, just as Rommel lost Alam Halfa during the first few hours of his attack, so Montgomery threw away the full fruits of his victory in the first twenty-four hours after its consummation.

The situation at dawn on the 4th is described dramatically in the *History of the Fourth Indian Division*, whose 5 Brigade in its attack during the night, just south of Tell el Aqqaqir, had secured one of the two shoulders of the corridor for the 'break-out'.

> At the first streak of light in the east, the infantry came into broken ground. They saw before them the kidney-shaped contour which they had been shown on the map. The guns lifted and were done; there was quiet but for the crackle of small-arms fire. Out in front little figures scuttled madly, seeking holes. A carrier platoon went out to bring them in. Then another noise, thunder out of the east, and more thunder. The roar mounted. The tanks came plunging through—hundreds of tanks, lunging to the west through the gap the Wedge had made, and wheeling north for the kill. The sun rose on the last of Alamein.

But the thunder soon decreased, and the tanks did not lunge very far: nor did they make a kill.

Tuker, perhaps the most intelligent and percipient of Eighth Army's divisional commanders, had already, on the 3rd, instructed his two uncommitted brigades of the Indian Division to be ready for pursuit as soon as a break occurred, 'for we knew we were the only fresh, desert-worthy troops now left. . . .' They aimed at spurting to Halfaya Pass, some 250 miles away, and achieving there another Beda Fomm. Their intention was to be at Halfaya and Sollum early on the 6th, but, says Tuker in his *Approach To Battle*, 'there was no pursuit. Ponderously, crawling through those congested corridors, heavy tanks and heavy infantry went forward with no burning sense of urgency.' These remarks might be thought to reflect the natural acerbity of a disappointed man, but in fact they reflect the truth. Just as some of the troops in Normandy needed to be urged forward on D + 1, so now there was an understandable reaction on the part of weary officers and men most of whom had fought for nearly a fortnight with very little sleep. (For the armour, in particular, darkness did not mean repose. Re-fuelling, re-stocking with ammunition and essential maintenance consumed much time.) This was the moment when a firm hand and the feeling of conforming to a 'predetermined pattern' were essential. But the relevant staff-work was missing. The records contain many references to the absence of efficient traffic control, and the advancing divisions found themselves relying on their own provost units (most of whom, also, had spent sleepless and dangerous nights manning the minefield gaps).

4 Indian Division, alert and on its toes, having taken little part in the main battle, was merely instructed to hand over its troop-carrying transport to the Greek Brigade and start picking up salvage. The first phase of the chase was made the business of 10 Corps, with 1 Armoured on its right, 7 in the centre and 10 on the left. (See map on p. 92.) The New Zealand Division was ordered to swing west and north round the southern flank of 10 Corps, with 4 Light Armoured Brigade (some 79 tanks), in the lead, followed by 9 Armoured Brigade (now reduced to one regiment of 24 tanks). Freyberg, like Tuker, had caught the scent of victory and, also on the 3rd, had told the New Zealanders to load with eight days' water and rations, petrol for some 500 miles, and an adequate stock of ammunition. The old desert hands were not lacking the prevision born of experience—and this includes Raymond Briggs of 1 Armoured, who has described to me how he too sensed well in advance that the end was coming, and pleaded to be allowed to reload his transport (disproportionately filled with ammunition for the break-out battle) with supplies for a pursuit. Briggs reckoned he could have been ready with 24 hours' notice, bearing in mind that his different types of tank required three different kinds of fuel, and their various types of gun various types of ammunition. But his request was rejected.

Montgomery himself displayed a confidence which was not fully justified by the facts. At 0915 on the 4th he issued the following message:

> The present battle has now lasted for twelve days, during which all troops have fought so magnificently that the enemy is being worn down. The enemy has just reached the breaking point and he is trying to get his Army away. The Royal Air Force is taking heavy toll of his columns moving west on the main coast road. The enemy is in our power and he is just about to crack. I call on all troops to keep up the pressure and not to relax for one moment. We have

the chance of putting the whole Panzer Army in the bag and we will do so. I congratulate all troops on what has been achieved. Complete victory is almost in sight. On your behalf I have sent a separate message to the Royal Air Force thanking them for their quite magnificent support.'

But a detailed examination of the performance of the New Zealand Division on the 4th—a division which prided itself, rightly, on its experience and skill in desert manoeuvre—is sufficient to demonstrate that the Army Commander's exhortations could not explain the absence of a 'predetermined pattern'.

The initial moves laid down for the New Zealanders and 10 Corps on the 4th were—Freyberg with his two mobile infantry brigades, the 5th and the 6th, and preceded by 4 Light Armoured and 9 Armoured Brigades, to cut westwards across the desert and then turn north for Fuka (some 60 miles from the Rahman track); 1 Armoured to make for El Kharash, due north west of Tell el Aqqaqqir; and 7 Armoured to aim for Ghazal. Then 1 Armoured followed by 10 was to be ready to move on, parallel with the coast, to Fuka. A glance at the map on p. 92 will indicate that what was envisaged was a broad wheel to the north by Eighth Army's advancing front, the key to the operation being the point just west of Fuka where the coastal road climbs up the escarpment. If this bottleneck could be blocked in time, there was just a chance that the retreating *Panzerarmee* would be caught between two fires. But the wheel jammed as soon as it began to revolve.

Freyberg's first problem was to assemble in clear ground west of the minefields the separated elements which were to constitute his flying column. 'It was quite impossible,' says Kippenberger of 5 Brigade, 'to move in formed bodies. All we could do was to work our way through the gaps in the minefields in single file, the armour leading. It was all most confused and difficult.' 4 Light Armoured, which was to take the lead, was four hours late in emerging. 9 Armoured and 5 Brigade found that the congestion and the pulverized dust in the lanes hampered them from even getting into the forward area. 'There appeared to be no traffic control,' Kippenberger noted. The confusion was worse confounded by the simultaneous movements of 10 Armoured Division. At dusk, in consequence, the head of the column had only got to El Agramiya, 9 Armoured Brigade was only just beyond the Rahman track, and 6 New Zealand Brigade had hardly stirred; it only caught up in the early hours of the 5th, guided by wireless which directed it on to a burning truck— the result of a skirmish in the dark between 5 Brigade's rear and a group of Axis fugitives. The many flares rising and falling all over the desert made direction-finding difficult, with the result that Freyberg, who intended to close up his force during the evening and move on at 1300 hrs., was compelled to delay his start until 0530 next morning. Between dawn and dusk on the

7 *North Africa : Leese, Montgomery and Lumsden*

8 *North Africa : Gurkhas at the Mareth Line*

4th, therefore, the rate of advance of the New Zealand 'flying column' was . . . 4 Light Armoured, 35 miles; 9 Armoured, 12 miles; 5 Brigade, 28 miles; and 6 Brigade, 2½ miles.

For the armour of 10 Corps the day was even less rewarding. The relative tank strength of the two armies was now: Eighth Army, about 600; the Afrika Korps, 20; the Italians, under 100. Nevertheless, 1 Armoured, delayed by 21 Panzer, was only eight miles further ahead by the evening. Until about four in the afternoon 10 Armoured was engaged, as it reported, in 'systematically destroying enemy tanks and anti-tank screen'. It was only then (when, as will be seen, 7 Armoured had eliminated Ariete and Rommel had issued final orders for a retreat) that the links between the Germans and the Italians fell apart, and 10 Armoured was able to set its 8 Armoured Brigade in motion to work round the rear of the Afrika Korps. But darkness soon intervened, and though two of the regiments asked to be allowed to press on through the night towards the coastal road, the brigade halted (having only moved one and a half miles), because its third regiment was in difficulties. 7 Armoured Division's advance, which began at 0900, went well for the first five miles: then it hit a defended ridge, and had to deploy. More and more enemy tanks and guns came into action—the remnants of the Italian Ariete Division fighting a desperate rearguard. It took 22 Armoured Brigade all day to break their resistance, and though by dark it had virtually annihilated Ariete, 7 Armoured now went into leaguer for the night. The total picture presented by Eighth Army on 4 November, therefore, is scarcely one of remorseless, dynamic pursuit in the spirit of the oft-quoted words of Marshal Saxe, '. . . attack, push, and pursue without cease. . . . All manoeuvres are good then: it is only precautions that are worthless.'

This failure partly arose from the fact that though Montgomery at first had an embryonic plan, he abandoned it. The matter is put succinctly by the *Official History*.

> Because of the course taken by the battle since 23rd October there was no strong mobile formation fresh, concentrated, and poised for distant pursuit as, for example, had been Allenby's Desert Mounted Corps at Megiddo in September 1918. Nevertheless a plan had been made for a force under Major-General C. H. Gairdner (commander of the skeleton 8th Armoured Division), with an air component, to be formed ready to dart forward to some point in the enemy's back area, possibly even as far as Tobruk. This force was to be self- contained for several days, but as it could only be made up of units taken from here and there General Montgomery cancelled the project and decided instead to use formations already in the forward area.

In his eighties Montgomery still defends himself on the ground that he flung 10 Corps (from which Gairdner's force was to be drawn) wholesale into

North Africa : The Hat

the winning of the set battle, and there was 'Nothing left, nothing left.' I remember the fanatical intensity with which he told me that towards the end
of Alamein he was informed that his ammunition stocks were running low.
' "Use it all," I said. "Use it all. Nothing matters but winning." ' And the same
with the tanks of 10 Corps. *Tout le monde à la bataille!* Yet Montgomery has
always advocated the policy of forming reserves for the decisive blow, and
rightly takes pride in his application of this policy before SUPERCHARGE.
Eighth Army was certainly not short of tanks when the set battle ended, and
before it Montgomery had talked largely about a *corps de chasse*. It does not
seem an unreasonable usage of hindsight, therefore, to ask why such a corps
was not available when the need for it arose. In criticising Montgomery's
performance at this stage one is doing no more than applying to it his own
high standards of generalship—standards which he has constantly expounded: the need to think ahead, the need for a clear-cut plan well understood by subordinates, the need for leadership from the very top, all ensuring
that operations are inevitably conducted according to a 'predetermined
pattern'.

But when that is said it must still be remembered, in fairness to the Field
Marshal, that considered from Rommel's viewpoint the activities of Eighth
Army on the 4th appeared in a very different light. By the end of the day
Rommel was in despair. He had started it still paralysed by Hitler's order to
stand fast, and not encouraged by the fact that on the previous evening he
had dispatched his A.D.C., Lieutenant Berndt, to explain to the Führer how
obedience to his orders would mean the destruction of his army: when Berndt
got to Mersa Matruh he telephoned Rommel, to say that he had travelled
down the coast road for four hours under non-stop attack by hundreds of low-
flying planes, and that 'the road was blocked at many points by burning
vehicles and vast traffic jams had developed. In many cases drivers and men
had abandoned their vehicles and fled westwards on foot. Abandoned tanks
and vehicles stood at many points on the road.' During the morning of the
4th Field Marshal Kesselring visited Rommel, and they discussed Hitler's
order, Rommel taking the line that 'until this moment we in Africa had
always had complete freedom of action. Now that was over.' (According to
a foot-note by Rommel's son Manfred, in *The Rommel Papers*, Kesselring
said that he thought that as the man on the spot Rommel should take whatever action he thought correct.) But, for the time being, the fight continued.
Then Rommel received a message from his Chief of Staff, Westphal, that
the Italian divisions on his right were disintegrating. Finally, at 1300 hrs.
Bayerlein reported that General von Thoma had disappeared in the front line
and was probably dead (he was actually taken prisoner) and that Bayerlein
himself, who then took over the Afrika Korps, had escaped on foot from an

imminent armoured attack. By the early afternoon Rommel realised that his front was crumbling, irretrievably, and at 1530 hrs., in spite of Hitler's embargo, he sent out orders for a general retreat which—by then too late— were duplicated next morning by signals from Hitler and the Italian High Command. 'So now it had come,' Rommel wrote subsequently, 'the thing we had done everything in our power to avoid—our front broken and the fully motorised enemy streaming into our rear. Superior orders could no longer count. We had to save what there was to be saved.' In this sense Montgomery's prophecy in his morning message had come true: the enemy had cracked. But 'the whole Panzer Army' was by no means 'in the bag'.

'The pursuit proper,' Montgomery says in his *Memoirs*, 'began on the 5th November.' But it was at least a day too late. In spite of attrition in many rearguard actions, and more severe losses in a number of formal battles, the Afrika Korps continued to preserve an entity throughout its long withdrawal to Tunisia, and its units were never 'put in the bag' *en masse* until the day of the final surrender of the Axis armies in North Africa. There were three places where Rommel might have been intercepted during the first phase of the retreat—Fuka, Mersa Matruh, and Sollum—but in each case he was able to break contact in time, as misfortune or miscalculation held back the Eighth Army. Rommel himself reached Fuka and set up an H.Q. there by the early hours of the 5th, and during the day a considerable portion of the Afrika Korps, 90 Light and some Italian motorised troops had arrived. But by the evening of the 5th none of Montgomery's spearheads was in a position to strike: none, at least, was prepared to do so.

The reasons were varied. The New Zealand group was on the move well before dawn, with the escarpment above Fuka its target, and 4 Light Armoured Brigade soon had a useful skirmish, catching a German column at breakfast, putting out of action some tanks and capturing the general commanding the Italian Trento Division. But at noon the advance was halted by an apparent minefield, covered by artillery fire, and though this was in fact a dummy (laid, it seems, by the South Africans during the summer retreat from Gazala), it was sufficient to hold Freyberg up until dusk, and he paused for the night with the head of his group still ten miles short of Fuka. 10 Armoured Division, having been re-directed on to Galal station (half way between El Daba and Fuka) got there by early afternoon, having destroyed an Italian column and finished off 44 tanks. Its 8 Armoured Brigade then swept some nine miles up the road towards Fuka, but it too stopped at 2000 hrs., still short of its objective, while the infantry brigade was ordered *east-wards* during the evening to mop up enemy stragglers on the way to Daba, which was 7 Armoured Division's goal at the start of the day. After Montgomery appreciated that Daba was empty, however, he re-orientated 7

Armoured in a westerly direction and ordered it to make a deeper thrust, for the airfields near Sidi Haneish and Qasaba. Its centre-line, unfortunately, took it across the rear of the New Zealanders, a check which was repeated when it met the dummy minefield; so this division also went into leaguer for the night, not many miles south of the New Zealand group. 1 Armoured, after reaching Daba, was dispatched on an even wider sweep to the south west, with orders to work round on to Mersa Matruh from the rear. Its march, however, did not begin until 1800, and during the night it was diverted by an enemy leaguer, while its wheeled transport began to scatter in the darkness.

Thus it is fair to say that on the 5th Montgomery was starting to think with a larger scope: but his ideas were still not bold enough, nor were his subordinates ruthless enough in pressing forward. It may also be doubted whether the dispersion of his forward divisions was his best policy. By dawn, anyway, the bird had flown. Rommel intended to stay at Fuka long enough to give his marching infantry (and especially the Italians in the south*), a chance to extricate themselves, but he soon appreciated that a stand would be hopeless, and during the night of the 5th/6th, realising that he must abandon his infantry to their fate, he ordered his mobile troops to pull back to Mersa Matruh, 'a wild helter-skelter drive through the pitch-dark night'. He was harassed by the Desert Air Force, which during the day—presumably because of the difficulty of distinguishing friend from foe among the columns scattered about the desert—had been surprisingly quiescent . . . 367 sorties of all kinds as against 641 on the 4th and 1,094 on the 3rd. But Montgomery, nevertheless, continued to enjoy a virtually unchallenged superiority in the air. Tedder, in *With Prejudice*, summarises in a telling fashion what this meant to the Eighth Army.

> This phase of the campaign demonstrated again the unique advantages of air power as a flexible instrument of war. Aircraft could be switched rapidly from one task to another as the situation demanded. They could be summoned from bases and theatres widely separated. The bombers operated by day and night against Benghasi and Tobruk. Aircraft from Egypt and Malta made carefully co-ordinated attacks against Rommel's seaborne supplies from Europe. Beaufighters blasted trains and transport beyond the range of normal fighters. Torpedo Swordfish loaded with flares ranged the desert, seeking out targets, and calling up the Wellingtons to deal with them. Fighters covered barges and coastal shipping, so that our seaborne supplies should keep pace with the advance.

During the pursuit, it is true, the actual destruction caused from the air was somewhat less than might have been expected in view of the magnificent targets offered by the enormous traffic jams: but the German records are

---

* The prey of 13 Corps, which was left behind to tidy up this inanimate mass.

unanimous in remarking on the damage done to the morale of their retreating army by a surveillance from the sky which seemed uninterrupted by day and by night.

'A modern battle,' Montgomery has written in describing his doctrine of command, 'can very quickly go off the rails.' The operations of 7 November vividly illustrate this commonplace—a day of which Rommel observed that 'although the enemy must have been aware of our weakness, he still continued to operate with great caution'. It was not, however, caution which hampered Eighth Army in the more enterprising movements which it had started on the 6th: it was rather human miscalculation and an Act of God . . . too little petrol, in other words, and too much rain!

During the morning the Afrika Korps was making its way back to Matruh, in spite of indescribable conditions on the road, columns jammed between minefields, vehicles on tow. 15 Panzer and 90 Light came in safely: but 21 Panzer, immobilised by lack of fuel, was caught by 22 Armoured Brigade (at the head of 7 Armoured Division) as it drew near to the edge of the escarpment just south of Qasaba. First 1 R.T.R., however, and then 4 County of London Yeomanry and then 5 R.T.R. were also grounded with empty tanks, and though by noon they were sufficiently replenished to be able to form a half-circle round the Panzers, which had taken up a 'hedge-hog' position, the Voss Reconnaissance Group, left behind as a rearguard at Fuka, came up on the British rear and helped 21 Panzer out of its predicament. The result was that though the latter lost guns and 16 tanks, its survivors were able to extricate themselves and, aided by a small replenishment of fuel, escape to Matruh . . . by which time the rain which had started to fall heavily during the afternoon had so ruined the going that 7 Armoured made no further progress.

1 Armoured had a similar experience. Its 2 Armoured Brigade was well on the way, after dawn, to intercept the enemy at Charing Cross, the track junction to the south of Mersa Matruh through which those of Rommel's troops taking an inland route would have to pass. But after 16 miles the Brigade ran dry—sad news for the divisional commander, Briggs, who, it will be remembered, had sought at Alamein to be allowed to jettison his excess ammunition and stock up with petrol for the chase. The Brigade's transport (scattered during the night's march) did not catch up till 1100, and even then could only partly replenish two regiments. The second line supply column was far away, lumbering over the deeply rutted tracks, and the onset of rain caused it to bog down, immovable, some 40 miles from the point where it should have been re-filling the first-line lorries. 10 Armoured Division got no further than Fuka before it, too, had to pause for the night on the escarpment, water-logged. As for the New Zealand group, Kippenberger best describes

its predicament. After it had reached the Baggush area 'the bottom fell out of the desert . . . my car sank down to the axles'.

Montgomery has always used the rain as a scapegoat. On 10 November he wrote to Alan Brooke, '. . . what saved him was the rain; I had nearly reached Matruh and was getting in behind all his transport when torrential rain turned the desert into a bog. . . .' But this is implausible. The Lord sendeth rain on the just and on the unjust: the *Panzerarmee* suffered equally. 'Torrential rain fell during this period,' says Rommel, 'making many tracks impassable and forcing us to rely almost solely on the coast road, which became hopelessly jammed up with traffic at many points.' Moreover, as has been seen, a number of attempts to block the retreat had already been made, to no effect, *before* the rain fell. Liddell Hart's comment is nearer the truth than Montgomery's special pleading:

> In analysis it becomes clear that the best opportunities had already been forfeited before the rain intervened—by too narrow moves, by too much caution, by too little sense of the time-factor, by unwillingness to push on in the dark, and by concentrating too closely on the battle to keep in mind the essential requirements for its decisive exploitation. If the pursuit had driven deeper through the desert, to reach a more distant blocking point such as the steep escarpment at Sollum, it would have avoided the risk of interception either by resistance or weather—for while rain is a likely risk in the coastal belt it is rare in the desert interior.

'At Sollum': where Tuker's 4 Indian Division, now reduced to a salvage corps, had planned to arrive early on the 6th!

Throughout the 7th three of Montgomery's divisions made no move, stranded as they were in the sodden sands, and still without fuel. 1 Armoured, indeed, could work along the road, and had enough petrol to do so: but even its probe towards Matruh was foiled by an enemy road-block, and it was not till early next morning that the way was clear. Patrols entered Matruh only to find that Rommel had disengaged during the night, his aim being to get through the Halfaya/Sollum bottleneck before he was outstripped.

Between the 8th and the 20th, when Eighth Army's advance elements reached Benghazi, there was not so much a pursuit as a procession. Montgomery steadfastly refused to abandon the 'masterplan' which he later set out, nakedly, in an address to the New Zealand Division on 4 January. 'In the various battles we have fought out here you may have noticed that we have intervals where we sit still and do nothing, and you may wonder why. The reason is that part of my military teaching is that I am not going to have out here in North Africa any failures. . . . I definitely refuse to do anything until we are absolutely ready administratively, until we have built up sufficient strength to be certain there will be no failures. . . .' Even when Gatehouse reported to him on the morning of the 8th that 10 Armoured Division, 'the strongest in Egypt and with a complete B echelon', was ready for action, and asked to be allowed to drive for Sollum and Tobruk, Montgomery was unwilling to risk 'a mad rush' and a kick-back by Rommel. It is clear that he was haunted by the débâcles of previous years, and sensitive to the feeling among his older hands (which increased perceptibly as Benghazi and Agheila drew near), that Rommel might achieve another miracle, turn at bay and hurl them back along the reverse route of 'the Djebel stakes' or, as it was some-times called 'the Benghazi handicap'. 'As one officer expressed it to me: "We used to go up to Benghazi for Christmas and return to Egypt early in the New Year." I was determined to have done with that sort of thing.' Yet at this distance in time it is difficult to see what he had to fear but fear itself. Inclined though it was to over-estimate the capacity of the Afrika Korps, Eighth Army intelligence was not grossly inefficient. By now the prisoners taken, the transport and tanks destroyed, the sustained sinking of trans-Mediterranean shipping, the picture presented by air reconnaissance of an enemy in disorder and the knowledge of his own relative strength ought to have persuaded Montgomery, as it certainly would have persuaded O'Connor or Patton—or Rommel—to concentrate all his available resources in a final attempt to stop and shatter the *Panzerarmee*. 'Balance' and administrative orthodoxy seem during these days to have acted more as a soporofic than as a stimulus to aggressive action. The following table* of the strengths of the principal German formations on or about 10 November speaks for itself.

Formation	Men	Artillery	Tanks
90 Light	1,000	10 a/t guns 2 troops Fd. arty.	Nil
15 Panzer	1,177	5 a/t guns 11 Fd. guns	Nil
21 Panzer	1,009	5 a/t guns 6 Fd. guns	11
Ramcke Para. Brigade	700	5 a/t guns 2 Fd. guns	Nil
19 Flak Division	?	24 88mm. 40 2cm. Light a/a guns	
164 Light (on 17 Nov.)	2 bns.	2 troops Fd.	Nil

At Matruh Montgomery had a narrow escape whose implications are reminiscent of 24 November the previous year, when Rommel, after his

* Reproduced from *The Official History*.

controversial 'dash to the wire' in the middle of CRUSADER, spent the night with some of his senior staff in a lonely Command vehicle, lost and desolate on the frontier of Egypt while his enemy's transport and despatch-riders sped past him in the darkness. Montgomery was moving with a small escort behind his leading troops. A reconnaissance party, including his stepson Dick Carver, went down the road to the shore east of Matruh to select a site for a Tactical H.Q. Unfortunately this party was captured by a German rearguard, and had Montgomery's group not been halted by a skirmish he might well have followed his stepson down to Smugglers Cove, as it was called; it is intriguing to reflect on the possible consequences.

As Matruh was being cleared on the 8th, the news broke which Montgomery had been expecting and which for Rommel, after Alamein, was his true *coup de grâce*—TORCH had begun. Anglo-American convoys were pouring men ashore at the western end of the Mediterranean. Rommel immediately grasped the significance of this threat to his rear: it 'spelt the end of the army in Africa'. He held a conference with Bayerlein, and there formed the opinion that he must hasten his retreat westwards . . . even that the Axis must now evacuate North Africa. Henceforth an allied presence in Algeria and Tunisia was a permanent factor in the calculations of the opposing commanders— who, however, could not know in the days immediately after the landings that Hitler would switch the main weight of his reinforcement from the Afrika Korps, already meagrely supplied, to the sustenance of his bridgehead around Tunis.

Indeed neither Hitler nor Mussolini evinced any sympathy for Rommel in his new predicament. The latter wished to avoid a pitched battle at all costs, and aimed at pulling out of Cyrenaica and falling back along the shore of the Gulf of Sirte as rapidly as possible. The Duce, by contrast, sought to retain a foothold as far east as possible for as long as possible. On 22 November Hitler ended a protracted and acrimonious argument by ordering that the Agheila bottleneck must be held. Like Wavell and Auchinleck, in fact, Rommel was about to learn in full measure what Alamein had already begun to teach, that the military appreciation of the man on the spot can weigh light in the scales against the political requirements of a Higher Command. This widening gulf between the Axis dictators and the General of the *Panzerarmee* was naturally of the greatest value to Montgomery, brimming as he now was with self-confidence, enjoying the firm support of Alexander and steadily winning the Prime Minister's approbation.* The seal was set on the latter by Montgomery's capture of the Martuba airfields on the 15th, followed by those at Derna ('Martuba by mid-November' having been one of the strategic purposes of the Alamein battle): and though rain kept Martuba out of service

* On 11 November, Montgomery was promoted to the rank of General and awarded the KCB.

until the 19th, on the 20th the vital *Stoneage* convoy reached and revived Malta—the Eighth Army entering Benghazi the same day. A second convoy reached Malta a fortnight later, and thereafter the island was never seriously at risk.

Montgomery can thus legitimately argue that though criticism may be levelled at his handling of the pursuit through Egypt and Cyrenaica—as it may—he had nevertheless fulfilled his contract. He had broken the Alamein line within the time-limit predicted, he had routed Rommel, he had reached Martuba by the necessary date and Malta had been relieved. While Rommel now sought to establish a position in the Mersa Brega/Agheila area (into which he retired on the night of 23/24 November), Montgomery screened him with light forces, and paused to review his own situation. And this, the first major lull since 23 October, provides a convenient point at which to make a preliminary assessment of Montgomery's generalship.

. . . . .

Fortunate in his appointment, Montgomery was also fortunate in two other respects—the support he received in the air and the wealth of *matériel* available to him were of an order of magnitude which none of his predecessors, nor Rommel, ever enjoyed. The account I have given of his manoeuvres on the ground can only be seen in correct perspective by remembering that at every stage, before, during and after the battle of Alamein, Montgomery and his army could count on superiority in the sky. The period of congestion in the minefields when, as General Carver puts it, 'the whole area looked like a badly organised car park at an immense race meeting held in a dust bowl', would otherwise have been inconceivable. Rommel's perennial lack of mobility, moreover, was directly due to the aggressive hunting down of his supply ships by the R.A.F. (and the Navy) and to the persistent bombing of their ports of arrival. Interrogated after his capture, von Thoma declared that 'your bombers put all my batteries out of action, and pounded my H.Q. all night long'. Rommel summed up more simply: 'The British command of the air was complete.'

The figures of stocks held at the Middle East Base are portentous. In October there were 272,000 tons of ammunition in store; 253,000 tons of military supplies came in from overseas in that month alone. The number of vehicles received in September and October was 18,480. In August local manufacture produced no less than 530,000 anti-tank mines—about the total Rommel employed in constructing his Alamein defences. Under Lieut.-General Sir Wilfred Lindsell, who from July superintended the base installations,* and Brigadier Sir Brian Robertson, who was responsible for Eighth Army's administration, the forwarding of these riches to the front proceeded smoothly. Sir Brian's comment in February 1943 was: 'Having said what he is going to do, a commander must not cheat. He must not beat the pistol, nor wangle additional troops, nor sneak his troops further forward than he said he would. A good administrative staff does not over-insure and cannot be cheated without unfortunate consequences. Some Generals have no morals. Fortunately, General Montgomery does not cheat—whether that is due to his innate honesty or to the fact that I watch him like a cat does not matter—and moreover he doesn't let other people cheat. . . .'

Montgomery did not, in fact, tend to cheat; though his disposition, unlike that of his opponent, was towards over-insurance, sometimes excessive, rather than towards risky gambles. Nor can one see him, like Patton in N.W. Europe, forcing the hand of his superior and the supply services by getting his army into a situation where replenishment beyond the allocated scale became inevitable.

Of course there were minor, local, or temporary difficulties and shortages. Replacement tanks, as has been seen, were not always delivered in the right condition, in the right place or at the right time. During the advance there were some doubts about water supplies. And, as Montgomery reiterates in his writings, his 'administrative situation' denied him a sufficiency of fuel for a swift, sustained pursuit.

Since this is a critical issue, it is worth observing, first, that unlike Rommel during his drive to Alamein (with which Montgomery's advance is sometimes adversely compared) Montgomery had to supply the Air Force as well as his army. The warmer collaboration which he had instituted, and the expertise of Tedder, Coningham and their staffs, produced an astonishing degree of close support: ground crews and essential equipment were flown into forward airfields within hours of their capture and clearance, to be followed immediately by the fighters. This involved an administrative problem with which Rommel was never faced to the same degree. Moreover the planes working over the Mediterranean (for example from Martuba), also required those services and supplies which were normally the Army's responsibility. Of these the largest item was aviation fuel and petrol for transport. The overall tonnages needed were—by 28 November, 400; by 2 December, 800; by 9 December, 1,050; and by 16 December, 1,000 at Tobruk and 400 at Benghazi. West of the Egyptian frontier, during the first phase of the advance, no less than 11,500 R.A.F. and A.A. personnel (the latter for airfield

---

* It was part of Montgomery's good fortune that these installations had been laid down initially by a far-sighted Wavell on a scale much larger than his instructions from the Chiefs of Staff required.

defence), had to be maintained . . . and, until the port of Benghazi was captured and put in working order, a very high proportion of the ferrying had to be done along the single coastal road. Moreover Montgomery, wisely, gave the Air Force a special priority.

But those sudden shortages of fuel which delayed the striking force on several crucial occasions cannot be simply explained away by referring to the R.A.F., or to the weather or the going. The many changes of direction which Montgomery imposed on his formations played their part: but the fundamental factor was the absence of a clear-cut operational plan for the pursuit. Since this was lacking, there was no carefully premeditated and properly organised scheme for ensuring that the pursuers were always adequately maintained. Montgomery, the proponent of foresight and good husbandry, cannot avoid criticism in this regard, even though it be argued that after fighting the battle of Alamein he reached Tripoli, 1,415 miles from Alexandria, in three months during which Rommel evacuated Egypt, Cyrenaica, Libya and Tripolitania.

What of the battle itself? Some critics claim that it should never have been fought—for two main reasons. There are, first, those who believe that Montgomery could and should have eliminated Rommel immediately after repelling him at Alam Halfa. I have explained in Chapter 3 why Montgomery's decision not to do so seems valid, and would simply add that such critics tend to forget that Rommel was most dangerous when organising an offensive/defensive. Sick though he was, it cannot be imagined that he would have collapsed after Alam Halfa without a stern fight. A renewed British offensive would surely have caused him to fall back on the minefields so close to his rear, and set up there one of his typical anti-tank defences—creating, possibly, a new 'Cauldron'.

The second view is presented with the most extravagant emphasis by Correlli Barnett in a book which has been widely read, *The Desert Generals*. Barnett's thesis is that, because of the menace of the TORCH landings (which did not, of course, occur until 8 November), 'it is certain that, even if Montgomery had not fought his battle, Rommel would have been out of Egypt within a month and in Tunisia within three'. Alamein was therefore 'an unnecessary battle'. Even including the 12 days of Alamein, and in spite of a number of skilful rearguard actions by the Afrika Korps, Montgomery nevertheless drove Rommel over the Tunisian frontier to Ben Gardane on 26 January 1943, only just over three months from 26 October! But let that pass: the proposition is wholly unrealistic. Was Montgomery to stand idly by while Malta succumbed? Were the 300 Shermans and 100 self-propelled guns which Roosevelt generously dispatched to the Middle East after the fall of Tobruk to remain silent and immobile while American troops fought their way to Tunis from the west? Would Churchill, only persuaded by 'blackmail' to accept October as a deferred date for Alamein, have calmly bowed to a policy of even further inaction? And, finally, would Hitler and Mussolini have for one second permitted Rommel to withdraw except under the compulsion of irretrievable defeat?

Assuming, therefore, that Montgomery was right to attack at Alamein (which had, it must be remembered, been Auchinleck's intention), did he set about it in the most efficient fashion? He was certainly correct—as Auchinleck would have been—in choosing the northerly sector of the line for a breakthrough. To have penetrated in the south would have involved a subsequent right wheel—a Gazala in reverse*—with the difference that the Germans would undoubtedly have defended themselves far more effectively than did the British in the June disaster. Such a manoeuvre, moreover, would have made it difficult, if not impossible, to benefit from the Eighth Army's massive preponderance in artillery. But to attack between the centre of the line and the sea meant, inevitably, that the assault would go in just where the *Panzerarmee*'s minefields were most elaborate and most extensive.

This is the crux of the matter. If it be true that a battle—and a victory—at Alamein was both a political and a strategic necessity, and if a battle in the north was tactically preferable, then it is in these terms that Montgomery's generalship must be evaluated. It is pointless for critics to dismiss him, as some do, simply as a soldier who had learned nothing and forgotten nothing since the First World War: the real point is that at Alamein Montgomery was the only British commander in the desert to be faced with a situation that was commonplace between 1915 and 1918. His problem was to break through a continuous line, lacking open flanks round which to manoeuvre, organised in greater depth than any defensive position before or since on any of the North African fronts, and manned by a resolute† enemy, skilful and tenacious in defence, who had been blessed with enough time to strengthen his shield. Circumstance and Rommel imposed on Montgomery very considerable limitations. If the options open to him are compared, say, with those open to Cunningham before CRUSADER in 1941, it will at once be seen how restricted was his freedom of choice as to the nature of the attack he had to undertake. At Alamein, in fact, the only freedom Montgomery enjoyed was whatever

* Although he achieved a final victory, Rommel was in such administrative difficulties after his left wheel at Gazala—he had, in particular, virtually run out of water—that at one point he asked a captured British officer to translate into English a request for terms of surrender. This was, of course, before Ritchie had thrown away his initial advantage. (Information supplied by Sir Ian Jacob.)

† Resolute, as the battle showed, in spite of exhaustion, lack of air cover and ammunition, bad rations and a progressively hopeless situation. Even some Italian units fought hard; the Folgore Division, for example, and Ariete.

dexterity and imagination could generate within the predetermined limits of a battle of position.

Yet here, too, he was fortunate: time and chance presented him with a problem for whose solution he was ideally equipped by temperament, by experience, and by a lifetime's study and contemplation. The very qualities which inhibited him in mobile operations lifted him above the ruck as an orchestrator of the set-piece battle. Montgomery would never have swept like a whirlwind through Georgia: but before the gates of Richmond he would have been completely at home.

I suppose the Eighth Army at Alamein was as intelligent and in many respects as experienced a formation as the British Commonwealth ever sent to war. This is true of all ranks. Units like the 11th Hussars and other members of the old Western Desert Force had run through the whole gamut of victory and defeat since 1940. The New Zealand Division had not only faced Rommel before: they had survived, unbroken, the disasters of Greece and Crete. The 4th Indian Division had endured the fearful ordeal of Keren in Eritrea as well as desperate actions in CRUSADER. Mingled with these and other veterans were the novices—51 Highland, 44 Division, a number of armoured regiments. Montgomery's first achievement at Alamein was to inspire the whole of this army, both the wary and cynical old hands and the apprehensive, unblooded newcomers, with an all-pervading confidence. Veterans cannot be hood-winked for long, while tyros soon lose their trust in a commander whose promises prove to be empty. But the high morale with which the Eighth Army entered the engagement persisted throughout, in spite of the heavy casualties sustained by some units and the long-drawn-out 'slogging match'. To write of this is to attempt to describe the uncommunicable: it had to be felt. But its reality can be sensed over and over again in personal recollections and in regimental and other histories. To bond such a multifarious army with a unity of purpose in so short a time—well under three months— was an extraordinary *tour de force*.

Montgomery passed a further test. Had his direction of the battle been merely that of the cold-blooded, self-centred, uninspired butcher which is the caricature of him offered by some commentators, then his army (as it might have said) would have 'rumbled' him. 2,350 officers and men killed, 8,950 wounded and 2,260 missing, though a relatively modest total, was still a figure liable to cause immediate disenchantment if the troops had suspected that they had been seriously mishandled and that lives had been needlessly sacrificed. But the Eighth Army never felt about Montgomery as, for example, Gough's army felt about his handling of them at Passchendaele. On the contrary: morale remained high after Alamein and increased steadily during the advance along the African shore, until, by the time Tunisia was reached, it was exuberant. To imagine that this was merely the effect of a few gimmicks and some carefully organised personal publicity is to over-estimate the gullibility of the British soldier.

If to inspire a whole army is a rare gift, another is the capacity to surprise an opponent well versed in war. Here, too, Montgomery was successful. There is little evidence to indicate that his present of Himeimat to the enemy, or his attempts to suggest a forthcoming attack in the south (about both of which he congratulates himself), did much to raise Rommel's suspicions. The infantry on the right of the Axis line were chiefly Italian—which is suggestive—and the retention of 21 Panzer and Ariete behind them was largely the result of lack of fuel. But on the main front of the attack Montgomery obtained a genuine tactical surprise, in spite of grave difficulties. It is true that he had the tremendous advantage of superiority in the air. But nevertheless it was only by the most meticulous precautions that security was maintained and the great forward dumps, vehicle parks, and agglomerations of infantry and armour were so assembled that both the date and the precise point of the attack were kept secret.

Wavell began his classic lectures on 'Generals and Generalship' by referring to the various expositions he had read of the virtues considered necessary for a general, and observed that 'I found only one that seemed to me to go to the real root of the matter: it is attributed to a wise man named Socrates.' After quoting Socrates Wavell went on to say 'the first point that attracts me about that definition is the order in which it is arranged. It begins with the matter of administration, which is the real crux of generalship, to my mind. . . .' Here again Montgomery was exemplary. The benefits of a well-stocked Base, an abundance of all necessities and a particularly competent Staff might well have been squandered by indecision or inability at the highest level. But under Montgomery all the infrastructure for his attack moved smoothly into place—the most complicated operation of its kind carried out by a British general since 1918.

In mounting this 'First World War' offensive Montgomery was short of the very weapon which in the main battles of 1914–18 was available in relative abundance—infantry: and for a 'break-in' his strength in armour was not an adequate substitute. This deficiency, noticeable from the second night onwards, was only partially met by frequent changes in the direction of his thrust-line (which meant that individual infantry units were not pushed to the point of annihilation), and by the unconventional use of armoured brigades in an assault rôle. Lumsden and Gatehouse were pardonably anxious, on the night of 24/25 October, for another infantry attack to be launched to clear the mouths of the corridors: but, seen from Montgomery's more widely ranging view-point, what in effect they were pleading for was that rifle companies should be sacrificed instead of tanks. This, particularly in the early stages of what he had appreciated would be a long struggle, was a price Montgomery was rightly unwilling to pay. But in this context it might well be asked why so little significant use was made of the superb 4 Indian Division until the last hours of the battle.

The employment of the armour at Alamein has been criticised for two other reasons. The first—and it is a valid point—is that Montgomery was over-optimistic about the progress his infantry could make on the first night of the battle; should not 10 Corps, it is reasonably asked, have been held back until it was certain that clear lanes had been established through the minefields, from which the tanks could swiftly debouch into the open instead of piling up head to tail in a confused mass? The other cavil is that the armour was not poured through in overwhelming strength on a broad front, which Rommel certainly expected and feared. But even to clear narrow lanes proved difficult enough, and expensive enough in casualties to the engineers. It is easy to forget that a deep minefield in open country, covered by constant defensive fire, presents formidable problems to an attacker, and that what may seem deceptively simple on a map can be infinitely complicated on the ground.

On balance Montgomery has received more praise than blame for his conduct of Alamein: and the blame has not always been objective or un-prejudiced. The praise is justified. He kept his head, and his boast to Alan Brooke that Rommel had been compelled to dance to his tune is supported by the facts. His mixture of powerful drives and short stabs from firm bases paid dividends, for he was never seriously unbalanced and his army was not excessively over-taxed. He revealed an effective flexibility of mind in the switching of his attacks 'now here, now there', and perhaps particularly in grasping the case made by his subordinates for aiming SUPERCHARGE down a line to the south of the coastal road, and altering his plan. If he was lavish in the use of metal, the answer is that he could afford to be, and that the total cost of Alamein in human casualties was about a quarter of those suffered by Haig's armies on the very first day of the Somme. Unlike Haig, however, he had decisively won a victory of immense strategic importance within the period he had set for himself: and if, as he pondered at Benghazi, he was unable to feel self-satisfaction at having put Rommel 'in the bag', he could at least contemplate with confidence the likelihood that the Djebel Stakes would never have to be run again.

6

Forward to Tripoli

'Pushing on smartly is the road to success . . . in war something must be allowed to chance and fortune, seeing it is in its nature hazardous and an option of difficulties.'

General Wolfe

Rommel had already lost the war in Africa, and knew it: but Montgomery showed no signs of having realised that he had won it. His measure had now been correctly taken by his opponent, and it was of the greatest value to Rommel, in a situation of delicate poise, to be able to comfort himself with the knowledge that the Eighth Army would only move with caution under a man to whom, in Rommel's own words, 'bold solutions were completely foreign'. The German's view was entirely justified not only by what happened but also by Montgomery's personal statement of his principles of action, as declared in *El Alamein to the River Sangro*. 'I did not rely on the effects of Rommel's defeat to ensure that he would not try again to invade Egypt. From the time the pursuit from El Alamein began I gave much thought to the problem. I planned to preserve the strategic balance of the Army by maintaining, in a series of chosen areas, a force which would ensure against the effects of any local failure or surprise being turned to important advantage by the enemy.' It was in the light of these principles that Montgomery devised his next moves, ignoring the useful maxim that circumstances should not be made to fit plans, but plans to fit circumstances.

Broadly speaking, his immediate intention was to grasp the Agheila bottle-neck and hold it in strength as a long-stop for his troops advancing westwards, and to place 10 Corps (now under Horrocks, Lumsden having been eased out) to the S.E. of the Djebel Akdar, around Tmimi, his idea being that it could block any drive towards Tobruk and also threaten the flank of a by-passing enemy. This would have been sound enough in 1941, or 1942; but now? There is a point beyond which steadfastness of mind turns into obduracy: and Montgomery's weakness was always the *idée fixe*. It is worth while, therefore, looking back in this context to the night of 11/12 August when, as Montgomery flew to meet his destiny in Cairo, he brooded about North Africa and finally resolved his cogitations about its topography in these terms: 'The four main features that I must work into my plans were: the coast road to Tripoli,

10 *North Africa : the end in Tunisia*

11 *Tea-time in Sicily*

12 *Italy : farewell to the 8th Army*

13 *Italy : with Alexander and Alan Brooke*

the ports along the coast, the Jebel between Tobruk and Benghazi, and the Agheila position.' He had now gained the first two objectives. As to the third, it seemed to him that night that 'if held strongly, with forces trained to attack southwards from it, it would be a valuable feature to possess and could not be by-passed'. So now, in December, he was going to justify his August thinking by implementing the third and fourth of its 'main features'. But as he pondered in his plane he could not *know* how his campaign would develop; he could only guess and estimate, and his ideas must be necessarily contingent. Now he was faced with a real situation and a shattered Afrika Korps. Before describing the sequence of actions which followed the conquest of the Benghazi bulge, and only terminated in the Tunisian hills, it will be useful to ask whether Montgomery had assessed this situation accurately—whether his 'approach to battle' was on the right lines.

It is clear from his *Papers* and other post-war publications that Rommel now felt his situation to be desperate, although he had miraculously managed to hold his army together. Given a free hand, he would have immediately withdrawn westwards from Agheila and established a strong defensive position at 'the Gabes gap'. Here, 120 miles from the Tunisian frontier (and another German army), vehicular movement is for all practical purposes confined to the 12 miles between the sea and the Chott Jerid, a maze of marsh and impassable lakeland. Here would be fought in due course the battle of Akarit.

But Rommel's hand was not free. It was held in several clamps. The prospect of the Führer's agreement to such a retreat was a pipe-dream. Additionally, Rommel was subject to two Italian controls. *Delease (the Delegazione del Comando Supremo in Africa Settentrionale)*, had been set up in August as a military delegation to provide a link between Rommel and *Comando Supremo* to whom Rommel was directly responsible. Now, in November, a more hampering device was produced, in the form of a head-quarters establishment called *Superlibia*, under Marshal Bastico. As had been the case earlier in the campaign, Rommel found himself Bastico's subordinate. He was thus driven to a dual course of action. Fully aware that it could be outflanked from the south and that his resources were insufficient to sustain a severe frontal assault, he set about making the stop-line at Mersa Brega/El Agheila as firm as possible, while at the same time endeavouring, in his out-spoken Württemberger fashion, to negotiate with his masters the right to retire.

In the latter he was inevitably unsuccessful. Mussolini ordered that the line must be held regardless of cost. On 22 November Rommel and the Italian general Navarrini argued their case with Bastico: 'We either lose the position four days earlier and save the army, or lose both the position and the army

I

four days later.' Bastico would not budge. On the 24th Kesselring and Marshal Cavallero, the Italian Chief of Staff, arrived for a conference, and again Rommel was rebuffed: indeed, soon afterwards Mussolini requested an attack on the British!

In despair, Rommel took the ultimate step: he flew north to plead with Hitler, who interviewed him on 28 November in a furiously hostile mood. All that Rommel got was the gift of Goering, who was sent back with him to act as plenipotentiary in what proved to be another fruitless round of talks in Rome. 'Flying back to Africa,' Rommel wrote, 'I realised that we were now completely thrown back on our resources': yet in *matériel*, and particularly in fuel, the Panzer Army had reached starvation level. During November, for example, it received only 5,000 tons of petrol—another 8,100 tons having been sunk in transit.

Montgomery, by contrast, 'held the initiative and had the superior force', as the *Official History* points out. True, the war-weary Eighth Army had progressed 800 miles . . . but so had Rommel. It was forward in strength. There was 30 Corps, now consisting of 7 Armoured, 51 Highland, 2 New Zealand, to be joined later by 50 and 4 Indian Divisions from 13 Corps (whose units were distributed, 1 South African and 9 Australian Divisions returning home, while the unlucky 44 Division was disbanded). And 10 Corps was busy re-grouping in preparation for its 'blocking' rôle. In the Desert Air Force there was an abundance available to hold the skies above the army, and to harass the enemy, for the technique for establishing advanced landing grounds and rapidly bringing them into use was working well. As to supplies, what Rommel called 'the Quartermasters' are inherently pessimistic, and this certainly proved the case at Benghazi, for the tonnage of cargo discharged there during the first half of December was twice as much as had been anticipated, while the advancement of the railhead to Tobruk on 1 December increased by nearly a third the number of General Transport Companies working the road-ferry from Tobruk to the front.

Though Montgomery lacked the opportunity of reading the *Rommel Papers*, and could hardly be aware in their entirety of what Rommel called 'the mismanagement, the operational blunders, the prejudices, the everlasting search for scapegoats', he nevertheless had, one would have thought, ample evidence from which to estimate his opponent's military situation. He could not have known that in Rome Goering had the effrontery to accuse Rommel in front of Mussolini of having left the Italian troops in the lurch at Alamein: but he did know the results of anti-shipping strikes in the Mediterranean.

Thus it is extraordinary to read in *El Alamein to the River Sangro* that Montgomery found it 'interesting to conjecture why Rommel failed to stand and fight at Agheila'. Is this not, for example, what he himself would have done had the rôles been reversed? It was the correct *military* answer. It is extraordinary also to read that 'the Agheila position was immensely strong'. Rommel knew better: 'as soon as I arrived in the area I pointed out that fortifications, however strong, could not help us, as the enemy could outflank the whole line—even though with some difficulty'; which Freyberg was shortly to prove. Here, surely, was a situation to which Montgomery might have applied a phrase recurrent in his personal *patois*, 'We'll bounce them out . . .': a situation where to push on smartly might well have been the road to an earlier success. Instead of 'bouncing out', Montgomery took his time. Benghazi had been entered on 20 November. The plan of attack issued on 29 November indicated that it would not go in until the night of 16/17 December. The risk of an earlier move aimed at keeping Rommel 'on the run' might well have been justified. It is sometimes said that he who has not fought the Germans does not know what war is: a secondary truism is that he who *has* fought the Germans should never give them a chance to dig in. But while the Panzer Army was doing just this, Montgomery took time off to fly down to Cairo for a weekend, see Alexander, get some new clothes and read the lesson at the Cathedral's Sunday morning service: Leese, in the meantime, was charged with the preparation of plans for the attack. Montgomery would not have taken time off before Alamein! Indeed, his actions at the time and his subsequent writing seem in direct conflict with the clear statement in the *Memoirs*: 'I decided that I must get possession of the Agheila position quickly: morale might decline if we hung about too long looking at it.'

The character of the Agheila position may be easily visualised. Slightly to the east is the little anchorage of Mersa Brega, and here began a sweep of defended posts and intermittent minefields which ran due southwards for some 40 miles to Maaten Giofer. A track from here continues southwards via Sidi Tabet to an oasis called Marada, where Rommel maintained an outpost. Further depth was given to the defences by a ring of mines encircling El Agheila itself, and by a mine-protected anti-tank ditch at El Mugtaa, some 17 miles to the west. On paper this looks formidable enough. But the weakness of the position was the fact that El Agheila was not the Alamein line: its southern flank lay open. The going was difficult but it was viable; what finally made Rommel's position untenable was the fact that, aware as he was of the danger to his right flank, he was so pitifully short of petrol that he could not let loose his armour on whatever force Montgomery might—as he obviously must—send to the deep south. With all this in mind, and in spite of his overlords, Rommel was psychologically prepared to give way at the first excuse. All that was necessary was a push.

Eighth Army's patrol reports gave some indication of this. And rightly, for in fact Rommel had started to filter his unmotorised Italians towards the rear from the night of the 6th onwards. To prevent Rommel slipping away without a fight, Montgomery advanced his timing, and ordered heavy raids by 51 Highland to be made on the main position from the night of the 11th (hoping thus to pin Rommel down) while the full attack was to begin on the 14th. The New Zealand Division, which from El Haseiat, well behind the British front, was to carry out a 200-mile envelopment, was due to start its move on the 12th. But much went awry.

What was the concept behind the plan? Montgomery himself is ambivalent about El Agheila. In *El Alamein to the River Sangro* he declares that he first wondered whether 'by bluff and manoeuvre on the open flank I could frighten the enemy out of his positions. . . . *I eventually decided to go all out to anni-hilate the enemy in his defences*' (Author's italics). . . . 'I decided that bluff would not remove him and planned to get behind his German forces and capture them.' By the time that he published his *Memoirs* in 1958 this had been scaled down to 'I therefore decided to bluff and manoeuvre, and to bustle Rommel to such an extent that he might think he would lose his whole force if he stood to fight.' The actual dispositions for the attack leave little question that Montgomery had more in mind than bluff. 51 Highland was to attack straight down the coast through the Mersa Brega defences, with 7 Armoured moving on its left flank, infantry first and armour following. This, with the long march of the New Zealanders, looks like the making of a battle.

But to all intents and purposes there was no battle. El Agheila was a non-happening. The initial raids by the Highland Division, and the supporting gun-fire, quickly convinced Rommel that *Der Tag* had arrived. 'Soon there was no more doubt—the enemy offensive had opened.' He therefore pulled out his remaining troops as swiftly as possible, aiming for the temporary safety of the anti-tank ditch at El Mugtaa. In his *Papers* he has the last word. 'The British commander's planning had contained one mistake. Experience must have told him that there was a good chance that we would not accept battle at Mersa el Brega. He should not, therefore, have started bombarding our strong-points and attacking our line until his outflanking force had completed its move and was in a position to advance on the coast road in timed co-ordination with the frontal attack.' This, while being a perfectly just com-ment, also weakens Montgomery's observation in his *Memoirs* that 'the enemy began to withdraw the moment our frontal attack developed'.

Everything now lay with the New Zealand Division. Freyberg was sup-posed to reach the Marada line by the night of the 15/16th: he had, working with the Division, 4 Light Armoured Brigade which contained two regiments of armoured cars and the Royal Scots Greys. But when battles run awry they have a way of continuing to do so, and Freyberg's operation was marred by a sequence of technical hitches which, as will be seen, robbed him in the end of his prize. The Greys had just received a batch of Sherman tanks requiring, as usual, adjustments and replacements. The runners in the Regiment on 12 December were 17 Shermans, 4 Grants, 15 Stuarts—a very light force with which to cut off even an emaciated Afrika Korps. Then, having on the 13th received a signal to increase speed (in view of the advance in timing for the general operation)—a signal which was nearly nine hours in transmission—Freyberg ran into difficulties over fuel. 'On the 14th one petrol convoy did not catch up until 5 p.m., another did not find the Division, and a third which was quickly called forward could not finish its issues until 11 p.m.' In spite of a night march, Freyberg was still held up by the lagging Greys—on whom he must rely to engage the anticipated enemy armour. Finally, by the evening of the 15th, he had got his two infantry brigades up to the area of the coast road. Unfortunately they were still six miles apart, and as Freyberg reported, 'enemy in small columns including tanks passed through at high speed . . . most difficult to intercept . . . majority escaped round our flanks'. The total bag in the 'battle' of Agheila was estimated to be 450 prisoners, 25 guns and 18 tanks.

To all of this Montgomery's reply might well be: 'Yes. You accuse me of lack of dash. But please remember that it was not until the Casablanca Conference in the latter part of January 1943 that a firm decision was taken to invade Sicily as soon as possible after victory in Africa; it was not until the end of April was set as a terminal date for this victory, if advantage was to be taken of the good summer weather to mount the invasion, that a complete clearance of the African shores became *pressingly* urgent. Of course I felt the need to keep moving, but I saw no case for taking unnecessary risks. I had Rommel where I wanted him, retreating between me and TORCH. And, granted my strength in men and armour, granted my superiority in the air, it still was something to have done what no previous desert commander had achieved—I mean, with a minimum of casualties to have expelled Rommel from the Agheila bottleneck. Moreover, if you consider my next three actions —the drive for Tripoli, Medenine and the Mareth Line—you will observe that I was not lacking in *brio* in the first and third of those operations, while the second was a classic example of a completely decisive defensive action. My case rests.'

Rommel withdrew his army swiftly to the west, relying on mines, demolitions and booby-traps, and his dogged rear-guards, to slow down his enemy. But in spite of brushes at Nofilia and Sirte, Montgomery's spearheads were breasting up to the next main stop line, at Buerat, by 29 December. Rommel had heard a broadcast by Cairo Radio which reported that his army was in a bottle which Montgomery was about to cork. His reaction was to observe to his staff that the bottle would soon be empty if only they could get their tanks full: the point was well illustrated at Nofilia, where a shortage of petrol made it seem as though elements of the Afrika Korps might be cut off. 'When the petrol ration came through, the units which had been threatened with encirclement streamed back along it' (the coastal road) 'to the west.'

Neither Rommel, nor, indeed, Marshal Bastico was sanguine about holding the Buerat position for long: and Rommel was already looking over his shoulder towards Tunisia and the danger of an Anglo-American attempt to cut off his retreat by seizing the Gabes gap. However, in reply to a request for permission to fall back Mussolini on 19 December sent a signal saying, in effect, 'Resist to the uttermost, I repeat, resist to the uttermost with all the troops of the German-Italian Army in the Buerat position.' Nothing could have better suited Montgomery. His plan was simple: to crack the defences at Buerat and in one fluid movement to thrust straight for Tripoli. In the higher ground curtaining Tripoli Rommel might have been able to establish a better blocking position, had he withdrawn. As it was, if the crust could be broken at Buerat, the rest should now be relatively easy.

However, Rommel was a powerful debater, and in the end extracted on 31 December an order to Bastico from *Comando Supremo* that he might use his own judgement about a withdrawal if he was seriously menaced. Rommel had already set his Italian troops in motion. The consequence was that when the attack finally went in at Buerat the *Panzerarmee* was somewhat scattered, and commanded by a man who was still yearning for the greater security of Gabes.

Montgomery's plan for the breakthrough, which began on 15 January, was simple. 30 Corps would launch a two-pronged attack, 50 and 51 Divisions along the coast and 7 Armoured and 2 New Zealand Divisions sweeping round the open right flank of Rommel's position and then making a bee-line for Tripoli. Montgomery was working to a narrow margin. He allowed ten days for the whole operation. He had assembled 450 tanks, by stripping 1 Armoured Division which still lay back with 10 Corps. To maintain his forces therefore raised enormous administrative problems (from Buerat to Tripoli was 230 miles: from Benghazi to Tripoli 675), and it was of paramount importance that the build-up of supplies before the attack should be sufficient to sustain it all the way through to Tripoli: it was equally important that off-loading in the Tripoli docks should start at the earliest possible moment.

Rommel was nearly saved, and Montgomery thwarted, by an Act of God. On 3 January a gale breached the mole at Benghazi. A number of ships were either sunk or badly damaged. Berths were destroyed and storehouses flooded. For two days nothing was landed, and further gales in the middle of the month kept the average daily rate of discharge low. But foresight had been used. The danger had been anticipated, and there was a plan. Montgomery had intended to move 10 Corps up to Agheila: that idea was immediately dropped, and Horrocks was given the task of organising with the transport of his grounded Corps a supply lift from Tobruk and Benghazi. 50 Division was also taken out of the battle-plan. All in the end went well, and early on the 23rd elements of 11 Hussars, 50 R.T.R., and 1 Gordon Highlanders were in Tripoli, whose formal surrender Montgomery accepted at noon that day, from the Italian Vice-Governor of Tripolitania.

The Highlanders were early into the city because Montgomery showed an effective flexibility in evolving a plan which provided him with options. He could decide in the light of circumstances whether to push home his attack down the coast, or with his mobile outflanking forces. In the end he opted for the coastal drive. He had taken charge of this himself, leaving Leese to look after operations further inland, on the ground that the two wings of the attack were too far separated for one Corps H.Q. to control them. He proved a hard taskmaster, forcing the Highland Division onwards by day and night, issuing 'rockets' to Wimberley, the unfortunate divisional commander, and by sheer ruthlessness overcoming what he described as 'a lack of initiative and ginger'. But the job was done, and the reward, for Montgomery, was a seizure of a harbour through which the supplies might pass to enable him to undertake his next major task; which was, obviously, the breaching of the Mareth Line. The Navy, aided by the Eighth Army, worked wonders, for though they found that the port installations had been thoroughly wrecked, and the harbour mouth completely blocked, as a result of their efforts the first ship came in on 3 February, the first convoy on the 9th, and by the next day the daily rate of discharge was over 2,000 tons. The Eighth Army was now in tremendous fettle (as was its commander): this was increased by a visit from the Prime Minister early in February, when the Army marched past him in what, considering the circumstances, was an astonishing degree of smartness.

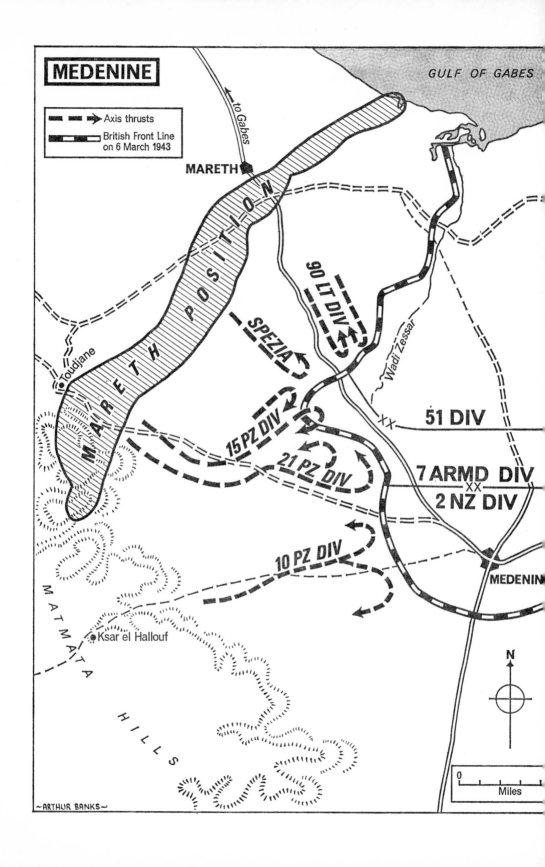

MEDENINE

Axis thrusts
British Front Line
on 6 March 1943

GULF OF GABES

to Gabes

MARETH

MARETH POSITION

90 LT DIV

SPEZIA

Wadi Zessar

Toudjane

XX

51 DIV

15 PZ DIV

21 PZ DIV

7 ARMD DIV

XX

2 NZ DIV

10 PZ DIV

MEDENINE

MATMATA

Ksar el Hallouf

HILLS

N

0
Miles

~ARTHUR BANKS~

Mareth and the Mountains

He watches from his mountain walls
And like a thunderbolt he falls.

Tennyson, *The Eagle*

The pattern of the African war was now changing. One of the results of the Casablanca conference was that Alexander's responsibilities were enlarged. He was appointed Deputy Commander-in-Chief of the Allied Forces in French North Africa on 17 February, and Eisenhower's directive telling him this continued:

> 2 This appointment takes effect on 20th February, on which date you will take command of all Allied forward forces engaged in operations in Tunisia. These consist of the British 1st Army, which exercises command over the United States and French forces operating in Tunisia, the British 8th Army, and such reserve formations as may be placed under your command.
> 3 Your mission is the early destruction of all Axis forces in Tunisia. . . .

Here was the formal recognition of a fact: the two theatres of war were being progressively unified. The TORCH landings had been beneficial for Montgomery from the moment they were announced. The Allied threat to Rommel's rear was an ever-present menace which grew stronger as the weeks passed, while the diversion of the main flow of supplies from the Germans facing the Eighth to those facing the First Army starved the Afrika Korps when its need was most urgent. But these were imponderable effects, substantial though they might be. Alexander's elevation coincided realistically with the point in time when actual operations in the two previously separated theatres now began to bear directly upon one another. This process would gather momentum until the last symbolic battle, when divisions from both armies swept side by side down the Medjerda valley in their *Blitzkrieg* assault on Tunis.

But the logic of time and space also applied to the enemy. Rommel had extricated his army from the complicated terrain surrounding Tripoli and, by the beginning of February, the greater proportion of it was established in the Mareth Line. The boundary between Rommel and von Arnim, commanding the German forces in Tunisia, was fixed just north of Gabes. 21 Panzer Division had already joined von Arnim. The two fronts were thus meshing together, and the closer they approached one another the greater was the advantage to be derived from an exploitation of their 'interior lines'. But unfortunately this harmonious relationship of the fronts was weakened by a lack of harmony in the Higher Command. Rommel's retirement from Tripoli had been far too precipitate to please the Italians, and they, Kesselring (the German Commander-in-Chief, South), and Hitler's staff were all after his blood. This resulted in a message from *Comando Supremo* on 26 January instructing Rommel that his bad state of health entailed his replacement by General Messe, who had commanded the Italian Expeditionary Corps in Russia. Moreover, there was a temperamental gap between von Arnim and Rommel which prevented their acting in concert. By coincidence, therefore, just when the Germans should have been immensely strengthened by the fusion of their forces they were subtly weakened by a series of personal factors which came into play at the very time when Alexander, so deft at smoothly manipulating a force of mixed nationalities, was about to piece together the jig-saw of First Army and act as a bridge between it and the self-conscious Eighth.

Rommel was indeed unfit, but he had lost none of his resilience. By 8 February he was writing to his wife: 'I've decided only to give up command of the army on orders, regardless of the state of my health.' And indeed he was soon in action. The interplay between the two fronts can be seen most clearly from the reasons for that action and the course it took. Put simply, the aim was so to shatter the Anglo-American forces in south-western Tunisia as to eliminate the possibility of their breaking out via Gafsa, splitting the newly unified German grouping of armies. The core of this operation (which suffered much from von Arnim's distaste for Rommel) was the latter's brilliant and famous victory-without-a-morrow, at Kasserine Pass. Here Rommel inflicted a crushing defeat on the Americans, and all appeared wide open. The main assault was launched on 20 February: but a crisis of confidence affected Rommel's 10 Panzer Division (transferred from von Arnim) after it had been held beyond Kasserine, at Thala, by a 'thin red line' (mainly the British 26 Armoured Brigade). On 22 February this division and the portion of the Afrika Korps Rommel had brought west with him fell back from the furthest point of advance, and thereafter the threat dwindled away.

The reason for referring to the Kasserine Battle in a study of Montgomery is because it clearly illustrates how the Eighth and First Armies were beginning to be indivisible. Alexander took up his new command on the 19th. Kasserine began on the 20th. That day, Montgomery says, 'General Alexander sent me an urgent request for help, urging me to exert all possible pressure on the enemy. . . .' His troops had already entered Tunisia: 7 Armoured was up to Ben Gardane, together with one brigade from 51 Division. But there is little evidence of any impressive activity on Eighth Army's front. Rommel, moreover, is absolutely explicit, in his *Papers* (which reveal no concern about Eighth Army); writing about the 22nd he says 'at about 1300 hrs. I met Field Marshal Kesselring. . . . We agreed that a continuation of the attack . . . held no prospect of success and decided to break off the offensive by stages.' It is thus somewhat misleading of Montgomery to state in his *Memoirs* that 'I speeded up events and by the 26th February it was clear that our pressure had caused Rommel to break off his attack against the Americans.' However, here at last was an outward sign that the two armies were being thought of as one.

More forcible evidence came on 14 March, when Alexander issued a directive instructing 2 U.S. Corps to move on Maknassy and Gabes, thus threatening the German line of communications, while Eighth Army was to seize the Mareth Line. For this Montgomery's preparations were well advanced. There was no sloth now. A supply line stretching some 200 miles back to Tripoli had not only to serve a striking force of two Corps but also to enable dumps to be established close to the front, at Ben Gardane, from which a pursuit consequent on a victory at Mareth might be fostered. All this was done, though Montgomery had a phase of anxiety, between 28 February and 3 March, when he felt there was not enough strength forward to counter the return visit from Rommel which he rightly anticipated. This was indeed a time when he had a weight on his mind, and its clarity and imperturbability were both necessary and obvious. Already nominated as one of the Task Force commanders in HUSKY, the proposed invasion of Sicily, he had much to think about in long term—and, as will be seen, his thinking was to some purpose. In the nearer distance lay the battle of Mareth, a dour business for which highly complicated preparations must be made. And close to him, in the foreground of his thought, lay Medenine, the outpost of his army on which he expected an attack to fall at any moment.

On 23 February Rommel, surprisingly, became the Alexander of the enemy. Reluctantly, he accepted the order of *Comando Supremo* nominating him as commander of a unified Army Group Africa. He took over at an inauspicious moment, for in N.W. Tunisia von Arnim's ill-judged OCHSEN-KOPF offensive was grinding away uselessly among the hills, sacrificing in the end some 71 tanks against an Allied loss of 16. Rommel broke this off as soon as possible and embarked, in a spirit of desperation, on what he had always envisaged as the strategic counterpart of a successful hammering of the Americans—a riposte at Montgomery. He chose Medenine as the point of conflict and Ben Gardane as the objective because he saw that an assault on the Mareth Line was inevitable: if he could catch Montgomery off balance at Medenine he might manage to defer the ultimately inescapable.

But Montgomery was not off balance. By 4 March his anxieties were over and he had a sense of poise. 'We worked feverishly to prepare ourselves. . . . Rommel had missed his opportunity, and we all breathed freely again.' So Montgomery's Chief of Staff writes; and Montgomery himself draws the frequently-made analogy with Alam Halfa, saying that he determined to meet Rommel on ground of his own choosing. Of course the general area was predicted by Rommel: it was Montgomery's dispositions within it, and his complete control of the shape of the battle, which were the dominating factors.

The position to be defended lay inside the great curve formed by the Matmata Hills to the west and then, running to the sea, the defensive localities which took their name from Mareth. It consisted of the broken, higher ground to the N.W. of Medenine, linked with the valuable anti-tank obstacle of the Wadi Zessar. 2 New Zealand Division defended the Medenine area: to their right was 7 Armoured Division with its infantry brigade forward and 8 and 22 Armoured Brigades echeloned in the rear; and 51 Highland completed the line by holding 20,000 yards of the Wadi (whose effectiveness had been increased by some 70,000 mines). 201 Guards Brigade had been placed temporarily under 7 Armoured, and filled an important gap between this division and the New Zealanders by occupying a hill called Tadjera Khir which dominated the whole of 30 Corps' defences. But though Medenine was akin to Alam Halfa in that it was a defensive battle which preceded a victory, it introduced certain new features into the repertoire of the Eighth Army. The first was the Pheasant. I well remember sitting by the side of the coastal road as my regiment was moving up to Mareth, seeing large objects shrouded in canvas sweep by behind their tractors, and wondering what this apparently secret weapon might be. It was the 17-pounder anti-tank gun, now coming into action for the first time, low-mounted, hard-hitting, the British answer to the 88mm. Secondly, the anti-tank armoury was used (as never before) in its proper rôle: guns were sited, often in enfilade positions, where it was calculated that they could best kill tanks, not to suit the convenience of infantry or artillery anxious to shield their nakedness.

This was a sign of absolute self-confidence which was manifested in several ways at Medenine. For example, on the right of Kippenberger's 5 New Zealand Brigade was a wide wadi over which observation was poor. The night before the battle they received 500 mines, and 3,000 yards of wire with the necessary pickets. But as Kippenberger had a squadron of tanks under command he decided not to sow a minefield in case it made difficulties for his own armour, and instead put up a wire fence covered by a couple of six-pounders. The ruse worked. During the battle German tanks shied away from the wire, and five of them were finished off by the two guns. (Kippenberger had, in fact, gone so far as to ask his supporting field artillery not to engage German armour unless requested to do so, since he wished the targets to be saved for his anti-tank weapons.) He was ready and happy, full of a confidence which flowed downwards from the Army Commander. 'We always thought this Medenine position,' Kippenberger recalled, 'was our masterpiece in the art of laying out a defensive position under desert conditions.'

The plan and conduct of the German attack were decidedly *not* master-pieces. Rommel, disillusioned, weary and ill, more or less abandoned hope even before the guns began to fire. His instinct was to attack in the north where, though a set-piece action would have been required, surprise might have been achieved. Instead he seems, in the end, to have delegated decision to a sort of soviet of his subordinates, Messe, Ziegler (commanding the Afrika Korps), and the commanders of the three Panzer Divisions which were to make the assault, 10, 15 and 21 Panzer. The soviet selected ground further to the south, where the tank-runs were better—and the anti-tank guns wait-ing. Through the morning mists on the 6th, therefore, two blocks of armour, 15 and 21 Panzer, were observed emerging from the hills and groping forward along the road which connects Medenine with Toujane, at the inland end of the Mareth Line. About the same time 51 Highland faced an infantry attack by 90 Light and the Italian Spezia Division. Then a further armoured force—10 Panzer—was spotted pushing down towards Medenine from the Hallouf Pass.

The British field and medium artillery blasted the advancing Axis troops relentlessly, while the anti-tank guns held fire until the last possible minute. There was virtually no penetration of the British positions, and by noon the enemy had been drawn back to re-organise. It was observed that the co-ordination between his tanks and his infantry was poor, and that the normal dynamism of the Afrika Korps was missing. This, however, is not surprising in view of the fact that General Cramer arrived to take over the Korps from Ziegler on the eve of the battle: that, during the battle, Messe seems to have been an 'absentee landlord'; and that 10 and 21 Panzer, already badly shaken by the abortive OCHSENKOPF enterprise, only joined the attacking force very shortly before it began to move forward to the start lines.

Reorganisation brought no better dividends. In view of the morning's experience the three armoured divisions' commanders, after conferring together, sent in their infantry in front of their tanks. It was a forlorn hope. The infantry, drenched by British shell-fire, wavered and broke, the tanks made only a half-hearted showing, and 'at 8.30 p.m. Rommel gave the order to end what was to prove to be his last battle in Africa'. Some statistics tell their own story. In the course of the intermittent fighting during this one day the British artillery fired some 30,000 shells, and whereas the British losses were minute, Rommel had 635 casualties and, more importantly, lost over 50 tanks—the actual number is imprecise, Montgomery in his *Memoirs* claiming 52 and the *Official History* more cautiously saying 'between 44 and 56'.

It is Montgomery's misfortune that his critics tend to ascribe all his victories to a superiority of *matériel*, while his failures are put down to bad generalship. Montgomery was certainly not impeccable: but his success at Medenine, equally certainly, cannot be simply explained away as a by-product of weight of metal. The relevant figures for 30 Corps are tanks 300, anti-tank guns 460, field and medium guns 350. The Italo-German equivalents are much smaller in each category. There is no doubt that Montgomery had a discernible advantage in all these respects. But a student can read a battle as an expert can read calligraphy, noting the salient characteristics and the overall style. Medenine offers to the connoisseur a perfect specimen of Montgomery at his quintessential—fighting, at his best, the kind of battle that suited him best. There are no flaws to mar the whole, as Alam Halfa is marred by the conduct of its final phase.

Montgomery's art was now to be exposed to a sterner test. Built by the French in their palmier days as a deterrent to an Italian invasion of Tunisia, the Mareth Line ran inland, for 22 miles, from the sea to the base of the Matmata hills (see map on p. 127). The hills themselves, stark and high, prolonged the defences until, to the west, the apparently impassable Dahar (a sand-sea) offered a powerful flank-guard. Moreover, about equidistant from the Wadi Zigzaou (the core of the Line) and the Wadi Zessar, which 51 Highland had manned at Medenine, there ran the Wadi Zeuss, a useful outpost. The Germans had gradually made up the deficiencies in the defences which existed when they took the Line over. For example, the concrete pill-boxes built by the French were too small to accommodate the larger German weapons: nevertheless, there were posts in the line capacious enough to accommodate a battalion, and the Germans worked up this mini-Maginot into something if not impregnable, at least most difficult to breach. Forward positions were established between Zeuss and Zigzaou, which itself was turned into a formidable anti-tank obstacle averaging 60 feet in width and between 8 and 20 feet high. It was also a water-course carrying a stream sometimes 30 feet wide and 8 feet deep. A lavish use of mines—to the extent of 100,000 anti-tank and 70,000 anti-personnel—together with 19 miles of wire improved the natural obstacles. The banks of Wadi Zigzaou had been scarped (i.e. dug into steep slopes), and it was not difficult to spot possible crossing-points and arrange appropriate defensive fire from artillery and mortars, or to set up machine-guns to cover the crossings on fixed lines. This was the position which now challenged Montgomery's skill. But in fact it was

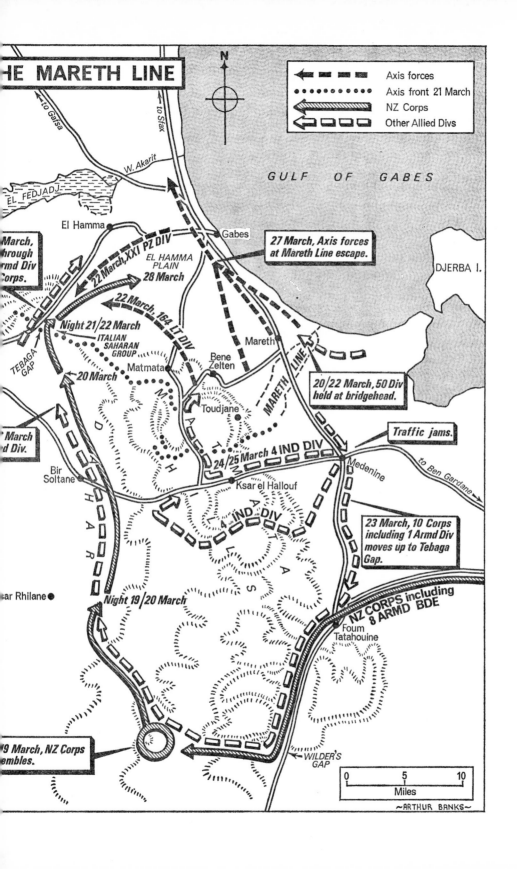

HE MARETH LINE

Axis forces
Axis front 21 March
NZ Corps
Other Allied Divs

to Gafsa

to Sfax

EL FEDJADJ

W. Akarit

GULF OF GABES

El Hamma

Gabes

March, hrough rmd Div Corps.

22 March, XXI PZ DIV

EL HAMMA PLAIN

28 March

DJERBA I.

27 March, Axis forces at Mareth Line escape.

22 March, 164 LT DIV

Night 21/22 March

ITALIAN SAHARAN GROUP

TEBAGA GAP

20 March

Matmata

Bene Zelten

Mareth

20/22 March, 50 Div held at bridgehead.

MARETH LINE

Toudjane

M A T M A T A

Traffic jams.

March d Div.

Bir Soltane

24/25 March 4 IND DIV

Ksar el Hallouf

Medenine

to Ben Gardane

D A H A R

4 IND DIV

H I L L S

23 March, 10 Corps including 1 Armd Div moves up to Tebaga Gap.

ar Rhilane

Night 19/20 March

NZ CORPS including 8 ARMD BDE

Foum Tatahouine

9 March, NZ Corps mbles.

WILDER'S GAP

0   5   10
Miles

~ARTHUR BANKS~

not the only route to the west. There were narrow but adequate roads winding through the Matmata Hills, to which little artificial protection seems to have been added. And finally there was the 'impassable' Dahar, on whose far side lay the Tebaga gap through which could be reached the plain of El Hamma, Gabes and the sea. As a precaution this gap had been mined and wired, though the arrangements were not as elaborate as in the Line proper.

Montgomery's success at Mareth turned on a simple fact—it *was* possible to cross the Dahar. Thinking well ahead, Montgomery had dispatched the Long Range Desert Group on a reconnaissance as far back as December, when he was still at Marble Arch. About the third week in January the L.R.D.G.s were able to report that they had found a gap which made viable an out-flanking operation, and on this, the famous Wilder's Gap (named after Lieutenant Wilder, the discoverer), Montgomery's planning pivoted. The Germans were not unaware of these possibilities, for in their hands was a report of a similar reconnaissance made by General Catroux and Colonel Gautsch in 1938. This report indicated that three divisions could pass to the west via Ksar el Hallouf and Bir Soltane in a space of six days, and actually mentioned the gap to be known as Wilder's. In the event, the Germans did betray a certain nervousness about their right wing, but Rommel put the matter in a nutshell when he wrote: 'It was impossible, with the forces we had, to deal with one British attack on Mareth, another at El Hamma, and an American attack on Gabes.' And the Germans' first-hand information was out-pointed by the British, who had as advisers a former Chief of Staff of French Troops in Tunisia, and no less a person than a Captain Paul Mezan who was Garrison Engineer of Mareth.

The accumulated stock of information about the Mareth Line and its environs, added to steadily by the operations of 285 (Reconnaissance) Wing of the R.A.F. which had been active over the Line since the end of January, provided Montgomery with one of those possibilities of an option which he always welcomed. The drive-by-the-sea and the inland hook were the almost inevitable alternatives along the African shores, but there was much greater merit in the two-fisted attack if either blow could be developed to the point of a knockout, instead of one being merely a feint. The planning for the Mareth battle supplied the groundwork which enabled Montgomery, having struck hard and ineffectively with his right, to make a rapid switch and strike hard but decisively with his left.

It was the left hook that began to swing first. For this Montgomery created, *ad hoc*, a New Zealand Corps which was in effect Freyberg in charge of 25,000 odd men and 150 odd tanks, 2 New Zealand Division being stiffened by 8 Armoured Brigade, an armoured car regiment, extra artillery and

14 *Sicily: Patton, Eisenhower and Montgomery, on the occasion of presentation to the latter of the highest order which the USA can bes upon a soldier of another nation—that of Commander of the Legion Honour*

a Free French column.* Against the main position 30 Corps was to attempt the breach: its 51 Highland Division held the front line, and through this 50 Division and 23 Armoured Brigade with its obsolete Valentine tanks would pass to make the assault when H Hour came at 2315 hrs. on 20 March. The final objective of the Army, as laid down in Montgomery's orders, was Sfax: this would conform well with the American thrust towards Gabes and Maknassy demanded, as has been seen, by Alexander. To take the shock from these powerful masses (behind whom, of course, lay the uncommitted 10 Corps in Army Reserve) Army Group Africa had what, on paper, looked a relatively feeble array. The left of the line, touching the sea, was occupied by the Young Fascist Division (respected by Eighth Army); then in sequence came six infantry battalions of Trieste, seven battalions from 90 Light, then Spezia, and then Pistoia. This covered the front as far as Toujane. Up in the Matmata Hills, further to the right, was a weak 164 Light. As to the armour, 15 Panzer with 32 battleworthy tanks lay close behind the line, in a useful reserve position some five miles from Mareth. 21 Panzer at Gabes and 10 Panzer at Sousse, who jointly could produce 110 tanks, might be moved fairly rapidly to deal with any *Schwerpunkt*. But it was the natural strength of the terrain which gave the Italo-German miscellany a threatening posture.

Freyberg's Corps had started to assemble at Foum Tatahouine, about half way between Medenine and Wilder's Gap, during the night of the 11th/12th. By the 19th it was well west of the gap, and by the 20th it was in position ready to break through the Tebaga Gap and fight on to El Hamma and Sfax. Facing it there was only a raggle-taggle force called *Raggrupamento Sahariano*, a trivial body which one New Zealand Intelligence Officer wrote off as 'Mannerini's mannikins'. This move was a considerable feat, even though it was not interfered with by the enemy. Tracks had frequently to be bull-dozed out of the sand, and much movement was by night. The experienced Kippenberger thought that 'we never did more difficult and tiring marches'.

It is an interesting game, when reading Official Histories, to spot the points at which it is clear that the author or authors would have said more had they been writing unofficial histories. One such point where impartiality begins to waver is in the British *Official History*'s account of the Mareth battle. 'General Nichols,' it says, '(commander of 50th Division) was given the 30th Corps' outline plan on 4th March, and thereafter was left largely to his own devices.' A foot-note comments, 'H.Q. 30th Corps was at first entirely pre-occupied with the forthcoming battle of Medenine, and thereafter seems to

---

* This was 'L' Force, the distinguished Free French unit commanded by General Leclerc, who, having formed it in Chad in French Equatorial Africa, reported with it to Montgomery at Tripoli on 26 January 1943. It should be distinguished from the Fighting French Flying Column, a small mobile force which had been in Eighth Army since Alamein.

Before D-Day : telling the troops

have felt that the planning of the main attack was perhaps best left to the commander who had to carry it out.' To this apathy at Corps level must be ascribed at least some of the reasons for the failure of Montgomery's first option—for the assault on the main defences of the Line certainly appears to have been intended as a body-blow. During the preparatory phase of the battle, Montgomery held one of his conferences at which he explained 'personally to officers down to the rank of Lieutenant-Colonel throughout the Army' that his plan depended on a major attack on the eastern end of the Mareth Line as well as a powerful outflanking movement. If the enemy 'concentrated against one then I would succeed with the other'. Kippenberger, who was present, is a most reliable witness. The impression he gained was that 'he expected the frontal attack to be decisive'. An infantry division and an armoured brigade, supported by the fire of 13 field and three medium regiments, together with various ancilliaries, certainly looks like a group meant to do business.

Whatever Montgomery's intentions, the operation was a total and unmitigated failure. Even his statement in *El Alamein to the River Sangro* that, at the point when he called the attack off, 'I knew that his reserves were now definitely committed on the eastern flank', provides no alleviation, for the reinforcements thrown in during the battle came mainly from 15 Panzer, already placed close behind the front, and 90 Light who were already in the line. 10 and 21 Panzer, as will be seen, were not affected.

It was 151 Brigade of 50 Division which, on the night 20/21 March, attempted to secure a bridgehead across the Wadi Zigzaou. Nobody seems to have realised that the technique for even a small river-crossing, which in effect this was and which had to be made a myriad times in Italy, requires a high degree of skill and experience, especially if it has to be achieved at a predictable place under predicted enemy fire. Yet such was the situation. General Nichols, the divisional commander, inevitably sought a portion of the wadi where the opposition looked weakest, the water shallow, and the banks not impossibly steep. Thus there was no surprise, because surprise was unattainable. Nevertheless the attack was launched at 2345 hrs. on the 20th, having been preceded by a substantial artillery programme. Flail tanks worked through the minefields, and with the aid of scaling ladders and in spite of heavy defensive fire 151 Brigade made its crossing and captured two of the larger strong-points. When it came to the turn of the supporting tanks, however, everything went wrong. 50 R.T.R. was the regiment that night. The idea was for the tanks to carry large fascines which could be dropped off in the wadi to provide a makeshift roadway. The heat of the tanks' exhausts ignited many of these, and in any case the leading tank drowned in three feet of water, thus jamming the route. Engineers made a by-pass which enabled three tanks to get to the other side, but after further blockages only one more tank crossed before 50 R.T.R. were ordered to withdraw.

The Wadi that night was like the mouth of Hell. The point of crossing was so obvious to the enemy that all his available fire, from artillery, mortars and machine-guns, could be concentrated on it. No praise could be too great for the infantry who fought through it to the relative peace of the enemy positions on the further bank, or, more particularly, for the steady courage of the engineers who could not cross but had to stay in mid-stream, trying to improve the route for the tanks, until, as happened to a high proportion of them, they were wounded or killed. Their waning strength made it impossible to attempt more than one of the three crossing-places which had been envisaged. During the following night 151 Brigade, reinforced by 5 East Yorks from 69 Brigade (the other Brigade in 50 Division), tried again and had a superficial success in that 42 more tanks joined the lonely four on the enemy bank. There was only a superficial gain because in churning their way across the second batch of tanks made it impossible for any vehicle or, especially, anti-tank gun to follow them. This was fatal. Early next afternoon 15 Panzer put in a vicious counter-attack, eliminating 30 Valentines and thrusting 151 Brigade back to the verge of the wadi. By 0200 hrs. on the 22nd Montgomery saw that he had been foiled. The assault troops—such as survived—were withdrawn, 151 Brigade was commanded by a VC, Brigadier Beak, and during this abortive action it acquired another, awarded to Lieut.-Colonel Seagrim.

What went wrong? With all the detailed information available to him, it seems strange that Montgomery selected for a main thrust an area where everything was in the defender's favour and little or nothing in the attacker's. Might there not have been a better case for a feint at Mareth properly timed to coincide with a properly prepared left hook? Properly prepared—because, as will be seen, there was a large element of extemporisation about the left hook which actually occurred. Assuming that an attack was to be mounted, the use of 23 Brigade seems dubious. Of the 51 runners available in 50 R.T.R. on the first night, 43 carried the 'pop-gun' 2-pounder and only eight the 6-pounder. Of the 32 tanks available in 15 Panzer, 14 were the long-barrelled Mk. IV Special which was superior to the 6-pounder. 23 Brigade was part of an Army which had just carried out a model anti-tank action at Medenine. The 'form' was perfectly understood. In view of the inadequate arrangements for ensuring that anti-tank guns followed the infantry at the earliest possible moment, it seems baffling that the dash and ardour of 151 Brigade and the stolid endurance of the engineers was provided with so feeble a support. Mareth was badly stage-managed: it was the first sign of a symptom which would become progressively more noticeable—that Eighth Army formations were slow to re-adjust themselves to changed conditions of warfare. This process could take a considerable time: the performance of 7 Armoured Division in Normandy is a good example.

It was not that the men were laggard. Since Gazala in June 1942 50 Division, made up of proud battalions of steady soldiers from the north of England, the Green Howards, the East Yorks., the Durham Light Infantry, had been out of the limelight and was ready for a little more glory. It happened that my battery position at Mareth was just behind the start-line for the attack, and I remember the D.L.I. passing through our gun positions in high spirits and bursting with confidence. (I remember two days later seeing Brigadier Beak standing on the rim of the bowl in which we lay, endeavouring to rally the stragglers from the assault as they drifted back.) I remember spending a morning with the 50 R.T.R. a day or so earlier: no sign there of hesitancy or doubt. The men were good but the plan was bad.

Montgomery swiftly cut his losses. He shifted the weight into his left hand, converting Freyberg's Corps, with reinforcements, into his main instrument for a breakthrough. 30 Corps was left to engage the enemy's attention as much as possible on the Mareth front, while 4 Indian Division was given the task, congenial to it, of forcing a way through the Matmata Hills: the latter now seemed feasible because during the night of 19/20 March, 164 Division began to move away from the position which it held in the hills before the attack and towards the Tebaga Gap. This movement had been observed.

10 and 21 Panzer were also alert to Freyberg's threat. But after their remarkable approach march the New Zealanders were functioning sluggishly. Although Montgomery had signalled to Freyberg that he wanted him to get through to El Hamma as soon as possible, and then on to the Gabes area and the rear of the Mareth defences, there was no atmosphere of urgency. At midnight of 21/22 March the brigadiers of both 8 Armoured Brigade and 6 New Zealand Brigade were willing to attempt to burst through the Gap, but Freyberg was lukewarm. Even the New Zealand Official Historian observes 'an opportunity was lost'. Nobody could doubt Freyberg's fighting spirit. In the First World War alone he had won the VC and the DSO with two bars. Winston Churchill, who nicknamed him 'the Salamander', once in the 'twenties asked Freyberg to show him his wounds: the count was 27, and three more were to be added. What was restraining Freyberg now was a sense of being in an exposed position which might expect a heavy counter-attack, and also his perennial nightmare—the problem of using and yet conserving what was in effect a national force representing a small country with limited manpower. On the 23rd, however, he received a personal signal from Montgomery saying that 1 Armoured Division would reinforce him, together with 10 Corps H.Q.—i.e. Horrocks.

Orders to this effect were issued by Montgomery within hours of his decision to break off at Mareth. As Freyberg had missed his chance of a breakthrough, it was obvious that Freyberg's Corps would not be strong enough to tackle the reinforcements which the Germans must be rushing to Tebaga. Moreover, Montgomery knew his Freyberg, and how far he could drive him. He knew the insurance of extra infantry brigades he had needed to add to be sure that Freyberg would undertake SUPERCHARGE at Alamein. He must have sensed that Freyberg was being 'sticky', as he would put it, and in need of 'ginger'. The eager Horrocks was just the man for this. Montgomery produced, however, a Gilbertian situation. Horrocks shrewdly pointed out that Freyberg, of all people, would not take kindly to another Corps H.Q. being inserted over his head, and suggested to de Guingand that all signals and instructions should be sent to the pair of Corps Commanders jointly. De Guingand agreed (he named the pair Hindenburg and Ludendorff), and the consequence was letters which began 'My dear Generals . . .'

But Horrocks had far more important things to concern him than protocol. Because the move of his Armoured Division was an after-thought and not part of a careful, pre-planned operation, it had all the appearance of what the Navy calls 'a lash-up'. The worst feature was a failure in co-ordination between two Corps H.Q., for as 1 Armoured of 10 Corps was due to pass through the bottle-neck of the village of Medenine, there entered from another direction a brigade of 4 Indian Division, 30 Corps, on its way to carry out the Division's new directive to cut through the Matmata hills. Worse than that, the tanks of one of 7 Armoured's brigades followed straight on after 1 Armoured, thus costing 4 Indian some 24 hours' delay.

If Horrocks had cause for concern, so much the more had Major-General Raymond Briggs. It was his direct responsibility to steer his 1 Armoured Division through an enterprise unparalleled, so far, in British military history. Starting at 2000 hrs. on the 23rd, it began its journey with a night march (and the traffic jam at Medenine) and continued steadily via the route pioneered by the New Zealanders until the Division was up at the point of action, the last vehicles reporting in no more than half an hour before there began a battle in which 1 Armoured was again to establish a record. 21 Panzer had now taken up positions to guard the Gap, and it was clear that a stiff fight would be necessary to open it.

For the battle-plan which made this possible there are several putative fathers. Horrocks reached Freyberg on the afternoon of the 24th, and though he was received frostily he and Freyberg were soldiers, not children, and they immediately dealt with a proposal from Montgomery for an attack that day under air cover. At 1530 they made their reply, pointing out the topographical features which made Montgomery's plan unsuitable, and offering three alternatives. Out of these and other exchanges emerged the final scheme, which in effect consisted of a break-in by Freyberg's Corps and an immediate follow-up and break-out by Briggs. It was Briggs who overcame the desire of Horrocks and Freyberg for a daylight attack: as a result, Freyberg was to start operations at 1600 hrs. with a final objective set at 4,500 yards from the start line. Briggs would then pass through to a point of rest some 3,000 yards further on. Here 1 Armoured would await the moon, and as soon as enough light was available it would drive straight for El Hamma. Nothing like this had been previously attempted. The initial assault was to be supported by 'a real low-flying blitz', as Air Vice-Marshal Harry Broadhurst—A.O.C. the Desert Air Force, and the man who devised it—described the continuous flow of low-flying fighter-bombers and cannon-firing planes which, since the front of attack was so narrow, had a devastating effect. Broadhurst seems to have worked out the plan on a suggestion of de Guingand's: he displayed not only originality of thought in so doing, but also moral courage, because his superiors in his own Service disapproved and actually tried to stop him. They approved afterwards.

Montgomery had given the attack the code-name of SUPERCHARGE. It was even more smoothly successful than its illustrious predecessor. Freyberg's opening gambit gained the necessary ground, 1 Armoured Division's tanks rolled through to their pause-line on time, and soon after 2300 hrs. the moon rose. Though it was obscured by cloud, at midnight Briggs set the armour in motion and, as the light cleared, there was an extraordinary spectacle as British and German sped side by side, and sometimes intermingled, towards the goal of El Hamma. The British were just outstripped. Acting with extreme energy von Liebenstein, the commander of 164 Light, raked together a thin line of field and anti-tank guns which caused a halt a few miles south of the village. Thereat the action guttered away, but in any case the enemy was now retiring of his own accord, and by the 29th the New Zealanders and 51 Highland were en route through Gabes.

Montgomery had got his victory, and justifiably so. It was not absolute, and it might have been more comprehensive, and within the victory was contained the defeat at Mareth. Nevertheless, there it was: in spite of the obstacles of unfavourable terrain, and an enemy whose spirit was un-quenched, Eighth Army was at Gabes. Military historians of the future are likely to follow the most reliable of those of the post-war epoch in judging that in the opening stages of the battle Montgomery made a two-fold error: in deciding to make a powerful assault over the Wadi Zigzaou and, having made it, allowing it to happen with inadequate preparation and inadequate strength. But all will commend his speed in switching from a loser to a potential winner, though some will have reservations as to whether he should not have pre-planned the final left hook from the start. No pre-planning could have made Briggs do better during his night drive at Tebaga. Horrocks was justified in replying to Freyberg's doubts, before the battle: 'If we punch the hole will the tanks really go through?' 'Yes,' said Horrocks, 'Yes, they will, and I am going with them myself'. It was a cunning move of Montgomery's to send off Horrocks into the wilderness, for he injected a dynamism into the armoured attack which Freyberg certainly could not have instilled then—and perhaps never. What a better plan for the left hook might have given Montgomery is time—that extra 24 hours (and probably no more were needed) which might have enabled his spearheads to thrust right across the Hamma plain to the sea and give him a large haul of prisoners, if not the whole of Messe's army. But when all is said, two things stand out—Montgomery's foresight which resulted in the early discovery of Wilder's Gap, and the absolute self-confidence, and confidence in his men, which enabled him to send first Freyberg's Corps and then, by a forced march, Briggs' 1 Armoured Division to make their way across the 'impassable' and fight at the end of the journey.

The simultaneous operations in the north of 2 U.S. Corps, under their new commander General Patton, were at first fumbling and never decisive. Patton needed time and experience before his fervour could be correctly channelled and his troops trained in the way they should go. Still, the interlocking of the fronts was well illustrated by the fortunes of 10 Panzer, last mentioned as ingloriously present at the battle of Medenine. Drawn back again to its home ground, von Arnim's command, it was very badly battered on the 23rd by 1 U.S. Infantry Division. A wounded 10 Panzer in the north instead of an active one at El Hamma was much to be preferred.

21 Panzer helped to cover the withdrawal of Messe's army to the stop line of the Wadi Akarit, some 20 miles north of Gabes, and then, during the 30th and 31st, turned away to join their comrades of 10 Panzer, and the Italian Centauro Division, in stemming the pressure from 2 American Corps. A study of the implications is worth while in this context. Usually the two theatres—that of First and that of Eighth Army—tend to be displayed on separate maps and the reader is insensibly led to think of them as being in different compartments. But this move vividly and visually demonstrates their unity: demonstrates, too, the wisdom of the Casablanca Conference in seeing the need for an overall ground commander. Every mile gained and every tank destroyed by the Americans had its relevance, however small, for the British: and vice versa.

Rommel had always desired, as has been seen, to pull back to what he called the 'Gabes Gap', by which he really meant the defensive line along the Wadi Akarit. Had he been able to retreat from, say, Agheila, he might have had enough time to put the defences into sufficient shape for him to maintain a reasonably prolonged resistance. There is a true bottleneck. One flank of the line rests on the sea and the other, 12 miles inland, on the salt marshes and lakes of Chott Jerid through which the going is impossible. This narrow neck is strengthened by the presence five miles in from the sea of a saddleback feature, some 500 feet high and a mile long, called Roumana, and, further west, the foothills climbing up to the heights of Fatnassa. 'This freakish and outlandish agglomeration of high ground,' it has been said, 'is reminiscent of a Disney drawing.' All this, with time, Rommel could have developed into a position possibly stronger than Mareth, in that the chance of being out-flanked did not arise. But there was now no Rommel* nor any time.

Horrocks set 1 Armoured and the New Zealanders to work at reconnaiss-ance as early as the 29th. He proposed another blitz attack, but Montgomery turned this down, and by the 31st Horrocks had to admit that his men alone could not penetrate the line. Montgomery then decided on a routine assault by the infantry of 30 Corps, which the mobile 10 Corps would exploit. It is interesting, in connection with paragraph 3 on p. 135, to notice that he told Alexander, referring to the Americans, that '. . . if that Corps could come forward even a few miles it would make my task very simple'. Zero Hour was set for the night of 4/5 April.

At a conference at the beginning of April Montgomery outlined his plans to his generals. They were textbook and uninspired. 51 Division would attack on the right and make the hole through which 10 Corps would exploit, and 4 Indian Division, on the left, would move forward on to the lower ground beneath Fatnassa. Even assuming 51 Highland took Roumana, the whole battlefield would be overlooked from Fatnassa. But this was to reckon without Major-General Francis Tuker of 4 Indian. In his typical way he had insti-tuted a system of energetic patrolling as soon as his division entered the line, and from patrol reports and his own personal reconnaissance he had drawn certain conclusions. The first was that the proposed plan was disastrous and the second was that 4 Indian Division could take Fatnassa. After the con-ference, therefore, he nobbled Wimberley of 51 Highland and, finding him favourably inclined, tackled Leese and guaranteed that if his division could attack Fatnassa in the dark, with surprise and no supporting fire, it could capture the menacing feature in a night. Leese, won over, tackled Mont-gomery, and the result was a modified plan giving Tuker what he wanted and, because the opposition now appeared stiffer than was at first thought, adding 50 Division on the right. (Montgomery, ungraciously, mentions Tuker's

* Of his final departure from Africa on 9 March 1943 Rommel wrote: 'Orders were issued by the Führer's H.Q to maintain the utmost secrecy concerning my recall.' This was certainly effective in the case of Montgomery, who did not realise until well after the war that Rommel had not opposed him to the end.

brilliant amendment neither in *El Alamein to the River Sangro* nor in his *Memoirs*: but Tuker was his own worst enemy, always outspoken in his criticism of plans handed down from above and—even more irritating!— original and very frequently right in the alternatives he proposed.)

The formal attack began at 0400 hrs. on the 6th, in the dark, thus catching Messe on the wrong foot. He had anticipated that Roumana would be the prime target and that Montgomery would wait for the moonlight which was not due, from the moon at its full, for another ten days. But Montgomery was in a hurry. On 3 April Alexander had issued to both his armies a joint pattern of operations designed to prepare the way for a knockout blow. A central feature in this was to be an absolute interdiction of the enemy's potential in the air: and indeed the 5th, the first day of Operation FLAX (the cutting of the trans-Mediterranean air supply route), saw the destruction of many German and Italian planes. Montgomery was now keeping his part of the contract.

Hours before Zero, Tuker's Gurkhas were infiltrating the posts on Fatnassa, and, gradually backed up by more and more of the division, executed their task with such silent efficiency that all was in 4 Division's hands by morning. According to Tuker, Horrocks visited him at 0845 and was told that 'the way was clear for 10 Corps to go through; that immediate offensive action would finish the campaign in North Africa'. But 10 Corps did *not* go through. Whether or not Tuker had made a practicable gap, the right of the British front was in disarray. 50 Division had a fierce struggle over the anti-tank ditch and among the minefields beneath Roumana. On Roumana itself 51 Highland, though it had gained ground on the ridge, nevertheless endured such desperate counter-attacks by both Germans and Italians that the Divisional Intelligence Summary stated: 'There is no doubt that the day marked the fiercest fighting that the Division has experienced in this campaign.' But their gallantry did not cause the retreat of some 88mm. guns which sat in enfilade positions below Roumana; these, picking off tanks of 8 Armoured Brigade as they probed ahead of the New Zealand Division (intended to be the forerunner of 10 Corps, which Leese had transferred to the right flank), provided an effective barrier. Montgomery had sent off to Alexander a signal full of euphoria: but in fact Eighth Army made no significant jump forward on the 6th.

Yet the battle was already won. During the afternoon the senior officers of the African Army were conferring in despair, and, though hardened divisions like 15 Panzer and 90 Light fought with normal ferocity, their generals had lost all hope. On the 7th, therefore, the front suddenly crumbled, and Messe set his men in motion towards the west. By 12 April the Italo-German forces opposing Montgomery were virtually all established in their last bastion. This was at Enfidaville, the little village where the mountains of the central Tunisian *massif* drop down to the sea, leaving only a narrow plain which, running between the two, carries the road and railway due north to Tunis—to Tunis which had been the *leit motiv* of Montgomery's stirring Message to his Army before Mareth. Para. IV of this Message read: 'We will not stop, or let up, till Tunis has been captured, and the enemy has either given up the struggle or has been pushed into the sea.' The final paragraph exclaimed: 'FORWARD TO TUNIS! DRIVE THE ENEMY INTO THE SEA!' These are words to which due weight must be given in reviewing the course of events after, on 13 April, advance elements of the New Zealand Division closed up on the Enfidaville defences. If they do not sufficiently reveal Montgomery's climate of thought during these April days, then one has only to refer to Alexander's Operation Instruction of the 16th, part of which states:

> Eighth Army will:
> (a) draw enemy forces off First Army by exerting continuous pressure on the enemy.
> (b) by an advance on the axis Enfidaville-Hammamet-Tunis prevent the enemy withdrawing into the Cap Bon Peninsula.

To this Instruction Montgomery replied '. . . All my troops are in first class form and want to be in the final Dunkirk.'

The rights and wrongs of the situation are too detailed and technical to argue here, but, in sum, it would seem that Alexander, who certainly intended the *coup de grâce* to the Axis Forces in Africa to be delivered in the good tank country further inland and further north, in this Instruction bent over too far in a generous endeavour to meet Montgomery's, and Eighth Army's, natural desire to be in at the death. In fact the Army was going to have a proper representation. 1 Armoured had already been detached, to join 9 Corps in First Army. And ultimately 7 Armoured and 4 Indian would travel round the corner to take a leading rôle in the final drive for Tunis and put those desert veterans, 11 Hussars, into the city before anyone else—if the counter-claim of First Army's Derbyshire Yeomanry be ignored! But there was no Montgomery there. Yet he had clearly cast himself in a leading rôle. Apart from the tone of his messages and signals, there is the significant fact that on 11 April, with the arrival of Eighth Army at Sfax, Montgomery actually asked Alexander if 6 Armoured Division of First Army, then making for Kairouan, could be put under his command, to enable him to leave 1 Armoured at Sfax and 'help my supply arrangements'. Alexander's response, an order for 1 Armoured to join 6, should have shown Montgomery the writing on the wall. But he misinterpreted the situation of himself and his Army, and in consequence made at Enfidaville some of the worst battle-judgements of his career.

It was a period of error, personal as well as professional. When on 10 April Eighth Army entered Sfax Montgomery dispatched a signal to H.Q. North

Africa Command. 'Personal. Montgomery to Eisenhower. Entered Sfax 0830 this morning. Please send Fortress.' The origin of this signal, as strange a missive as any sent from one commander to another, was a bet which Montgomery believed he had made with Bedell Smith, Eisenhower's Chief of Staff, that if he entered Sfax by 15 April Eisenhower would send him a Flying Fortress for his personal use. This was at best infantile behaviour: a complete absence of the *tact des choses possibles*. Bedell Smith's reaction is vividly described in a note in the Alan Brooke *Papers* which begins 'My morning interview with Monty was another of those instances when I had to haul him over the coals for the trouble he was creating.' The occasion was a visit by Brooke to Algiers at the beginning of June. Even then he found Eisenhower 'boiling with rage' over the incident; for though Bedell Smith had naturally treated the matter as a joke, he had had, in the face of Montgomery's pertinacity, to lay the problem before his commander who, to maintain a good relationship, surrendered to Montgomery a Fortress with an American crew. The incredible thing is that Brooke makes it clear, in his account of his interview with Montgomery, that the latter was convinced that 'Ike' had thought the whole business great fun. Here, in fact, can be observed once again the irredeemable small boy 'trying it on'. But the sad truth was that, though Eisenhower himself was big enough to forgive and forget, there were many others in the American—and British—forces who heard these and similar stories, embroidered no doubt in the telling, and whose reactions towards Montgomery were very much less charitable. It was by this kind of behaviour that, from time to time, he poisoned his future.

When Montgomery's Eighth Army ran up against the Tunisian mountains its existence ceased to have any great purpose, except as a holding force to keep as many of von Arnim's troops as possible away from the decisive area— the Medjerda valley and the flat lands which are the natural gateway to Tunis. This had always been First Army's territory, and it would remain so to the end. Alexander had made that obvious in his reply to Montgomery's request on the 11th to take over 6 Armoured. But no hint from a senior was necessary: a mere glance at a map, or even better a personal reconnaissance, should have indicated that any form of attack at Enfidaville must necessarily be expensive in relation to ground gained; a breakthrough was impossible, except at such a cost in men and munitions as to make Enfidaville a word of ill fame like the Somme or Passchandaele. Horrocks, in the end, came to see this, when he told Montgomery 'we will break through, but I doubt whether at the end there will be very much left of the Eighth Army'. Many good men died in demonstration of that simple truth.

I know the ground well. The guns of my battery were in one of the huge olive groves at the foot of the mountains. I had an Observation Post far to the right flank, in the seaward plain, which gave one an enfilade view of the whole Eighth Army front. And immediately after the surrender I clambered up into the hills to examine the enemy positions from the other side. Thus one built up a complete panoramic picture in one's head. The two salient features were the ability of the enemy to see practically everything that happened on the plains below, and the immense natural strength of the fire positions dug in just below the crest-lines, quite untouchable by the Eighth Army's particular asset, its artillery.

The small village of Enfidaville lies about five miles inland from the sea. The village and the seaward gap were partially defended by an anti-tank ditch. But these were only forward posts. The keep was formed by the row of forbidding hills towering to the north, the 1,000 foot high Djebel Garci on the west of the village with Mdeker to Garci's north rear and, running north-eastwards, Blida, Mengoub and Tebaga. The coast road runs west and east through Enfidaville and then bends due north, to pass between mountain and sea towards Bou Ficha and Tunis. Where Djebel Tebaga swings down towards this road, forming a tighter bottleneck, the enemy had established another anti-tank ditch. Such was the maze through which Montgomery was to attempt to find a way. And at the gate of the maze stood a sentinel—the curious crag called Takrouna, which broke out of the ground just N.W. of Enfidaville, a rotting stalagmite dominating the whole battle area.

Montgomery's first step was to 'square up' to the enemy line, and try to 'bounce' him out of it. His hopes for so simple a decision were based partly on an inaccurate estimate of the opposition's strength; an estimate partly grounded on the knowledge that some reinforcement of the vital defences in front of Tunis must have occurred. But Messe had some tough soldiers to deploy: from left to right of his line he emplaced 90 Light, the Young Fascists, Pistoia (with the remains of Centauro), 164 Light, Spezia—and 15 Panzer in reserve. Armour, fuel and ammunition were all low: but the infantry were desperately determined. An attempt by a New Zealand battalion to attack straight off its approach march, and 'bounce' Garci, was instantly thwarted, and this and other probes led Montgomery to mount a full-scale, set-piece attack, which started during the night of the 19th/20th. Its plan was for 4 Indian to take Garci, 2 New Zealand Takrouna and the surrounding area, while 50 Division had a holding rôle on the right and 7 Armoured looked after the left and linked up with First Army's 19 French Corps. The most stagger-ing feature of the plan was the contemplated second phase: in this 4 Indian, having got a firm hold of Garci, were to strike across the rugged hills and uplands in a north-westerly direction, fighting as they marched some 12 miles, and to emerge on the coastal plain roughly where the anti-tank ditch cut the road beneath Tebaga. Both Montgomery and Horrocks, the responsible Corps Commander, keep quiet in their memoirs about this second phase —and very wisely, because when the night came 4 Indian, a two-brigade division, found in the end that it had committed four out of its six available battalions without obtaining more than a finger-hold on Garci. For this infinitesimal gain it lost between 500 and 600 men.

The New Zealand Division also paid a heavy price. Kippenberger's 5 Brigade was given the daunting task of taking Takrouna, whose sheer sides were crowned by a small village: the buildings and the crinkled ground offered good cover for a defender. There was great confusion as the night wore on, and the New Zealanders were exposed to vicious defensive fire. Quite early in the attack the advanced dressing station was reporting that from the Maori Battalion alone eleven officers, including all company commanders, had been brought in. Still, a weak platoon of the Maoris, two sergeants and seven men, pressed on to an epic achievement. By the time they had reached and seized the 30-yard-square summit of Takrouna only four of the assault party were left: but 150 prisoners had been taken and 40 or 50 killed. And these, it should be noted, came from, among others, the first-class Italian Folgore Division and the German 104 Panzer Grenadiers. There was much shelling and counter-shelling, and attacking and counter-attacking, but by the afternoon of the 21st Takrouna was firmly held. In this and the accompanying operations, however, the New Zealanders lost some 500 casualties. How this can bear on a force coming from a small nation of limited manhood can be seen quickly: 21 Battalion, assault party 360, losses 159; 23 Battalion, assault party 383, losses 116; Maoris, assault party 319, losses 131, including 12 out of 17 officers.

Between 23 and 26 April Montgomery was in Cairo attending to the planning for HUSKY, the Sicilian venture. But before he went he told Horrocks, 'I want you now to work out a plan to break through to Tunis by a strong attack up the coastal plain.' Horrocks describes this period as the most unpleasant in his life, for he knew that his battle-wise divisional commanders, Freyberg and Tuker, had no confidence in the further application of desert warfare concepts to North-West Frontier conditions. The First Army had by now discovered, but Eighth had still to learn, that fissured hillsides can devour the man-power of an attacker and make the defender virtually impregnable. Montgomery finally abandoned this project: but one of the key reasons for making him do so was what happened to 56 London Division. By one of those evasive statements which have a way of slipping into his writing Montgomery says, 'I called forward 56 Division from Tripoli. . . .' In fact, as the *Official History* makes clear, the Division 'had come overland from Kirkuk in Iraq, a journey of 3,200 miles in 32 days. It was without experience in battle. . . .' One of its brigades, 167, did not arrive until the 28th. Yet this raw formation was sent into night operations on the 26th/27th and 28th/29th. On the morning of the 29th 169 Brigade was counter-attacked and driven in disorder off Djebel Srafi, just south of Terhouna. It is impossible to justify such a wanton waste by a seasoned commander except on the grounds that he is mad, ill, or otherwise pre-occupied. Though people asked, when Montgomery in 1939 was carried on ship-board strapped to a stretcher, 'Who is that mad general?', his wits, as future events would show, were unimpaired. But at Enfidaville he *was* ill: so unwell that on the 30th he had to signal to ask Alexander to visit him. And he was now deeply pre-occupied with thoughts about Sicily: both the attack plan and the extrication from the front line of divisions he wanted to rest and train for HUSKY. There was undoubtedly a marked deterioration in the quality of high command during the Enfidaville operations. As Messe said of Akarit, looking at it from his own point of view, *'Non e stata una bella battaglia. . . .'*: 'This was not a good battle.'

For Horrocks, however, and for the troops pinned down at Enfidaville, relief arrived on 30 April. Horrocks was summoned by Montgomery, who had Alexander with him, and was instructed to take 4 Indian Division, 7 Armoured Division, and 201 Guards Brigade, and move round to the First Army's front where he would take over command of 9 Corps. 'You will then smash through to Tunis and finish the war in North Africa.' And this of course Horrocks did, in the great *Blitzkrieg* drive from north of Medjez el Bab and up the Medjerda valley into the heart of Tunis.

At the beginning of March—so near and yet so far—Montgomery had had three main anxieties: the imminent battle of Medenine, the approaching battle of Mareth, and the invasion of Sicily for which, he knew, he had been cast in a leading rôle. His first two anxieties were over. They had passed into history as victories. There now remained the third.

8

Sicily to the Sangro

'Somewhere, at some time, the reconquest of the Continent must
begin with the first British or American soldier wading ashore
out of the sea. . . .'

John Ehrman, *Grand Strategy*, Vol. V.

'Christ! What a steep hill. . . .!'

Reflections of an Intelligence Officer
of 231 Infantry Brigade

For Montgomery the personal significance of HUSKY, the invasion of Sicily,
was that from the moment he was nominated as one of the Force Commanders
until the very end of the war he was committed to fighting in consort with
American troops and officers and serving under the direction of an American
Supremo. The old days of an almost absolute independence as a plenipotentiary master of the Eighth Army, under an indulgent Alexander, were over
—for ever. He would have to come to terms with American personalities and
comprehend American ideologies, while always, waiting in the wings, there
would be the American press, swift and cruel in its exploitation of the barrack-
room rumour. In the case of a man with Montgomery's temperament, im-
perious, self-centred, absorbed in what he himself conceived to be the military
truth, the astonishing thing is not his frequent failures to achieve accommodation and understanding but the considerable extent to which an efficient
harmony was established. Without this the story of D-Day might have been
very different.

But Normandy was still not a certainty during the spring and early summer
months of 1943 in which the plans for HUSKY were slowly matured and rapidly
executed. And for Montgomery in particular, and the British in general, there
were already signs of a disharmony which would be increased during the arguments about how the battle for Sicily should be fought and also during the
fighting itself. As to Montgomery, his candid friend Alan Brooke put the
matter succinctly in a diary note of 3 June, made while he and Churchill were
on a visit to Algiers to discuss Sicily and the consequences of success. 'Montgomery . . . requires a lot of educating to make him see the whole situation and
the war as a whole outside the Eighth Army orbit. A difficult mixture to
handle, brilliant commander in action and trainer of men, but liable to commit

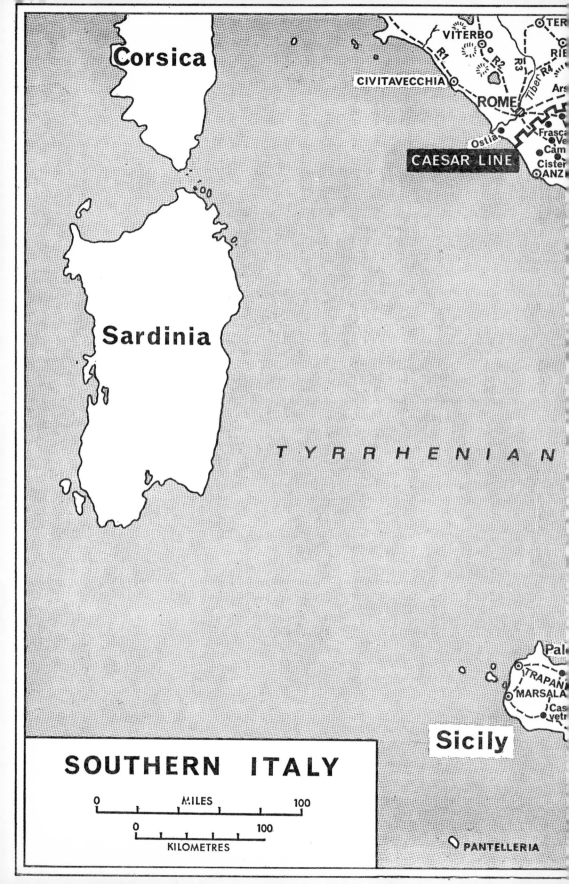

Corsica

Sardinia

VITERBO

CIVITAVECCHIA

ROME

Ostia

CAESAR LINE

Frasca
Cam
Cister
ANZ

TER

RIE

R1 R2 R3 R4 Ars

T Y R R H E N I A N

Pal

TRAPAN
MARSALA

Cas
vetr

Sicily

SOUTHERN ITALY

0   MILES   100

0   100

KILOMETRES

PANTELLERIA

PESCARA
GUSTAV LINE

ADRIATIC

SEA

R16
Chieti
Orsogna
Casoli
Ortona
oli
Sangro
Vasto
escina
Termoli
no
R17
C.di
Sangro
Isernia
Campo-
basso
GARGANO
PENINSULA
Fortore
CASSINO
Venafro
Vinchiatura
R17
Foggia
R16
Ausonia
R7
R6
Volturno
Caserta
Capua
BENEVENTO
R90
Ofanto
Barletta
Canosa
Bari
NAPLES
AVELLINO
Teora
Melfi
ALTAMURA
Vesuvius
Scafati
SALERNO
Battapaglia
R94
POTENZA
BRINDISI
CAPRI
Sorrento
Auletta
Taranto
GULF OF
SALERNO
Sele
Paestum
R18
Vallo
Sapri
GULF OF
TARANTO
CASTRO-
VILLARI
R19
Scalea
R18
R19
SEA
R106
CALABRIA
CROTONE
CATANZARO
GULF OF
GIOIA
LIPARI IS.
Gioia
C.Milazzo
Bagnara
C.
Orlando
Brolo
Messina
S.Fratello
REGGIO
R113
Stefano
Tortorice
Barcellona
Scaletta
R114
ee
Troina
Randazzo
Bronte
Taormina
Petralia
R120
Nicosia
Leonforte
Adrano
Mt.
Etna
Acireale
IONIAN
R121
Agira
Paterno
ENNA
Catania
SEA
Calta-
girone
Lentini
Licata
Augusta
Gela
SYRACUSE
Vizzini
R124
Ragusa
Vittoria
Avola
R115
Pachino

~ARTHUR BANKS~

untold errors, due to lack of tact, lack of appreciation of other people's out-look. It is most distressing that the Americans do not like him, and it will always be a difficult matter to have him fighting in close proximity to them. He wants guiding and watching continually and I do not think that Alex is suffi-ciently strong and rough with him.' The inept affair over the Flying Fortress 'bet' had done nothing to improve relations with Eisenhower and Bedell Smith. Then there was Patton. After Rommel was checked at Kasserine, and Patton took over the American 2 Corps on the right of First Army's front, Major-General Sir Charles Dunphie (who had commanded at Thala the British 26 Armoured Brigade which finally contained Rommel's attack), was attached with other experienced officers to Patton's Corps as 'advisers'. At this time, Sir Charles told me, Patton held Eighth Army in high regard. It is a straw in the wind, however, that General Omar Bradley remembers, in *A Soldier's Story*, that when he heard of how the Eighth Army had stopped dead outside Enfidaville he said to one of his colleagues: 'Let's radio Monty and ask if he wants us to send him a few American advisers to show his desert fighters how to get through those hills.' And then there followed Mont-gomery's lectures at Tripoli on the conduct of the desert war, to which repre-sentatives from First Army were bidden. Of these some rosy accounts have been published: there are also stories to the effect that when Montgomery complained that First Army had sent its second eleven and was told that the top men were fighting a battle he snorted, 'Much better have been listening to me.' What is certain is that the effect on Patton was disastrous. The late Major-General Bateman was sitting a few feet from Patton during one lecture and told me his face was a study. Patton's subsequent bemused comments have often been quoted. Here, I think, was the germ of a competitive hostility which grew in Patton's mind, was fostered by events in Sicily, and developed into dangerous proportions between Normandy and the Rhine.

Because Montgomery was so obvious a focal point, he suffered also from the lack of general rapport between the men of the sands and the men of the hills. It would be otiose to recapitulate the vast numbers of accounts in regi-mental histories, and reports in analyses of the African campaigns, describing the overwhelming sense of superiority which the Eighth Army displayed in regard to the First—and the Americans in particular. This was natural, almost inevitable, and infinitely to be regretted. It was natural because the high morale of the Eighth Army had been built up on the principle that they were the sons of God, and there was no other God but Montgomery; it was almost inevitable because information about First Army operations was very sparse —we knew about Kasserine, for example, but not about Thala; and it was to be regretted because the British elements on either side were in the end part of the same national Army fighting a common enemy. Matters could, however, reach such a pass that a battalion from the desert would look down its nose at a battalion from the hills which belonged to the same Regiment! Differences in vehicle camouflage, differences in dress, differences in discipline all widened the gulf. And if the gulf was wide between fellow-countrymen, how much the wider did it yawn between the Eighth Army and the Americans, who represented a strange and alien entity (and vice versa!).

Particular events had intensified the strain. Apart from the affair of the Fortress, there was the matter of Coningham's signal. When on 1 April Patton, on Alexander's instructions, put in an armoured drive towards Gabes, he was greatly frustrated by the *Luftwaffe*. (Dunphie, his 'adviser', was then wounded.) His Intelligence Officer noted: 'Total lack of air cover for our units has allowed German air force to operate almost at will.' This SITREP reached Coningham, commanding the Tactical Air Force. He sent back a stupid and offensive reply which included such words as '. . . it can only be assumed that 2 Corps personnel concerned are not battleworthy in terms of present operations . . . it is requested that such inaccurate and exaggerated reports should cease . . . this false cry of wolf'. Patton was furious, Eisenhower was furious, Tedder was shocked. The latter made Coningham withdraw the signal, and took him to meet Patton and apologise in person. But something stuck. Bradley in telling the story refers to 'a sensitivity that can result in bitter misunderstanding under the most trivial of circumstances'. Finally there was the case of Crocker at Fondouk. After the battle of the Fondouk Pass on the First Army front at the beginning of April, in which the American 34 Division acquitted itself badly, Crocker, commanding 6 Armoured Division, was asked by an American mission to state, in what he assumed to be confidential terms, the reasons for 34 Division's failure. Unfortunately there was a press leakage. While it appears that Crocker's comments were justified, Patton and Bradley were distressed and offended, and the matter had to go up to Alexander. The affair was smoothed over, but it left a bad taste.

Since Montgomery's relationships with his American allies are so vital an element in the pattern of war which he was henceforward to follow, it should also be pointed out that the desert victories which, for the British, had been an occasion for ringing church bells were, seen from an American point of view, rather less remarkable. As they evaluated Alamein and the advance to Tunisia, many shrewd American minds detected a lethargy and caution which fitted in ill with their own native urge for the forceful, the violent, the energetic. It did not matter if their evaluation was as faulty as Eighth Army's verdict on First Army's performance. What they thought was what mattered. As they would put it, they tended to cut Montgomery down to size.

The clear decision at the Casablanca Conference that Sicily rather than Sardinia (which had many supporters) should be the next target triggered off a sequence of events which only concluded on 12 May with a final invasion plan approved by the Combined Chiefs of Staff. This left a mere two months to the estimated D-Day, 10 July, a date fixed to suit the variant degrees of moonlight required by the different services. But there were good reasons for this lapse of time. The surrender of the Axis forces in Africa did not take place until 13 May—though the end of April, it will be remembered, had been the target date. Following the decision at Casablanca the Combined Chiefs of Staff nominated Eisenhower, on 23 January, as Supreme Commander of HUSKY, with Alexander as his Deputy, Admiral Cunningham as Naval Commander and Tedder as Air Commander. Eisenhower was told to create a special staff, with its own Chief, to plan and prepare. Alexander was put in overall command of ground operations. This lead to the establishment of a central planning agency set up at Algiers on 12 February, with Major-General Gairdner (whom we last met at Alamein as commander of the unfortunate 8 Armoured Division) as co-ordinator. The subordinate commanders were nominated by Eisenhower on 11 February and the agreement of the Combined Chiefs of Staff was received two days later: on land the men were Montgomery, to lead the Eastern Task Force, known initially as Force 545 but in fact the Eighth Army, with two Corps, 13 and 30; and Patton, whose Western Task Force, Force 343, consisted of 2 U.S. Corps, under Omar Bradley, which was ultimately to be upgraded to 7 U.S. Army. The two Task Forces were to operate under the direction of Alexander's H.Q. which, during the planning phase, was known as Force 141 but later became 15 Army Group by the simple mathematics of adding together the numbers of its two armies.

A consideration of the names and dates listed above suggests immediately that though the appointments were excellent the planning of HUSKY had delays built into it from the very beginning. The African campaign was in its last critical stages, and until collapse became a certainty men like Alexander, with his 18 Army Group; Montgomery with Eighth Army; Patton with 2 U.S. Corps; Bradley, Patton's Deputy; and Tedder with his many responsibilities were all deeply involved in a shooting war. Planning had thus to be delegated to representative staffs who had responsibility without power—that power to decide and dictate which, in the British military system, resides only in the office of commander. In the American army the system differs, in that a staff officer acting in a commander's place is deemed to assume his authority. (Montgomery, it will be remembered, adopted a somewhat similar system within his own army in August 1942, when he appointed de Guingand his Chief of Staff with plenary powers.) But in operational planning it is usually essential that the man who is going to run the battle is identified with the planning at the earliest possible stage: otherwise, and generally for sound reasons, the field commander is liable to insist upon changes, major or minor, which may throw right off gear a carefully calculated scheme. This was about to happen to the plans for HUSKY. When we come to examine the planning for OVERLORD, the invasion of N.W. Europe, it will be seen that matters follow a similar and almost inevitable course. Almost, because first-class fighting commanders of the most senior ranks tend to be few, and there is a reasonable likelihood that the man you want to lead in the next action is still engaged in finishing off the last one.

There were other causes of delay. The divisions to serve with Eighth Army in Sicily had to be assembled from the following sources: 1 Canadian, England; 51 Highland, Tunisia; 78 Division, Tunisia; I Airborne, Tunisia; 7 Armoured, Tripoli; 5 Division, Egypt-Palestine-Syria; 50 Division, Palestine-Syria; 231 Infantry Brigade, Palestine-ex-Malta. In addition, the H.Q. of the High Command, the most senior operational commanders, the sister services and the administrative centres were scattered along the African shores in Algiers, the N. Tunisian front, Cairo, Malta, Sfax and Sousse. It hardly needs to be pointed out that with all the benefits of modern communication the integration of an army and the concerting of agreed plans is not improved by such a dissipation.

And those concerned, it must be remembered, were new to the game, for all their manifold experience. What was being prepared was to be the first opposed Amphibious Operation since Gallipoli. New techniques, new equipment would be required—the last-minute arrival, for example, of the American amphibious trucks, the D.U.K.W.s, made a tremendous difference to off-loading of stores over open beaches. Crews for landing craft (for whose training Combined Operations H.Q. in England had made wise preparations) needed to be brought to key pitch for what would be their first active experience. The use of airborne forces was contemplated: so pilots of tug-planes and paratroop-droppers also needed to perfect their skills, especially as most of the pilots of the planes normally had other functions. (It will be seen how failure in this vital matter led to tragedy.) All these were problems the Americans shared, along with many others.

There was, for example, the fundamental question of Intelligence: and at the heart of that lay the question whose answer would predicate success or defeat—how many and what kind of Germans were or would be on the island? Here there was a novel difficulty. In a land battle patrols beyond the front line, prisoners, and many other attainable indications make it usually possible to form a picture of the opponent's strength and dispositions. Now touch had been lost and No Man's Land was the sea. But Tedder was co-ordinating an extensive and extended effort in the air which, among its other benefits, made possible a complete and detailed photographic survey of the 10,000 square miles of the island. It was also necessary to scrutinise carefully some 300 miles of coast to establish which beaches were and which were not suitable for landings. This study revealed that 36 could be counted as possible (of which 26 were in fact used): but it was thought that only two offered all the appropriate facilities. Thus two main needs—the capture of a port or ports, and efficient air cover—were dominant in the planners' thoughts. Some ingenious methods of obtaining information were devised. For example, a mathematical formula was invented to establish the slope of a beach. A calculation of the distance between the wave-crests under certain wind conditions, as revealed in air photographs, gave the answer. And careful censorship at the Cairo traffic-centre of the mail distributed to 700,000 Italian prisoners-of-war considerably aided the process of building up an enemy order of battle.

I have pencilled in this general background to indicate how Montgomery was now but a cog in a very large wheel. Still, he was a very large cog! This became plain as soon as he was free to devote concentrated effort to the project. The staff H.Q. of his Force 545 began to operate in Cairo on 22 February (Patton's opened at Rabat a day later). The man chosen to head this staff was Major-General Dempsey, who had been brought out from England to take over the redundant 13 Corps H.Q. which, it will be remembered, remained as a rump when 13 Corps' divisions were distributed at Benghazi. No longer a rump, 13 with 30 Corps was to form the British section of Alexander's Army Group of Sicily. Dempsey, later to command the British Second Army from Normandy to Germany, was a man Montgomery had long wanted at his side: equable and efficient, loyal without hero-worship, he was an admirable foil to his commander. Dempsey, therefore, dealt with the first phases of the Army planning until in mid-April de Guingand, released from the demands of the battle-front in the west, could take over as Chief of Staff in Cairo and free Dempsey to apply himself to the particular problems of 13 Corps. Shortly before his death Dempsey, a man not given to overstatement, told me that in his opinion the part Montgomery played in evolving the final plan for HUSKY was his finest hour. How could this be?

The British and American planners did not begin with a blank sheet of paper. As early as 1941 the possibility of an invasion of Sicily as an exploitation of success in the great CRUSADER offensive had been examined—and dismissed. Then in November 1942 the British Chiefs of Staff proffered an outline plan, so that when Eisenhower after Casablanca received his directive as Commander-in-Chief he was given with it 'a Memorandum setting out the various considerations and the outline plan for the operation which formed the basis for this study . . .' Because of the current pre-occupations of the senior officers involved, Eisenhower circulated this plan (insufficiently studied by himself) not so much as a commander's fiat as a tentative blue-print which could serve as a basis for discussion. From this act, inevitable in the circumstances and in view of the time factor (Churchill was vociferous for a D-Day in June!), much confusion flowed, making HUSKY a dubious example of how to plan a major Amphibious Operation involving two allies.

The embryonic Chiefs of Staff scheme might be called 'the Ports-and-Airfields plan'. It was founded on certain assumptions later proved false. A glance at the map of Sicily (p. 144) reveals three port areas: Messina on the straits in the N.E., ruled out as a target because of its proximity to the mainland and the impossibility of air cover; the Syracuse-Catania-Augusta complex in the S.E.; and Palermo in the N.W.—the relative daily intakes being Messina 4,000–5,000 tons, Syracuse 1,000 tons, Catania 1,800 tons, Palermo 2,500 tons. The plan plumped for Syracuse and Palermo, the Americans to take the latter and Montgomery the former. Air supremacy would be essential, but apart from the large forces available from Allied airfields it was assumed that some of the main island fields would be rapidly seized. Put summarily, this initial plan meant that three British divisions were to make separate landings along 100 miles of coast, while Americans came ashore 60 miles to their west: after that, on D + 2, the Americans would land again in the N.W. to take Palermo while 140 miles away the British landed at Catania. As part of the operation British and American airborne forces were to be dropped on various airfields.

It will be seen that inherent in this plan was a high degree of dispersion of effort. Slight changes, but important ones, were proposed by Alexander— no splitting of divisions unless essential, use of parachutists to capture beach defences rather than airfields—but in substance the plan was approved in principle by Eisenhower on 13 March. It was not, however, approved by Montgomery. Dempsey alerted him, and Montgomery signalled to Alexander 'in my opinion the operation as planned in London breaks every commonsense rule of practical battle-fighting and is completely theoretical. It has no hope of success and should be completely recast.' His glove was in the ring. From this point until the emergence and acceptance of a final plan the debates are continuous and tortuous and the movement of the spokesmen is confusing. But the salient considerations are clear enough. Montgomery was convinced that the nub of the matter was a successful seizure of the S.E. corner of Sicily, containing the Catania-Syracuse-Augusta ports; that this could only be ensured by a proper concentration of force; and that if this meant the sacrifice of plans for taking other ports and airfields, it was just too bad. Finally, by the beginning of April, it began to look as though some compromise might emerge if the British could produce out of the hat one more division with the necessary shipping.

It is at this point in time that an element of comedy enters the scene. The Deputy Prime Minister, Mr. Attlee, on 13 April minuted to Churchill: '. . . have we anyone of directing mind and commanding will-power directly in control of the joint planners? Should not their deliberations be directed to essentials by some ruthless and forceful personality?' No better description than this could be given of what Montgomery was actually *doing*—and it is in this, I take it, that Sir Miles Dempsey perceived an outstanding achievement. The essentials, in Montgomery's view, were Catania and concentration, and with a ruthless singleness of purpose he pressed the deliberations of his peers to the point where his view prevailed. His 'commanding will-power' was ready to offend American susceptibilities, to increase a distaste for him on Tedder's part which had begun in North Africa, and even to be insolent to Alexander. The sad thing was that a right-minded plan seemed to be emerging from a swollen head. Already on 23 March he had stated 'Army Commander intends to throw cloak of 8th Army name and prestige over operation and therefore intends use as many his own veteran Divisions as possible, also 8th Army name not Eastern Task Force.' On 23 April, as we have seen, he was able to leave Enfidaville and fly down to Cairo for discussion with de Guingand and his staff. By this time seven plans had already emerged, and none satisfied Montgomery. On the 24th he sent Alexander a long message which contained three essential points. 1. All planning was suffering because everyone was trying to make something of a plan they knew could never succeed. 2. Montgomery insisted on making his own Army plan. 3. Eighth Army must land between Syracuse and, in the south, the Pachino peninsula. 'I am not,' he added indifferently, 'able to judge the repercussions of this solution on the operations as a whole.' These, when examined at a meeting called by Alexander at Algiers on the 29th, seemed formidable. Tedder rejected the plan on the ground that it left uncaptured far too many airfields and air supremacy could not be guaranteed. Cunningham felt that because of this the off-shore shipping would be unprotected against air-strikes. Alexander thought the basic idea was sound from an army point of view. Eisenhower now asserted his right, and called, on 2 May, a summit conference. The upshot was that Montgomery put forward a radical new scheme whereby the Americans would abandon the idea of attaining Palermo in the early stages, and instead land along the south coast at Gela, while Eighth Army landed as he had already proposed. In the end this was the plan adopted for the invasion of Sicily.

It was probably the best: Montgomery deserves great credit for grasping the simple essentials and refusing to budge. And in the event, as will be seen, the fears of Tedder and Cunningham proved quite unjustified. But there was a serious flaw. Montgomery had propounded his case with an unfortunate arrogance—or so it was felt. Moreover, sound though his plan was, it reduced the efforts of the Americans, in the early stages, to that of a minor rôle. Here was their big chance to prove their coming of age and to show that they had digested the lessons of Tunisia. Patton was not a man for the second rank. Thus there was, inevitably, a wounding of susceptibilities. Eisenhower was fully aware of this, and it is yet another example of his dedication to a common cause rather than to narrow national interests that he accepted Montgomery's plan. Indeed, after mature consideration he still maintained in 1948, when he came to publish *Crusade in Europe*, that his decision to invade with British troops moving against the eastern coast and Americans against the eastern part of the southern coast was correct.

It was important that the decision should be correct and that Montgomery's rigidity was soundly based, for the venture, as Sir Arthur Bryant points out, was of an extreme complexity unmatched even by the TORCH operations. 'It involved transporting in more than two thousand ships, under an escort of twelve hundred naval vessels, including eight battle-ships and two aircraft-carriers, a force of 160,000 men with 1,800 guns, 600 tanks and 14,000 other vehicles. These had to be carried through waters heavily mined, guarded by U-boats, a powerful battle-fleet and German and Italian air forces operating from shore airfields, to storm open beaches and conquer an island defended by more than twice as many troops, a substantial part of them German.' Actually, the Italian fleet could be virtually ignored as a menace. As to the threat from the air, the very simple answer is that fears enunciated during the planning stage proved unfounded in fact, and that Tedder, deploying a mass of over 4,000 aircraft, neutralised the Mediterranean airfields within striking distance of the island while on the island itself, on 10 July, there were only two fields in action and 50 per cent of the enemy airforce had left. There remained the men to be met on the ground. Early in July there were 200,000 Italian troops, half from four normal divisions and the rest from coast-defence formations, and 32,000 Germans (excluding *Luftwaffe* technical staff). The Germans consisted of 15,500 in the Hermann Göring Panzer Division and 16,000 in the 15th Panzer Grenadier Division, both scratch new formations recreated under the names of famous African divisions. But Montgomery was absolutely right in brushing aside all theories that the defences of Sicily would fall at a push. He spelled his views out in plain language in his signal to Alexander of 24 April: they form the third paragraph of his message from Cairo.

3 Planning to date has been on the assumption that resistance will be slight and Sicily will be captured easily. Never was there a greater error. Germans

and Italians are fighting well in Tunisia and will repeat the process in Sicily. . . .
We must plan for fierce resistance, by the Germans at any rate, and for a real
dog fight battle to follow the initial assault.

This prescience was justified in the event: by 13 July Hitler had decided
to thrust two more German divisions in to Sicily, and a Corps H.Q. under
General Hube, an experienced Panzer Corps commander from Russia.
Moreover, control and defence of the Messina straits was fully 'Germanised',
and steadily but quite intentionally the Germans, as the fighting progressed,
took over direction of the fighting and, particularly important, of the evacuation. Kesselring, as German overlord in the South, came to Sicily as early as
the end of June and imposed his views on the local Italian commander,
Guzzoni. The result was that Montgomery was faced, in the south-east
sector, by a 16 Corps which contained the Napoli and Livorno Divisions,
sundry smaller units and, last but not least, the Hermann Göring Division
plus an infantry group from 15 Panzer, whose armour was held further west.
This force was likely to increase rather than diminish.

Wind and sea were unfriendly when the Eighth Army landings began in
the very early hours of 10 July. But Montgomery's requirement was fulfilled:
the Royal Scots Fusiliers of 5 Division took Syracuse the same evening. It
was the same story on the front of 30 Corps further south in the Gulf of Noto.
The Americans had a rougher passage. Their landings along the southern
shore exposed them to the effects of wind and water, while resistance from
the shore was more active and some troublesome air attacks occurred. Nevertheless, the day's end saw all three divisions of their assault force ashore and
established. But within a story of deceptive success is concealed that of some
tragic losses. For example, the capture of Syracuse was made possible by 1
Air Landing Brigade, which dropped around the Ponte Grande, a bridge over
the river Anapo just south of the city. When the brigade left Kairoan during
the night of 9/10 July it was 2,075 strong. 69 gliders fell in the sea. 56 more
were scattered over 25 miles of ground beside the Gulf of Noto. Only 12
landed at the right place, and from 0630 on the 10th 87 men had to hold the
bridge until relieved by the advancing 5 Division. In this operation 252 men
of 1 Air Landing Brigade were drowned. A drop of 82 U.S. Airborne Division
inland from Gela was a similar fiasco. 3,400 men set off from the Kairouan
area: about three companies were dropped on the objective. Though play
was made about the distraction caused to the enemy by small groups of armed
and resourceful men suddenly appearing over a very wide front, the truth is
that even at this stage of the war the British and American knowledge of the
techniques of airborne operations was minimal. The training of pilots of both
tow-planes and gliders required more attention: the lesson had to be assimi-
lated that it is useless to ask an airborne armada to follow a complicated route;

and, as a further disaster in the Sicily campaign was to demonstrate, it is fatal to send such an armada over your own fleet by night, even though the ships have been warned to hold their fire. A good many, though not all, of the lessons of Sicily had been learned by the time of the Normandy landings.

If Messina is the gateway to Italy, Mount Etna, with its foothills and volcanic central mass, is an imposing threshold. Rearing up to the north of the Catania plain, it dominates the whole of the north-eastern corner of the Sicilian triangle. To take Messina one must pass by Etna, if approaching from the south or west. But though this geographical necessity was clear enough on any map, the plan for HUSKY did not make sufficiently plain how, once the landings had been made, Messina was to be reached. Montgomery in fact says that 'there was no master plan' and that 'the army commanders developed their own ideas of how to proceed and then "informed" higher authority'. By this Montgomery really means that, fighting in an area of his own choosing, he was brought to a standstill while Patton, having been denied Palermo, proceeded not only to capture it but also to precede Eighth Army into Messina. If there was no master plan for exploitation of the landings Montgomery could hardly complain, since he had been instrumental in devising the first stage of the operation, in spite of intense opposition.

Alexander knew what he wanted; 'the next thing to do was to split the island in half'. So also thought Montgomery, who signalled to Alexander on the 12th: 'My battle situation very good. . . . Suggest my Army operates offensively northwards to cut the Island in two.' But to do this, in Montgomery's view, entailed using 7 U.S. Army as a sort of static flank-guard. Patton had larger ambitions, and by the 13th already had his eye on Palermo. But that evening Montgomery signalled Alexander, who had just returned from a visit to Patton during which he had given permission for a limited forward move. This signal was to cause great affront. It arose from Montgomery's appreciation that availability of good roads was a necessity for a commander operating in the broken, hilly Sicilian countryside, and that there were only two good roads which offered possibilities for Eighth Army. One was Route 114, which ran roughly northwards past the eastern flank of Etna; this he proposed to exploit with 13 Corps. The other was Route 124, which, running in a north-westerly direction via Caltagirone-Enna-Leonforte, would enable him to by-pass the Germans in the plain of Catania. The only flaw was that Route 124 lay inside the American zone, and was intended by Bradley to provide for his 2 Corps an axis precisely the same as Montgomery intended to develop. All was made more uncomfortable by the fact that the British beat the gun: 51 Highland were discovered by the Americans on Route 124 during the evening of the 13th. This was followed at midnight by a *diktat* from Alexander, instructing Bradley to hand the road over to Montgomery.

Alexander seemed to Patton and Bradley to be rubbing salt into their wounds. Montgomery's advocacy had led to a revision of the plan for HUSKY which down-graded the 7 U.S. Army: now he was proposing, with Alexander's connivance, to rob them of a precious route and to enter Messina in triumph while the Americans were even denied Palermo. Patton was a soldier, and Patton obeyed. But it is in a wry mood that Bradley, in *A Soldier's Story*, describes how, long afterwards, Patton and Montgomery were discussing this episode and how, when the former complained of the injustice that had been done to him, Montgomery replied, 'George, let me give you some advice. If you get an order from Army Group that you don't like, why, just ignore it. That's what I do.' This from Montgomery, the arch-enemy of what he called 'belly-aching'! What he was proposing to Patton was, of course, a mode of behaviour that struck right at the roots of the American Army tradition, in which an order from a higher authority is sacrosanct.

Yet, as so often in war, hindsight presents the surrender of Route 124 in a very different light. Neither Montgomery's hopes nor the Americans' fears were to be realised. In the east German resistance stiffened steadily, under the remote control of Hitler who, via Kesselring, exercised his will. This modulated through stages, from an initial demand that the enemy be hurled back into the sea to a final decision that a bridgehead should be maintained in N.E. Sicily, behind which German and the more loyal Italian troops could be evacuated to the mainland. Hube would be in control. The main defence line or *Hauptkampflinie* was to run in a curve from San Stefano on the northern coast via Nicosia and Agira and Catenanuova to a point on the eastern coast six miles south of Catania. Two further 'lines', the 'Old Hube Line' and the 'New Hube Line', were envisaged as positions on which to dwell as the bridgehead inevitably contracted.

What this meant was that victory in Sicily, instead of becoming progressively easier, became progressively more difficult. The enemy was evolving a clear-cut plan and was concentrating in country both marvellously suited for defence and so broken and trackless that there was no scope for British armour. As General Jackson puts it in *The Battle For Italy*, 'It looked very much like Wellington's Lines of the Torres Vedras in Portugal': and the Lisbon in the situation, the straits of Messina, had as overseer the efficient Colonel Baade, who as Commandant, Messina Straits, (to which post he was appointed by Kesselring on 14 July), organised under central control a very powerful anti-aircraft and anti-naval defence system. Alexander saw what was foreshadowed. Montgomery was moving sluggishly down both his axes, and the Deputy Commander therefore informed the C.I.G.S. that he proposed to drive for Messina via Catania with 13 Corps, to send 30 Corps west of Etna to the coast at San Stefano and then turn it back on Messina, and then, and only then, to release the Americans for an advance on Palermo. Alexander, in fact, wanted to pressurise Montgomery and grasp Messina before the Germans so solidified their line that they could reinforce behind it from the mainland, and even attempt a breakout and counter-offensive. These plans he issued as a directive to his Army Commanders on 16 July. It gravely wounded the Americans.

'It confirmed my earlier suspicion,' writes Bradley. 'Only Montgomery was to be turned against Messina.' Patton, confident that he too could reach Messina, resented an assignment which seemed to leave him the soft end of the island to tackle. 'There was no glory', Bradley puts it, 'in the capture of hills, docile peasants, and spiritless soldiers.' When next day Patton was ordered to maintain his movement to the north and to cut the coastal road, one of his staff crystallised in a a phrase the feeling at 7 Army's H.Q 'And then,' he said, 'we can sit comfortably on our prats while Monty finishes the goddam war.' Patton was not one for sitting comfortably. He sounded his four divisional commanders and then flew to have it out with Alexander. He sought, primarily, a brief to go for Palermo: and Alexander, weighing up the situation, gave it to him. Yet theoretically the Eighth Army remained the chief striking force, and by the two axes running through Catania and Enna Alexander expected its divisions to reach the straits. Optimistic messages from Montgomery nourished this hope: on the 12th he hoped for Catania on the 14th, on the 16th he expected 'to get Catania tonight'. He had almost consistently advocated no more than a holding rôle for the Americans. Yet in so doing he deceived himself and misled Alexander.

All the same, there were no rational grounds for expecting what followed. Patton was known to Alexander and Montgomery not as the man who executed the brilliant cavalry charge across France in 1944 or the man whose Third Army, during the Ardennes campaign, carried out almost overnight a 90-degree change of front before rushing to the relief of Bastogne. The Patton of the Sicilian campaign was the man under whose new command the 2 U.S. Corps had greatly improved: but as yet he had shown no real signs of being a Sherman. This capacity he now began to demonstrate. The dates speak for themselves. On 22 July Patton's 'Provisional' Corps entered Palermo. The previous day Montgomery had accepted local defeat, by ordering 13 Corps to change to the defensive in front of Catania, and deciding to make his main effort on the left with 30 Corps. This his weary troops could only sustain if 78 Division were called in from the reserve in N. Africa —a movement which could not be completed before the end of the month. On 25 July Alexander held a co-ordinating conference at which 2 U.S. Corps was now given the task of driving eastwards. By 27 July the Americans had taken San Stefano and Nicosia, while the Canadians of 30 Corps, coming up from the south, had taken Agira. 15 Army Group was thus poised on the edge of the *Hauptkampflinie*: but since 26 July this line had acquired a new significance. Mussolini had been sacked.

The Germans now came fully out into the open in Sicily, taking over everywhere, whereas so far there had been a certain amount of tactful control from the background. Hube on 27 July was ordered by Kesselring to prepare for evacuation: and this, as swiftly but as safely as possible, is what the Germans now contrived. On the British front there was a steady forward movement which by 5 August brought 13 Corps to the neck of land between Etna and the sea, and 30 Corps to the delaying foothills on the other side of the volcano. But Montgomery had to fight hard to the end, even returning to the line 5 Division which had been withdrawn to prepare for the entry into Italy. Commandos from Eighth Army finally entered Messina during the evening of 16 August—to be received by 7 Infantry Regiment of 3 U.S. Division! For Patton had kept his men moving down the north coast, by leap-frogging units and trying the occasional, though usually abortive, amphibious outflanking operation.

What of the enemy? Allied air-power, massive though it was, could not disrupt evacuation to any important extent. The figures for the bombing sorties over the Messina area during the relevant few days are misleading, in the sense that they can give an impression of an overwhelming weight of metal dropped on a fleeing army. This is far from exact. Much damage was done to many shore installations, but it is extraordinarily difficult (as was to be learned in 1944 at the Seine crossings) to stop a determined enemy from passing over a waterway. The truth is that Hube withdrew both his men *and* their heavy equipment. The Germans made up their losses from the Italians; and General Jackson observes that most German units re-entered Italy more mobile than when they left for Sicily.

The campaign itself brought Montgomery few laurels, though it is mainly due to him that it was launched on the right foot. At the time, Eisenhower remarked, there cropped up the usual criticism of Montgomery's 'caution'— because he had not made a headlong assault on the Mount Etna defences. This is nonsense. Such critics should be asked to serve a few weeks in the torrid, dusty Catanian plain and then get up and advance on a German parachute unit settled into positions skilfully chosen in hillside crevices. A real 'Eighth Army set-piece attack' was hardly on administratively, and would certainly not have been an operation of war. The critic, by the way, would probably have had malaria. The figures for Sicily are:

Losses by	7 U.S. Army	Eighth Army
Malaria	9,892	11,590
Battle	8,375	9,000 approx.

Eisenhower's considered judgement, after subsequent discussion with Alexander and Montgomery, was that 'I believed then, and I believe now, that a headlong attack against the Mount Etna position, with the resources available in the middle of July, would have been defeated.' But, knowing what is now known about Patton's ability to maintain the momentum of a mobile force, it might be asked whether Eisenhower, Alexander and Montgomery were not all wrong in failing to observe that Montgomery in Sicily created something very like the strategic pattern he designed for Normandy, but in reverse. If, as soon as the possibilities became evident, Montgomery had taken upon himself or been ordered to draw to the east the maximum amount of opposition, and Patton had been given the task of breaking loose in one of his power drives at the earliest possible moment, the Sicily campaign might have had a different complexion. It was a victory, certainly: but within the victory lurks a defeat, in that too many Germans got away.* For Montgomery, briskly though he writes about it in his *Memoirs*, and applauded though it was at the time, it was, after Africa, a *diminuendo*.

In the high drama which now followed the over-running of Sicily and the subsequent Unconditional Surrender of the Italian people Montgomery had only a minor part to play: in the first act, and in a rôle which hardly allowed of a *bravura* performance. (It is a fascinating war-game, for example, to consider how Montgomery would have dealt with the problem of Cassino.) This no doubt partly explains why a certain acidity enters into his account of his share of the Italian campaign, and why his brief annals seem to be largely composed of the text of his letters and messages. 'We proposed to invade the mainland of Europe without any clear idea how operations were to be developed once we got there. The decision precisely where we were to land in Italy was not firm till the 17th August, the day on which the campaign in Sicily ended. So far as the Eighth Army was concerned I was to launch it across the Straits of Messina on the 30th August, but was given no "object".' When he published those words in 1958 Montgomery well knew the reasons for a lack of clarity in the concepts behind the invasion of Italy and an apparent dilatoriness in setting the assault in motion. From the strictly limited, strictly military point of view of an Army Commander he is of course absolutely right. But consider the situation from Eisenhower's lonely eminence. The Casablanca Conference in January had agreed on an invasion of Sicily. The TRIDENT Conference in Washington in early May, where future developments in the Mediterranean were on the agenda, had in the end given

---

* The respective casualty figures for Sicily are Italians some 132,000 (mainly prisoners of war); Germans some 32,000; and Allies 31,158. The O.K.W. figure on the 18th of Germans evacuated was about 60,000; roughly 75,000 Italians also got away. The Germans also evacuated 9,605 vehicles, 47 tanks, 94 guns and 17,000 tons of ammunition. For the allies it was not, as Churchill used to say, 'a fair cop'.

Eisenhower no clearer guidance than 'to plan such operations in exploitation of HUSKY as are best calculated to eliminate Italy from the war and to contain the maximum number of German forces'. Even at the Quebec Conference, QUADRANT, in August, an agreed Anglo-American policy was only squeezed out in the vaguest terms. The reasons for all this are a commonplace—the persistent disagreement on strategic fundamentals between a strong American faction, headed by General Marshall and to a large degree supported by Roosevelt, who put a cross-Channel invasion first and feared to be drawn into political entanglements in the Mediterranean, and an equally strong British faction, headed by Churchill and Brooke, who in the traditional British way sought to destroy Germany by 'knocking away the props', were lukewarm about a re-entry into the Continent from the north, and saw political advantages, especially vis-à-vis Russia, in the pursuit of operations along the northern shores of the Mediterranean. This was Eisenhower's dilemma: the Italian policy which emerged from these debates was a political compromise, and political compromise may produce for the soldier a short-term Object, but rarely provides a long-term Objective. Indeed, the only long-term objective about which Eisenhower was certain from TRIDENT onwards was that he would have to surrender from Italy seven seasoned divisions by 1 November at the latest, for future use in OVERLORD.

Confusion was worse confounded by the imminence of an Italian surrender. Between 31 July, (when two emissaries were sent from Rome, one to Lisbon and one to Tangier, to make preliminary contact with British representatives) until 8 September (when the surrender was at last announced) negotiations proceeded *sub rosa* amid so many complicating factors and with so much obscurantism on the Italian side that it is not surprising that Eisenhower found it difficult to give his subordinate commanders a clear lead. Nor is it surprising that a multitude of plans proliferated, each intended to insert an Allied force into some portion of the Italian south. There was GOBLET and SLAPSTICK and MUSKET and FIREBRAND and BRIMSTONE and BUTTRESS and GIANT I and GIANT II and AVALANCHE and BAYTOWN. The significant survivors of this plethora were the last two. AVALANCHE was the code-name for an assault landing to be made at Salerno on 9 September by General Mark Clark's Fifth Army with the port of Naples as an objective. It was to be preceded by BAYTOWN, and that was Montgomery's affair.

It was appropriate that Clark's Army drew close to Salerno as the fact of Italy's surrender was being broadcast to the world, while Montgomery's Army set forth during the early hours of the day on which the Italian negotiator, General Castellano, put his signature to the actual terms. That day was 3 September, and the hour 0430, when hundreds of shells began to whine across the straits of Messina. They came from the massed artillery of 30

16 *Before D-Day: a salute for the dockers*

17 *Warming up the factories before the invasion*

18 *Normandy : with Croker*

Corps, given extra weight by the inclusion of 80 medium and 48 heavy guns on loan from Patton's 7 U.S. Army. 15 warships simultaneously bombarded the defences of Reggio at the southern end of the strait, while inland heavy bombers made their contribution. All this was the grand overture to BAY-TOWN, whose purpose, after much protest about lack of orders, Montgomery obtained from Alexander in a handwritten note on a half sheet of paper on 20 August. It read:

> Your task is to secure a bridgehead on the toe of Italy, to enable our naval forces to operate through the Straits of Messina.
> In the event of the enemy withdrawing from the toe, you will follow him up with such force as you can make available, bearing in mind that the greater the extent to which you can engage enemy forces in the southern tip of Italy, the more assistance will you be giving to AVALANCHE.

It was to this end that the guns were firing on the morning of the 3rd (it pleased Montgomery to be returning to the European mainland on the anniversary of the outbreak of the war) and that some 300 landing craft and ferries were transferring to the further shore, in what was almost a gala mood, 5 Division and 1 Canadian Division of 13 Corps. But in fact there was little to be cheerful about. There had been no concerting of plans with Mark Clark, and in any case Montgomery's supply arrangements were apparently based on the assumption that his Corps would make a pause on the Catanzaro neck, the narrow strip of land, some 60 miles north of the straits, which separates the gulfs of Squillace and Sta Eufemia. It was also something of an anti-climax to find that all the protective fire had been wasted: there was no German in sight. 29 Panzer Grenadiers had been in the area, but had withdrawn two days previously. It was not in fact men but demolitions and difficult roads that proved a hindrance. Nevertheless, by 10 September the Catanzaro line had been reached, a creditable move of 100 miles in seven days in the face of great difficulties.

The arrival was timely, for Clark's divisions at Salerno were in grave danger. Indeed, on that same afternoon Alexander signalled to Montgomery emphasising the urgent need for him to maintain pressure on the Germans to relieve AVALANCHE. Montgomery did what he could in the circumstances. He was genuinely short of administrative transport; the two roads down the flanks of the toe, which had been the axes for his two Divisions, were not of the highest quality; the Eighth Army was not on top priority for shipping supplies from Sicily; and, finally, one obvious step for him was to take and make viable the airfield at Crotone to enable more fighters to go in at Salerno. He therefore pushed light forces forward as far as they could go; captured Crotone with the Canadians on the 11th; and prepared 5 and 1 Canadian

M

Division for further action. At the same time he had to take over responsibility for Taranto, where 1 Airborne Division landed on the 9th and made a small bridgehead, adequate enough for it to be planned that 8 Indian Division, coming from Egypt, should land there. Montgomery also felt able now to order forward from Sicily the veteran 78 Division.

It cannot justly be maintained, as it sometimes is, that Montgomery crawled to the aid of Clark. Using the same technique of amphibious 'hooks' as he had employed when advancing up the toe, Montgomery had 5 Division at Auletta and 1 Canadian at Potenza by 19 September. Even so, the supply lines were severely strained. A major move by Eighth Army did not seem possible before 1 October, by which time a second Corps H.Q., 5 and 8 Indian Division would have reported in. But in the meantime Montgomery continued to push down the east side of Italy, soon to become Eighth Army's private territory, and with a group called Force 'A', consisting of elements of 78 Division, armour, and some Special Air Service troops, on 27 September drove German paratroops off the vital Foggia airfield complex.

From now on the story of Eighth Army's activities in Italy under Montgomery is one of steady advance from one river to the next. The first main obstacle was the Biferno. This was neatly outflanked by a Commando landing by which Termoli on the Adriatic was captured undamaged, harbour and all, on the night 2/3 October. Further inland 78 Division made a bridgehead which Kesselring in person ordered to be eliminated: but it held, after fierce fighting, and the same problem presented itself as the Germans withdrew northwards behind the line of the river Trigno.

Here the Eighth Army met the realities of the Italian front. First, the north bank of the Trigno was the Adriatic end of the Bernhardt Line; and 20 miles north, resting on the river Sangro, was the Gustav Line, with Cassino at its heart; and behind these would be other lines culminating in the great Gothic Line, the Germans' last redoubt before the Alps. All these lines would be stoutly manned and formidably armed: and when one was taken there would always be another. Secondly there was the weather. General Jackson, evidently writing with some feeling, says: 'Even under summer conditions the road network in southern Italy was barely adequate for two armies of some 11 modern mechanised divisions. Given the demolition of practically every bridge and culvert, add water in gushing torrents from each river and rivulet, churn up the improvised crossings over them with tanks and heavy vehicles and you have a morass where roads used to be. The task of the engineers became impossible while it lasted. There was only one answer—wait till it stopped—but few commanders were willing to do so.' It was in such conditions that Montgomery gathered together his Army and stock-piled supplies for the Trigno battle, and it was in thick mud, and cold, and drenching rain, that his divisions forced from its positions on the further bank the German 76 Panzer Corps.

The Eighth Army was now organised into two Corps. 5 Corps lay on the right, with its flank on the Adriatic, and contained 78 and 8 Indian Divisions. The rested and reformed 2 New Zealand Division was now in Italy, and was brought forward to Foggia by Montgomery to act as an Army reserve. Across the Trigno were 16 Panzer, opposite 78 Division; 1 Para Division opposite 8 Indian; while 26 Panzer opposed 13 Corps on the British left, and the 65 Infantry Division constituted a German reserve behind the Sangro. Montgomery's plan was inevitably simple. 13 Corps put in a distracting attack on Isernia, engaging the attention of 26 Panzer, while the main thrust was made on the sea flank by 78 Division, strongly supported from the sea and the air. The river-banks became mud, and movement for vehicles was only possible on a road. The Germans had skilfully fortified the characteristic mountain villages. The infantry found digging in the rocky ground very difficult, and had to revert to sangars,* while mules were increasingly employed for carting equipment and serving outposts. All this would become the elementary grammar of mountain war in Italy, but here was not the setting for a tutorial. Nevertheless, by 19 November the Eighth Army was over the Trigno and in possession of the south bank of the Sangro. Its next hurdle was the Gustav Line.

The battle for the Sangro and its hinterland was Montgomery's last in Italy; the first stage in the battle for Rome (though the city was not to fall till the following June); and a step forward in the co-ordination between Fifth and Eighth Armies, since the Sangro attack was to be followed by a northward thrust on the allies' western flank, including an amphibious landing south of the Tiber which won ultimate fame as Anzio. Unfortunately, though this was the first major 'Montgomery-type' operation in Italy, it was doomed to frustration from the start—through no fault of its commander. Subsequent months were to prove that since Hitler had adopted the optimistic policy of Kesselring (to hold as tightly as possible south of Rome), rather than the pessimistic policy of Rommel, (to fall back on the Alps), there was no method by which the Anglo-Americans could achieve a clean break through the mountain fastnesses other than a manoeuvre on the largest possible scale, involving good weather, the combined forces of both Armies, elaborate and successful deception, and the unobserved concentration of a superior mass at the right place and at the right time. This was finally achieved in 1944 by Operation DIADEM which gave the Allies Rome just as the OVERLORD landings were due. But in Italy no smaller scheme, even at Army level, could make

* Self-protection attempted by building up bits of stone above the ground where the ground was too hard to burrow beneath the surface: a technique developed on the N.W. Frontier of India.

more than a penetration which was bound to be sealed off. Already this had become evident: the Sangro battle would prove the case.

With the Eighth Army commanding the escarpment which formed the south bank of the river the Germans, in their normal style, only held the three miles or so of flattish ground on the northern side with light posts. Their chief line of defence was along a ridge, Li Colli, which ran inland from Fossacesia by the coast through Mozzagrogna to Santa Maria and Casoli. It then followed amid high ground the E/W Route 84 to Castel di Sangro and Alfredena. On their 40 miles of front the Germans had four divisions (and all the advantages of ground). For the attack Montgomery had five, including the fresh New Zealand Division: but his infantry was now very weary, and officers in particular were well below strength. It is worth remembering, for example, that during the last six months 78 Division had sustained 10,000 casualties.

Nevertheless, 78 Division was to go in again, for the pivot of Montgomery's plan was an attack by 78 and 8 Indian Divisions of 5 Corps along the coast. This made sense in that here was the route Montgomery would in any case have to control to bring forward the supplies and munitions necessary for the hoped-for advance. On their flank, but some 15 miles away, ran Route 81, parallel to the coast road, down which the New Zealanders would attack on the axis Casoli–Chieti. 13 Corps, finally, were to make it obvious that they were apparently about to attack towards the line Castel di Sangro–Alfredena. Preparations were elaborate, since in his usual way Montgomery had been working out well ahead what would have to be done. Constant and aggressive patrolling was carried out nightly over the river—no easy task, since the fields either side are sodden and the height of the river can oscillate alarmingly according to the amount of rain or snow in the mountains. The historian of the Royal West Kent Regiment gives a vivid account of one battalion's purgatory. A 'Patrol Master' was instituted to co-ordinate activities and reports. About 60 men were out nightly, on mine-clearing, protecting engineer and tank reconnaissance parties, drawing enemy fire so that positions could be pin-pointed. Each patrol was interrogated on return and a large panoramic map of the battalion front was gradually compiled. Sometimes it was necessary to swim the river to start a patrol, and always necessary to wade (and it was winter). In this battalion several men were drowned on patrol duty. More ambitious endeavours included a wireless deception scheme aimed to suggest that Montgomery's Tac. H.Q. had moved west to 13 Corps' area. 1 Airborne Division, about to return to England, mounted embarkation exercises to imply an amphibious hook directed at Pescara. And the Alamein trick was used of concealing the growing dumps on 5 Corps' front and emphasising with dummies the 13 Corps' administrative points and gun-sites. For the attack itself the usual massive air support and artillery programme were planned. The target date was 20 November.

But . . . 'Thenceforward the weather rapidly deteriorated. Heavy rain frequently continued for two days, only to be followed by one or two further days of drizzle and mist. Snow was falling in the mountains and the state of the country became wet and very muddy.' So Montgomery describes the days before the main operation—days during which the Sangro could rise or fall as much as six or seven feet in 24 hours. And it was in such conditions that the preliminary moves were attempted, the New Zealanders, the Indians and 78 Division all seeking a secure foothold. But this was not easy when, as during the night of the 23rd, a flood could rush down from the mountains and sweep away three strenuously established bridges, or when an Indian brigade could make a successful advance only to be cut off by rising floods in its rear. It was not until the 29th that the situation improved, with Mozza-grogna captured, and by the evening of the 30th Li Colli was wholly in the hands of 5 Corps. Now, after re-shuffling to give 78 Division a rest, Montgomery chose as his next two targets Ortona further up the coast, for 5 Corps; and Orsogna on the left of the line for 13 Corps. The Canadians had patrols in Ortona on 20 December, but it was in the hands of 3 Para Rgt. of 1 Para Division, and the regimental commander was a past-master at street fighting. So there followed a whole week of battling from house to house before the Canadians in the end compelled their brilliant opponents to retreat, neither side presumably realising that they had assisted in what, for all future compilers of military textbooks, would be a model example. The New Zealanders, however, in spite of armoured support had only been able to nibble at Orsogna, and the German defences held firm until gradually the sounds of battle died away and Montgomery, in effect, accepted defeat.*

The German front had been heavily reinforced—that was one reason. But it was the weather (always, of course, the unsuccessful general's excuse) which truly undermined the whole project. On the New Zealand front six men were being used to carry one stretcher down the mountains: and nothing could better illustrate the inhumanity of the elements than Kippenberger's heart-broken account of how a platoon of his beloved New Zealanders, the veterans of Greece and Crete and CRUSADER and Alamein and a hundred other affrays, had to be court-martialled for refusing, when in the front line, to go into action. In 78 Division, during December, five men died from cold and there were 113 cases of exposure.

It was sad that Montgomery could not remain with them until the sun and the spring, the flowers in the fields and the hard going on the tracks.

---

* Those interested in unravelling the skeins of Montgomery's complicated psychology should note that the story of the Sangro battle is missing from his *Memoirs*.

Much distinction in Italy still awaited Eighth Army: but not under Montgomery. He was aroused 'very early in the morning' on 24 December to read a War Office signal instructing him to return to England to take over command of 21 Army group, the British force preparing its contribution to the Second Front. Montgomery found the news 'a relief and an excitement'. The cause for excitement is obvious. But the relief requires explanation. For reasons by no means wholly military (and this is not the place to expound them) the Allied situation in Italy on Christmas Eve 1943 was unpromising. In his eyes there was 'no grand design for the opening of a new theatre of operations; no master plan; no grip on the operations; a first class administrative muddle . . .' One remembers that letter to de Guingand in 1934—'I am not used to backing the wrong horse. . . .'

Farewells were a problem. The old Eighth Army of desert days had virtually vanished—50, 51 and 7 Armoured Divisions had preceded him to England. He first, on the 27th, flew over to Algiers to see his future Supreme Commander, Eisenhower, and Bedell Smith who was to remain as Eisenhower's Chief of Staff: and there he was told by Eisenhower that he was to be in complete charge of the initial fighting on land, while the American armies in England would fall under his control for D-Day and subsequent developments. They discussed the need for Anglo-American collaboration at staff level, (Montgomery had already sent a signal to the War Office about the members of his own staff whom he wished to take back with him). Then he returned to his H.Q. at Vasto, and in the Opera House faced 'a great gathering': and quietly departed.

But his mood was to remain neither quiet nor sentimental nor nostalgic, for his route back to England took him via Marrakesh, where Churchill was convalescing. On New Year's Eve the Prime Minister handed him the draft plan for OVERLORD—long ago established as the code-word for the invasion of Normandy. In spite of Montgomery's protests Churchill insisted on his reading it and formulating his first impressions. Earlier on that New Year's Eve Montgomery had been instructed by Eisenhower, a fellow guest, that he was unhappy about the plan, from what he had seen of it, and that while Eisenhower was in the States seeing Roosevelt Montgomery was to act as his representative in London during his absence and 'analyse and revise the plan and have it ready for him on his arrival in England about the middle of January'. Montgomery therefore excused himself at the end of dinner and retired to his room with OVERLORD. The typed report he handed to Churchill in his bed next morning can be summarised in one of its sentences:

'My first impression is that the present plan is impracticable.'

9

Overlord: the master plan

'Well, there it is; it won't work, but you must bloody well make
it.'
> C.I.G.S., (Sir Alan Brooke) to
> C.O.S.S.A.C., (Lieut.-General Sir Frederick Morgan)
> Spring, 1943

'As yet there is no immediate prospect of the invasion.'
> Field Marshal von Rundstedt,
> *Situation Report*, 5 June 1944

1,200 fighting vessels, 4,000 assault ships of various types and some 1,600 merchant craft were required to protect, deliver and supply the Allied soldiers who landed in Normandy on 6 June 1944, the D-Day of OVERLORD. Before the landings Great Britain carried such a surcharge of men and *matériel* that, as Eisenhower wrote, 'it was claimed facetiously at the time that only the great number of barrage balloons floating constantly in British skies kept the islands from sinking under the seas'. Over 3,500,000 troops from many nations had been crammed into the United Kingdom—of which some 1,750,000 were in the British army and 1,500,000 in the U.S. army and air force. There was also the staggering quantity of 13,000 aircraft—apart from thousands more for training and replacement, and apart, too, from 3,500 gliders. Yet all this array was but the end-product of the extensive and unparalleled efforts which had made the assemblage possible. How far back must one trace the roots of OVERLORD's strength? Certainly to BOLERO, the immense trans-shipment of American man-power across the Atlantic: and certainly to the victory, during 1943, in the battle of the Atlantic which made BOLERO possible. The great Anglo-American assault on all aspects of German air-power, including the increasing missile threat, was also a vital contributory factor to OVERLORD's easement, while the divisions struggling northwards through Italy, and thus drawing more German forces into Italy itself and the surrounding Mediterranean lands, also played their valuable diversionary part. And in other ways that were manifold—the inventors, the subverters, the deceivers, the resisters —what might be called the pre-fabrication of OVERLORD had long been under way. It is hardly possible, one might think, to detect within this vast complex of continuous activity the specific contribution of a single man.

In Montgomery's case, nevertheless, such an assessment can be made with ease and accuracy for two sound reasons. The first derives from the character of the man: his native gift for striking to the heart of a matter and lucidly and summarily expounding his reasoning and intentions was not only invaluable, during the first five months of 1944, in identifying correctly the tasks for his Armies and putting across to them their duties—it also greatly aids the historian of the period, because all that Montgomery thought and said and did is definite and intelligible. As in the old days of his Staff College lectures, there is not a shadow of doubt as to his meaning. This was no small achievement, for many of the discussions and debates of the time—especially those between the British and the Americans—are shrouded in a penumbra of indecision and uncertainty.

The second reason, of course, is that Montgomery himself *was* the heart of the matter. After all the forecasts and calculations and head-scratchings of the Planners there always comes a moment, when, in a famous phrase of Army folklore immortalised by Lord Wavell, 'Private Snodgrass must march straight to his front.' At H Hour of D-Day many thousands of men would have to march or sail or fly straight to their front, and it was for this climacteric moment that the laborious months of preparation, the pouring out of millions of pounds and dollars on munitions, the sacrifice and the study had been devoted: to make D-Day succeed. Montgomery, under a directive issued by Eisenhower on 10 March, was 'responsible for planning and for the command of all ground forces engaged in the operation until such time as the Supreme Allied Commander allocated an area of responsibility to the commander of the United States First Army Group' . . . which in effect meant that until 1 August, when Patton took over in Normandy the American Third Army and Bradley assumed command of the American Twelfth Army Group, Montgomery had entire responsibility, under Eisenhower, for the land battle: and it was the land battle which, in the end, was of predominant importance. Thus in every sense, direct or indirect, whatever was said or done about OVERLORD affected Montgomery and his command. During the ratification and execution of the Master Plan for D-Day it was he, in the last analysis, who was master.

The proposals for OVERLORD which Montgomery peremptorily, and rightly, rejected as he examined them in his bedroom at Marrakesh on New Year's Eve had already been subjected to much stern scrutiny. They had been passed by the British Chiefs of Staff before the QUADRANT Conference at Quebec in mid-August 1943, and there, after much discussion, the Combined Chiefs of Staff registered that 'We have approved the outline plan of General Morgan for Operation OVERLORD, and have authorised him to proceed with the detailed planning and with full preparations.' Churchill had also agreed, though the soldier in him made him very properly declare that 'every effort should be made to add at least 25 per cent to the first assault', and also that there should be landings, additional to those proposed, on the eastern beaches of the Cherbourg peninsula known as the Cotentin. What was under consideration, and what failed to convince Churchill, Eisenhower and Montgomery was a recommendation that the crucial Anglo-American invasion of western Europe should take the form of 'an assault across the Norman beaches about Bayeux' with an initial frontage of only three attack-divisions. Nobody at the time pointed out, so far as I have been able to trace, that for this vital enterprise it was suggested (and accepted by the supreme military authorities in the form of the Combined Chiefs of Staff) that the wall of Fortress Europe might be breached by a force smaller than that considered necessary to make the first impact across the beaches of Sicily and Salerno. How had such a meagre plan emerged? And why was it called General Morgan's outline plan?

Its ancestry reached back over many years, and its parentage was multiple. One can observe its embryo, for example, in that amateur landing exercise carried out in 1938 by Montgomery's 9 Brigade at Slapton Sands, (where in 1944 many troops were to train in disembarkation for Normandy): one can sense the spirit behind it in the words of a famous minute:

Prime Minister to General Ismay   V.VI.40
'. . . The completely defensive habit of mind which has ruined the French must not be allowed to ruin all our initiative. It is of the highest consequence to keep the largest number of German forces all along the coasts of the countries they have conquered, and we should immediately set to work to organise raiding forces on these coasts where the populations are friendly . . .'

The decisive turn in the plan's history, however, occurred in January 1943 when, at the Casablanca Conference, it was established between the Anglo-American leaders that preparations for a cross-Channel assault should be actively pursued, and that to this end there should be appointed a staff drawn from both the allied armies, with a British Chief of Staff and an American Deputy. Pending the appointment of a Supreme Commander, which was to be deferred, the principal officer would be entitled 'Chief of Staff to the Supreme Allied Commander (designate)'. On 1 April Lieut.-General F. E. Morgan was nominated to this post, with Brigadier-General Ray W. Barker, an American officer with a deep understanding of the British, as his Deputy. Morgan soon reduced his unwieldy title to COSSAC, and it was by this self-generated code-word that his swiftly expanding empire was usually known. 'The business premises of the firm consisted of a room we had found unoccupied in Norfolk House, and I regarded it as an omen that this was the room in which I had first met Ike Eisenhower. The equipment consisted of a couple of desks and chairs we found in the room, and we were lucky enough also to find a few sheets of paper and a pencil that someone had dropped on the floor.' Territorial demands increased as COSSAC got to grips with their directive, which after discussion was refined into an instruction from the Combined Chiefs of Staff of 25 May 1943, giving as the object of OVERLORD 'to secure a lodgement on the Continent from which further offensive operations could be carried out'. A supplementary directive allocated five divisions to be immediately loaded for the assault, with two more for a quick follow-up, plus two airborne divisions for D-Day. 20 more divisions were to be available for the build-up. But COSSAC's staff calculations established that the shipping then allocated for OVERLORD could sustain an initial attack by no more than three infantry divisions—and that on a reduced scale of equipment. These were the strengths which, through no fault of COSSAC's, were embodied in the plan which the Prime Minister showed to Montgomery at Marrakesh.

Morgan and his team were fully conscious that they were working on a basis of inadequate resources—in men, in shipping, in planes for the airborne auxiliaries, in techniques and equipment for supply over open beaches. 'It won't work, but you must bloody well make it' was no recipe for victory. And in all these calculations Morgan was aware of the gravest deficiency of all— the lack of a designated Supreme Commander, and a land commander of recent battle experience. As to the latter, he had to deal with General Paget, who from July 1943 commanded the British 21 Army Group, composed of the Second British and First Canadian Armies: the invasion force. Paget had done a superb job, as is recognised in all quarters, in supervising the training in England of the men who would shortly cross to France: but he was not Montgomery.

Indeed, it was Montgomery's recent practical experience in Sicily and Italy which, at Marrakesh, directed his eye immediately to the basic flaw in the COSSAC plan. The second paragraph of the hurried memorandum which he delivered to Churchill in his bed on New Year's Day, 1944, was of such significance that it must be quoted in full.

2 The initial landing is on too narrow a front and is confined to too small an area.

By D + 12 a total of 16 divisions have been landed on the same beaches as were used for the initial landings. This would lead to the most appalling confusion on the beaches, and the smooth development of the land battle would be made extremely difficult—if not impossible.

Further divisions come pouring in, all over the same beaches. By D + 24 a total of 24 divisions have been landed, all over the same beaches; control of the beaches and so on would be very difficult; the confusion, instead of getting better, would get worse.

My first impression is that the present plan is impracticable.

Churchill said 'he had always known there was something wrong in the proposed plan, but that the Chiefs of Staff had agreed with it and that left him powerless. Now a battlefield commander had analysed it for him and given him the information he needed—and he was grateful.'

A battlefield commander—that is the point. What had passed the Chiefs of Staff (the Americans, no doubt, in their anxiety to start crossing the Channel and the British, perhaps, because in their hearts they were still bound to the Mediterranean and wanted to retain a northern Second Front only as an option) had been pounced on immediately by the man who would have to fight the battle: on the Johnsonian principle of 'Depend upon it, Sir, when a man is to be hanged in a fortnight, it concentrates his mind wonderfully.' It is improbable that even Eisenhower, in spite of his known reservations about the plan, would have been able to lay his finger on it and say '*That* is what is wrong: and *this* is what we must do'. As will be seen, as soon as he got to London Montgomery followed up his diagnosis with swift and surgical activity: from that moment the presence of the Supreme Commander's plenipotentiary, a man who could order, and demand, and if necessary browbeat, gave a new impulsion to the whole elaborate mechanism of the preparations for D-Day.

Perhaps even more important than the question, '*What* to land?', was the question '*Where?*' A satisfactory answer to this strategic fundamental could only be the sum of a series of answers to secondary, but each in its way all-important, queries. What ports could be taken for maintenance of supplies? Where could the vitally necessary fighter cover be ensured? The landing beaches proposed—would they be of the right consistency and gradient, and would the tide table be right? If you got on to a beach, could you get off it— *exits*—and what sort of country would lie in the hinterland? Good or bad for deployment so as to spread the beach-head and make room for the build-up? Flooding—if so, where? Could forward airfields be rapidly established? And where was the enemy? In what immediate local strength, and with what capability of reinforcement? How exposed were his communications with the battle-area to interdiction by bombing and sabotage?

Shortly after Montgomery's arrival in London a presentation by COSSAC of the plan in its latest form was staged for himself and de Guingand. This made clear how much study had been devoted to all these points, and indeed Eisenhower's verdict on Morgan in *Crusade in Europe* can stand: 'He had in the months preceding my arrival accomplished a mass of detailed planning, accumulation of data, and gathering of supply that made D Day possible.' But of course Morgan himself, when he took up his post early in 1943, entered into a vast miscellaneous scatter of major or minor studies made by units large and units small ever since the evacuation of France in 1940. There was, for example, the original and energetic activity of Combined Operations H.Q. There was all the groundwork which preceded the Dieppe raid in 1942 —for the name Dieppe had not just been picked out of a hat. A single instance beautifully illustrates the organic growth of such researches— recorded by Donald McLachlan in his book on Naval Intelligence, *Room 39*. 'It is a striking coincidence in the history of NID 6,* that the stretch of French coast about which they made in June 1940 their first primitive beach report was the same that they later studied and described down to the finest detail for the Normandy landings of June 1944. The skimpy collection of photographs pasted on to brown paper of folio size, linked with text, was to become the elaborate and beautifully produced work, in thousands of copies, of a University Press.'

Of all COSSAC's legacies possibly the most valuable was the result of a continuous study carried out for many months before Morgan received his directive by a group loosely named 'the Combined Commanders'. This embodied Paget as C.-in-C. Home Forces and, at various times, the Air Officer Commanding-in-Chief, Admiral Sir Bertram Ramsay, Eisenhower, Mountbatten and other lesser lights. Under them a planning staff 'summarised among other things an exhaustive collection of information on the nature of the whole seaboard from Holland to the Bay of Biscay'. This survey took into account every imaginable factor which could affect an assaulting army and its opposition. And though when Morgan first addressed his COSSAC officers he said, 'The term "Planning Staff" has come to have a most sinister meaning—it implies the production of nothing but paper,' nevertheless the final document handed down by the Combined Commanders was far more than *paperasserie*. Entitled 'The Selection of Assault Areas in a Major Operation in North-West Europe', it dismissed the notion of a multi-point attack and, as a considered by-product of its careful topographical review, nominated the Baie de la Seine in W. Normandy as the best target for a *Schwerpunkt*. Around this core COSSAC's thinking coalesced, and it was onto the shores of the Baie de la Seine that the plan bequeathed to the Supreme Commander and Montgomery proposed to launch the three assaulting infantry divisions with their airborne accompaniment.

Montgomery's reaction to the plan, now that it had been presented to him in fuller detail, was still highly critical. He did not dispute the choice of target, but before settling for it he ordered a further review of the possibilities for landings in Brittany and on both sides of the Cotentin. This conclusively demonstrated that the Baie de la Seine was preferable, and henceforward it remained a constant. It was known as the NEPTUNE area, since NEPTUNE was the codeword for the actual assault on D-Day: and I will now continue

* NID—abbreviation for Naval Intelligence Division.

to use it in this special context rather than OVERLORD, which had wider implications. (Incidentally, Sir Arthur Bryant, commenting on Alan Brooke's wide-ranging amphibious strategy, calls him 'Neptune's General'; in all the circumstances a name, surely, more directly applicable to Montgomery!)

The radical flaws in the plan, to Montgomery's way of thinking, were the extent of frontage, the weakness of the assault, and the faulty arrangements for command. He therefore proposed to extend the frontage for D-Day so that it ran from the area at the base of the Cotentin, north of the Vire estuary, to the eastern side of the river Orne. This entailed an attack by two armies side by side, 21 Army Group on the left with three divisions in line, First U.S. Army on the right with two divisions. The original plan had proposed that all the landings should be controlled by one Corps or Task Force H.Q. The Montgomery-modified plan (which also included a drop of 6 British Airborne Division beyond the Orne and 82 and 101 U.S. Airborne Divisions on the far right) thus produced what was at once a stronger and a simpler structure. The increase in strength is obvious. Greater simplicity was achieved because the two national armies would each have its own area of entry and exploitation, to which its supplies and reinforcements could flow without confusion. It worked out well, as a matter of convenience, that the Americans should be *en bloc* on the right, since their troops were massed in the western part of the United Kingdom and it was at Cherbourg, whose early capture was anticipated, that men and materials sailing direct from the United States would be offloaded. Moreover, the pattern of attack was now such that individual Corps would control their own beach areas, which immensely simplified the problem of ensuring a smooth flow of follow-up and build-up units. Finally, this pattern also meant that there was now available a normal chain of command from Montgomery to the Army Commanders and through them to Corps and Divisions. NEPTUNE, in Montgomery's language, was now 'tidy'. Of course the new ideas were not all his own: Bradley, for example, was equally anxious about there being an airborne operation on his flank, and Morgan, as has been seen, would ideally have gone for greater width if his resources had allowed. Montgomery was simply in a much stronger position to stake out a larger claim, having Eisenhower behind him and occupying, himself, a post of assured authority. Still, there was something characteristic in that he made his plan in the light of military logic and then took it for granted that the extra resources would somehow be produced. The assumption was, of course, enormous: but it was aided by the agreement to the revised plan of Admiral Ramsay and Air Chief Marshal Leigh-Mallory, who were respectively responsible to Eisenhower for naval and air matters, and in whose fields the greatest shortages were evident.

There was no grave problem about extra divisions, either for an enlarged assault or a bulkier build-up. But ships and planes were a difficulty.

To make it possible to drop within the 24 hours of D-Day the three airborne divisions now postulated for NEPTUNE meant that 200 more troop-carrying aircraft would have to be available; and available, in England, two months before D-Day. Moreover eight extra fighter squadrons were necessary to provide top cover for the additional convoys and the extended battle-zone. These requirements were met with greater ease than Admiral Ramsay's.

Immediately on Eisenhower's arrival in England to take up, formally, his post as Supreme Commander the Revised Outline Plan was submitted to him by his three subordinates, on 21 January, and approved by him. His acceptance was ratified by the Combined Chiefs of Staff—and now NEPTUNE and OVERLORD began to look like realities. There was a Supreme Commander with his headquarters (called Supreme Headquarters Allied Expeditionary Force or, more comfortably, SHAEF: located, by Eisenhower's firmly expressed wish, outside London—at Bushey Park. It should have been at Bushey Heath, near to the H.Q. of the Air Commander-in-Chief at Stanmore—but the American Engineers got the address wrong!) There were Commanders-in-Chief for the three arms, air, sea and land, all appointed and all functioning. There was a practical plan. Everything was beginning to look workmanlike and promising—except for a paralysing shortage of shipping. This was Ramsay's headache.

At the conference on 21 January, and in forwarding his recommendations to the Combined Chiefs of Staff on the 23rd, Eisenhower took at least two steps which showed that he meant business as the supreme authority. First, he accepted responsibility for rejecting the powerfully argued case put up by his Air Commander-in-Chief, Leigh-Mallory, for abandoning the idea of dropping airborne forces west of the inundations at the base of the Cotentin peninsula. Leigh-Mallory claimed that the German flak was so strong in these parts that a loss of up to 75 per cent in planes and personnel must be contemplated. Montgomery both disagreed with Leigh-Mallory's forecast and reiterated his requirement, in which he had Bradley's support: for only in this way, they felt, could the Americans capture the crucial port of Cherbourg without unacceptable delay. Eisenhower backed Montgomery and Bradley against Leigh-Mallory—thus, as will be seen, laying up further trouble for himself before NEPTUNE was consummated. His other decisive act was, in view of the shortage of the shipping essential for the new plan, to recommend to the Combined Chiefs of Staff immediately that NEPTUNE should be delayed a month and, moreover, that ANVIL should be converted into a threat rather than developed as a fighting operation.

To mention ANVIL is to refer to one of the most controversial issues* that distracted the British and American war directorates between Pearl Harbour and VJ Day. Much of the story has no direct bearing on Montgomery's history, but in this special matter of NEPTUNE its influence was crucial. ANVIL was the code-name for a landing by, it was estimated, two divisions in the south of France, designed to mesh in with the OVERLORD operations further north. Strong arguments in its favour, such as the capture of Marseilles as an entry-port for divisions piling up in the States, concealed a fundamental fact—the dislike of the Americans, and particularly Marshall, for an involvement in Italy. The immediate point was that ANVIL required landing craft, and if ANVIL coincided with NEPTUNE it would be impossible to switch such craft from the Mediterranean to the Channel to make up at least some of the huge deficiencies with which the planners were now faced. For in effect, as a result of Montgomery's enlargement of the front of attack, Admiral Ramsay needed some 150 extra minesweepers, 240 warships, and 1,000 landing craft.

The British Navy was already fully stretched. As late as the Cairo Conference in December 1943 it had been confirmed that for OVERLORD—the confirmation relates, of course, to the still unmodified COSSAC plan—Britain should supply all the warships and of the 3,323 landing craft required the United States were only to produce 1,024, or 5 per cent of American strength in this field at the end of 1943. British shipyards had long been overworked: there was no available slack. Indeed, to honour the existing OVERLORD commitment the building of a fleet carrier, four destroyers and 14 frigates, all urgently needed, had been postponed for three months so that 75 extra tank landing craft could be constructed. The upshot of intense and extended argument (bedevilled by an important technicality, a difference between the British and U.S. planners about the potential load of a landing craft) was in the end satisfactory—but only just. The postponement on 1 February, by the Combined Chiefs of Staff, of D-Day for OVERLORD from 1 May to 31 May made possible a further month's output of craft. And on 25 February they agreed that ANVIL *might* have to be postponed to aid OVERLORD; but it was not until 24 March that a final decision was taken to defer ANVIL until OVERLORD was so well established that craft could be returned to the Mediterranean. In a sense, however, this long debate, not finally resolved until *ten weeks* before NEPTUNE happened, was wholly unnecessary. (Montgomery himself, buoyed up during these months by a supreme and infectious confidence, was probably not over-burdened by it, strong as he was in the faith that all would be well. But the uncertainties, indecisions and changes of front

* The connoisseur of such controversies will find of interest the 'Memorandum from General Ismay to the Prime Minister on 28th April, 1944, concerning the Discussion on OVERLORD and ANVIL, January–April', printed as Appendix VII in John Ehrman, *Grand Strategy*, Vol. X, H.M.S.O.

taxed to the uttermost the endurance of his and Bradley's subordinate staff, daily concerned with those minute and multitudinous calculations on which the success or failure of an amphibious operation can depend: Montgomery has indeed put on record that many of his staff were exhausted before battle even began.) Yet this strain had been caused by a debate which was unnecessary; because there was no *Allied* shortage of the essential craft. Admiral King, the redoubtable C.-in-C., U.S. Fleet, records in his *U.S. Navy at War, 1941–1945* that on 1 May 1944 he had available 31,123 landing craft of which, and unwillingly, he had supplied 2,493 for OVERLORD. Granted the nature of the Pacific War, this still seems an extraordinarily disproportionate contribution of an irreplaceable piece of equipment by an ally who, consistently in theory if not always in practice, had adhered to the partnership's first priority—the elimination of Nazi Germany. If Eisenhower and Montgomery had been firmly appointed in the spring of 1943, at or about the time when COSSAC was set up, operational difficulties like this one might have been disclosed and fought over far earlier, with time to achieve a sensible resolution. For landing craft were not the only naval problem. To provide those extra 240 warships Ramsay needed, the Admiralty used every possible means, reducing escorts for Atlantic convoys, holding back ships for the Far East and recalling others from the Mediterranean, and so on: but it was not until 15 April that Admiral King brought relief by disgorging three battleships, two cruisers and 22 destroyers. The extra merchant shipping was produced with great difficulty, but no inter-Allied strain: the main burden fell on the British, since many of the ships had to be extracted from the coastal fleet which normally carried coal and other essentials.

From the preceding pages it will be seen how all these great debates and controversies,

> 'hi tanti motus atque haec certamina tanta'

impinged directly on Montgomery and his personal task, the success of the NEPTUNE landings and their prolongation into that substantial lodgement area in Normandy from which an all-out land offensive on Germany itself might be mounted. But, 'having got an agreed plan', he writes, '(or so I thought at the time!) I left the details to de Guingand and his staff and devoted my main efforts to ensuring that the weapons we were to use would be fit for battle'. Once again, in fact, he was employing the well-tested technique of concentrating on essentials and then letting his staff alone to work out details, while he, in turn, was left free for other matters. And so, in the spring of 1944, he set out to do what no other commander of a British expeditionary force has ever done: he embarked on an exhausting series of journeys which enabled him to show himself and explain his policies not only to a large

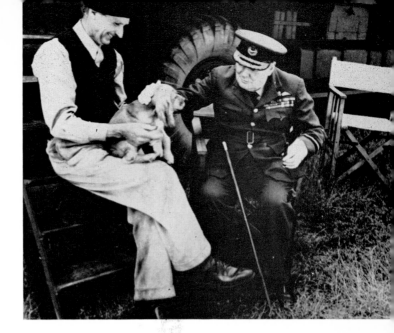

19 *Normandy : the Prime Minister visits the beachhead*

20 *Leaving Caen cathedral*

proportion of the troops whose lives lay in his hands but also to great numbers of civilians, especially the hardpressed workers in the factories. This was a carefully calculated operation. Having got his plan agreed, Montgomery decided that 'confidence in the high command by one and all was the next essential': to observe the necessity was, for him, to take the necessary action. By so doing, Montgomery increased the confidence of the army in itself and confirmed the confidence of the people in the army. Apart from Montgomery, no living Englishman in 1944—except Churchill—was capable of such a feat: certainly not Brooke, certainly not Slim, certainly not Paget, and certainly, for all his skills, not Mountbatten. What was required was a reputation, indeed, but also a sort of elemental simplicity of temperament which bridged the gulf between Brass Hat and Common Man; and a liking for the job. There is no doubt that Montgomery responded emotionally to the great demonstrations he received, and, like a true actor, was warmed by his audience.

This mode of self-presentation was, indeed, one which gave him much self-satisfaction, and increased a natural vanity which had developed slowly but dilated as manifest success bred assurance. There is, for example, a certain naive wonder in the passage in his *Memoirs* describing the short visit he paid to Cairo during the halt at Benghazi. When he read the lessons in St. George's Cathedral he 'created quite a stir'. 'It is a strange experience,' he comments, 'to find oneself famous and it would be ridiculous to deny that it was rather fun.' But when he visited London briefly before the Sicily operation his reaction when he was warned off attending a Thanksgiving Service in St. Paul's (on the grounds that his visit must be kept a secret) was an indication that he knew, *and knew that it was known*, that he was a man of unusual note. 'Yet to my delighted surprise, wherever I went I was followed by crowds. The incident made me realise that if I were pretty popular with a lot of people, I was not too popular in some circles. Perhaps the one explained the other.' The fact seems to be that Alamein released in Montgomery a previously pent-up desire to play to the gallery and a genuine ability to stimulate the gallery (or most of it) which had, until then, only found partial expression in his brilliant lectures and some of his more unorthodox training devices. However that may be, it is clear that in the months before D-Day his 'whistle-stop' tours, in spite of their value, did cause concern in a number of quarters. There was muttering in the Service Clubs. Even Churchill, who could never 'bear, like the Turk, a brother near the throne', was impelled on 19 January to minute to Ismay: 'It would seem to be about time that the circular sent to generals and other high commanders about making speeches should be renewed. . . . There seem to have been a lot of speeches and interviews lately.' And around Westminster some politicians began to scent a potential rival

Normandy : with the Beachmaster after landing on the shores of France

now busy building a platform for a future career. The last suspicion seems absurd in retrospect, though perhaps it had a little justification at the time. For with hindsight it is clear that, even had he wished to enter politics, Montgomery's post-1945 career demonstrates that this would have been a disastrous step for him to take. (That shrewd observer Lord Shinwell who was Secretary of State for War, 1947–1950, at a time when Montgomery was C.I.G.S., once remarked of that period: '. . . as a fighting general he was supreme, and as a man, a human being, forthright, honest beyond question. But as a politician—quite infantile.') In the United States there was a different situation. With their racial memory of soldier-politicians the Americans had good reason to ponder about the possibilities of 'MacArthur for President'. (They did, after all, get Eisenhower.) But in the wholly different British context, such fears about Montgomery were groundless. In any case, just as before Alamein, so now those incapable of understanding how to inspire the national army of a modern, sophisticated, democratic society misinterpreted Montgomery because of their own myopia about what he was trying to do before D-Day.

The method was simple. In 'Rapier', the specially equipped train which had been used by the Commander-in-Chief, Home Forces, he visited informally every one of the OVERLORD formations and calculated that, in so doing, he had talked, by the middle of May, to more than a million men, had looked at them and had been looked at by them; Americans as well as British and Canadians—and the exiles, the Free French, the Poles, the Dutch and the Belgians. He would usually inspect a parade of about 10,000, and after slowly walking past them, 'at ease' so that they could see as much of him as possible, he would stand on the bonnet of a jeep, call them round him, and quietly tell them what they were going to do, and why. Whatever the gentlemen in the clubs might splutter, there was a genuinely positive response on the part of his audience, which is well summarised in an unsolicited testimonial sent to him by Bedell Smith on 22 June. It was an excerpt from 'a report on attitude and state of mind of American troops in action'. The relevant passage read:

> Confidence in the high command is absolutely without parallel. Literally dozens of embarking troops talked about General Montgomery with actual hero-worship in every inflection. And unanimously what appealed to them—beyond his friendliness, and genuineness, and lack of pomp—was the story (or, for all I know, the myth) that the General 'visited every one of us outfits going over and told us he was more anxious than any of us to get this thing over and get home'. This left a warm and indelible impression.

His senior officers had a rather different form of induction. As early as 13 January he summoned to his H.Q. at St. Paul's school the generals of his armies, (Dempsey, Second British; Bradley, First U.S.; and Crerar, First Canadian, with Patton, Third U.S., whose troops were not in the first wave). Here he gave them—another of Montgomery's special terms—the 'atmosphere'. By this he meant his concept of the battle and the way he intended to run it. The conference might well be compared with Nelson's indoctrination of his Captains before Trafalgar, as described by him in a letter to Lady Hamilton. 'When I came to explain to them the "Nelson touch", it was like an electric shock. . . . It was new—it was singular—it was simple! It must succeed.'

This meeting was of considerable importance in another way. During discussion it emerged that certain rearrangements in the structure of a division were necessary for OVERLORD, and that though the War Office had been informed, nothing had happened. Montgomery agreed with his generals, and ordered that the changes be made immediately. But there were present some War Office representatives, who reported back to their masters this irregular action by a 'new broom'. The Secretary of State for War, Sir James Grigg, was of at least as strong and independent a character as Montgomery, and when he heard of the latter's action he was displeased. A displeased Grigg was a formidable animal. However, the pair had lunch together, Montgomery apologised but explained the urgency of all that he had to do, and a lifelong friendship was started. The importance of this episode was that in terms of 'the Establishment' Montgomery had done what, militarily, he always sought to do: he had created a firm base. Brooke as C.I.G.S. was his backer; the Prime Minister was more than favourably disposed; and now he had come to terms with the Secretary of State for War. The circle was complete—for even the King, though at first put out by Montgomery's idiosyncratic 'desert-type' turnout, and disregard for dress regulations, accepted them as the whim of a *grand chef*.

The soldiers Montgomery was seeking to invigorate by his inspections fell into three main types. 21 Army Group, the last major force that Britain's declining man-power could produce, summarised in its constitution all that had happened on land since the outbreak of war. There was 7 Armoured Division, many of whose officers and men had served since and even before Wavell's annihilation of the Italians in the 40/41 African campaign—and with them 50 and 51 Highland Divisions, veterans of the desert, of Sicily and Italy (though all three divisions contained, of course, new drafts); there was 3 Division which, like 50, had been blooded before Dunkirk—there was also a Highland Division in France in 1940, but its casualties were such that the Division which made a fresh start at Alamein was virtually a reconstituted formation; and there were divisions like 43, 15 Scottish or 11 Armoured which had been waiting and training back in England for years, but which, in Normandy and after, would prove themselves no less efficient or ardent than their more seasoned fellows. Montgomery endeavoured to spread the seasoning by a certain amount of cross-posting of old hands to less experienced units, a painful but sensible process. There was also a surgical excision of officers assumed, for age or other reasons, not to be battleworthy. (This, however, did not always work out according to theory: in my own regiment there was one comparatively mature officer so removed who was on parade to greet our follow-up division when it landed at Arromanches—he himself having been there with a Beach Group since D-Day!) Such excisions should, however, be seen in due perspective: by the end of August 1914 Joffre had already disposed of one Army commander, three out of 21 Corps commanders and 36 out of 83 divisional commanders.

Apart from the army, there was the people. Montgomery held a genuine conviction that a jaded and war-weary citizenry needed a tonic if the fighting spirit of his soldiers was not to be diminished by apathy or scepticism on the home front, and if the supplies and munitions for the battle ahead were to be restricted by langour in industry. (It is relevant here to note that the COSSAC team, when considering the question of propaganda and morale, recommended 'the early appointment to the British Army in England of some colourful personality who might impart the dynamism, that we judged to be in short supply, through the army to the people'. Following his own train of thought, Montgomery carried out COSSAC's requirement to the letter.) Under the aegis of the Ministry of Supply, therefore, he visited many factories, especially those where on overtime the workers were producing urgently required OVERLORD equipment. The theme was always the same: 'we were all one great army, whether soldier on the battle front or worker on the home front; their work was just as important as ours. Our combined task was to weld the workers and soldiers into one team.' This sort of thing sounds, after a quarter of a century, as banal as a speech at a school prize-giving: but it has to be evaluated in relation to the conditions of the day—and contrasted with the inability of the Services during the First World War to assist as effectively in applying dynamism during the Munitions Crisis.

Montgomery's domestic crusade took him to many a strange rostrum— strange, at least, for a soldier. On 22 February, for example, he spoke for one and a half hours at Euston Station to a broad cross-section of the railway workers, whose co-operation was so vital. 'When I had finished speaking, the Secretaries of the Trades Union pledged their full support.' On 3 March it was London Docks, where he talked to some 16,000 dockers, stevedores and lightermen. Then there was National Savings, with the 'Salute the Soldier' campaign whose high point was a Mansion House luncheon on 24 March at which the chief speakers were Grigg and Montgomery. 'I decided that my speech would be a call to the Nation to inspire the Army going forth to battle with the greatness of its cause.'

The indoctrination for OVERLORD culminated in the two-day exercise held at Montgomery's H.Q. on 7 and 8 April, attended by all the generals in the Allied armies, and a final presentation of the ultimate plan of action which was taken by Eisenhower, also at St. Paul's, on 15 May. Brooke's reflections, in later years, are revealing. 'A charming personality and good co-ordinator. But no real commander. I have seen many reviews of impending operations, and especially those run by Monty. Ike might have been a showman calling on various actors to perform their various turns, but he was not the commander of a show who controlled and directed all the actors. A very different performance from Monty's show a few days previously.' This was less than fair comment. It is a solecism for a dramatic critic to censure an actor for playing badly a part for which he has been wrongly cast. This was not Eisenhower's rôle to have at his finger-tips that microscopic knowledge of his mission which befitted an Army Commander. Very many large and varied matters came within his purview, and his essential function was, by sagacity and personality, to maintain an effective unity between the numerous divergent interests within his command. Montgomery, incidentally, thought better of him: 'Throughout the day Eisenhower was quite excellent; he spoke very little but what he said was on a high level and extremely good.' There was, however, little doubt concerning Montgomery's conduct of his own 'exercise'. 'A wonderful day,' was Brooke's reaction; and it is the general consensus that the Commander-in-Chief displayed to his senior subordinates a complete grasp of OVERLORD.

From the Army point of view, Montgomery explained, the NEPTUNE area fell into five separate parts or points of landing, each being distinguished by a code-name and allocated to a different formation. The second main step, after the accomplishment of NEPTUNE, would be further aggressive action to bind these parts together within a single beach-head. Reading from west to east the areas of assault were UTAH, 4 U.S. Inf. Div. (the Cherbourg peninsula, to the north of the Vire estuary); OMAHA 1 U.S. Inf. Div. (from UTAH's right flank to Port en Bessin); GOLD, 50 British Inf. Div. (from OMAHA's right flank to the river Provence); JUNO, 3 Canadian Div. (from GOLD's right flank to St. Aubin sur Mer); and SWORD, 3 British Inf. Div. (from JUNO to the river Orne). Two naval Task Forces, one for the American assault Army and one for the British, had been assembled and so sub-divided that each of the individual divisions moving in at H Hour would be supported by its own 'Naval Assault Force'. Air Support was to take so massive and multifarious a form that it can only be summarised here by remarking that on the day, operating to a carefully integrated plan, the number of heavy, medium and light bombers, fighters and fighter bombers, troop carriers and transports, Coastal Command planes, reconnaissance and air/sea rescue aircraft amounted to 5,510 British and 6,080 American, a grand total of 11,590. Such was the broad picture which Montgomery was able to present to his generals. But how were the landings to be exploited? Where, the generals might well have asked, do we go from here? Montgomery's answer was at once explicit and cautious.

It is best expressed in the words he used during the second presentation on 15 May. 'Last February,' he said, 'Rommel took command from Holland to the Loire. It is now clear that his intention is to deny any penetration: OVERLORD is to be defeated on the beaches. . . . Rommel is an energetic and determined commander; he has made a world of difference since he took over. . . . He will do his best to "Dunkirk" us—not to fight the armoured battle on ground of his own choosing, but to avoid it altogether by using his tanks well forward. . . . We must blast our way on shore and get a good lodgement before the enemy can bring up sufficient reserves to turn us out . . . we must gain space rapidly and peg out claims well inland . . . once we get control of the main enemy lateral Granville-Vire-Argentan-Falaise-Caen and have the area enclosed in it firmly in our possession, then we will have the lodgement area we want and can begin to expand.'

Such was the main intent, which, thickened up by descriptions from Ramsay and Leigh-Mallory of the support their Services would provide together with talks by Army Commanders and others, gave the audience a clear and definite objective—particularly when what has been quoted is taken in conjunction with two other statements of policy Montgomery made to his subordinates, one firm and one tentative. Each of these was subsequently so misunderstood or so distorted that, as a result, the quality of Montgomery's leadership was called into question both in the press and, more importantly, at SHAEF and in Whitehall. Today it seems that the statements Montgomery made about his strategy and intentions are so crystal clear that only malice or stupidity could miss their meaning—statements, that is, issued well before D-Day to which, as the next chapter will show, his conduct of affairs after D-Day most closely conformed.

The first statement of policy related to the fundamental strategic idea round which the whole of the Normandy campaign revolved, an idea of such classical simplicity that for some it was incomprehensible and for others inadequate. Montgomery took the city and adjacent area of Caen as a pivot on which the whole of the Allied front must swing. The Germans *must* defend Caen fiercely, or endeavour to recover it if captured, for Caen was the chief communications centre in that part of Normandy. If, therefore, 21 British Army Group could attract and wear down the bulk of the German armour around Caen, this would enable the rest of the line to swing eastwards in ever-enlarging curves until finally 1 Canadian Army was lining the Seine north of Rouen, 2 British Army between Rouen and Paris, and the Americans from Paris southwards. It will be seen that this concept involved the British in a slow 'slogging match' with small territorial gains, while the Americans, once they had cracked the relatively light enemy crust, would have the opportunity for an impressive break-through which could send their armour hurtling eastwards. Chester Wilmot neatly observes that this policy should have been intelligible to the Americans, since in terms of their own Civil War it cast the British in the ponderous rôle of Grant, 'the apostle of direct approach', and the U.S. Armies in the more glamorous role of the hard-riding Sherman. Patton, who was to be galloper-in-chief with his Third U.S. Army, certainly seems to have understood Montgomery's intentions as early as the Army Commanders' briefing by Montgomery on 13 January, for de Guingand recalls that he was downcast at learning that he was not to get on the move in the opening phase; but 'when he heard what his task was to be—to over-run the Britanny peninsula and exploit the break-out by the First U.S. Army, he cheered up, and told us what he would do to those "Goddam sons of bitches." '

The second cause of confusion and misunderstanding was the 'phase line map'. This was a diagram produced by Montgomery's staff as far back as April.* It provided visually a broad forecast as to how the bridgehead would expand. Curved lines across the blank landscape of Normandy and Brittany showed the estimated points of advance by $D+17$, $D+20$, $D+25$, $D+35$, $D+60$, and a final position at $D+90$ which set the Armies along the length of the Seine as described above. The danger of such maps is that they are essentially professional tools which, if misused, can do damage. They have two sound purposes. Every commander planning an operation must have a rough idea, at the least, of where—taking into account all possible mischances —he may get to as his attack progresses. Phase maps are thus useful for such a commander (with all the possible mischances in his mind) as a diagrammatic representation of his hopes. But they can obviously mislead those unaware of the many possibilities of things not going to plan which are daily present in the commander's head. (Perhaps the symbol used in commercial correspond-ence should be stamped on all such maps—E. & O.E., or 'Errors and omis-sions excepted'.) A phase line map in fact represents a rational estimation of a possibility, rather than the committal of a cast-iron guarantee. As such, it is of great value for those responsible for the difficult task of logistical fore-casting. A yardstick, however frail, is better than nothing as a basis of

---

* See diagrams 1, 2 and 3 reproduced on pp. 357 and 359 of L. F. Ellis, *Victory in the West*, Vol. I, H.M.S.O. These are simplifications of the more detailed map, which can be found as Map 2 in Montgomery, *Normandy To The Baltic*, Hutchinson.

measurement. The trouble was that not amateurs but highly placed professionals were, later on in OVERLORD, to take the qualified predictions of the phase lines as absolute promises. Montgomery's own view was that 'while I had in mind the necessity to reach the Seine and the Loire by D+90, the interim estimates of progress could not, I felt, have any great degree of reality'.

Mentioning Rommel in his mid-May address, Montgomery singled out the man who by his defensive policies was both to cause the Allies much inconvenience and concern, and also to play right into their hands. The diagnosis Montgomery delivered of how Rommel would react on D-Day was proved correct in the event—and this is not surprising, because the diagnosis of Rommel's general philosophy in 1944 was also precise—'not to fight the armoured battle on ground of his own choosing, but to avoid it altogether by having his tanks well forward'. Montgomery acknowledges the importance of this evaluation of Rommel's intentions by Brigadier Williams, his Chief Intelligence Officer. 'If Rommel failed to "see us off" on the beaches, he would try to "rope us off" in the bocage': this was the method employed by the German command in Normandy, and when Rommel was put out of action by wounds in mid-July it was far too late to make a change. As a method of opposition, it fitted like glove to hand with Montgomery's method of attack. Yet things might have been otherwise. Rommel, after his African experiences, was wholly despondent about the possibility of armoured manoeuvre without air superiority. He saw the irrecoverable weakness of the *Luftwaffe* in western Europe, and therefore, as the Commander responsible for the Netherlands, 15 Army between Ostend and Le Havre, and 7 Army between Le Havre and the Loire, stood out with some success for his system of armour-behind-the-beaches against the joint view of von Rundstedt, the Commander-in-Chief, West, and Geyr von Schweppenburg, the general commanding Panzer Group West, who both wished to employ the orthodox method of holding the panzers well back, *en masse*, and striking solidly and decisively when the main point of thrust had been identified.

But it was other aspects of Rommel's defensive plans which were more disturbing. Since his Army Group B took over responsibility for the northwestern coasts of *Festung Europa*, Rommel had applied his exceptional energy and resourcefulness to improving the inefficient condition of what the cynical von Rundstedt had described to him as a 'Propaganda Wall'. The rate of inland mine-laying was tripled, some five to six millions being laid before D-Day. Reconnaissance photographs of potential dropping-zones showed that what were nick-named 'Rommel's asparagus-beds' were increasing alarmingly; these were forests of large stakes driven into the ground in close proximity and capable of ripping the bottom out of a glider. Most disturbing of all, however, were the signs of intensive activity on the foreshores.

From February onwards it became evident that obstacles of various shapes and sizes were being established on every possible landing beach. Study revealed that they fell into several groups—'hedgehogs', which were seven-foot-long steel girders so fastened together that they offered a set of sharp points on which a landing craft might impale itself; 'tetrahedra' a ton in weight; stakes with mines or shells to be exploded on impact, and other variants. The emplacement began at highwater mark and proceeded steadily seawards till by June the half-tide mark was being approached. The problems presented to the captain of a landing craft during the last seconds of his run-in were thus enormously increased: but these were as nothing compared with the fundamental issue now raised for Montgomery and his naval advisers. All the months and years of preparation, planning, production would be put at hazard by what happened to a few thousand men at the time they were disembarking, assuming their craft had come through, and until they were safely ashore. Considered dramatically, the margin was as narrow as that. No landing—no follow-up. No follow-up—no build-up. No NEPTUNE—no OVERLORD. If highwater mark was chosen for disembarkation, almost certainly a high proportion of craft would be holed. If lowwater mark, then equally certainly there would be a new Gallipoli as the infantry made their way over the beaten zone of open beaches swept by German fire. Weighing up all the factors, which included the strong request by the Navy (based on Mediterranean experience of supported landings) for a daylight phase as early as possible, to allow of observed fire, Montgomery settled for an H Hour between three and four hours before high water and some forty minutes after 'nautical twilight'—an abstruse concept which is established by the presence of the sun twelve degrees below the horizon. Moreover—and this was to prove a brilliant decision, as was revealed at the time by their presence or their absence—Montgomery decided to bring in the floating or D.D. tanks immediately on the next wave, to provide the closest possible fire support for the infantry when they were most naked.

This was a vital question to which a sufficient answer was found. But to answer the larger question raised by these hectic activities was less easy, because the data were less easy to assemble. Had the Germans finally selected Normandy as the most likely area for the invasion which they had every reason to anticipate? There were several ways of attempting a reply; the one most likely to contain a possible truth would be based on an interpretation of what was happening to Rommel's 15 Army standing on guard in the Pas de Calais. Any significant movement of this army's divisions to the west would certainly be of immediate import to Montgomery and his intelligence staff, for the British realised that, like themselves, the Germans must have apprehended that there were really only two options which made sense for anyone planning a cross-Channel invasion. One would be to go for Normandy and the other, superficially the more attractive, would be to go for the Pas de Calais, which offered a shorter sea voyage, a quicker turn-round of craft, better opportunities for fighter cover, and so on. The heavy coastal defences and the presence of 15 Army, together with sundry other indications, had suggested that so far the Germans had given the Pas de Calais priority. But now? There was reason for suspicion if major troop movements were observed from the Pas de Calais to the West. Assuming that Hitler had *finally* settled for Normandy as the most threatened area, he must obviously decide to reinforce it, for though the 'Propaganda Wall' had been much strengthened, 7 Army had never been treated as an élite. The source of good reinforcements nearest to hand was 15 Army.

There were no grounds for any real fear. Hitler and his commanders continued to see the Pas de Calais as the chief danger-spot. Any developments in Normandy were simply due to Rommel's energetic carrying out of a task allotted to him, and to a last-minute intuition of Hitler's that Normandy and Brittany might be the subjects of strong secondary attacks by the Allies to divert attention from their true target. Such troop movements into Normandy as occurred during the critical period before D-Day were, it was noted with relief by Montgomery's staff, of no sinister magnitude. This is clear from the following figures:*

	April 4	*May 28*
Static coast divisions	26	25
Infantry field-force and parachute divisions	14	16
Armoured and mechanised divisions	5	10
Reserve divisions	10	7
Total	55	58

The main significance of these figures is that the number of tanks in 7 Army was 752 at the beginning of the year; 1,403 by the end of April; and almost certainly more by D-Day.

Montgomery would have had even less cause for fear had he been able to deduce the Germans' frame of mind not only from intelligence reports but also by observing at first hand their reactions to two major deception programmes, undertaken on his behalf to keep 15 Army east of the Seine both before and after his landings. There existed a comprehensive cover/deception

* Taken from L. F. Ellis, *Victory in the West*, Vol. I, p. 117, H.M.S.O.

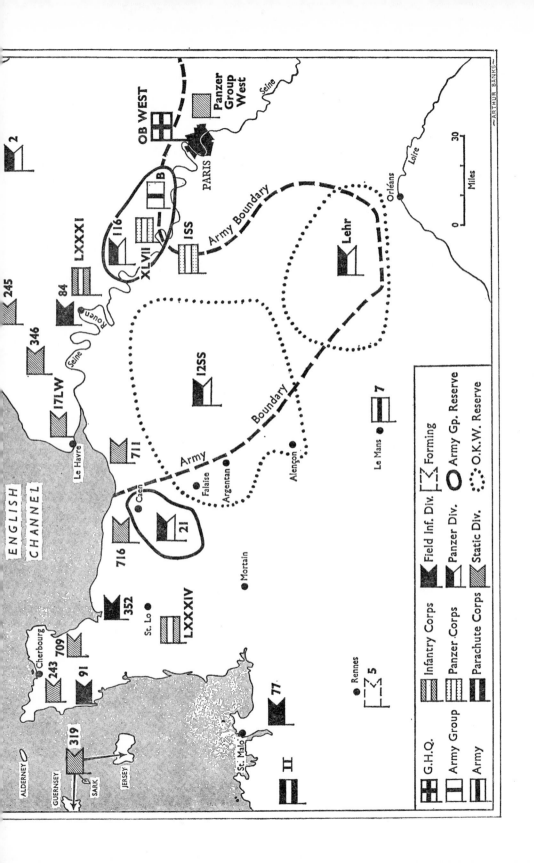

ENGLISH CHANNEL

ALDERNEY
GUERNSEY
SARK
JERSEY

319

243   709
91

352

716   21

711

17LW

346

245   84

116

XLVII   155   XLVII

LXXXI

2

OB WEST

Panzer Group West

PARIS

Seine

Seine

Rouen

Le Havre

Caen

St. Lo

LXXXIV

Mortain

Falaise

Argentan

Alençon

Army   Boundary

12SS

Lehr

Orléans

Loire

Le Mans

7

Army Boundary

B

Army Boundary

Cherbourg

St. Malo

Rennes

5

77

II

G.H.Q.	Infantry Corps	Field Inf. Div.	Forming
Army Group	Panzer Corps	Panzer Div.	Army Gp. Reserve
Army	Parachute Corps	Static Div.	O.K.W. Reserve

Miles
0   30

—ARTHUR BANKS—

plan for the total strategy of the Allies in Europe; and within this, called BODYGUARD, was a scheme specially devised for OVERLORD's benefit. Named FORTITUDE, it consisted, in essence, of an attempt to convince the Germans that the main invasion would be launched about the third week in July (over six weeks after the true D-Day), and that it would be preceded by a Scottish-based invasion of Norway, about which Hitler was always nervous. At the same time the idea was to be sown that anything happening in Normandy was a mere feint.

The highly elaborate method consisted of the faking of the presence of a complete army and ancillary air force in South East England. The scheme was aided by the remains of various installations, 'hards' for landing craft, and so on, which had been built in the area the previous year for similar purposes. Of course there were some troops normally based there: but their numbers were inflated enormously (in the enemy's imagination) by the skilful use of underground channels, by a managed press and diplomatic media. Convincing headquarters, camps, and all the appurtenances of invasion were simulated, while wireless traffic in the area was increased to a level consonant with what might be expected. Montgomery's forward H.Q. moved down to Portsmouth at the end of April, but to lend verisimilitude to FORTI-TUDE wireless signals were carried from Portsmouth to Kent by landline and broadcast from there, so effectively that, for example, Rommel noted on 21 May: 'The formation of the Allied *Schwerpunkt* in Southern and South-East England is again confirmed by the location of Montgomery's H.Q. south of London.' The 'Order of Battle' built up by the deluded Germans—S.E. England being, incidentally, the only area where the *Luftwaffe* could do cut-and-run reconnaissance—is conclusive evidence of the plan's success: as are three reports. On 4 June Admiral Krancke, commanding Naval Group, West, wrote that 'he was doubtful whether the enemy had yet assembled his invasion fleet in the required strength'; on 5 June Army Group B recorded that concentrated air attacks in the Dunkirk/Dieppe region still indicated the Pas de Calais as the threatened coast; and the same day von Rundstedt summarised his views in his weekly report by saying 'The main front between the Scheldt and Normandy is still the most probable place of attack.'

These stratagems were reinforced by the airmen. In all-out efforts, aimed chiefly at helping OVERLORD in the short or long term, the R.A.F. and U.S.A.A.F., between 1 April and 5 June, lost about 12,000 officers and men and 2,000 aircraft. Apart from strategic targets, those closer to the NEPTUNE area included bridges, railways, radar stations, airfields, and coastal batteries. The benefit for NEPTUNE was incalculable: for as part of the deception plan the air forces worked on a formula; for every target attacked in the NEPTUNE area two must be attacked in the Pas de Calais. Of the railway targets chosen the greater percentage were outside the area. Montgomery had special cause to be grateful to the airmen for carrying out these deception tasks so meticulously, since undoubtedly men and planes were lost, in the 'duplication' process, on targets which otherwise were not always of very high priority.

Of the many last-minute problems that arose, two should be mentioned. The first was the Prime Minister. Never able to grasp the difference between a modern army and what he himself had been used to, he grumbled continuously about the proportion of fighting troops to the administrative 'tail'. This was a point he had chosen from the presentation on 17 May. At the time he gave Brooke three quarters of an hour on the subject: but it still rankled, and indeed spilled over into his *Memoirs*. 'I was told, for example, that two thousand officers and clerks were being taken across the sea to keep records, and I was given the following statement, which showed that twenty days after the landing—D+20—there would be one vehicle ashore for every 4.77 men. . . .' Montgomery heard that the Prime Minister wanted to have this out with his staff. He therefore invited him down to Portsmouth to dine with the staff on 19 May. When Churchill arrived Montgomery firmly took him into his room—'I sat at my desk,' he told me, 'and he sat in a chair. That was the right way round'—and without beating about the bush told his Prime Minister that he was NOT going to interrogate his staff. Churchill became very emotional. He saw he had lost. Then with typical resilience and humanity he walked out of the room with Montgomery, passed down the waiting line of staff officers in silence, turned, and with the Churchillian twinkle simply observed: 'I wasn't allowed to have any discussion with you gentlemen.' In Montgomery's autograph book he wrote, that night:

> On the verge of the greatest Adventure with which these pages have dealt, I record my confidence that
>
> all will be well
>
> and that the organisation and equipment of the Army will be worthy of the valour of the soldiers and the genius of their chief.
>
> Winston S. Churchill

Of more serious significance for Montgomery was Leigh-Mallory's return to the attack, at the end of May, on the question of the western air-drop. This was a vital element in the plan to capture the essential port of Cherbourg at the first possible moment. Until 25 May there existed an arrangement, agreed between Montgomery, Bradley and Leigh-Mallory, whereby to meet the latter's objections the main drop during the first night would be of paratroops from 82 and 101 Airborne, with 100 gliders following at dawn and a further 200 at dusk. The news on 25 May that a German division had arrived in the area allocated to 82 Airborne led Bradley to urge that the latter should be dropped further east, close to 101, so that jointly they could support the landings on UTAH which would otherwise have to be abandoned. Leigh-Mallory still rebelled; and though Montgomery supported Bradley and was upheld by Tedder, who as Eisenhower's Deputy supervised all air matters relating to OVERLORD, Leigh-Mallory tackled Eisenhower himself, saying, in short, that the operation would involved the sacrifice of 50 per cent of the parachutists and 70 per cent of the glider loads. Eisenhower decided that the whole was greater than the part. NEPTUNE was imminent: this was no time for fundamental changes. He ordered the airborne operation to proceed, thus making a decision which cost him more mental stress than the decision to set NEPTUNE in motion. After the landings, Leigh-Mallory wrote to Eisenhower the most graceful admission that he had been in the wrong. But none of this was settled until 30 May: and now the final decision had to be made.

All the conditions of sea and sky—the right tides, the right moonlight, etc., —could only be fulfilled on 5, 6 and 7 June. Of these, in Montgomery's view, 5 was best, 6 was acceptable, and 7 was just tolerable though it allowed two hours' daylight before the first wave of landing craft had touched down. The unthinkable alternative was postponement for a fortnight, when conditions would next be tolerable.

A quick chronology indicates why postponement was so fearful a prospect. D-Day had been provisionally settled by Eisenhower as far back as 8 May, and this decision had not been revoked by the beginning of June. Thus the preliminary moves built into the D-Day plan were automatically started. On 31 May blockships for use in the artificial MULBERRY harbour began their last voyage from ports in Scotland. On 2 June H.M.S. *Nelson* left Scapa for the south, and a Bombarding Force sailed from the Clyde, while two midget submarines, the markers for SWORD and JUNO, set off across the Channel to pick up their stations. The Commanders were now meeting twice daily with Eisenhower to consider the weather reports, which got steadily worse. Nevertheless no change was yet made, and on 3 June two Bombarding Forces left the Clyde, as well as H.M.S. *Rodney*; a further Bombarding Force left Belfast; and later that day actual assault convoys put out from Dartmouth, Salcombe and Brixham. To put into reverse such a volume of seaborne traffic was both difficult and distasteful. Still, by the evening the prospects were so threatening that a postponement seemed unavoidable. Eisenhower deferred his decision until a meeting summoned for early next morning, the 4th. The forecast then was still so menacing for the 5th that Eisenhower signalled the Combined Chiefs of Staff to inform them that he had put off D-Day until the 6th. His chief reason, says Tedder, was that a successful D-Day could only be made possible by the exercise of overwhelming air-power. If the air power could not operate, the operation must be postponed.

The good sense of the decision was confirmed that evening, as the storm intensified, and again at 0400 on the 5th, when the conference re-assembled to reach an absolutely final decision about the morrow. Most of those present have at some time or other described this fateful occasion; described how the rain poured and the wind howled outside, while to the meeting the Chief Meteorological Officer, Group Captain Stagg, reported that the worst appeared to be over and that fairer weather lay ahead for a few days. Eisenhower walked up and down the room, apart, hands behind back and head sunk forward in thought. Montgomery appeared impatient, as if the answer was only too obvious. But the answer was Eisenhower's to give, as lonely a decision as a man has had to take, in the sense that it was not a matter of his own life being at risk—a relatively simple decision—but the lives of millions of others in the free and occupied countries, the well-being of all those he represented and, at that moment in the early morning of 5 June 1944, he alone. He stopped his pacing. 'O.K. boys,' he said. 'We will go.' He then walked out of the room, in an agony of responsibility which found expression in the provisional announcement he scribbled on a scrap of paper during the day. It read: 'Our landings in the Cherbourg-Havre area have failed to gain a satisfactory foothold and I have withdrawn the troops. My decision to attack at this time and place was based upon the best information available. The troops, the air and the navy did all that bravery and devotion to duty could do. If any blame or fault attaches to the attempt it is mine alone. June 5th.'

10

Normandy: mastery achieved

'We have never before played for so great a stake, and the whole
world is watching how we conduct the game upon which our
national honour and our prestige and position among nations
depend. I need not tell you that a large proportion of the spectators
devoutly hope that we may lose this game, and that England may
henceforward take rank as a second or third-class power, and it
is therefore all the more incumbent on us to win it. I do not permit
myself to doubt that we shall do so because we are determined
upon it. . . .'

Lord Clarendon (then Foreign Secretary) to
Lord Elgin, 1857—à propos the Indian Mutiny

'Whereas anyone can make a plan it takes something quite out of
the ordinary to carry it out.'

Lieut.-General Sir Frederick Morgan, C.O.S.S.A.C.

By a natural chauvinism the British tend to think of D-Day as *theirs*, their
triumph, and of Normandy as a private preserve, whereas Americans have
quite different ideas. Both points of view are understandable: just as Pershing's
doughboys were more conscious of the Argonne than of Ypres, of St. Mihiel
rather than Cambrai, so Bradley's G.I.'s remember Carentan rather than
Caen and St. Lô rather than Villers Bocage. And *vice versa*: particularly as,
for the British, there existed as a background to combat in Normandy the
racial memory of a thousand years of invasion and counter-invasion across the
Narrow Seas. For the Americans, apart from the fact that their inflowing
armies soon made them the predominant Allied power on the Continent,
there is a statistical justification for feeling an equivalent sense of possessive-
ness about NEPTUNE. On their two beaches some 57,500 troops came ashore
on D-Day, with an additional airborne element of 15,500: about 6,000 became
casualties. The joint British/Canadian figures were 75,215 landed by sea, plus
7,900 airborne: of these approximately 4,300 were either killed, wounded or
missing. To weigh these figures impartially is to see that on this day of blood-
brotherhood there was a community of sacrifice: that chauvinism is not
enough.

Such had to be Montgomery's outlook. Though he was formally the British
Army Group Commander, and only temporarily commander of all the allied
land forces, it was his duty to endeavour to steer the battle without any sense

22 *Germany, February 1945, Montgomery with Horrocks and Thom*
G.O.C. 43rd Division

23 *The Liaison Officers*

24 *Normandy : Montgomery's first press conference after D-Day*

of nationality—an abnegation also made by Eisenhower, in his post as
Supreme Commander, to very nearly the limits of his capacity as a human
being who happened to be an American. When he arrived off the beaches in a
destroyer on the morning of 7 June, therefore, it was appropriate that Montgomery first visited Bradley in his command ship, before seeking out
Dempsey; there then followed a conference with Eisenhower and Ramsay on
the latter's flagship. Early next morning Montgomery set foot ashore and
occupied his Tac. H.Q., which had been established at Creully, a hamlet near
to Bayeux. It was sensible for him to have chosen the British sector for his
initial H.Q.—though as overall land commander he might have preferred to
be nearer to Bradley, and indeed, on 22 June, did move to Blay, just inside
the American zone to the west of Bayeux, for precisely this purpose. But
during those tense early days the inevitable headlines in the American press
may be imagined . . . 'Monty looks over Bradley's shoulder!' In any case,
at Creully he had beside him Dempsey's 2 Army H.Q. and that of his old
African colleague Air Vice-Marshal Broadhurst, whose 83 Group was in
support of Dempsey. As to Bradley, the General is his own witness. There
were undoubtedly disagreements over policy, and misunderstandings of
Montgomery's intentions, but in Normandy these were never allowed to
distort a harmonious relationship: in *A Soldier's Story*, Bradley stated firmly,
during this period Montgomery 'exercised his Allied authority with wisdom,
forbearance and restraint. . . . I could not have wanted a more tolerant or
judicious commander. . . .'

If Churchill had had his will, he would probably have smelt powder even
before Montgomery, since he determined as early as the night of the 4th to
establish himself on a cruiser and share the start of the battle. Like a small
child, he kept his plan secret from Brooke, well knowing that his C.I.G.S.
must veto the idea. Fortunately this was done by the King himself, and in fact
Churchill was not allowed into Normandy until the 12th. Untroubled by
visitors, therefore, Montgomery could calmly piece together the jig-saw
created by the assault. His very presence on French soil within 48 hours of
the landings was eloquent of success: but how much success, and where?

In spite of the monolithic master plan, the different sectors of the front
must have seemed to the troops on D-Day to have had something of the
lonely separateness so familiar to the American amphibious forces in their
advance across the Pacific from one island stepping-stone to another: the
Battle was the beachhead.* By the end of the first day this isolation was
virtually unaltered. On either flank the airborne troops had once again proved
that such élite units can achieve the impossible even if dropped inefficiently:

---

* In the 24 miles of the British sector none of the five invasion beaches was much more than
a mile wide.

o

but the Normandy drop, unfortunately, showed that not all the lessons taught by Sicily had been adequately digested and applied. Yet on one point at least Montgomery had solid grounds for satisfaction. That decimation of the American airborne troops and their conveyors which Leigh-Mallory had predicted did not occur. Losses were not excessive. What *did* occur, however, was a dissipation of manpower and equipment due to inaccurate dropping or landing. This is partially explained by the complicated route the aircraft had to follow (Sicily had shown the dangers of complication), and partly because just before the run-in to the Dropping Zones cloud confused some of the pilots while others, inexperienced, were distracted by anti-aircraft fire and started to 'weave' to avoid it. In the event, though 805 troop-carrying planes were used on this front, only 20 were lost; but 101 Airborne was dotted about over an area 25 × 15 miles, by dawn only 1,100 men out of 6,600 were where they should be, and even a day later less than half had been gathered in. Still, by dark they had seized the western end of the five causeways over the inundations. 82 Airborne had better luck. A large proportion of its leading paratroop regiment came down within three miles of the correct spot, and quickly took over Ste. Mére Église, a vital blocking-place on the Carentan-Cherbourg road. They were followed by 22 out of 52 gliders. An uncovenanted blessing was the confusion which these determined and self-sufficient soldiers, 'sprinkled', as Chester Wilmot puts it, 'over the country-side from some giant salt-shaker', caused to a bemused enemy. This is, of course, the classic apologia for an inefficient airborne operation: but in the riverain swamps and orchards of the Merderet valley it does seem, during the early hours of D-Day, actually to have been the case. No firm link-up, however, had as yet been achieved with the seaborne 4 Division at UTAH.

Chester Wilmot himself flew in, as a B.B.C. War Correspondent, with the British 6 Airborne Division whose task was to secure the eastward flank of the landings, around and beyond the mouth of the river Orne. His enumeration of the contents of the first of the planes which were to drop parachutists into the divisional area to act as pathfinders describes a characteristic cross-section of Montgomery's army. All volunteers, they were '. . . at the point of the invasion spearhead, a Berkshire hod-carrier and a toolmaker from Kent, a brick-layer from Edinburgh, a Worcestershire kennelman and a lorry driver from Dumfries, two "regulars", a deserter from the "army" of the Irish Free State and a refugee from Austria, led by a young lieutenant, who, when war began, had been in the chorus of a West End musical comedy. Three of them had been at Dunkirk, one had fought in Africa, but the rest were going into battle for the first time.' 6 Airborne also had difficulty with dispersed drops, but its essential tasks were fulfilled—to secure the crossings over the Orne, and the canal between Caen and the sea, which would be the main line of communication between east flank and main bridgehead; and to capture the coastal battery at Merville which could enfilade SWORD beach disastrously. The evening reinforcement by 6 Airlanding Brigade, in 145 gliders, came in smoothly, and by that night Major-General Richard Gale, commanding 6 Airborne Division, had a useful force of six parachute battalions, two air-landing battalions, some light tanks and artillery, and about 50 anti-tank guns with which to face the predictable counter-attack next day. Like the Americans, he still lacked a link-up.

But the airborne operations were essentially an insurance policy, taken out to cover the vast capital investment in men and metal represented by the seaborne assault: and for Montgomery the critical question was, what dividends had the investment produced? In the American sector, unfortunately, the immediate visible profit was not encouraging. At UTAH, true, much had been gained. 4 Division benefited from the location of its beach: under the lee of the Cotentin its landing craft were exposed to less ferocious seas, thus having an easier run in, and, because highwater mark was not unusually high, beach obstacles were sufficiently exposed. 269 medium bombers accurately carpeted shore defences just before zero hour. Of 26 D.D. tanks launched 3,000 yards from shore, all floated safely in: and within an hour, in fact, demolition parties had established safe approaches for the follow-up landing craft. . . . UTAH was the only beach on which this occurred during D-Day. With these advantages, and faced by a relatively feeble enemy, 4 Division, after a bridgehead had been seized, was thwarted more by the inundations and lack of exits from the beaches than by human opposition. At the end of the day over 23,000 men had been landed, and a sufficient space carved out for manoeuvre and build-up.

OMAHA that same night presented a very different picture and potential. Though more than 34,000 men were landed they had gained, as an American historian puts it, 'a toehold on the enemy shore nowhere more than a mile and a half deep'. Total disaster was prevented, in a final analysis, by two factors: the guns of the Navy and the guts of 1 U.S. Division—'The Big Red One'—a formation hardened by TORCH and Sicily, unit-proud, and capable of demonstrating this day, as many a battered fragment of American soldiers was to demonstrate in the Ardennes, that in extreme adversity they could fight in the spirit of 'I care not; a man can die but once; we owe God a death.'

The object of these OMAHA landings, a bridgehead 16 miles wide and five or six miles deep, was reduced to a 'toehold' because inadequate foresight led to inevitable slaughter. The configuration of the coast in the OMAHA sector made it an obvious point of attack, which the Germans had fortified heavily, with strong-points and trenches enfilading the beach and copious mines sown across all possible exits. The Americans knew of this threat: but on D-Day at

OMAHA Eisenhower and Bradley paid with American lives for what, on their part, was either a lack of insight or an inhibiting nationalistic pride. The facts are that as early as January—i.e. shortly after they took up their appointments—Eisenhower and Montgomery were shown the capabilities of the various forms of specialised armour which, within his secret 79 Armoured Division, had been developed by General Hobart to overcome the difficulties of an amphibious assault noted at Dieppe and in subsequent operations. The flail-tank to breach minefields; the flame-tank; the bombard-tank for blasting concrete; the bridging tank—all these and others were available in Hobart's 'zoo'. Only one type was ordered by Eisenhower immediately, nor were others sought by Bradley and his staff when the matter was handed over to them. Yet the ability of an American to decide and act was shown by Eisenhower's response to the D.D. tank, which he ordered in quantity. Blueprints were flown to the U.S.A. immediately, and the first 100 D.D. Shermans were across the Atlantic within six weeks.

This unfortunate story must be contrasted with Montgomery's reaction to what he was shown. Hobart was enormously impressed by Montgomery's quick grasp of the specific value of each piece of equipment. The value was proved, as will be seen, on the British beaches on 6 June: and Montgomery's steadily increasing appreciation of its worth is indicated by the fact that in February 1945 Hobart's division had expanded into the only all-armoured formation in the British Army—17 regiments, 21,430 officers and men, and 1,566 tracked pieces of equipment. (An average armoured division would have about 350.) This was modern warfare; it was modern warfare in the American style; yet it was Montgomery, so often accused by the Americans of being cautious and set in his ways, who applied imaginatively this variable new technical aid—Montgomery, the British and, under the brilliant Simonds, the Canadians.

These were the very weapons which 1 Division desperately lacked at OMAHA. The seas were rough: yet the landing craft were launched *12 miles from shore*. Thus, as the U.S. War Department's account of OMAHA observes, 'men who had been chilled by their wetting, cramped by immobility in the small and fully-loaded craft and weakened by sea-sickness were not in the best condition for strenuous action on landing'. But this was not all. Of 29 D.D. tanks launched from four miles off-shore only two reached the land. And because of cloud the Eighth American Air Force's bombers were not able, like the mediums over UTAH, to bomb on sight; the use of pathfinders and bombing-on-instruments meant that the beach and its defences were hardly touched, whereas there was a good scatter up to three miles inland. The infantry were, in effect, stranded defenceless on the shores of France—those who got there—and stranded, too, before an enemy stronger than they had expected. They had assumed they would meet only elements of the weak 716 Division. Evidence that the sound and mobile 352 Division was moving up from St. Lô towards the coast was rejected by the Americans, in May, as too frail. But on 6 June units of 352 Division were on the OMAHA front. What was meant to be a successful invasion thus soon degenerated into a struggle for survival; and it was only by sheer will-power that this was gradually converted into a minor victory—a determination symbolised by the leadership of Colonel G. A. Taylor, of 1 Division, with his magnificent cry, 'Two kinds of people are staying on this beach, the dead and those who are going to die—now let's get the hell out of here.' A toehold had been purchased: the price was 3,000 casualties.

On the British/Canadian front the general picture was one of uniform if qualified success. The objectives laid down were certainly too great. Apart from getting ashore, those who passed through GOLD, JUNO and SWORD were expected to get into their grip the very considerable rectangle formed by the coast from the mouth of the Orne to Port-en-Bessin, the line Port-en-Bessin—Bayeux (inclusive), the Bayeux-Caen road, and the eastern flank formed by Caen (inclusive) via the Canal de Caen and its parallel, the river Orne, to Ouistreham on the sea—with a bridgehead flung over the waterways to create a link with 6 Airborne. Montgomery probably knew he was asking too much of his assault troops: Dempsey certainly did. When I asked him about this he was frank—he had, after all, seen landings happen in Sicily—and confessed that in an amphibious operation it is wise to fix your objectives well ahead in order to overcome the inevitable reaction which sets in (and on some British beaches did set in) as soon as your troops find they are ashore and actually still alive.

Montgomery's foresight was cheated in one respect, but justified in another. The high, choppy seas, driven by an on-shore wind, forced the tide unexpectedly far up some of the beaches, so that many craft had to ride in over armed obstacles already under water, while the demolition squads' work was delayed. This caused much confusion and many casualties both to craft and their contents. On the other hand a high proportion of the D.D. tanks landed either as soon as or shortly after the infantry, and the armoured engineers were sent in with their specialised equipment immediately behind the first wave: this was an inestimable benefit. In spite of misadventures and stiff resistance, there was never any likelihood of any of the three beaches becoming an OMAHA. The whole paraphernalia of mechanised beach clearance was in action from the beginning and almost consistently along the whole front. One example will suffice.

'A bridging tank of the sappers laid its bridge against the dunes and three flail tanks of the 22nd Dragoons went up it. The first had flogged its way for about forty yards through the minefield when a mine exploded under its track; the second was stopped by mechanical trouble and the third so entangled in wire that it could not get further. Progress was now impeded by a German tank trap, fifteen feet wide and nine deep. A fascine was laid in it and a bulldozer set to work to fill it in. Beyond the trap the flooded stream had passed through a culvert; this had been blown up and a huge crater full of water took its place. Another fascine-carrying tank tried to fill it but the "tank slid into the crater and gradually disappeared from view except for its fascine". The crew baled out but were all killed or wounded by mortar fire before they could reach cover. Other sappers freed the fascine by explosives and a bridge "was dropped from the seaward side on the sunken tank which acted as a pier but left a gap on the far side; this was filled with logs . . ." About 0915 the first D.D. tank got across. More followed. Then field guns arrived but the first "totally misjudged the bridge and bellied itself on it . . ." Three bulldozers were linked together but failed to pull him off; two AVRES were therefore brought up and, after a lot of trouble, succeeded in getting him off.'*

That, in essence, is the justification for Montgomery's confidence in Hobart's ingenuity—and it is curious to see two brothers-in-law, so different in temperament and experience, profitably converging at so critical a moment in their country's history. It was with such assistance, and more from the sea and the air, that 50 Division in the GOLD area, in spite of fierce opposition from unsubdued strong-points, managed to land all four of its brigades by the afternoon and thrust inland to just short of Bayeux. The Canadians too, on JUNO, had an uncomfortable landing: of their 306 landing craft 90 became casualties during the day. But for the Canadians this was not Dieppe repeated. With armoured aid, and in spite of the fact that the beaches became blocked with vehicles as clearance of the exits was delayed, the 3 Canadian Divisional Group was in the end able to break free and press sideways and forwards until some of its armour actually reached part of the day's objective—the Caen-Bayeux road at Bretteville L'Orgueilleuse and Carpiquet, south of which lay one of the desired aerodromes.

For Montgomery the fortunes of the British 3 Division in the SWORD area was of particular significance during a day when all had meaning. It was here that his overall policy for the Normandy battle would be put to the test in its most crucial aspect—what would the Germans do with their armour? SWORD, of course, came most closely to Caen, threatening as it did the south of the city. Caen, for the Germans, held the master-key to their western front: it was the Ypres of Normandy.

The location, handling, and command arrangements for the German

* L. F. Ellis, *Victory in the West*, Vol. I, p. 182.

armour during D-Day turned out, in fact, to be symptomatic of what was
later to happen. Rommel* had 21 Panzer under command in Army Group B:
thought by the Allies to be stationed S.E. of Caen, it had actually moved
some elements into the city, and at 0700 was given to 84 Corps to assist in
dealing with 6 Airborne's landings beyond the Orne. 12 S.S. Panzer was south
of Rouen, and Panzer Lehr near Chartres, but both were under the direct
command of Hitler as part of O.K.W. reserve. Rundstedt made tentative
efforts to bring them into the battle, but at 1000 hrs. was told that though 12
S.S. could move north, Panzer Lehr must stay put, and *neither* must be committed to action without O.K.W. approval. Not till 1430 hrs. was permission
given to move Panzer Lehr and 12 S.S. into the line: but this was far too late,
and by midnight advance elements of 12 S.S. were still south west of Caen.

This paralysis of command prevented an OMAHA on the British left. As a
result 3 Division, which had also had to fight its way off the beaches and had
been rather slow in exploitation, was nevertheless able to deal with some
difficult strong-points, reach out along the coast to Ouistreham, and by midnight relieve the airborne troops holding the canal bridges. To the south they
had taken the important Périers ridge and other features and villages—and
all this without disastrous interruption by the Panzers. Even the division on
the spot, 21 (with a strength of 127 Mk. IV tanks, 40 assault guns and 24
88s), was dispersed and mishandled. It had battalions either side of the Orne,
the 88s on the Périers ridge, other artillery in or around Caen, and its tanks
mainly near Falaise. At first two battle-groups were sent down the east side
of the Orne to deal with 6 Airborne: then they were pulled back to share a
general move by 21 Division into the Caen area. This however was observed,
and a continuous air attack was launched. Consequently, when Feuchtinger,
the Panzer divisional commander, put in an attack on 3 Division in the afternoon which ought to have broken through to the sea, he found the British
well placed to receive him and rocket-firing Typhoons active in the air: and
the thrust failed. By the evening 21 Panzer had only 70 tanks. But fingers of
3 Division had reached within three miles of Caen.

Though Montgomery was not ashore to receive detailed reports, he could
feel satisfied with the broad picture of the day's results. Along a reach of 24
miles the British and Canadians had penetrated to a depth of four to six miles.
OMAHA had proved only a partial disaster. UTAH showed some promise. The
airborne flanks were solidifying. German reactions had been slow and in-
conclusive. The allies held the air. And, according to plan, the German tanks
were being drawn by the magnet of Caen.

---

* Though the unsuspecting Rommel was absent on D-Day—with his family near Ulm, on his
way to see Hitler at Berchtesgaden. His Chief of Staff, Speidel, took charge till Rommel returned
in the evening.

Still more was this the case on D+1. Events on the eastern flank during this day must be considered against the background knowledge that FORTITUDE, the great deception scheme to convince the Germans that the Normandy landings were a feint, still held sway in the minds of the Higher Command—from Hitler downwards. 7 Army must operate with its own resources. The five infantry and two panzer divisions which could have been moved from 15 Army stayed motionless. And even 7 Army's strategic reserve of tanks was not immediately available. 12 S.S. and Panzer Lehr had been drawn to the battle: but 17 S.S. was 200 miles away, below the Loire; 1 S.S. was in Belgium; while 2 S.S. was as far away as Toulouse. Thus the German strategy of holding the Americans with infantry while driving the British into the sea with armour, grandiose on paper, looked less so to Dietrich, the commander of 1 S.S. Panzer Corps who was given the job to do by Rommel. He could muster at best 160 odd tanks from 21 Panzer and 12 S.S., (Panzer Lehr was not expected till 8 June); and his attempt at a concerted drive past the strongpoint at Douvres la Délivrande, which still dominated a wide-open gap between the Canadians and 3 Division, was foiled from the start. Shortage of petrol* delayed the grouping of 12 S.S., and by the time they got on the move 21 Panzer was already involved heavily with 3 Division. 12 S.S. simultaneously were drawn off by a Canadian thrust at the Carpiquet airfield. In consequence the major breakthrough to the sea by 160 tanks, planned for the morning, was whittled down until all that could be raised for this important enterprise, later in the day, was 17 tanks and a battalion of infantry. In any case, by this time the gap had been closed.

Already, in fact, Montgomery was making the enemy dance to his tune. The immediately available armour had been directed on Caen, as expected, and put into the attack piecemeal, as had been hoped. By drawing attention to his left Montgomery had aided his right, where aid was most welcome: for the Americans at OMAHA had been held by a crust behind which were virtually no immediate reserves, and now, with extraordinary resilience, they were pushing aggressively to extend beyond that crust their narrow bridgehead. Very heavy fighting had occurred at the base of the Cotentin, but here too the Americans had held attacks and made gains, while the Germans had been tardy in summoning from Brittany the necessary reserves. These too, as they began their march on the 11th, were damaged and slowed down by the ubiquitous fighter-bombers. As Montgomery sat in his forward headquarters at Creully for the first time, on the morning of the 8th, and reviewed in detail the shape which the battle was now beginning recognisably to

---

* This was a perennial difficulty for the Germans in Normandy. The main stocks lay in 15 Army area. Damage to the railway system meant transport by road (and by night), and the Allied fighter-bombers were quick to destroy anything to do with fuel.

assume, he saw much that was developing well: but to establish his campaign on an absolutely firm footing he demanded three prerequisites—a binding together of the beachheads into one continuous front; a maintenance of the initiative, which was so far in Allied hands; and the establishment of smoothly working administrative arrangements within the narrow zone of occupation before the enemy asserted himself in strength. There was, of course, another factor constantly before Montgomery's mind—the weather. 'That was the element,' Churchill observed, 'which certainly hung like a vulture poised in the sky. . . .'

His first objective was achieved on 12 June, when the Allies finally established their hold in a solid territory over 50 miles in length and between eight and 12 miles in depth. A sign of this coming achievement was the entry in the German 7 Army's Telephone Log at 1730 hrs. 9 June: 'there would be a return to the defensive in the sector between the Vire and the Orne . . . the counter-attack should be postponed until all preparations have been completed'. This order of Rommel's was a tacit admission of the defeat of 12 S.S. in its attempt to over-run the Canadians at Carpiquet on the 8th, and the shattered condition in which Panzer Lehr had at last reached the Bayeux area the same day. This counter-attack, however, never occurred. Its planning was put in the hands of Geyr von Schweppenburg, Commander of Panzer Group West. Unfortunately for him his H.Q. had been located, and on the evening of the 10th it was so precisely bombed that almost all the staff (except Geyr) were killed or wounded. Moreover Dempsey had been warned of a possible attack, and as counter-measures he ordered an air raid on Caen and a redeployment of the Canadians. All these events persuaded the disheartened Germans that, far from putting in a major attack themselves, they must expect one from the British. Such events indicate how Montgomery was gaining the moral as well as the tactical initiative. On the 12th, the day of the bridgehead's consolidation, Dempsey attempted to implement Montgomery's will.

The chance this time was offered by the Americans, and is a singular proof of the courage and energy they had displayed in extricating themselves from OMAHA—for it was on their extreme left that the opportunity arose. Bradley drove on his tired troops relentlessly, day and night: by the evening of the 11th Carentan had fallen, and next morning the Americans were into Caumont, far inland from OMAHA and several miles south west of Tilly-sur-Seulles, on the right-hand corner of the British front, where 7 Armoured were stuck before the shield of Panzer Lehr. Dempsey's plan was for 7 Armoured to break contact, swing west and south to Caumont, and then, turning sharply to the east, move fast via Villers-Bocage and penetrate into the hinterland of the thin defensive line which the Germans had established from the Orne right across to Tilly and beyond. The point was that behind the line was little by way of a completed defence system; and Dempsey's manoeuvre, classic in conception, might have produced a 'rolling up from the flank' whose consequences are incalculable. But he had selected the wrong instrument. Their magnificent desert *expertise* was of no use to 7 Armoured in the lanes and hedgerows of the *bocage*. They were never at home in Normandy. Their deployment was laboured; one column was caught at the halt in Villers-Bocage, and in a sharp encounter with Tigers lost 25 tanks, 14 armoured trucks and 14 carriers. Though 50 Division maintained pressure on Tilly, taking it on the 19th, and though there was heavy fighting along the rest of the front, especially east of the Orne where 51 Highland was now engaged, it was clear that 7 Armoured lacked enough infantry to proceed. On 15 June it was pulled back to between Caumont and Tilly. (But, as in the case of several of Montgomery's apparently unsuccessful moves in Normandy, there was profit as well as loss in the balance. The tanks of 7 Armoured had fought hard and the infantry of 50 Division had battled on in their dour northern fashion. The consequence was that afterwards Bayerlein, the very experienced commander of Panzer Lehr, said: 'My chance to drive to the sea was lost. We had lost about a hundred tanks against the British.')

Even if this 'failure' caused natural disappointment, that was as nothing compared with the atmosphere prevailing in the German headquarters. Montgomery's absolute moral defeat of his enemy is dramatically demonstrated by the individual reports which, by mutual agreement, von Rundstedt and Rommel sent to Hitler, the former on the 11th, the latter on the 12th. Their gist was that the striking power of the German armoured divisions had had to be used *for defence*; reinforcements, even as they arrived, were being steadily fitted into the defensive line. Here were two German commanders describing, out of immediate experience, what Montgomery had already predicted. Further despairing messages from the west made Hitler decide to fly to meet his commanders on the 17th at a summit conference at Margival, near Soissons, which for them was wholly abortive. No retreat, whether tactical or strategic; not even a division to be moved without O.K.W. permission; reinforcements would come; the Allies would not break out, they would be driven into the sea. The spirit of unreality in which the discussion (or monologue) was conducted is illustrated by a signal Hitler sent off to Dönitz, the Naval C.-in-C., during the meeting, telling him that the only way to help the situation on land was to 'eliminate or neutralise the enemy's naval forces, particularly his battleships'!

Montgomery, however, like other commanders, had to subject himself to the elements—to rain, wind and storm.

Temporary aid was on its way for the depressed Rommel. Shortly after the Hitler meeting, on the 18th, Montgomery issued a new directive stating 'We

must now capture Caen and Cherbourg as the first step in the full development of our plans.' This was the old story but with a new emphasis, for by
now the Americans had over-run a broad corridor right across the Cotentin
peninsula. The capture of Caen was to be effected by a supporting attack east
of the Orne, and a major outflanking attack by the newly arrived 8 Corps
which was to seize the high ground south of Caen at Bretteville sur Laize and
gain control of the exits from the city. In the Channel, however, a strong gale
from the north had worked up to 30 knots by the afternoon, raising huge
waves. This continued for three days. Montgomery had selected for the
moment to deal a death-blow to Caen—a time when Rommel was frantic for
reinforcements—the week in which the Channel was savaged by the worst
June storm for 40 years. The catalogue of disaster is unending—800 craft
shattered and stranded; two and a half miles of steel roadway sunk on tow;
ferries, breakwaters, blockships damaged or destroyed . . . and so on. Inside
the chaos, of course, a great truth was concealed: the artificial harbours—
by no means completed as yet—justified themselves by providing sanctuary
off the British beaches. (For technical reasons those off the American beaches
were virtually useless.) Yet all this was happening at a moment when two
major offensives were in preparation. To list the consequences would be
wearisome; one instance is vivid enough—before the storm 2 British Army
was short, on the landing schedule, of two brigades; when the storm flagged
on the 22nd, the shortage stood at three divisions. And the attempt on Caen
was postponed; the supporting attack in the east to the 23rd, the important,
major attack until the 25th.

The end of June was a significant turning-point in the Normandy campaign. On the 30th NEPTUNE formally ended and OVERLORD passed into its
next phase with the departure to England of the British naval Task Force
Commander, Admiral Vian, who was followed immediately by his American
counterpart, Admiral Kirk. The more junior naval officers responsible for the
individual beaches ashore were also withdrawn, and replaced, in the British
sector, by a *land-based* Flag Officer British Assault Area, and in the American
by Flag Officer West—in each case a Rear-Admiral. This transformation from
the amphibian to the terrestrial was a symbol of the confidence now felt in
the security of the expanded bridgehead—a confidence buttressed by two
other simultaneous events which, in fact, represented an attainment of the
last two of the three prerequisites enunciated by Montgomery on 8 June as
essential 'to establish his campaign on an absolutely firm footing'.

On 1 July there ended Operation EPSOM, the great hook to the south of
Caen whose postponement to 25 June had been caused by the Channel
storm. This failed to make as much ground as had been hoped, but it did
something much more important: it brought about a decisive defeat of the

German armour. On the previous day, after a magnificent American drive up the Cotentin which culminated in the fall of Cherbourg's massive fortress and its supporting batteries, the first Allied vessel, a British motor-launch used for minesweeping, delicately entered the harbour. The significance of these two events was first that, after EPSOM, the Germans were never again to be able to mount a properly concerted counter-attack by massed armour —if one excludes Hitler's later and lunatic Mortain offensive—and second that the Americans, now freed from the compulsion to capture Cherbourg, could turn wholeheartedly to the south and west. Montgomery's second prerequisite, 'a maintenance of the initiative', had been granted in good measure. The little craft creeping into Cherbourg harbour, forerunner of the deep-draught ships which began to anchor there on 16 July, was also a promise that Montgomery's third requirement, administrative stability, was on its way.*

EPSOM was the first major British operation: it was therefore singularly appropriate that taking part in it was Lieut.-General Sir Richard O'Connor, that superb leader of mobile troops who, in Wavell's first offensive in the African desert, had annihilated by skill and daring a vastly superior Italian army. Later a prisoner of war in Italy, he had now returned to action again in Normandy at the head of 8 Corps (II Armoured, 15 Scottish and 43 Wessex Divisions) which had just landed. This Corps was to bear the brunt. 30 Corps, who had been in the battle since the beginning, was to form a flank guard on the far right by first taking Rauray, securing the line Rauray-Juvigny, and then pushing southwards. 8 Corps had the heavier and more dramatic rôle of forcing its way from the old-established Canadian positions on the Caen road west of Bretteville l'Orgueilleuse down past Cheux to the river Odon, then battling eastwards to the river Orne, forcing more crossings, and finally establishing itself in a position to dominate the southern approaches to Caen. A fearful task for an unfledged formation—especially among the Norman lanes and hedges. On the credit side was unchallenged airpower, much artillery (with the aid of 30 Corps on the right and 1 Corps on the left 700 guns were on call), three cruisers and a monitor, but above all the high ardour and ability of three new divisions whose performance, now and later, would put them all in the top rank.

To summarise a bitter battle, 8 Corps only managed to consolidate a bridge-head beyond the first river-barrier, the Odon, before the end of the fighting: but though a deeper thrust would of course have been rewarding, territorial gain was not the main profit from EPSOM. The real truth is to be found in the pessimistic signals made during the conflict by Army Group B, the Panzer

---

* This must of course be seen in conjunction with the astonishingly swift reorganisation of the beaches and harbours, and recovery of the supply services, after the storm.

Corps and German Divisional Commanders. In effect, the threat created by EPSOM was such that not only was the German armour locally available thrown in to hold the line, but also divisions coming from a distance: reserves for a future counter-attack were unavoidably frittered away in defence. Round the bulge made by 8 and 30 Corps a ring was finally drawn by 12 S.S., 1 S.S., 10 S.S. and 9 S.S. (the two latter the menacing components of 2 S.S. Panzer Corps, just arrived from Russia), 2 S.S. and Panzer Lehr. 1 S.S. had struggled from Bruges: 2 S.S., during its long crawl from Toulouse, had been greatly hampered by the Resistance and air-attacks, and was unable to contribute a complete formation. Also present on the British front were 2 and 21 Panzer. The Americans, freed from the Panzers, were therefore able to execute their violent and fruitful manoeuvres which led to the fall of Cherbourg without the embarrassment of armoured interference: in which they were more fortunate than they knew, for in the latter days of June Hitler was pressing his commanders hard to shift their weight to the west, telling von Rundstedt on the 27th, for example, that 'the Führer holds firmly to the idea of attacking not the strength, but the weakness of the enemy west of the Vire where weaker American forces are located on a broad front'. He was wrong about American weakness! Still, he wanted four or five Panzer divisions to be transferred from the EPSOM front, and it was only the realism of his commanders on the spot that retained them. Even so, on the 28th von Rundstedt and Rommel had to set out for Berchtesgaden to plead their cause.

The logic of the military argument seems to speak for itself. In human terms what it amounted to was this: at present both the British and American armies each had ashore the rough equivalent of 16 divisions. In England there awaited nine American and six British or Canadian divisions. From the U.S.A. further divisions were making ready, to bring the total American complement up to 61 divisions; whereas for the British the maximum would be 20. Yet Montgomery, following the strategy which he conceived to be correct, had so far intentionally manoeuvred in Normandy to bring the whole power of the Panzers against his own national army—an irreplaceable army. For this he received at the time and has since received much criticism. When it was not born of malice or pique, however, much of this criticism can be traced to incomprehension.

The incomprehension grew from a failure to understand that Montgomery was not a newspaper editor—or a Prime Minister. He was not, at bottom, interested in capturing ground or towns for their own sake, to make a good showing in the press next morning or a good mark-up on a map in Whitehall; like a chess-player, he would make a gambit or even accept a rebuff with the equanimity of a man who has a long-term plan in mind. His critics, and some of his superiors, soon began and continued to clamour for short-term successes which would have an immediate popularity. In the case of the Americans the misunderstanding was—to a degree—venial. The subtle and the indirect are not normal characteristics of the American military mind, which tends to pay lip-service to Stonewall Jackson but to follow Grant in practice. This was Eisenhower's instinct—'everybody attacks all the time'—and in spite of his disclaimers it is doubtful whether he ever really grasped the devious, long-term character of Montgomery's strategy. In his heart the fall of Caen would signify more than the containing of the German armour. As late as 1948, when he published *Crusade in Europe*, he was still writing: 'As the days wore on after the initial landing the particular dissatisfaction of the press was directed toward the lack of progress on our left. Naturally I and all of my service commanders and staff were greatly concerned about this static situation near Caen. Every possible means of breaking the deadlock was considered and I repeatedly urged Montgomery to speed up and intensify his efforts to the limit. Montgomery threw in attack after attack, gallantly conducted and heavily supported by artillery and air, but German resistance was not crushed.'

Nor was Montgomery's situation improved by the presence in Eisenhower's entourage of several men who suspected and misinterpreted his motives.* The airmen passionately sought for airfields in the Caen area. Tedder, Eisenhower's Deputy, was deeply anxious on this point, while Coningham, commander of the British Tactical Air Force, felt an almost frenetic hostility. Arguing their case, both airmen got the military facts wrong. Coningham, for example, on 14 June 'said that the 7th Armoured Division had suffered a severe setback, and described the situation as being *near crisis*'. (Author's italics.) Later he called the great Channel gale 'an excuse but not a reason for inaction on the left flank'. And even after EPSOM Tedder referred to a letter of Eisenhower's as reflecting the latter's conviction that 'attacks by the British Second Army had recently been made on a scale of two or three divisions only'. Moreover C.O.S.S.A.C. Morgan, now holding the post of Deputy Chief of Staff to Eisenhower, was quick to comment on what he held to be Montgomery's failure to execute the manoeuvre which Morgan and his planners had originally advocated, a British break-out at an early stage through Caen-Falaise to the south. Morgan's references to Montgomery's 'incurable defensive-mindedness' helped to poison the brew.

Yet the facts, as set out in the table on the next page, are inescapable. During this period the maximum number of Panzer divisions on the American front was three and the minimum less than one: on the British the

---

* But not Omar Bradley. See *A Soldier's Story*, pp. 325–326, which give a shrewd and balanced assessment.

	Tanks opposite *1 U.S. Army*	Tanks opposite *2 British Army*
15 June	70	520
20 June	210	430
25 June	190	530
30 June	140	725
5 July	215	690
10 July	190	610
15 July	190	630
20 July	190	560
25 July	190	645

maximum was seven and a half and the minimum four (on 15 and 20 June). As to infantry battalions, the maximum number attracted by the Americans was 87 and the minimum 63: the British maximum figure was 92 and the minimum 43.

But even more evidential than this tabular statement are the proceedings and consequences of the Berchtesgaden confrontation on 29 June. Von Rundstedt and Rommel had requested from Hitler, in writing, permission to exercise a free hand—in other words, to be allowed to disengage from his remote control of the conduct of the battle. 'A free hand' meant, and was certainly understood to mean, freedom to withdraw. The journey of the Field Marshals was undertaken as a last attempt to make military sense of the German position in the West.

It was a fruitless errand. Far from receiving the option of flexibility which they requested, the Field Marshals found themselves exposed to a general discussion in which Hitler, promising wonder-weapons and demanding control of the air and sea, expounded his thesis that 'We must not allow mobile warfare to develop, since the enemy surpasses us by far in mobility. . . . Therefore everything depends on our confining him to his bridgehead, by building up a front to block him off, and then on fighting a war of attrition to wear him down and force him back.' His mind, it must be remembered, was coloured by the continued success of FORTITUDE. The Weekly Report of Army Group B declared on 26 June (though at this time there were only 15 divisions for the supply of drafts), that 'in England another 67 major formations are standing to, of which 57 at the very least can be employed for a large-scale operation'. In other words, 15 Army and the Pas de Calais were still menaced, in his mind, and the British must not be allowed to make any further ground to the east.

Returning empty-handed to their headquarters, von Rundstedt and Rommel were handed Hitler's new directive, issued by O.K.W. late the previous evening, the 29th. This virtually confirmed the Berchtesgaden discussion.

But von Rundstedt also found two other documents waiting for him. One was from the acting commander, 7 Army: Hausser (commander of the ex-Russian 2 S.S. Panzer Corps) had replaced Dollman who had died of a heart-attack on the 28th. The other was from von Schweppenburg, of Panzer Group West. Both advocated withdrawal to the south. Von Rundstedt immediately, on his own authority, authorised Rommel to prepare for a retreat from Caen, and sent the reports—his courage must be admired—to O.K.W. with a covering letter of his own fully endorsing them. The inevitable response was threefold. On 1 July von Rundstedt received a signal from O.K.W.: 'The present positions are to be held.' The following day he was told he had been superseded, and on the 3rd Field Marshal von Kluge, whom Hitler had mistaken grounds for thinking of as his creature, arrived for the takeover. Next day von Schweppenburg was replaced by General Eberbach.

Whatever the rights or wrongs of Montgomery's policy in Normandy so far, it can at least be claimed on his behalf that it had led to the dismissal, on the field of battle, of two of the most senior and experienced of his opponents because they believed he had presented them with an intolerable military situation. Rommel shared their views; but his reputation made it more difficult to dismiss him at this stage. What Hitler did not know was that to a substantial degree Rommel was involved in the preliminaries of the Plot which would lead to action on 20 July, while von Kluge, who had been fully aware of earlier plots, was also a deeply divided man of whom Chester Wilmot rightly remarks, 'intellectually von Kluge had long since joined the opposition and only his oath had kept him in uneasy allegiance to Hitler'.

At this turning-point in the Normandy campaign, therefore, though it was more evident to Montgomery than to his American colleagues or some of his countrymen in England, the battle was proceeding along the right lines towards the desired consummation: while the spirit of Montgomery's opponents can well be summarised in the famous telephone conversation between Keitel and von Rundstedt at the end of the last—and for the Germans disastrous—day of EPSOM.

> Keitel: 'What shall we do? What shall we do?'
> von Rundstedt: 'Make peace, you fools, what else can you do?'

25 *Normandy: entertained by George Form*

11

Normandy: the coup de grâce

'This thing has busted wide open. We may be the spearhead that broke the camel's back.'

General Leland S. Hobbs, commander
30 U.S. Division, 27 July 1944

Before Montgomery could set in motion his majestic Schlieffen Plan—before the American scythe could begin to swing to the east—Bradley had first to secure a suitable start-line for his army. This was not simple. 'Although this offensive that was to carry our Allied line to the Seine had been outlined months before in England, the attack had yet to be fitted to the peculiarities of our situation in France.' So Bradley subsequently wrote: and his situation at the end of June certainly displayed some peculiarities. First, giving priority (as was correct) to the capture of Cherbourg, he had left St. Lô to be taken later—but any start-line he might devise must include that essential road-centre. Secondly, half his army was still tied up in the Cotentin north of the Carentan marshlands. He therefore attempted to thrust his 7 and 8 Corps out of the Cotentin and well beyond the soft going to Coutances, intending to make the St. Lô-Coutances road that desired line. But this movement, beginning on 3 July, never became more than a crawl: in 12 days 8 Corps only advanced 12,000 yards while 7 Corps, under General Collins, was also making slow progress. Bradley therefore retired to his tent—literally. A man who, like Auchinleck in the desert, lived as hard as his troops, he had to 'acquire' a mess tent and, against the protests of his camp commandant, be supplied with some planking to cover the muddy ground before he could set up his maps in front of which, for two nights, he paced in search of inspiration. By 10 July he had found the answer: he would use a more northerly road as his launching point, that which runs north west from St. Lô via Périers to Lessay on the coast. Moreover, just outside St. Lô he selected a rectangle of ground three and a half miles wide and one and a half deep: this he proposed to drench with saturation bombing by the U.S. Air Force, the planes flying parallel to the road which would clearly indicate to them their own front line. Through this rectangle of death his main thrust was to pass, swiftly developing pace until it had become Liddell Hart's classic 'expanding torrent'.

Normandy: 'still good friends'. A meeting with Omar Bradley

Bradley's tent in the mud was the birth-place of COBRA,* the mortal strike by 1 U.S. Army which, later in the month, would paralyse the enemy. But the Americans, too, paid a price. Between 3 July when preliminary operations started, and 19 July when St. Lô was occupied, their army sustained 40,000 casualties.

Bradley's inability to mount COBRA earlier derived not only from difficulties of terrain but also, in part, from the after-effects of the June storm: shortage of ammunition was a factor. The result was that Montgomery's intention to begin a breakout was implemented later than he had wished, since the directive he issued to the two Army Commanders on 30 June had envisaged, for the American part, 'that it would be possible to strike straight through, without pause, to the line Caumont-Vire-Mortain-Fougeres. Subsequently operations would continue with minimum delays. . . .' The British contribution was to be 'to continue to pin and fight the maximum enemy strength between Villers Bocage and Caen. . . . At the same time it was to ensure that our east flank positions remained firm.' Thus Montgomery, so severely criticised—especially by Americans—for sloth was in fact inhibited from achieving the breakout in the west which 'had been outlined months before in England', and which at the end of June he had ordered to start (under a month from D-Day), by a hold-up, very pardonable, *in the American sector.* His requirement for the British to pin and fight the enemy on the eastern front was therefore intensified during July so that 1 U.S. Army might be exposed to minimal pressure, and enabled to put its vital offensive in hand. All this Bradley well understood. It was a need, however, which generated in many quarters much misunderstanding at the time, not least because, as Bradley put it, 'had we attempted to exonerate Montgomery by explaining how successfully he had hoodwinked the German by diverting him toward Caen from the Cotentin, we would have also given our strategy away. We desperately wanted the German to believe this attack on Caen was the main Allied effort.'

Certain sinister signs began to appear. New German infantry divisions were identified—16 G.A.F. Division east of the Orne on 3 July and 276 Division on the 4th—while on the 7th 83 U.S. Division was attacked heavily by 2 S.S. Panzer, which had moved over from the British sector on the Odon. The implications were that the enemy was preparing to withdraw his armour from the line to refit and regroup, which he had so far been prevented from doing, while at the same time his interest in the Americans appeared to be increasing. Montgomery therefore decided to provide a major distraction by finally capturing the city of Caen.

* Though Chester Wilmot ascribes the saturation bombing plan to a suggestion of Montgomery's.

Three divisions under 1 Corps were to attack in line; 3 on the left, 59 in the centre, and 2 Canadian on the right. (On the 3rd/4th the Canadians had already made some progress by taking Carpiquet village west of Caen, though not, as yet, the airfield—objectives they had just failed to reach on D-Day.) The attack was to be massively supported by Bomber Command, by the 16-inch guns of the battleship H.M.S. *Rodney* (firing at 25,000 yards), by a monitor and two cruisers, and by a miscellany of specialised tanks from 79 Armoured Division. Strength was essential, for by now the Germans had brought the defences of Caen to a high degree of sophistication. Elements of 21, 12 and 1 Panzer Divisions were on the front, as well as a Nebelwerfer brigade and infantry units. But the real menace of the defences was the pattern of interlinked anti-tank ditches, minefields and weapon pits which had gradually been bound together into a defensive belt between two and three miles deep, containing a series of villages which, according to the *Official History*, 'were by now virtually tank-proof'. In this battle I was with 59 Division and thus saw something of these village-fortresses. Of one I wrote at the time: 'The defence of Galmanche consisted of a small château and farm buildings, set in a wilderness of gardens, orchards and shrubbery. Very careful preliminary work had rendered these few hundred square yards a magnificently defended locality. Behind every hedge which lay on the peri-meter an inter-connecting system of fire-positions, crawl trenches and com-munication trenches had been expertly dug and camouflaged. The trees provided excellent cover for snipers who, in their dappled tunics, were extraordinarily difficult to detect. Dug-outs, with thick roofs of earth and logs, were scattered round the position. A few anti-tank guns had been well sited to cover possible approaches, and the care which had been taken in the preparation of the strong-point was indicated by a row of trees from which the outer branches had been lopped and allowed to fall and lie, while a passage had been burrowed behind them to enable free and unobserved movement from one fire-point to another.' This copybook lay-out was characteristic of the defensive belt which, with dug-in tanks and assault guns inside it, and a substantial force of artillery and multi-barrelled mortars behind it, must now be penetrated by the divisions of 1 Corps.

At 2150 hrs. on 7 July 450 heavy bombers struck within an hour at a target area in the northern outskirts of Caen, preceding the infantry attack which began at 0420 next morning. Though a great tonic for morale, the bombing was not wholly satisfactory. Because it was the first of its kind in this theatre, a safety margin was allowed, and this was calculated to require a bomb-line 6,000 yards from the nearest troops. Secondly, though considerable damage was done to the Germans—and more to real estate—it is doubtful whether this effect, and the hampering of German reinforcements, outweighed the disadvantage of not being able to follow up the attack immediately. Finally, the lessons of Cassino had clearly not yet been digested or understood, for the impediment to the advancing troops next day of cratering, and of streets blocked by demolished buildings, was enormous. Still, considering all the unknown factors, it was probably the best arrangement Montgomery could make.

In spite of the bombing and the usual barrage, the Germans' reaction was predictably violent. Their defensive fire was heavy and effective, and in the clearance of the village strongpoints fanatic fighting 'to the last man and the last round' occurred. But at a cost of 5,500 casualties the infantry of 1 Corps got into the city, to be greeted by some 20,000 liberated inhabitants, on the morning of the 9th, and by the evening the whole of that part of the town on the west bank of the Orne—apart from mopping up—was firmly held. All the river-bridges were either destroyed or blocked by rubble, and at this point the attack was called off. Though not an absolute success, therefore, it had served Montgomery's purpose well by engaging the enemy's attention and also by eliminating the German bridgehead west of the Orne, a move essential for his future policy. This was to extend the British holding beyond the east bank of the river sufficiently widely to enable him at once to have room to build up a force that might strike to the south while, at the same time, making quite certain that his eastern flank remained strong enough to repel any possible counter-attack. The latter requirement, the inviolability of the eastern flank, is the reiterated *sine qua non* of Montgomery's OVERLORD strategy. To be able to manoeuvre, however, he would need good east-west routes running to the south of the Caen bottleneck, which was now less a 'communications centre' than a mason's yard: the victory on 8/9 July had taken him some distance in this direction, and the matter must be rounded off. Such, in part, is the background to the next major operation of 2 British Army, the battle called GOODWOOD, which for a variety of reasons was more misunderstood and brought Montgomery into deeper disfavour than any other operation of the Normandy campaign.

GOODWOOD began on 18 July. The concept was simple: three armoured divisions would cross the Orne to the eastern bank and attack in a southerly direction. But the apparent simplicity is deceptive unless the territorial objectives of the operation are clearly apprehended, and unless its relationship to COBRA is properly grasped. This relationship was explained by Montgomery to Dempsey and Bradley at a meeting on 10 July. It was further explained to Eisenhower by Montgomery in a telegram on 13 July which is so explicit that it must be quoted: 'Am going to launch a very big attack next week. Second Army begin at dawn on 16 July and work up to the big operation on . . . 18 Jul. when VIII Corps with three armoured divisions will be launched to the country east of the Orne. Note change of date from 17 to 18 Jul. First Army launch a heavy attack with six divisions about five miles west of St. Lô on . . . 19 Jul. The whole weight of air power will be required for Second Army on 18 Jul and First Army on 19 Jul. Have seen Coningham and explained what is wanted.'

To anyone like Eisenhower, long aware of the OVERLORD plan, this message ought to have made crystal clear Montgomery's initial intention, namely that the breakthrough leading to a breakout would be started by the Americans on the 19th, the British having begun a very powerful diversionary attack the previous day. Eisenhower's reply, which spoke of Bradley keeping his troops 'fighting like the devil, twenty-four hours a day, to provide the opportunity your armoured corps will need . . .', indicated that even the Supreme Commander could not comprehend what, at that stage, Montgomery had in mind—a tightly knit, unified scheme—an Anglo-American Battle. Still less, then, when the start of COBRA was postponed from the 19th to the 25th because of the delay in clearing the start-line and on account of bad weather which held back the American bombers, could the uninstructed see GOOD-WOOD in a true light. All those who were understandably eager for news of a blitzkrieg breakout from the constricted bridgehead, which would carry Montgomery's armies away from the *bocage* and on to the rolling plains of France, not unnaturally saw GOODWOOD as a British attempt that failed and COBRA, a week later, as an American triumph.

But the British were not attempting a blitzkrieg. I have spoken to Field Marshal Montgomery himself on this point, to the late Sir Miles Dempsey who commanded 2 British Army, and to General Sir Richard O'Connor who was in command of the armoured Corps which made the attack. All stated categorically that the purpose of GOODWOOD was *not* a breakthrough but, primarily, a continuation in another and more powerful form of the now long-standing effort by the British to act as a magnet for the Panzers. Exploitation was naturally envisaged—any sane general would have in mind the possibility of unexpected success proffering unexpected opportunities—but the basic intention was *not* that of COBRA; to smash a hole and pour through it. This Montgomery again made clear in a written instruction to Dempsey on 15 July, of which para. 5 reads: 'The three armoured divisions will be required to dominate the area Bourgebus-Vimont-Bretteville' (i.e. the high ground south of Caen) 'and to fight and destroy the enemy, but armoured cars should push far to the south towards Falaise, spread alarm and despondency, and discover "the form".' That is no prescription for a breakthrough: yet Dempsey told me that it was the only written order he received from Montgomery during the Normandy campaign—written 'for the record'. All other orders came to him by word of mouth in conversation or conference.

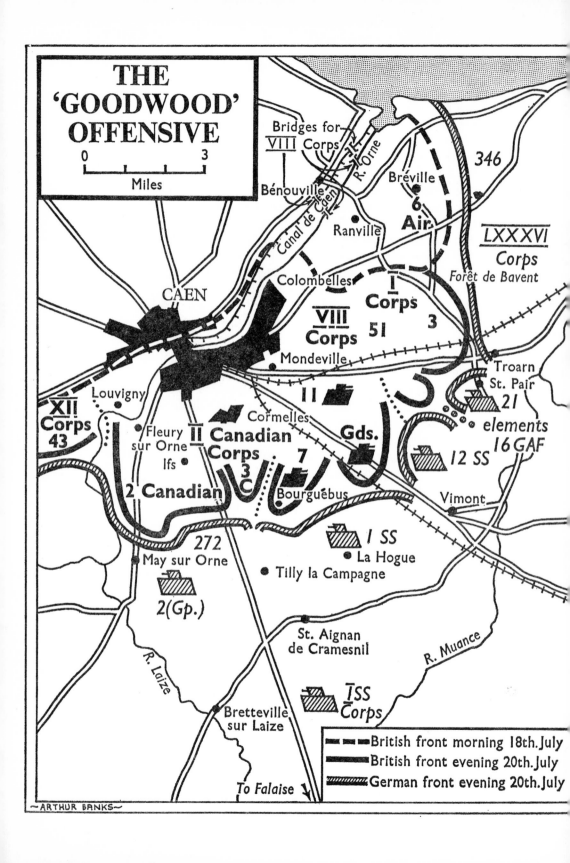

THE 'GOODWOOD' OFFENSIVE

0 _____ 3

Miles

Bridges for
VIII Corps

R. Orne

346

Bénouville

Bréville

6
Air.

Canal de Caen

Ranville

LXXXVI
Corps

Colombelles

Forêt de Bavent

CAEN

I Corps

VIII
Corps
51

3

Mondeville

Troarn
St. Pair

Louvigny

II

21

XII
Corps
43

Cormelles

Gds.

elements
16 GAF

Fleury
sur Orne

II Canadian
Corps

12 SS

Ifs

3
C

7

2 Canadian

Bourguébus

Vimont

272

I SS

May sur Orne

La Hogue

2 (Gp.)

Tilly la Campagne

St. Aignan
de Cramesnil

R. Muance

R. Laize

I SS
Corps

Bretteville
sur Laize

━ ━ ━ British front morning 18th. July
━━━ British front evening 20th. July
▨▨▨ German front evening 20th. July

~ARTHUR BANKS~

To Falaise

It was in fact Dempsey who propounded the idea, and Montgomery who at first shrank from it. Soon after the conference on 10 July (at which Bradley had shown concern about the Americans' progress, and had been told by Montgomery, without reproach, to take all the time he needed) Dempsey proposed that the British should put in a powerful attack on their own. Montgomery was at first unwilling, as the concept was counter to his strategy. He then saw advantages in a strong attack with limited objectives which, mounted east of the Orne, would pull the bulk of the German reserves towards it and thus keep Rommel off-balance when COBRA finally struck. At first, as is clear from his explanatory letter to the C.I.G.S. of 14 July, he was thinking somewhat more largely, in terms of 'to loose a corps of three armoured divisions in to the open country about the Caen-Falaise road', but even then he was at pains to send his Military Assistant over to the War Office to make clear that 'all the activities on the eastern flank are designed to help the American forces in the west while ensuring that a firm bastion is kept in the east.' When it became evident that COBRA would have to be postponed Montgomery therefore, as has been seen, further limited the scope of GOODWOOD; and it is, without question, on the basis of that limited scope that the battle was fought.

Yet in spite of all his concern and insurance against being misunderstood, Montgomery *was* misunderstood. This is partly due to his own carelessness, careful though he had been. When Churchill, for example, on the eve of the battle signalled 'God with you', it was probably unwise, knowing the Prime Minister's propensities, to answer with a message which (despatched on 17 July) ended 'Am determined to loose the armoured divisions tomorrow if in any way possible. . . .' Shades of Renton and Alam Halfa! 'When shall we set the armour loose?' With the airmen Montgomery also tended towards apparent overstatements which perhaps were a by-product of his anxiety to obtain their support. His message to Tedder of the 14th, containing the words 'if successful the plan promises to be decisive', was certainly capable of misleading a man already sharply critical of Montgomery's cautiousness and burning to hear of the over-running of more ground suitable for airfields.

In the event, it was fortunate for Montgomery that he had made no grandiose promises or pronouncements about GOODWOOD which contemporary critics or posterity might legitimately hold against him, for the opposition encountered was beyond everything expected, and to have effected a decisive breakthrough would have involved great slaughter. This was the result of Rommel's last achievement as a soldier. On 17 July he was returning from Eberbach's Panzer Group West H.Q., after making a final check of his defensive arrangements before the anticipated attack—for its imminence was obvious to the Germans from many indications—when his car was attacked by

British fighters and swerved into a tree; Rommel's injuries would have killed most men, but though he lived, he never fought again. Instead, on Hitler's orders he was murdered in the following October, on suspicion of complicity in the plot to remove the Führer which unsuccessfully culminated on 20 July, the day when a thunderstorm turned the country around Caen into a bog, and brought to an end the battle of GOODWOOD.

Under Rommel's eye Eberbach had created in the area to be assaulted the most powerful defence system ever established in Normandy. Two railway lines run east from Caen. North of the first, which goes from the suburb of Vaucelles, east of the Orne, to Troarn, two infantry divisions were positioned. Then came an armoured belt, 21 Panzer with 36 Tigers under command, plus a unit of 1 S.S. Panzer. The next defended zone followed the second railway, which runs south east from Caen to Vimont, and consisted of a dozen or so villages each manned by infantry and anti-tank gunners. The main gun line constituted the fourth defence belt, encompassing the Bourgébus ridge and the Secqueville woods and then curving north across the railway towards Troarn: the ridge villages were, as usual, made infantry strongpoints. Then came the fifth line, lying so far back as to be reasonably safe—45 Panthers of 1 S.S. and more tanks from 12 S.S. On the whole front were three infantry and two armoured divisions, well over 200 tanks, supported by 78 88s, 194 field pieces, and no less than 272 *nebelwerfers* as well as lighter anti-tank and anti-aircraft weapons.

And yet, efficiently though this defensive zone had been organised, the British ought, on paper, to have prevailed. The weight of metal on which they could call was out of all proportion to that available to the Germans, and in a *Materialenschlacht* should have proved irresistible. 8 Corps alone had 750 tanks: 1 Corps who were to operate simultaneously on the left and 2 Canadian Corps on the right added another 350. But the real strength of the Allies, which the Germans could never possibly match, lay in the air; on the first day of GOODWOOD there were employed 4,500 planes of all types, an unprecedented number for direct support in a battle of this scale. The bombing was to be on a new principle. This, broadly speaking, was that the heavy bombs were to be dropped along both flanks of the route to be taken by the armour, while selected areas aside and ahead of the route were to be dealt with by small high-explosive, fragmentation and incendiary bombs, thus avoiding cratering. There was a lavish supply of fighter-bombers and rocket-planes, on call from the ground. And, as in the attack on Caen on the 8th, heavy guns were to make their contribution from the sea.

But paper tigers are not necessarily all they seem: the British superiority in guns and bombs and armour was off-set to a substantial degree by geography. So far as possible the attack was to be a surprise—though in fact

Rommel was fully alerted and indeed reporting to von Kluge about 'the large-scale attack which is expected from the evening of the 17th for making a breakthrough across the Orne'. Aiming at surprise, however, the three armoured divisions, II, Guards, and 7, were held back west of the Orne until the night of the 17th, when in that order they would begin to cross the three available bridges over the river and the Caen canal: and—increasing the consequences of this appalling bottle-neck—most of the artillery, also held in the west, could not use the bridges till the armour had passed. The choice of a battlefield, in fact, inevitable though it may have been, at a stroke nullified many of Montgomery's advantages.

This truth soon became evident on the 18th. The bombing appeared to go according to plan—though, as later emerged, some targets were so obscured by dust that when the planes due to deal with them arrived they had to turn away and take their bombs home; other selected areas were accurately bombed only in part, and the unaffected part often contained tanks or anti-tank guns; while most of the 13,000 100-pound and 75,000 fragmentation bombs dropped by the U.S. Eighth Air Force fell widely scattered on the wrong places. Still, there was a spurious air of success as II Armoured crossed its bridges and moved steadily forward, finding many signs of a demoralised enemy. However, the first indication of impending difficulties soon appeared: by 0900 the advancing tanks had passed beyond the range of the supporting field artillery still imprisoned on the western bank. Moreover, there emerged simultaneously the pattern by which the rest of the battle would be dominated. At the bridges congestion was beginning to build up, while over the battlefront, and especially at the villages of Cagny, Émieville and Frénouville, the surviving tanks and guns of the Germans were taking an unwelcome toll. During the morning and afternoon there was much confusion, and such forward movement as was made was mainly affected by individual units of II and Guards Armoured Division. 7 Armoured were not able to struggle free of the bridges till midday, and had only one regiment in action by the evening: indeed, it was clear, at a conference held by General O'Connor of 8 Corps in the midst of the battle at 1400 hrs., that Major-General Erskine, commanding the division, 'regarded the whole operation', according to Chester Wilmot, 'as a gross abuse of armour and seemed determined to keep his tanks out of the maelstrom as long as possible'. On the left 1 Corps made small progress, getting no further than Troarn, which was still untaken by the end of the day. The Canadians did better on the right, seizing and clearing the shattered factory suburb of Colombelles (whose chimneys had provided the Germans with useful observation posts), working along the river bank, throwing out a bridgehead on the eastern bank and starting bridge-building.

Montgomery therefore seems to have been badly informed and was certainly ill-advised when, at 1630 hrs. that afternoon, he sent off a buoyant signal to the C.I.G.S. which began 'Operations this morning a complete success. The effect of the air bombing was decisive. . . . Situation very promising and it is difficult to see what the enemy can do at present. . . .' He also committed an act of what can only be described as blind folly by issuing that evening a special announcement which used of his troops the words 'broke through', and concluded 'General Montgomery is well satisfied with the progress made in the first day's fighting of this battle.' At best this was premature, for some of the gains Montgomery reported to London had not yet been achieved, and in fact during the next two days all that happened was that, in further heavy fighting, the Bourgébus ridge was partially secured and the strongpoints intervening between it and the start-line of the attack reduced. During the afternoon of the 20th there was heavy thunder overhead, and the torrential rain converted the soil of the battlefield, now a fine dust after the bombing and the movement of armour, into a morass. So far as O'Connor's tanks were concerned, that was the end. Next day the Canadians fought off a number of fierce counter-attacks on their positions east of the Orne, but for all practical purposes the day which ended with Hitler announcing to his people that a plot had failed to kill him also ended with the justification of the defensive zone which Rommel, later to be killed because of the plot, had been responsible for devising. On 20 July GOODWOOD was over.

Through misunderstanding of his intentions, both in the long and in the short term, and by his impetuous announcement of what seemed to be the breakthrough the people and the leaders of the Allies were impatiently waiting for, Montgomery had placed himself in the hands of his enemies and disconcerted his friends. Mingled with the disappointment and even desperation which the news of GOODWOOD's 'failure' aroused, there was certainly a malicious element of 'I told you so' in the comments of his habitual detractors. The press in England and America, having extracted from Montgomery's communiqué the fatal phrases 'break through' and 'open country' and displayed them in banner headlines, almost inevitably treated the news that the offensive had halted with the same dramatic emphasis. How far misunderstanding and ignorance of the true facts could go is summarised in a headline of the *New York Herald Tribune*, after GOODWOOD and on the eve of COBRA: 'Allies in France Bogged Down on Entire Front'—the eve of the strategic breakthrough!

Eisenhower was at a loss what to do—largely because he had an entirely wrong conception of what Montgomery ought to be doing. He visited his subordinate at his H.Q. on the 20th, and then sent him a letter next day 'to assure myself that we see eye to eye on the big problems'. After the usual generalities about being strong and so being able to hit the German hard and continuously, he went on to make this extraordinary statement. '. . . you should insist that Dempsey keep up the strength of his attack. . . . In First Army the whole front comes quickly into action to pin down local reserves and to support the main attack. Dempsey should do the same. . . .' If Montgomery had been as bilious as some of those near to Eisenhower he might justifiably have screamed with rage at this grandmotherly advice, for, apart from the almost total preoccupation of the German armour with the British front from D-Day onwards, between the start of Bradley's operations on 3 July and the *delayed* start of COBRA on 25 July five new infantry divisions (271, 272, 276, 277 and 326) had been identified opposite the British, as well as one new armoured division (116): during the same period only one new infantry division and the part of another had been identified by the Americans, as well as the Panzer Lehr armoured division which, as has been seen, had already been battered to weakness on the British front. But Montgomery wisely kept his head. It is a tribute to his equanimity (and self-assurance) that in spite of Eisenhower's incomprehension—a by-product of his thwarted desire for 'everyone to be fighting all the time' which finally found expression in his Broad Front policy—nothing irrevocable was uttered: a tribute to Eisenhower's good sense also, for he too never went beyond the tactfully emphatic, though at SHAEF and elsewhere he could hear voices urging him to exert his right and, as Supreme Commander, take over in France direction of operations on land from his incompetent subordinate. Chief among these sirens was his Deputy, Tedder, who as an airman had always a *penchant* for knowing how to run a battle on land. Tedder wrote to Eisenhower a letter commenting on his to Montgomery of 21 July, in which he specifically urged Eisenhower to come over to France and save the situation, ending persuasively 'in the hope that the expression of my views as your immediate British subordinate may be of some assistance to you and to support you in any action you may consider the situation demands'. Churchill was more easily appeased. He too had doubts; but a visit to Montgomery after GOODWOOD, during which all was explained to him, appears to have proved satisfactory.

Tedder's passionate petulance is, of course, explained to a considerable degree by the frustration which he and Coningham felt about their lack of forward airfields in Normandy—and to a considerable degree this was understandable. But was it justified? It is relevant to note that Montgomery, the arch-advocate of the need for air power to sustain modern military operations, never seems to have been disturbed during or after the battle by the air factor. In his review of the battle in *Normandy to the Baltic*, indeed, he speaks of 'the tremendous achievements of the Allied Air Forces' and adds, 'they maintained complete air supremacy over the battle area, so that finally the enemy became virtually immobilized during the hours of daylight'. That this was less than lip-service would be confirmed by anybody who was in Normandy at the time, and indeed the vast conglomeration of vehicles, stores and troops would otherwise have been impossible. The air marshals may have yearned for an empire larger than could be allotted to them in the crowded beachhead, but in practice, the enemy was kept out of the sky. Montgomery defined the fundamental differences in attitude when he wrote that 'Coningham wanted the airfields in order to defeat Rommel, whereas I wanted to defeat Rommel in order, only incidentally, to capture the airfields.'

The launching of COBRA was beset by difficulties. First there was the slow and costly sweep through the swamps of Carentan and the hedgerows about St. Lô. Then there was the failure to reap the full benefits of GOODWOOD by attacking on the 19th. Then the stormy weather which terminated GOODWOOD also had its effects on COBRA, for the bombers which were to prepare the ground for this attack were unable to operate until the 24th. Collins' 7 Corps, which was to follow up the air-strike, had been waiting since the 21st for a Zero Hour. And when, on the morning of the 24th, the bombers were at last due, heavy cloud gathered over the target area and the operation was again postponed, for 24 hours—unfortunately one group, not having received the message to return, had already dropped its bombs a mile short of the target and on top of 30 U.S. Division. Bradley was now faced with the kind of decision which demands the highest courage in a commander—the courage to face the possibility of an unnecessary sacrifice of the men he commanded. It soon became clear that the culprit bombers had not been flying parallel with the boundary road, but at 90 degrees to it. Leigh-Mallory, now at Bradley's H.Q., checked with Eighth U.S. Air Force H.Q. in England that this was the case: he confirmed that it was so, and that this was how they proposed to fly. Bradley was appalled; for, five days previously, he had himself visited Eighth Air Force at Stanmore in Middlesex to complete arrangements for the bombing, and had left convinced that the planes would keep to his plan and follow the road. Now this was not to happen. Assuming it was to happen, he had laid down a safety margin of 1,200 yards between his troops and the bomb-line; if the attack was to go in next day it was too late to rearrange matters. *He decided to proceed.*

On the 25th, when the assault went in, there was more inaccurate bombing. 9 Division was hit, and 30 for the second time, and there were several hundred casualties in dead and wounded, including the very able General McNair: but Bradley's decision was correct, for a further postponement would have meant that the Germans, already alerted by the first bombing, would have been able to thicken the St. Lô defences and COBRA might have lost the essential impetus it gained in the first 48 hours. Moreover, to press on with

COBRA was wise in a larger sense, for what Montgomery's critics could not then know was that he had created for it the most favourable conditions. Von Kluge was losing his nerve. Though he had arrived in the west an optimist, his experience had soon generated an absolute pessimism, so absolute that, though on the news of the 20 July plot he had immediately sent Hitler a message assuring him of 'unchangeable loyalty', he had followed this with Rommel's final judgement that 'the unequal struggle is nearing its end', endorsed by himself with the observation that 'discussion with the commanders of the formations near Caen' had convinced him that 'the moment has drawn near when this front already so severely strained will break'. At the same time FORTITUDE was continuing its deceit, for Speidel was signalling from Army Group B on the 24th that 'the sector of the Fifteenth Army from north of the Somme to the Seine is particularly threatened'—he thought there were still 42 divisions available in England—and that while the Americans would only advance their front to Domfront-Avranches, the British would break out via Falaise towards Paris. Such thinking was aided by an attack down the Falaise road which was mounted by 2 Canadian Corps with 7 and Guards Armoured, beginning at 0330 hrs. on the 25th, on Montgomery's strict orders that it should start then *irrespective of a decision when* COBRA *could begin and whatever the state of the weather*. He was worried by the premature bombing at St. Lô, and feared the warning it might give the Germans: the Canadian attack, he hoped, might suggest that the bombing was merely a feint. It was, indeed, precisely what Eberbach had anticipated, and during the 24th and 25th there was a general movement of Panzer units from the west towards or across the Orne.

COBRA, it should be emphasised, was an all-American activity. In the preparatory phases Montgomery, in spite of his overall responsibility, handled Bradley with great delicacy and understanding. He tacitly accepted the American command system whereby a subordinate is given a mission and left to get on with it. Bradley himself draws a contrast between Montgomery's 'interventions' in Dempsey's area, which 'Dempsey knew how to tolerate without jealousy or rage', and his recognition of 'the traditional independence of action' which an American officer assumed. Montgomery, Bradley says, 'never insisted upon scrutinising in detail our field operations'. Both before and after Normandy Montgomery at times displayed an obtruseness about American susceptibilities; but this, to his credit, he restrained during that vital period of the beaches and the *bocage* when it was essential that in their regular association Montgomery, Dempsey and Bradley should not only appear to be but should think like 'a band of brothers'. Moreover, while COBRA was American in its preparation, still more so was it in its execution. Lurking in the Cotentin, his presence a carefully kept secret, was General

Patton: he was supposed to be in England still, so far as the Germans knew—
FORTITUDE's General in Command of that phantom army. But shortly after
the start of COBRA, on 1 August, the 21 American divisions now on the Continent would be split between 1 Army under Hodges and a newly constituted
3 Army under Patton, the two forming 12 U.S. Army Group under Bradley.
When this occurred Bradley and Montgomery, as 21 Army Group Commander (1 Canadian Army under Crerar having become operational on 23 July)
would have parity of status under Eisenhower's supreme command, though
Montgomery was to retain a delegated power of surveillance over the whole
of the land battle until Eisenhower transferred his H.Q. to France and took
over full command. All this was in accordance with agreements made, and
fully understood by all parties concerned, long ago when the OVERLORD plan
was being prepared. Of course it was a secret arrangement, so that when
during August it leaked out to the press (SHAEF having unwisely put an
embargo on the story until 14 August) there was not unnaturally an outcry
in the British newspapers. Much though they had criticised him for excess
of caution, they rallied to Montgomery's cause when it seemed that in some
way Britain's most distinguished soldier was being slighted in favour of an
American. This was irrational but understandable, in that the size of Britain's
army had already reached its possible peak: competition with America could
only be in quality, henceforth, and never in quantity—and Montgomery
bestriding an American as well as a British army had in a very real sense
personified, for the British, a quality product. A proper public explanation
by Eisenhower of what had actually happened, and why, would have helped
to restrain comment, but he remained silent, and there is no doubt that the
unease aroused in Britain was an unfortunate background for the controversy
that would follow later in the year about the merits of having a single Ground
Commander. (All that has been said above applied in a reverse sense, of
course, in the United States.)

The 3,000-odd heavy, medium and fighter-bombers which, starting at
0940 hrs. on the 25th, saturated the rectangle designated by Bradley to the
west of St. Lô with high explosive, fragmentation and napalm bombs wrought
terrible destruction. Panzer Lehr was virtually eliminated: its commander,
Bayerlein, survived—to be later captured—and he described the scene after
the bombardment with a word which in recent years has become even more
intensely evocative because of the images it summons of arid, widespread
desolation . . . *Mondlandschaft*, a landscape on the moon. But though Bradley
had good reason to feel dismay, in view of the bombing his troops had
suffered, and of the delay caused by reorganisation as a result of these
casualties and the nature of the ground to be covered, torn fields and roads
littered with 'the black hulls of burned-out tanks, the mutilated bodies of

soldiers, and the carcasses of bloated, stiff-legged cattle', in fact Collins' corps achieved a break-in. By the end of the day it had advanced two miles, and on the 26th Collins put in his two armoured divisions, while on the right 8 U.S. Corps and on the left 5 U.S. Corps began to advance in échelon. On the 27th enemy resistance collapsed along the whole front, and by the 30th Avranches, the sally-port from Brittany, had been secured. There was con-fusion not only among the lines of defence but also among the German commanders in the rear: von Kluge was driven, on the 30th, to take over personal command of 7 Army and early next morning spoke to his Chief Staff Officer, Blumentritt, at C.-in-C. West's H.Q, to announce that 'the situation here is completely farcical . . . things are in a gigantic mess'. A 'Most Secret' report was sent to the same H.Q. a week later by Commander 7 Army, detailing the disintegration of his divisions, 'the 77th, 91st, 243rd, 275th, elements of 265th and 352nd and 353rd, 5th Parachute Division, 2nd S.S. Panzer Division and 17 S.S. Panzer Grenadier Division', whose survivors had straggled back in raggle-taggle groups, living off the countryside, the prey of the Resistance.

In the meantime Montgomery had been reviewing his plans. On the 27th he met Bradley and Dempsey. Applauding the American success, he stated that 'the object of everything done elsewhere must be to further American operations'. He therefore scrapped his ideas for more attacks by the British and Canadians to the east of Caen and the Orne, on the ground that operations here had probably served their purpose and that it was unlikely that more German divisions could be inveigled. Pointing out that all six Panzer divisions on the British front lay in the centre or to the east, he ordered Dempsey with all speed to mount a six-divisional offensive from the Caumont area right on the west of the British line, and next day, hearing how COBRA was progressing, he told Dempsey to 'step on the gas for Vire'. This order derived from his conviction that as the Germans pulled back before the American avalanche, they would pivot their eastward swing on first Caumont, then the inland reaches of the Orne, and finally on the uplands between Caen and Falaise. Dempsey's attack, Operation BLUECOAT, opened on the 30th, and it has two interesting features. The first is the high degree of expertise, at all levels, which made it possible. As the *Official History* says: 'Hardly a formation in the British and Canadian armies but had to adjust its positions or "up sticks" and move at once. Some of 8 Corps' formations who did not receive their orders till near midday on the 28th had to pull out from the other side of the Orne and drive forty or fifty miles along roundabout and crowded routes through the back areas, always mindful of the need for secrecy. Thanks to good staff work, good march discipline, and, above all, air superiority, all needed for opening the attack on the 30th were able to cross their start-lines (hastily briefed and a little breathless, perhaps) on time.' The second point is that BLUECOAT well illustrates, as do, for example, SUPERCHARGE at Alamein and the left hook at Mareth, the fact that although *strategically* Montgomery could prove stubborn and single-minded (once his mind was made up), *tactically* he was capable, within the battle, of rapid readjustment and reorientation when presented with a sudden opportunity or unexpected check.

The country to be tackled in BLUECOAT, that bounded by Caumont in the north, Vire in the south, and Thury-Harcourt on the Orne in the east, has been well described as *bocage* at its very worst. Moreover, in the centre the ground rises in broken hill features up to the dominant Mt. Pinçon ridge, 1,200 feet above sea level. In the two corps, 8 and 30, with which he was to attack Dempsey had a three to one superiority in armour but not great advantage in infantry, so that, considering the terrain and even though the enemy was disheartened, a dramatic advance comparable with what was happening on his right was out of the question. Moreover, this had been a static front for weeks, and both sides had copiously distributed minefields. The story for the first two days is therefore roughly the same for both corps— the arduous, dangerous and apparently unrewarding routine of in-fighting. But there was one favourable development: II Armoured during the night set up a bridgehead beyond the river Souleuvre at Beny-Bocage, about half way from Caumont to Vire, and here they linked up with troops of 5 U.S. Corps which was moving on the British right.

Montgomery's purpose had already been achieved. With 21 Panzer already involved, von Kluge on Eberbach's recommendation moved 2 S.S. Panzer Corps to meet Dempsey's *Schwerpunkt*—9 and 10 S.S. Panzer Divisions, a *nebelwerfer* brigade, and a heavy anti-tank battalion. Eberbach maintained that irrespective of what was happening elsewhere, the Caumont sector was decisive: even with the three armoured divisions, he doubted whether he could hold, and recommended retreat to the Seine. Hitler, too, appears to have started to think on similar lines: at a meeting on 31 July he ordered that a special O.K.W. staff should be created to examine a possible withdrawal, noting the pause-lines to be used in France and the work which would be required. At the same time the Commander-in-Chief West was to be left in absolute ignorance. 'Tell Field Marshal von Kluge that he should keep his eyes riveted to the front and on the enemy without ever looking backward,' was Hitler's message to him.

On 2 August II Armoured was almost in Vire: but on the 30 Corps front only slow progress had been made. 7 Armoured, counter-attacked the same day, was actually forced back to the position it held 48 hours previously. This was no recipe for victory, and 30 Corps' Commander, Bucknall, having been warned by Dempsey to 'get on or get out', was removed, as well as Erskine,

27 The Ardennes: Dempsey, Hodges, Montgomery, Simpson and Crer

28 *Germany : the thousandth Bailey bridge since D-Day*

29 *Forward to Osnabrück through the ruins of Goesfeld*

commanding 7 Armoured Division, together with his Commander, Royal Artillery, and his armoured brigade commander. This clean sweep caused much ill feeling at the time. Dempsey, however, who certainly knew his own mind and was no starry-eyed devotee of his senior, told me, when I asked him about Montgomery's alleged ruthlessness in sacking, that there was no dismissal of a senior officer in 2 British Army by Montgomery of which he did not know in advance and of which he did not approve. Bucknall's going happened to coincide with the availability of the dynamic Horrocks, who had just recovered from his Tunisian injuries and took over command of 30 Corps on 4 August. Whether it was through his influence or by a sudden burst of inspiration, 43 Division by hard and brilliant fighting were on the heights of Mt. Pinçon on the 6th, the same day as the Americans at last took Vire and the British 59 Division made, and in the face of bitter counter-attacks held, a bridgehead across the Orne at Thury-Harcourt. Two of Montgomery's three 'pivots' for the German retreat had now been seized, and plans were already well advanced for the capture of the third. But in the meantime, both the Americans and Hitler had provided Montgomery with much food for thought.

1 August 1944 was a great day for General George Patton. Hyperconscious of the harm he had done to himself by the slapping incident in Sicily, he was burning for an opportunity for redemption. When the news of the 20 July plot arrived, he came clamouring to Bradley for the chance of action before, as he feared, the war suddenly ended. Now he took over 3 U.S. Army on the very day when the Normandy campaign had reached the point where his exceptional talents could be displayed at their best. Bradley's plan, after the capture of Avranches, had been to use Patton's army to clear up Brittany— including the ports. But Brittany—excluding the ports—was already crumbling, and after a conference with Montgomery and Dempsey Bradley issued fresh instructions on the 3rd which laid down that Patton should use only 'minimum forces' for Brittany, while with the rest of his army he thrust south and east to clear the ground north of the Loire and then made, as Montgomery had specified in his directive, 'a wide sweep south of the *bocage* country. . . .' This was manna for Patton, who started off with, as he recalled, 'one of those things which cannot be done, but was'. Beyond the bridge at Avranches ran a single road, under regular Luftwaffe attack by day and night. Through Avranches and down this road Patton moved seven divisions in 72 hours, and the pace was thereafter maintained as his 15 Corps raced ahead through open country. By the 7th it was almost into Le Mans, thus fulfilling the spirit of Montgomery's directive of the 4th which declared that 'everyone must go all out all day and every day'. Early on the 3rd, however, Hitler had also issued a directive, with precisely the opposite object—a mortal blow to the wretched von Kluge, who had already reported back to O.K.W., soon

Q

after the fall of Avranches, that 'the whole western front has been ripped open'. Nevertheless he was now ordered by Hitler to draw back 7 Army's line, leaving it to be held by infantry only, and with the resultant armour, plus reinforcements that were more promises than facts, to put in a powerful counter-attack via Mortain with the purpose of seizing the Avranches bottleneck. Among all Hitler's military follies this is outstanding, and its executants were not deceived. Montgomery notes that Dietrich, commanding for the operation 5 Panzer Army (the re-named Panzer Group West), argued with von Kluge for an hour as he listed the reasons, all correct, which made the plan ruinous. Von Kluge could only produce in reply the word 'Führer-befehl' . . . 'It is Hitler's command.'

Though the Mortain offensive was, in Bradley's words, 'to cost the enemy an army and gain us France', it can be dealt with summarily. The first probes occurred during the early hours of the 7th, and by the 12th there were unmistakable signs of retreat. The victory, apart from the devastating rockets from British Typhoons, was entirely American: and if the Mortain attack looks somewhat like a miniature version of the Ardennes offensive, so here was to be seen in miniature the courage and adaptability of the American troops and command. The leading tanks hit, by chance (as in the Ardennes), a weary 30 U.S. Division which was 'resting'. This division held fast: one of its battalions, cut off and surrounded, fought for six days until relieved, and the four patched up Panzer divisions, all that von Kluge could collect for this crucial operation, made very little headway. Bradley remained calm, particularly in the early stages when he had to weigh the possibility of the 12 American divisions now south of Avranches being cut off. He took no wild emergency action, but quietly stopped, surrounded and squeezed the Germans while the Allied Air Force bombarded them mercilessly—there being, by good luck, a run of fine weather during these August days. Perhaps the most contemptuous comment to be made on Hitler's brain-child is that it never, for one moment, prevented Patton's advance: indeed, it was because Patton had advanced so far so fast that, with 15 Corps now speeding north from Le Mans towards Alençon, the Führer began to feel a concern about the rear of Army Group B and gave von Kluge, on the 11th, permission for a 'minor withdrawal' from Mortain. This kind of tinkering with disintegration was useless, for there was no firm line within reach on which von Kluge might retire. One day later, and Patton was telephoning to Bradley, 'We've got elements in Argentan. Let me go on to Falaise and we'll drive the British back into the sea for another Dunkirk.' This remark by an Army Commander to his Army Group Commander about a faithful ally was typical of Patton: it was not funny, it was certainly offensive, and it happened to be unjust. Montgomery had not been idle about Falaise. The truth was that while Patton's tanks had been burning up petrol along fast open roads and sweeping through thinly defended towns, the British and, more especially, the Canadians in the north had been struggling against the kind of ferocious resistance and difficult terrain which Patton did not experience until he ran head on into the fortifications of Metz and the Saar: there he discovered the significance of fixed defences—his army sustained 41,000 casualties in a month, or about half those of the whole of 21 Army Group between D-Day and the end of August.

As the Germans pulled slowly southwards from the Caen *enceinte* they maintained the thick defensive zone which had consistently characterised this sector of their line. Montgomery's problem was, how to crack it decisively so as to create a corridor through which a connection could be made with the Americans pouring up from the south, and thus tie the neck of the bag created by Hitler's insistence on pursuing the Mortain offensive. His tactics were two-fold. While he sought to tie the bag's neck, he also arranged with Bradley that the Americans should force their way onwards to the banks of the Seine, for it was now abundantly clear that Hitler had gambled unsuccessfully in retaining his divisions in Normandy: even though troops might filter through the Falaise constriction, an Allied presence on the Seine ought to result in a rich harvest of casualties and captured Germans. How to get to Falaise was a conundrum he remitted to 1 Canadian Army, as part of a general directive for the dispositions of the Allied armies which he issued on 4 August—i.e., well before the Mortain affair was concluded.

The operation, to start on the 7th, was put in the hands of Lieut.-General Simonds ('the best of my Corps Commanders', Dempsey told me) and his 2 Canadian Corps, whose two infantry divisions, one armoured division and one armoured brigade were amplified by 51 Highland, 33 Armoured Brigade, —and the Polish Armoured Division who were newcomers to Normandy. Patton might well have studied the intricate plans for this operation, codenamed TOTALIZE, for in daring and ingenuity they surpassed anything so far attempted with armour by the British army—or the Americans. Simonds' difficulty was this: he had to thrust down the Caen-Falaise road amid open country which, as several preliminary probes had revealed, gave ample scope to the 88s, the mortars and machine-guns in the strong enemy line. This hard crust he had to crack with his armour: but until his armour had reached the crust he must keep the heads of the enemy down without providing the conventional warning of an artillery preparation. He therefore adopted the wholly unconventional plan of using heavy bombers, *in a tactical rôle at night*, to carpet the flanks of his line of advance; meanwhile his assault troops moved in the centre, the forward infantry being transported in armoured troop-carriers made available by removing the guns from the tracked chassis of self-propelled artillery. Ingenious devices were also evolved for the maintenance of direction in this unprecedented attack: radio-directional beams for the tanks, target-indicator shells with coloured bursts, tracer from Bofors firing on fixed lines, and searchlights to illuminate the sky as the moon failed. Unconventional, too, was the mode of deployment: the main assault force was paraded in separate columns each on a 'four tank front', the vehicles packed nose to tail, and each column led by 79 Armoured Division's specialised flail tanks and armoured fighting vehicles. There were over 1,000 bombers in support of the attack, and as it moved forward 360 guns put down a barrage in its path.

The daring and ingenuity of the Canadians won only a partial reward. As so often had happened and would again happen, the material superiority of the Allies proved self-defeating. Only two-thirds of the heavy bomber programme could be carried out: the late-comers were unable to see their targets because of the dust raised by the bombs dropped by their predecessors. And the close-packed armour found forward movement to be difficult in the darkness, amid the smoke and dust. Nevertheless, Simonds' plan worked in so far as it showed that tanks and bombers could pass infantry through a defended line by night, for in spite of all the set-backs inevitable in such an operation 2 Canadian Division and 51 Highland were decanted before dawn and were seizing their objectives. The momentum of their attacks was slowed down first by the violent resistance in the German second line and the pockets which had been by-passed during the night, and also by the sorry failure of the American Fortresses who flew in at midday to further the advance. The failure was not wholly the Americans' fault: Bomber Command was due to do the job, but a complication of bad weather on the wrong airfields and other technical difficulties threw the burden on the Eighth Air Force. Of 678 planes under 500 dropped bombs, and very many of those fell wide of the mark—many, indeed, on the Canadian Corps which, as a result, had 300 extra casualties. Hard pressure continued during the next few days, but though the Canadians were still just short of Falaise when Patton contemptuously signalled to Bradley his desire to brush Montgomery's men aside, it was not, as they say, for want of trying. The pressure was intensified by Simonds on the 14th, when in an attempt to fulfil Montgomery's order to take Failaise he turned upside down his previous plan, and in Operation TRACTABLE sent his tanks in by daytime, in 'serried array', under the cover of thick smoke and, as before, convoying infantry in armoured carriers. Once again the unconventional succeeded—up to a point. By the evening the Canadians were indeed very close to Falaise, but during the afternoon Bomber Command, this time, had distracted and wounded them. Errors by nearly 10 per cent of 800 planes caused some 400 casualties.

From the Seine to the Rhine

'It was no summer progress. A cold coming they had of it at this time of the year, just the worst time of the year to take a journey, and especially a long journey in. The ways deep, the weather sharp, the days short, the sun farthest off, *in solstitio brumali,* "the very dead of winter".'

Bishop Lancelot Andrewes, 1620

'For the last time the Goodness of God smiled on his ungrateful children.'

Adolf Hitler, *Mein Kampf*

The Allies had reached the Seine too soon! Here is a classic illustration of the fact that phase lines should not be taken too seriously. The situation can be represented by numbers. In the OVERLORD plan it had been assumed that the left bank of the Seine would be over-run by D+90, and that thereafter there would be a considerable pause before forward movement began again. In fact, the river was reached on D+79: the Americans crossed almost on the march, and the British were not far behind. The problem that now faced Eisenhower and Montgomery was urgent, for whereas the original plan envisaged supplies for 12 American divisions on the Seine by D+90, with no further move till D+120 and even by D+150 no more than 'a minor advance beyond the Aisne', by 1 September, D+87, there were 16 American divisions on the far bank with leading elements 150 miles to the east. By the beginning of September 21 Army Group was also across the Seine in substantial strength.

It was not merely the speed of the Allied advance which posed a problem in logistics: there was also an Allied failure. Even the simpler situation forecast in the OVERLORD plan—support for Anglo–American forces at rest along the river bank—had predicated the use of the Breton ports through which it was expected that 14,000 tons per day would be passing by the beginning of September. But the ports had not been captured. The consequence was that all supplies had to be ferried by road (transport by rail was wholly inadequate) from administrative areas in Normandy fed mainly across the beaches; or else, on occasion, flown in from England. For Montgomery the result was that he had to ground one of his three corps, and he had no forward stocks of reserves.

It was a curious *bouleversement* that Montgomery, who had been so often and so bitterly criticised for his 'caution' during the Normandy battle, should now be finding himself in difficulties because the Germans, as a result of his master plan, had collapsed so much sooner than had been anticipated. Still, this was a time of optimism and enthusiasm, and what in other circumstances might have seemed a parlous state of affairs did not diminish the ardour of the two senior commanders. Eisenhower pressed steadily onward with his policy of pursuit on a broad front, while Montgomery brooded on the proposition so dear to him, a concentrated drive in overwhelming strength, under a single commander (himself) which would sweep through the disintegrating Germans past the northern flank of the Ardennes, take the Ruhr in its stride, and culminate in the capture of Berlin. Montgomery had discussed this project (which involved no mere 'pencil thrust', as is sometimes alleged, but a compact body of 40 divisions from 12 and 21 Army Groups), with Eisenhower as early as 23 August, but had found him adamant in insisting on a two-pronged advance, one prong to be thrust along the northern line advocated by Montgomery and the other to be aimed due eastwards, to the south of the Ardennes, the object being to enter Germany via the Saar. Nothing would persuade Eisenhower to ground American forces in order to facilitate the supply of a 40-divisional drive in the north. The furthest he would go was to offer Montgomery a limited reinforcement. On 29 August he sent to Montgomery and Bradley a long letter in which he defined his intentions with uncompromising clarity. It is strange that critics of Eisenhower allege that because of his inexperience of battle he was unsure, for a study of the prolonged correspondence exchanged between himself and the self-sure Montgomery, reveals little dubiety on Eisenhower's part—even though it is true that he sometimes expressed himself with a Delphic obscurity.*

Montgomery inevitably obeyed—without conviction: and, as will be seen, he pertinaciously continued to re-open the question from time to time until he wore Eisenhower's patience to shreds. His position, anyway, had now changed, for on 1 September Eisenhower, under pressure from Marshall, assumed direct command of the Allied armies, exercising no more than his right, for it had been agreed before D-Day that such a change in the command structure might occur once the battle for Normandy was over. At the same time Montgomery, in compensation, was made a Field Marshal: but from now on he had no more than a status equivalent to that of Bradley, under

---

* The five volumes of *The Papers of Dwight Eisenhower : The War Years* (The Johns Hopkins Press, published in 1970), demonstrate conclusively, as Michael Howard wrote in reviewing them, that 'from the very beginning his mind had a hard cutting edge, that he shouldered responsibility effortlessly; and that he grew at beanstalk speed to keep pace with his job. The human qualities which had made him famous were complementary to the professionalism which made him successful.' Neither Montgomery nor his *alter ego* Alan Brooke fully understood that the West Point man whom Marshall backed wholeheartedly was a man with a mind of his own. Much that went wrong derived from this misapprehension.

Eisenhower's Supreme Command. This was irksome for a man who had just won a great victory and was certain that he had the recipe for the final defeat of the Germans.

Since the debate between Montgomery and Eisenhower over the question of a 'single thrust' as opposed to a 'broad front' was to bedevil their relationship for months, it is worth a pause to ask what, in general, was the merit of Montgomery's thesis. This must be done without use of hindsight, for Montgomery's thinking was undoubtedly affected, as was that of many others in high positions, by the immediate climate of opinion. It appeared to be certain, in those halcyon days after the Germans had been expelled from Normandy, that the Reich was on the verge of collapse, for 7 Army's losses in men and equipment had been so colossal that it seemed inconceivable that a strong shield could be erected between the triumphant Allies and the German frontier. 40 divisions moving as one looked like an irresistible Juggernaut. There is no doubt that Montgomery's strategy was approved of in London. Sir Ian Jacob, who at Ismay's right hand saw everything from the centre, observed that 'at the time all the British in London thought that the correct strategy was to make one thrust north of the Ruhr into the N. German plain, holding back everywhere else'.* But would it have worked? Even supposing that Eisenhower had gone all the way with Montgomery, and grounded a substantial part of 12 Army to provide transport for the supply of the 40 Divisions, would it, (remembering how much was still being imported over the Normandy beaches, how many harbours were still in a state of siege, and that Antwerp still had to be captured and its approaches cleared) have been possible to maintain the necessary logistical support right up into Germany? Thinking of the rivers that had to be crossed, and the miles and miles of open flank which such a thrust would expose, was there not a grave danger that what would have started as a steam-roller might have been diminished, beyond the Rhine if not before, into something like a slender pencil?†

In any case, it was a concept doomed at birth. Even if it had been 100 per cent sound militarily, it was a political impossibility. Eisenhower put the facts in a nutshell when he said to Montgomery on 23 August, 'The American public would never stand for it; and public opinion wins wars.' Not only the American public: neither Roosevelt, nor Marshall, nor the American Chiefs of Staff can be imagined endorsing what, on the other side of the Atlantic,

---

* Private communication.

† It is fair to observe that since 1945 an impressive number of German generals, including von Rundstedt, Student, Westphal, Blumentritt and Speidel, have gone on record with the view that Montgomery's plan, especially after the fall of Brussels and Liège, must have succeeded. At that time a concentrated effort by as few as 15 divisions would, in their opinion, have taken the Allies to the Ruhr.

was bound to look like an outrageous betrayal. Montgomery never seemed able to grasp this crucial point, though Eisenhower drew it more than once to his attention. It is a striking example of his naiveté: of his inability to appreciate that in higher strategy political factors can sometimes have the same weight as purely military considerations.

Frustrated and unhappy, Montgomery decided on an operation which would show that he could move as fast as Patton. Like Patton he had to 'fix' his supplies ruthlessly: (the way that Patton fixed them does not bear examination, in terms of how a responsible senior commander should behave). Montgomery made a rational plan, which Chester Wilmot described succinctly:

'In Second Army's advance through Northern France, XII Corps had been able to follow XXX only because VIII Corps, and nearly all Montgomery's heavy, medium and anti-aircraft artillery had been grounded west of the Seine. By the start of September all the reserves of 21 Army Group were on the road. Imports were cut from 16,000 tons a day to 7,000 so that transport companies could be diverted from unloading ships to forward supply. This gain, however, was almost offset by the alarming discovery that the engines of 1,400 British-built three-tonners (and all the replacement engines for this particular model) had faulty pistons which rendered them useless. These trucks could have delivered to the Belgian border another 800 tons a day, sufficient to maintain two divisions. By reducing the daily tonnage of First Canadian Army, by bringing in fresh transport companies from England, and by such expedients as welding strips of airfield track on the sides of tank-transporters to convert them for supply carrying, 21 Army Group was able to provide enough supplies to carry Dempsey's two forward corps into Belgium, as far as Brussels and Antwerp, but with its own resources it could not go much further.'

Determined to get everything right for his dash to the east, Montgomery was as careful about his priorities at the level of command as he was about petrol. To stimulate XXX Corps he had employed Horrocks, the man who had injected dynamism into his drives in North Africa, who had been seriously wounded in Bizerta during an air raid, and who had been lying in a hospital in England, warned by his doctors that never again would he go to war. 'Within a few days his fresh and fiery spirit had transformed the Corps. A tall lithe figure, with white hair, angular features, penetrating eyes and eloquent hands, he moved among his troops more like a prophet than a general.' Those who have wondered, watching Horrocks' television performances, about his charismatic qualities should have no doubt about what he could do in war: I, like many others, having served under him, say that he could inspire. Certainly now, as in BLUECOAT, he inspired: whether it was the voice of a prophet or a general, it was undoubtedly compulsive.

The consequence was that Montgomery's tanks swept, within a week, 250 miles to the east. These dashes always look dramatic—large bold arrows on the maps—but if one is sensible one sees that much of the movement was motoring, as was the case in the great American gallops; and one observes that when Guards Armoured Division burst into Brussels on 3 September and II Armoured into Antwerp on the 4th, producing hectic joy among the war-weary inhabitants, they had tackled local resistance but nothing that could be described as a Front—which the Germans were powerless to consolidate. Everything looked gay and gorgeous: in the streets of those great cities the wine flowed, and there were hugs and kisses for the liberators. But Horrocks, with his onrush of tanks, failed to grasp the opportunity which was now offered, as, with his larger responsibility, did Montgomery.

It was a time when the British and their commander suffered from euphoria. Two men, however, immediately saw what was required. One was Admiral Sir Bertram Ramsay, Eisenhower's Naval Commander-in-Chief. On the day that II Armoured broke into Antwerp, capturing by their energy the docks undamaged, Ramsay sent a signal to SHAEF, 'for Action' (Author's italics). He passed copies to 21 Army Group, the Admiralty, and the Naval C.-in-C., Nore. Montgomery, therefore, should have been on the alert straight away, for the signal read as follows:

1. It is essential that if Antwerp and Rotterdam are to be opened quickly enemy must be prevented from

(i) Carrying out demolitions and blocking in ports

(ii) Mining and blocking Scheldt and the new waterway between Rotterdam and the Hook

2. Both Antwerp and Rotterdam are highly vulnerable to mining and blocking. If enemy succeeds in these operations the time it will take to open ports cannot be estimated.

The other man was Hitler. He and his staff instantly grasped that the approaches to Antwerp mattered as much as the capture of the city, and he therefore issued instructions to make the Scheldt impassable—by mines, by guns, by the presence of troops. Montgomery—and Eisenhower—were slow to take the point.

Dempsey, talking to me about Antwerp long after the war, was entirely honest. He said that in later years he had walked the course with the Canadian, Simonds, and that he then realised that his mind had been so set on Germany that he forgot about Antwerp. But the failure of Montgomery and Eisenhower to grip the problem posed by the need to clear the waterways leading to this vital port presents one of the most baffling questions raised by the whole campaign in N.W. Europe. Why did neither of them see what had to be done, and done urgently? Why were their quarter-masters not screaming?

Montgomery always insisted on a firm administrative base. He always, implicitly and sometimes explicitly, considered he was a better commander on the battlefield than Eisenhower. He took a pride in being able to penetrate to the essential. Neither he nor Eisenhower can be exonerated: during the climacteric weeks of September 1944 there was flurry and vagueness in the strategical direction of the campaign, but Montgomery, assessed by his own standards, must be considered the guilty party. Eisenhower was way back at Granville in the Cherbourg peninsula; from his H.Q. 400 miles from the front he was over-seeing the whole great operation. Montgomery had, in theory, his nose to the ground: he was fighting. Therefore he should have seen immediately, in spite of loose directives from SHAEF, the need to secure the approaches to Antwerp if his northern group of armies were to be provided with the sustenance they required. Eisenhower, for example, made a simple point in arguing with Montgomery about a thrust into Germany; what, he said, about railway bridges over the Rhine? Well, what? Without Antwerp, there was no possibility of moving across Europe the heavy metal. From this and other important points of view it might have been expected that Montgomery would have appreciated, like Hitler and Ramsay, the crucial significance of the river Scheldt and the fact that an unapproachable Antwerp represented a victory without a morrow. He failed to do so. Alan Brooke realised this. On 5 October he noted in his diary: 'I feel that Monty's strategy for once is at fault. Instead of carrying out the advance on Arnhem he ought to have made certain of Antwerp in the first place.' And, in fact, Montgomery subsequently realised this himself. Unwilling though he was ever to acknowledge an error, he did so without qualification in his *Memoirs* when he wrote: 'I must admit a bad mistake on my part—I underestimated the difficulties of opening up the approaches to Antwerp so that we could get free use of that port. I reckoned that the Canadian Army could do it *while* we were going for the Ruhr. I was wrong.' He was indeed—to the extent that while the town and port of Antwerp were captured intact on 4 September, the first Allied ship was not berthed in the docks until 28 November. Hindsight, that beguiling spy-glass, also indicates that in the good going of September 21 Army Group might have swept over the Scheldt on the run: when the Canadians were finally committed to finishing the job 'it was no summer progress . . . just the worst time of the year to take a journey'. My regiment was in their support in the clearance of the Breskens pocket and the capture of Walcheren: it was a matter of mud and flood, and for 3 Canadian Division it meant 2,000 casualties. It is also surprising that when II Armoured Division took the city of Antwerp neither its able commander, Roberts, nor Montgomery, saw the need to push *immediately* to the east and grab strong positions beyond the Albert Canal.

Yet these canals in the Lowlands were crucial for the next daring enterprise which Montgomery had in mind. There was an Airborne Army available, and he determined to use it for another bold stroke which would consummate his swift thrust to the east. Now he was wanting a bridgehead over the Rhine. By 10 September the Guards Armoured Division had made its way over the Meuse-Escaut canal, the Albert Canal having also been crossed, and the start-line had been secured for MARKET GARDEN—the code word for what is called 'Arnhem'.

On 10 September Eisenhower flew up to Montgomery's Tac. H.Q. and, in a summit conference in his aircraft, they agreed to differ but came to terms. Montgomery pressed hard for his Plan—what might be described as his monomaniac desire for a thrust in the north. He was so urgent that Eisenhower had to say, in his friendly and co-operative style, 'Steady, Monty! You can't speak to me like that. I'm your boss.' Montgomery replied, 'I'm sorry, Ike.' The upshot was an agreement that Montgomery's idea for an airborne operation to secure crossings over the main waterways ahead, which might have made possible an Allied advance into the North German Plain, should proceed. In *Crusade in Europe* Eisenhower readily admits that 'at the September 10 conference in Brussels Field Marshal Montgomery was therefore authorised to defer the clearing out of the Antwerp approaches in an effort to seize the bridgehead I wanted'. It was, in fact, a shared error. What was not shared was the conception of the next move: this was Montgomery's, and, in taking account of his generalship, his *panache* must be clearly seen, though Eisenhower blurs the picture in his memoirs by saying 'I believed it possible that we might with airborne assistance seize a bridgehead over the Rhine in the Arnhem region. . . .' Here the Supreme Commander was ungenerous, for of all Montgomery's strategic ideas this was the most cavalier. Indeed, Eisenhower wrote to Montgomery about MARKET GARDEN: 'I must say that it not only is designed to carry out most effectively my basic conception with respect to this campaign, but it is in exact accordance with all the understanding that we now have.'

There is nothing more to say about MARKET GARDEN (as the operation has been so often and so vividly described) except to comment on what went wrong. In effect, the American 101 Airborne Division got, in the end, their bridges, while 82 Airborne Division, whom Dempsey considered the most gallant single unit in the Allied armies, somehow . . . and one emphasises *somehow* . . . captured with the aid of Guards Armoured Division the valuable—indeed the vital—bridge over the Waal at Nijmegen. At Arnhem the

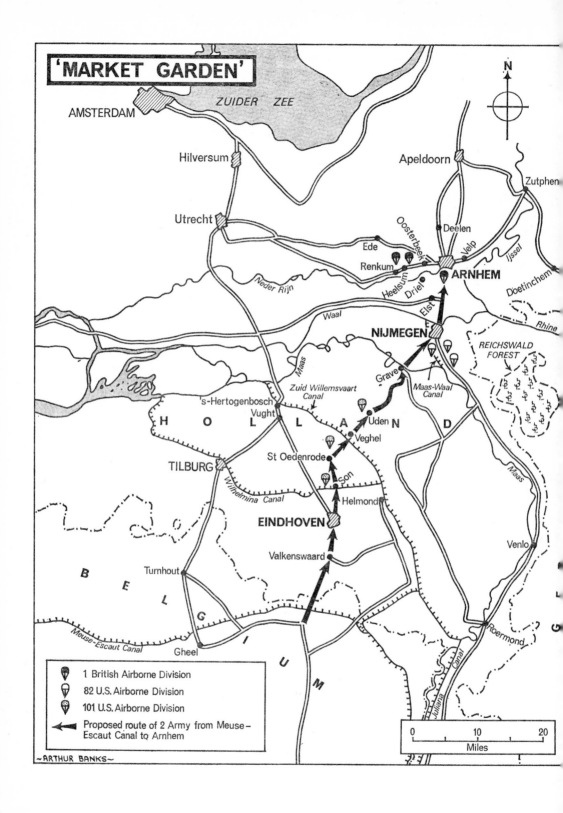

'MARKET GARDEN'

ZUIDER ZEE

AMSTERDAM

Hilversum

Apeldoorn

Zutphen

Utrecht

Ede

Deelen

Oosterbeek

Velp

Renkum

Ijssel

Neder Rijn

Heelsum

Driel

ARNHEM

Doetinchem

Waal

Elst

Rhine

NIJMEGEN

Maas

REICHSWALD
FOREST

Grave

Maas-Waal
Canal

Zuid Willemsvaart
Canal

's-Hertogenbosch

Uden

Vught

Veghel

H   O   L   L   A   N   D

St Oedenrode

TILBURG

Son

Maas

Wilhelmina Canal

Helmond

Valkenswaard

EINDHOVEN

Venlo

B   E   L   G   I   U   M

Turnhout

Roermond

Meuse-Escaut Canal

Gheel

Juliana Canal

N

1 British Airborne Division	
82 U.S. Airborne Division	
101 U.S. Airborne Division	
Proposed route of 2 Army from Meuse-Escaut Canal to Arnhem	

~ARTHUR BANKS~

0   10   20

Miles

British 1 Airborne Division failed. 101 and 82 Divisions suffered 3,542 casualties. The British figure was 3,716.

How did it happen that a total of 10,095 men, 92 guns, over 500 jeeps, 300 motor cycles and 400 trailers—the bulk of what came down at Arnhem—could only deliver, at the *point d'appui*, the Rhine bridge, about 700 men?

The answer is that for once Montgomery asked too much. The strategic concept was ambitious, but, built into it, there were too many flaws. Eisenhower is as much at fault as Montgomery, for he promised a logistical support which didn't quite materialise and an effort by the American First Army on Montgomery's right flank, an effort which, failing, meant that Montgomery had to use his precious transport to move up his VIII Corps to fill the gap. I remember talking to Dempsey, who was deeply involved in the planning of the battle. I remember—and Dempsey was not an emotional man—the way his right hand flapped as he said to me that the Americans were missing. By saying so he was not, of course, criticising their airborne divisions.

As Alan Brooke later observed, Montgomery was mistaken in trying to crash over the Rhine. Like so many of his peers he was gullible in believing that the Germans were finished: actually they were not, and actually the Allies—Eisenhower in particular—made a major *faux pas* in deferring their airborne assault from the beginning to the middle of September. During these days, by that extraordinary gift of improvisation which appeared to be a smile of the Goodness of God on his ungrateful children, 1 Parachute Army had been cobbled together (military slang alone can describe how it was done) under Student (who had commanded at Crete) to close the front between 15 Army in the north and the raggle-taggle divisions, in the south, who were trying to stop Patton.

Arnhem was essentially a *tactical* failure—once the doubtful commitment had been undertaken—and for a multitude of reasons for which Montgomery was not responsible. There must be grave doubt as to whether he was correct in thinking that Horrocks' Corps could link up with the Airborne Division at Arnhem: and there is no doubt that if he had made supplies to flow through Antwerp and persuaded the Americans to guard his right flank he would have been in a better posture. But what went wrong in the battle was beyond his control.

There was a cumulation of what might have been put right and what could not have been anticipated. A pardonable intelligence error: Model, one of the toughest German generals, happened to be on the spot, and 9 and 10 Panzer Divisions, tested in Russia and Normandy, were recuperating locally. Moreover, Student had in his hands within hours the Arnhem battle-plan taken from a map acquired from a shot-down American officer.

What was not pardonable was the planning which sacrificed these remarkable men.

Everything was wrong from the start. Urquhart, commanding 1 Airborne Division, had been an infantry brigadier: he had no notion—how could he have?—of how an airborne attack should be conducted. Dempsey said to me that he would have preferred to have had Gale in Urquhart's place: Gale whose 6 Airborne landed on D-Day and who believed that one should aim for a *coup-de-main* on the objective. Urquhart took the advice of the R.A.F. who told him that the flak around the bridge at Arnhem made a crash landing there impossible. So the landing grounds selected were too many miles away from where 1 Airborne must arrive—*at the bridge*.

There were other errors. A mistake in the scheme of air support denied to the embattled airborne troops the fighters who should have provided them with an umbrella: by an unfortunate misunderstanding there was a clause in the plan which laid down that where a drop or landing was taking place fighters should keep their distance. This was disastrous. So was a total failure in communications. Montgomery one supposes, could hardly have known how incompetent the *corps d'élite*, battle-experienced and rigorously trained, was in this crucial matter: but the facts are that during the first important days at Arnhem neither Browning, who had mistakenly flown with his Airborne H.Q. into Holland, nor 2 Army nor Whitehall had the least idea of what was happening, because nothing was received from the men on the other side of the Rhine. They fought in silence. This was because they were equipped with inadequate radio sets, and also because it could subsequently be seen that it was absurd for Browning to attempt to control the battle. Gale, expert in airborne affairs, seems to me to be right in thinking that the Arnhem division should have been tied in, directly and by efficient radio, to the Corps advancing in its aid, XXX Corps under Horrocks, as in Normandy 6 Airborne Division had functioned in close communication with the Corps coming up on its left and supplying it—a provision so important for weak airborne troops—with artillery support. Yet, having said that, one has to recognise that Horrocks could not advance with sufficient speed. Gallantly though his Guards drove in their tanks to Nijmegen and beyond, their thrust line was down a single road exposed constantly to flank attacks, and beyond the great bridge over the Waal the road was perched so high that every Guardsman was the target of an 88. The guns of XXX Corps might well have been brought to bear earlier on the Arnhem perimeter, and indeed when contact was made with a medium regiment the relief was perceptible. Dempsey would have liked to drop a parachute brigade at Elst, between Nijmegen and Arnhem, to command the naked road: but there were not enough planes.

Antwerp now came, at last, into the forefront. The first troops had been dropped at Arnhem on 17 September and the rump got away across the Rhine on the 24th. Montgomery was quite wrong in stating that his MARKET GARDEN operation had been '90 per cent successful', for in so doing he justified a strategical failure by underlining a tactical success. Though the Americans had secured their objectives, and though 2 British Army was established in and beyond Nijmegen, it was silly to brush aside the fact that the main intention, a crossing of the Rhine, had not been achieved.

But Eisenhower now acted. Montgomery was instructed 'to open the port of Antwerp as a matter of urgency'. Indeed, Eisenhower laid down that 'possession of an additional major port on the northern flank is an indispensable pre-requisite for the final drive into Germany'. It was an after-thought which had occurred none too soon.

This directive followed a stirring exchange of letters. On the 15th Eisenhower had written to his two subordinates, Montgomery and Bradley, in sanguine terms, saying that he hoped soon to be 'in possession of the Ruhr, the Saar, and the Frankfurt area'. 'Simply stated,' he went on to say, (and in the months to come his words would echo strangely), 'It is my desire to move on Berlin by the most direct and expeditious route.' Montgomery was appalled by this optimism, and three days later replied with an appreciation in which he reverted to his original idea for a push in the north by 21 Army Group, plus First American Army of nine divisions, adding that 'such a force must have *everything it needed in the maintenance line*'. Failing this, he was prepared to accept a drive by Bradley along the Frankfurt axis into central Germany. What he was not ready to accept was delay. Eisenhower refused to concede the point, and summoned a conference at SHAEF on the 22nd.

This Montgomery, rightly or wrongly, felt unable to attend. He justified his absence by pointing to the critical state of affairs at Arnhem, but it is more probable that he doubted his capacity to plead his case without rancour. In the event, he despatched to Versailles the supple de Guingand, who signalled to him 'Excellent conference. Ike supported your plan one hundred per cent. Your thrust is the main effort and gets full support.' How deluded can a Chief of Staff be! For there was no main effort. On 8 October Montgomery conferred with Marshall, Bradley and Hodges and the next day issued a significant and cautious order which, while emphasising the importance of Antwerp, mainly stressed the need to clear up the *west* bank of the Rhine. This was followed by a further letter from Eisenhower (dated the 13th but received on the 15th—a measure of the perennial delay, pregnant with misunderstanding, in communications between the Supreme Commander and the Field Marshal). It was a firm and elaborate comment on a paper put up by Montgomery on 10 October, entitled *Notes on Command in Western Europe*, whose tone can only be described as intentionally insubordinate. Arguing once again the moribund case for a single thrust and a single ground commander, it ended.

15. I do not believe we have a good and sound organisation for command and control.

16. It may be that political and national considerations prevent us having a sound organisation. If this is the case I would suggest we say so. Do not let us pretend we are all right, whereas actually we are very far from being all right in that respect.

Eisenhower's response was uncompromising. (His letter may be read in full in *Victory in the West*, Vol. II. p. 88.) How anyone who has studied it can consider Eisenhower a man of straw defeats understanding, for he put Montgomery precisely in his place. 'This,' he pointed out, 'is no longer a Normandy beachhead!' Montgomery replied in the only possible way; 'you will hear no more on the subject of command from me . . .' After this magnificent untruth he issued a further directive to 21 Army Group— about the clearance of the Antwerp approaches. It was much too late; and it was the fault, perhaps, of both great men: but at least, and at last, a decisive order had been issued, and, in the end, ships made their way into the Antwerp docks.

It is sometimes said that when a husband and wife, living in the same house, can only communicate by writing to one another their marriage is on the rocks; and something similar might be said about commanders. The fractious interchange of signals, messages and other missives between Montgomery and Eisenhower, of which I have only quoted a symbolic few words, and which was certainly not concluded, deeply underlines the tragic fact that a partnership, once harmonious, was now endangered.

Montgomery's directive had indeed come *in the end*, for the Canadians, who were given the task of breasting up to the Scheldt, faced a prolonged and bloody battle, in the worst possible conditions. They slogged from dyke to dyke. And when finally the R.A.F. breached with bombs the water-defences of Walcheren, and the Navy sought to put 4 Special Service Brigade ashore at Westkapelle, using 150 craft of various kinds as well as 27 boats armed with guns and rockets (with a battleship and two monitors for good measure), the casualties were frightful. In the support squadron alone 170 men were killed and 200 wounded out of a total of some 1,000, while 20 of its 27 craft were put out of action. An earlier endeavour would certainly have proved less costly. But the job was done.

Yet stalemate followed. By 28 November the first ships were working their way into Antwerp, but Eisenhower's orders, issued on 28 October and re-phrased on 2 November, were not fulfilled. He then stated and required

30 The final signature. Montgomery signing the Instrument of Surrende document. In the background General Admiral von Friedburg, Suprem Commander of the German Navy

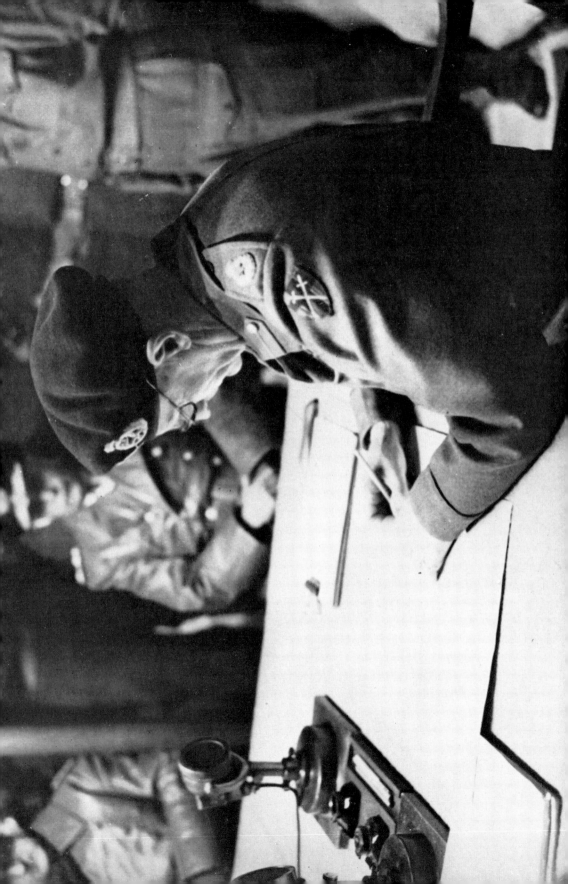

31 *The caravan: with Rommel, Himmler and Doenitz*

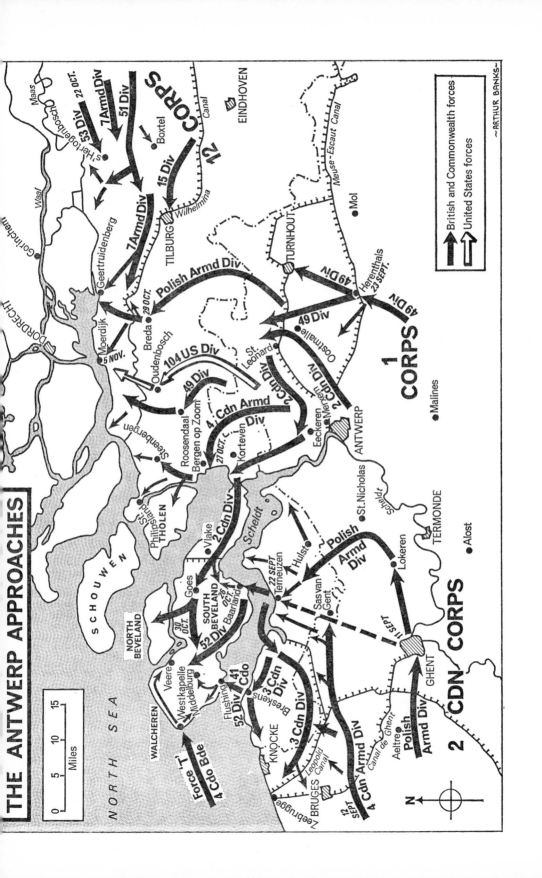

THE ANTWERP APPROACHES

~ARTHUR BANKS~

British and Commonwealth forces

United States forces

Miles
0   5   10   15

N

NORTH SEA

SCHOUWEN

NORTH BEVELAND

SOUTH BEVELAND

WALCHEREN

Veere
Westkapelle
Middelburg
Flushing
30 OCT.
52 Div
41 Cdo
Force 'T'
4 Cdo Bde

Goes
Vlake
Baarland
26 OCT.
2 Cdn Div

St Philips-land
THOLEN

Steenbergen
Bergen op Zoom
Roosendaal
49 Div
27 OCT.
Korteven
4 Cdn Armd Div

Oudenbosch
Breda
29 OCT.
5 NOV.
104 US Div
49 Div

Moerdijk
Geertruidenberg
7 Armd Div
Polish Armd Div

's Hertogenbosch
53 Div   22 OCT.
7 Armd Div
51 Div

CORPS
12

15 Div
Boxtel
TILBURG
Wilhelmina Canal

EINDHOVEN

Mol

Meuse-Escaut Canal

TURNHOUT
49 Div   23 SEPT.
Herenthals
49 Div
Oostmalle
1 CORPS

St. Leonard
2 Cdn Div
Merxem Div
Eeckeren
ANTWERP
Malines

Scheldt

St. Nicholas
TERMONDE
Alost

Polish Armd Div
Lokeren

Hulst
Terneuzen   22 SEPT.
Sas van Gent
11 SEPT.
GHENT
2 CDN CORPS

Brackens
3 Cdn Div
KNOCKE
Leopold Canal
Canal de Ghent
Aeltre
Polish Armd Div
4 Cdn Armd Div

BRUGES
Zeebrugge
12 SEPT.

Maas
Waal
GORINCHEM
DORDRECHT

that a main effort *in the north* should secure crossings over the Rhine, capture the Ruhr, and penetrate deep into Germany. At the same time, if possible, a further advance from the Saar should be prepared and ancillary operations conducted on the right of the Allied line. But all along the 'Broad Front' attacks stalled: most visibly on the front of the American armies, and especially in the case of Hodges' First Army's assault on the Hürtgen Forest. This was one of the bloodiest battles since the First World War. 9,000 Americans succumbed to trench-foot, combat fatigue and what were called 'respiratory diseases'. 24,000 were killed, wounded, captured or missing. The Official Historian of the American Army describes it as a basically fruitless battle which should have been avoided. On 28 November, therefore, the date of Antwerp's opening, when Eisenhower visited Montgomery at his Command Post the latter, in his abrupt way, told the Supreme Commander that he considered his directive of 28 October had failed and that the Allies were in disarray. His bitterness was pardonable. But Eisenhower rebutted his arguments, and even when the conflict was transferred to the level of President and Prime Minister Roosevelt blandly wrote to Churchill that 'our agreed broad front strategy is developing according to plan'. The fog of war was now blinding.

And greater confusion was shortly to follow. It is inexplicable why, during these weeks, the fertile and expert intelligence organisations of the Anglo-American Command both lost track of a newly created Panzer Army and failed to diagnose the *Schwerpunkt* of its forthcoming attack. Montgomery and Eisenhower have each been frank about the failure. Hitler, who masterminded both the creation of this extra Army and its subsequent assault, had already been explicit (though protected by the highest grade of security) about what he wished to be achieved.

The decisive day was 25 September 1944. The 'Napoleonic' concept which had been brewing in the Führer's mind then crystallised in urgent and imperative demand for action. He summoned an astonished Operations Staff and told them that his new Panzer Army must slash through the Ardennes, cross the Meuse, and strike for Antwerp. 'If all goes well,' he said, 'the offensive will set the stage for the annihilation of the bulk of twenty to thirty divisions. It will be another Dunkirk.' Actually what he envisaged was something more akin to the abortive Mortain offensive. He thought he could slice the Allies in half, as he tried desperately to do during those last days in Normandy: and now, as then, he was wrong. He was wrong because, as soldiers say, the operation was not 'on': and wrong because he refused to take the advice of his soldiers. Von Rundstedt, who had replaced poor von Kluge as a respectable Field Marshal in charge of the western front, had grave doubts, which he expressed. And Model, one of the best of the Nazi-orientated generals (in the sense that ideology did not excessively warp his military judgement)—Model, whose saying was '*Den lieb ich, der Unmöglisches begehrt*', 'I love him who craves the impossible'—observed, when the plan was expounded to him, 'to me the whole affair seems damned mouldy'.

Yet in the end Hitler dominated his generals once again, ensured that the operation given the cover code name of *Wacht am Rhein* was put in hand, made certain that 6 Panzer Army was secretly assembled to execute it (the movement of the various armoured divisions involved no less than 800 trains), and compelled his dubious officers to devise a deception scheme which, in its immediate effect, was as brilliant as the Anglo-American persuasion of Hitler himself, and his subordinates, that when D-Day occurred vast armies were due to descend on the obvious coast of Calais.

British, American, French and German authorities have meticulously surveyed the ensuing Ardennes offensive, and from Montgomery's point of view it is mainly necessary to ask what he contributed to its defeat and what he thought or said he had contributed. They are, unfortunately, two quite separate questions.

He has readily admitted that no more than SHAEF did he vividly anticipate this particular consequence of Eisenhower's 'Broad front' policy—the consequence being that to maintain a broad front you must take a calculated risk by thinning out *somewhere*, and that, for better or worse, Eisenhower and Bradley had taken this risk on precisely the front where the German blow was to fall. And while we know from *Intelligence at the Top*, the memoirs of the Supreme Commander's Chief Intelligence Officer, Major-General Sir Kenneth Strong, that on the day when the Germans attacked Eisenhower, Tedder and a small group were meeting at Versailles merely to discuss the increasing shortage of American reinforcements, we also know from Montgomery's own record that he himself was well behind the lines, playing golf.

Montgomery's interpretation of what he contributed was expressed at a fatal press conference held by him during the battle, on 7 January 1945. The Germans quickly and skilfully sub-edited his text and broadcast a revised version which had a disastrous effect on Allied solidarity. But the *actual* text was itself disastrous, containing as it did such passages as: 'Then the situation began to deteriorate. But the whole allied team rallied to meet the danger; national considerations were thrown overboard; General Eisenhower placed me in command of the whole Northern front. I employed the whole available power of the British Group of Armies. . . .' But was this really so? It is true that Bradley, by insubordinately evading Eisenhower's request that he should establish his H.Q. adequately far to the North, and by remaining in Luxembourg, found himself in an impossible position when the Panzers came pouring through the Ardennes and was unable to maintain proper contact with his left wing. It is true also that, had the Americans adopted a system of liaison officers like Montgomery's, and the *Phantom* intelligence network which had been suggested to them by the British they might well have appreciated as rapidly as Montgomery did the nature of the sudden cataclysm. Yet it cannot be argued that the reaction of the American troops to the power drive of 6 Panzer Army was so feeble that what Montgomery effected was decisive. For who was dying? The figures read as follows: U.S. Armies, killed 8,497; wounded 46,170, missing 20,905. British Corps (to 17 January): killed 200; wounded 969; missing 239. These are not figments of the American imagination: they are taken from the British Official History. The monstrous mistake that Montgomery made was to imply that in all he had done, and done so well, to provide calm and clarity, to maintain on the northern American flank an impregnable buttress, and to provide a solid wall on the *west* bank of the Meuse by putting his divisions into blocking positions, there was a personal triumph on his part and a particular triumph for British arms. No one would now wish to defend the latter thesis. 101 Airborne at Bastogne, Patton's great drive from the south, the activities of 2 American Armoured Division and a myriad other instances are now a part of military history. What Montgomery did was to destroy the *éclat* of a considerable but not astonishing achievement on his part by enacting the rôle of a saviour.

It is very strange that Montgomery should have so suicidally mishandled his press conference on 7 January, for only a week earlier his sustained pressure on Eisenhower for the appointment of a single ground commander had brought his professional career to a point of extreme danger. Marshall signalled to Eisenhower on 30 December 1944 'under no circumstances make any concessions of any kind whatsoever. You not only have our complete confidence but there would be a terrific resentment in this country following such an action. . . .' This was final, and yet no more than what Eisenhower had so often tried to make Montgomery see. Now the Supreme Commander's patience was exhausted. His court of advisers at SHAEF (and it is ironical that his American generals were always complaining that Eisenhower was cushioned and cozened against their interests by a British staff!) urged him to deal with Montgomery once and for all. De Guingand has tellingly described what followed: how Eisenhower reached the point of drafting a reply to Marshall which in effect said 'either him or me' and thus was bound to mean 'him'; how de Guingand rushed to Versailles, secured a breathing space, dramatically flew through the snows back to his master, persuaded a stunned Montgomery to draft an emollient letter to Eisenhower, and restored the situation when all was almost lost. One wonders how far it ever struck Montgomery that a personal disaster at this time would have

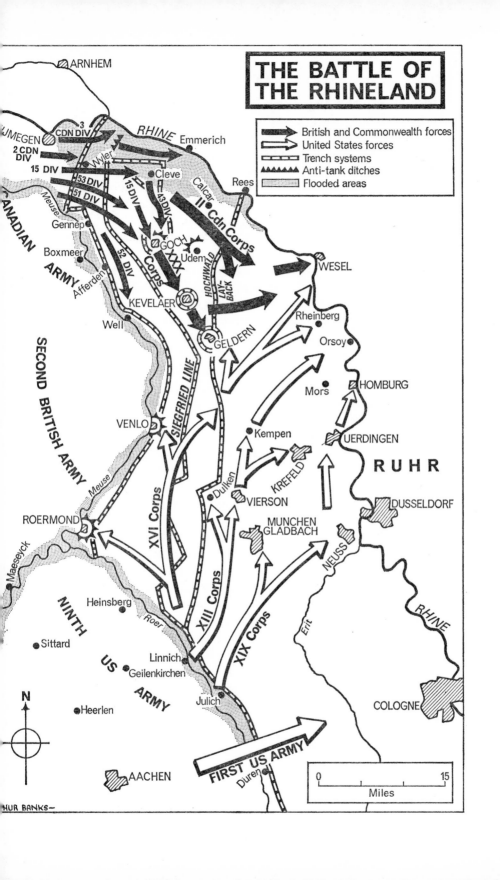

THE BATTLE OF
THE RHINELAND

British and Commonwealth forces
United States forces
Trench systems
Anti-tank ditches
Flooded areas

ARNHEM

RHINE   Emmerich

NIJMEGEN   3 CDN DIV
2 CDN DIV   Wyler
15 DIV   53 DIV   Cleve   Calcar   Rees
51 DIV   15 DIV   43 DIV   II Cdn Corps

CANADIAN   Meuse   GOCH   Udem   WESEL

ARMY   Gennep   Afferden   52 DIV   HOCHWALD
Boxmeer   Corps   KEVELAER   LAY-BACK
Well   GELDERN   Rheinberg

SECOND   SIEGFRIED LINE   Orsoy

BRITISH   VENLO   Mors   HOMBURG

ARMY   Meuse   XVI Corps   Kempen   UERDINGEN
KREFELD
ROERMOND   Dulken   VIERSON   RUHR
DUSSELDORF
Maeseyck   XIII Corps   MUNCHEN
GLADBACH   NEUSS

NINTH   Heinsberg   Roer   XIX Corps   RHINE

Sittard   US   Erft

ARMY   Linnich
Geilenkirchen
Heerlen   Julich   COLOGNE

N

AACHEN   FIRST US ARMY   Duren

0   15
Miles

ARTHUR BANKS—

been a tragedy for Anglo-American relations: how far, in fact, his imagination penetrated down the line which Hitler's intuition had suggested to him when he devised the Ardennes offensive—the notion that the Allies were like a vast mountain range incapsulating a rift. Find the rift, attack the flaw, and the structure might split. Hitler, of course, was wrong: like a self-sealing petrol tank, the alliance would have closed even over the wound of a Montgomery's passing. *Realpolitik* is like that. Still, Hitler had a point, as this episode uncomfortably (and inconclusively) revealed.

All was temporarily patched up: and though Montgomery might have retired to his tent, this was not his way. He had a good reason for so doing since, as the winter weeks dragged by, it continued to be clear that Eisenhower's 'broad front' policy was producing small dividends. Tapping, discursive operations by both Americans and British, all along the Rhine or its approaches, were getting nowhere. Intensive staff discussions, culminating at the Malta conference in late January, evolved a compromise and a formula. Both sides came a little way towards one another, and the Supreme Commander's final expression of intent was ratified in Malta on 1 February. 'You may assure the Combined Chiefs of Staff that I will seize the Rhine crossings in the north immediately this is a feasible operation and without waiting to close the Rhine throughout its length. Furthermore I will advance across the Rhine in the North with maximum strength and complete determination as soon as the situation in the South allows me to collect the necessary forces and to do this without incurring unreasonable risks.' It was as good as Montgomery could get, and perhaps more than he deserved.

But it opened the way to the penultimate major effort by the Commonwealth in N.W. Europe—Operation VERITABLE. The situation can be expressed diagrammatically. With its rear on the Rhine, a large German zone ran along the western bank from the Nijmegen/Arnhem sector in the north to a southern line linking Düsseldorf and Julich on the river Roer. This zone must be cleared before the full force of Eisenhower's armies, aligned along the Rhine, could master Germany. So 1 Canadian Army was given the task of sweeping over the northern sector, to the line Xanten-Venlo, in Operation VERITABLE, while in Operation GRENADE 9 American Army, having secured the dams which controlled the Roer valley, pressed north to effect a juncture. The last battle for the Rhineland, which now followed, like that for the Hürtgen Forest, approximated in this war in the west perhaps as closely as any except Cassino to the conditions of the Western Front in World War One. VERITABLE was unmitigated hell. Its other name is 'the Reichswald Forest'. The difference between it and the other forest battle, Hürtgen, (both of which recalled the horrors of the Wilderness Campaign in the American Civil War), was that while the latter was abortive Montgomery and his men, during a month when 1 Canadian Army sustained 15,000 casualties, attained their end. Hitler had once again made the fatal mistake of compelling his armies to resist *beyond* a river barrier, and by the beginning of March VERITABLE and GRENADE had shattered 19 German divisions which lost 90,000 men. The west bank of the Rhine was clear. God's Goodness had smiled on his ungrateful children for the last time. It had been a cold coming, and the ways had been deep. But the road to the east had been opened.

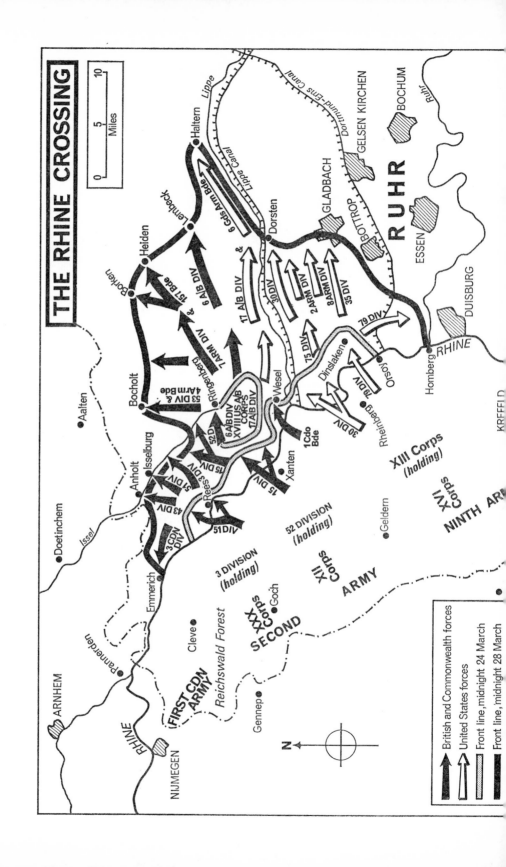

13

Germany without Berlin

'He who holds northern Germany holds Germany.'

General Blumentritt

'There is no greater fatuity than a political judgement dressed in military uniform.'

Lloyd George

For Montgomery and his 21 Army Group the crossing of the Rhine on 23/24 March 1945 was an appropriate *Götterdämerung*. For both, (and, in a longer and larger perspective, for the British Armed Forces) it was the last time that mountains of metal and many thousands of men would be thrown into a large enterprise on a limited front where British power was predominant. The passage over the river was Montgomery's consummation as a commander: the consummation, too, for those armies which had fought under him so far and so faithfully. I do not know whether it was by chance or design that during the night of the 23rd the two major assaults across the Rhine were made by 51 Highland Division (whose HD symbol had decorated the routes all the way from Alamein), and 15 Scottish who from Normandy onwards had shown how soon novices can become professionals.

But I would like to strike a last personal note, for retrospect brings much into clear focus. I was at the crossing of the Rhine with my regiment—now a Super Heavy Regiment—but its equipment was *American*. As the great Airborne Army flew over our heads exactly on time, and we cheered them, we did not realise that this was the last effective manifestation of such unquestionable power by the British. And when 51 Highland Division trudged through our gun positions towards the assault, and I met a gallant Company Commander with whom I had gone to Normandy in 59 Division, I did not clearly grasp then, as I do now, the reason why he was with the Highlanders: it was because 59 Staffordshire Division had been demolished to provide reinforcements in an irremediable shortage of infantry. The sands were running out. This was the last Big Show.

The truth became evident shortly after the river was crossed. From then until the conclusion of the war it was clear that Britain's forces in Europe symbolised a waning military strength which, despite Churchill's passion and persuasiveness, was firmly thrust, politically, into third place at Yalta. As we rolled triumphantly across the Bailey bridges over the Rhine we could hardly see, then, that such was the case: but so it was. A glance at a map setting out the final stages of Germany's collapse demonstrates this graphically: in the East, fat arrows all along the front, indicating Russian dominance, and in the West arrows darting in every direction, to indicate the irresistible thrusts of the American armies. Somewhere, in the northern sector, signs can be seen of the march of Montgomery's men—an entry into Hamburg, a brusque assault on Bremen, great work in Holland, a closing-up to the Elbe—but in scale and significance all this was no longer supremely relevant in terms of what the Russians and Americans were attaining. When one assesses Montgomery's last campaign these indisputable facts must be held in mind.

Why, then, should he cross the river in so elaborate a style? The question was often posed at the time by euphoric American generals, and has subsequently been more coolly discussed. It seems to me to be ill-framed. Montgomery was responsibly executing his Supreme Commander's plan. Eisenhower, indeed, later modified drastically his ideas about the ultimate defeat of Germany, but the record is definite: when Montgomery started the initial planning for the crossing of the Rhine, many months before the event, he did so in the good faith that his chief intended this to be the beginning of the end: and on 8 March Eisenhower confirmed that 21 Army Group must cross on the 24th.

Montgomery, who normally played safe, had now to do so for two reasons. The first was that, if he was going to cross the Rhine, he was determined to *ensure* that he would get to the other bank and far beyond. Of course it is true that at Remagen on 7 March the U.S. First Army luckily seized a bridge: but no one knew in advance—least of all the American Army Commander, or Eisenhower—that this would occur in a particular place at a particular hour on a particular day. Nor did seizure mean certainty. 'The captured bridge had finally collapsed under attacks by the *Luftwaffe*, artillery, floating mines and swimmers with demolition charges, but by the 24th eight newly constructed bridges were in use.' The taking of the Remagen bridge was a dramatic and laudable feat of arms: but few would maintain that luck like this should be counted on as a predictable factor in planning a major operation. It is true, also, that an exultant Patton, with his 3 American Army, got over the Rhine further south, at Oppenheim, on 22 March and pleaded that the world should be informed. And, of course, in the face of thin and ill-organised German defences to the east of the Rhine it was implicit in Eisenhower's 'broad front' strategy that an exploitable breakthrough might happen at any moment.

Montgomery, however, had to weigh a second consideration. Apart from his obsessional idea that he could strike to Berlin from the north, there were

political factors not far distant from his mind. It was a British purpose to
establish a presence in northern Germany—to free Holland, Denmark and
Scandinavia, and to enter important Baltic ports before the Russians penetrated to the west. So, unlike Bradley's generals, Montgomery had to ensure
not only a crossing of the Rhine but also a formidable follow-through, which
would place the British bargaining-counters (their troops), on the correct
squares of the chessboard. This follow-through would not be easy. By the
time the British reached the Elbe, after an advance of 200 miles, they had
built 200 bridges. For such a move, over so many waterways, enormous
stockpiles were necessary. To guarantee not only a crossing but also a drive
into an area which he thought to be militarily (and his superiors thought to be
politically) vital, Montgomery would have been irresponsible if he had tried
to act off the cuff, like Hodges and Patton: unlike them, he had to make
pre-dispositions.

Nothing, certainly, was missing in his effort to do so. For the battle two
corps of 2 British Army and one corps of 9 U.S. Army were committed. If
the German deception devices before the Ardennes offensive were remarkable,
they were as nothing compared with the screen behind which these masses of
men and their equipment were brought up to an obvious river line without
detection—and they got there. In a way it was Alamein over again: the
perceptible line of attack and the imperceptible attackers. The statistics
display Montgomery's problem. 118,000 tons of sundry supplies had to be
secretly stock-piled. During the first week before the assault some 662 tanks,
4,000 tank transporters and 32,000 other vehicles had to be moved, mostly by
night, into position; and 36 Landing Craft of the Royal Navy were also
ferried over the roads of Europe. The American Army dumped no less than
138,000 tons of ammunition. Moreover, complicated arrangements were
necessary to avoid the mistakes which had occurred at Arnhem in regard to
immediate support by the R.A.F. and U.S.A.A.F., and to plan the descent,
on the morning of the 24th, of 6 British Airborne Division, flying in from
England, and 17 U.S. Airborne Division which came from the Paris area.
When, on the night of the 23rd, 3,500 guns fired across the Rhine to give
cover to Montgomery's carefully contrived assault, all this was in hand,
and many other subsidiary aspects were in harmony—a harmony whose
concord would certainly have been broken without the crucial contribution of
superiority in the air: deception is easier if you are not over-looked.

For the last Big Show the Prime Minister was inevitably present, and has
movingly described what he saw—a consummation for him, too. All that he
had stood for in 1940 was now happening before his eyes. Churchill had
often been bloody-minded about what he often called *his* generals: he had
fought them; but Montgomery had survived, and here he was, able to pop

his Prime Minister into a boat and ferry him across to the country whose destruction had legitimately been his dream. When I think of Winston crossing the Rhine I remember W. H. Auden:

History to the defeated
May say Alas but cannot help or pardon

and I think of an unconquerable character: that moment of victory must have been very sweet.

Montgomery, the master-mathematician of the set-piece battle, had achieved a result which mathematicians, in their obscure calculations, describe as aesthetically elegant. Huge numbers of men, and much material, had produced a decisive success with small loss. Mass had not been wasted: there had been an economy of effort. By the 27th his armies were across the Rhine within a bridgehead 35 miles wide and 20 deep. 2 British Army had lost 3,968 casualties, and the Americans 2,813, but the lodgement was undoubtedly firm, and the prisoners taken were over 16,000. The guaranteed success which, as in Normandy, he was required in the circumstances of the time to achieve he had encompassed. Nothing had gone wrong. The *Götterdämerung* was not ignoble. But now that he was beyond the Rhine, what was to follow? American armies were also across the river in overwhelming strength, and in the east the Russians were moving towards the gates of Berlin.

Montgomery's reaction to his success was inevitable and reasonable, within the terms of the existing Allied plans as he understood them—to drive to the east as fast and as far as possible: first the Elbe, then Berlin. On 27 March he instructed his Army Commanders to this effect—on the left 2 British Army moving in a broad swathe with its northern wing directed on Hamburg, and 9 U.S. Army moving on the right, aiming at Magdeburg and thereafter being ready to co-operate with 12 U.S. Army Group in the annihilation of the Ruhr. 1 Canadian Army would simultaneously clear up the remaining occupied areas of Holland and thrust along the sea-coast towards the Elbe. There was to be no dilatoriness: armour and mobile troops were to gallop. It was a straightforward and sensible scheme. At 0610 hrs. on the 27th he signalled to Eisenhower: 'Today I issued orders to Army Commanders for the operations eastwards which are now about to begin,' and, after setting out the operational details, ended by saying '. . . my headquarters will move to Wesel-Munster-Wiedenbruck-Herford-Hanover—thence by autobahn to Berlin, I hope.' When Churchill received his copy of the signal he was naturally much excited by the implications of the last few words. Deeply concerned about the outrageous manner in which the Russians were already breaking the Yalta Agreement, his brooding mind was becoming increasingly aware of a need to establish firm bases from which to handle the political consequences of military success. A deep-seated distrust of the Russians was being almost daily confirmed. It now seemed to Churchill to be a paramount necessity that the Allies should make the first entry into the German capital. But there was a snag, soon to be revealed. Though Montgomery's instructions to his Armies correctly implemented what was still, apparently, the official intention, he had in fact jumped the gun, for only the Supreme Commander could formally direct the forces under his orders to make the final advance on Berlin: and Eisenhower now (and in British eyes disastrously), altered the whole concept for the concluding phase of the war in the west. In this new conception Berlin was not included as a target: but in devising it Eisenhower could rightly claim that he had considerable justification.

First, he was functioning in a political vacuum. Though, as Chester Wilmot tersely puts it, 'before the end of March the Yalta Agreement had been broken or disregarded by the Russians in every important case which had so far been put to the test of action'; though, during the last fortnight of March, Roosevelt had been engaged in a bitter exchange of correspondence with Stalin as a result of the latter's unfounded allegation that the Americans and British were trying to stab the Russians in the back over the question of *pour-parlers* with the Germans which might lead to a surrender on the Italian front; and though Churchill was now cabling to the President about the Russians that 'if they are convinced that we are afraid of them and can be bullied into submission, then indeed I should despair of future relations with them and much else', Eisenhower was wholly ignorant of the fact that the Grand Alliance was crumbling so fast and so fatally. He received no political directives from Roosevelt or Marshall: he was left, in the classic American tradition, as a commander in the field whose mission was to achieve military victory over the enemy by military means. This is how he correctly envisaged his obligation during the last weeks of the war: and if his military decisions are to be criticised on political grounds (which may be questioned), the blame must be firmly laid at the door of his masters.

Secondly, it is fair to recall that when the strategic plan was evolved for a main thrust in the north the Russians were still far from Berlin. But their early spring offensive had swept them westwards with unexpected speed, and now the situation was that, whereas the Allies were still some 200 miles from the capital, Zhukov was poised on the Oder, less than 40 miles from its heart, while other massive armies were moving up abreast of him on both his flanks. True, the Russians' advance on the city had latterly been halted: but from a military point of view it was reasonable to assume that they were in a better position than the Anglo-American armies to capture Berlin as and when they wished. Moreover, Eisenhower was haunted by the dangers which might arise from any unfortunate incidents following unexpected clashes as the two Allied fronts converged.

Thirdly, Eisenhower's judgement was led astray by a will-o'-the-wisp. This was the famous fantasy of the 'National Redoubt'. Evidence seemed to be accumulating from many quarters of a German intention to make a last, suicidal stand in the mountain fastnesses around Berchtesgaden. On 11 March the SHAEF Intelligence Summary was quite explicit. 'The main trend of German defence policy,' it said, 'does seem to be directed primarily to the safeguarding of the Alpine zone.' How to explain, otherwise, the transference of the only significant reserve, 6 Panzer Army, from the Ardennes to the *Danube*, when Berlin was so imperilled? Why were 'considerable numbers of S.S. and specially chosen units' being systematically withdrawn to Austria? Why were 'some of the most important ministries and personalities of the Nazi régime' already established in the Redoubt area? There were sinister references to more secret weapons; to vast underground caverns capable of containing armaments factories; to the preparation of an underground army of young men trained specifically for guerilla warfare. Though it is now known that, as the *Official History* mordantly observes, 'an examination of the contemporary German evidence available to us shows quite conclusively that the so-called "National Redoubt" never existed outside the imagination of the combatants', it was not unnatural that *at the time* Eisenhower should have felt bound to take the possibility into account. Moreover, on the same day as Montgomery's signal of 27 March reached Eisenhower there arrived in his office at Reims a message from Marshall. This also drew attention to the need to 'prevent the formation of any organised resistance areas. The mountainous country in the south is considered a possibility for one of these.' Marshall therefore asked for Eisenhower's views on 'pushing U.S. forces rapidly forward on, say, the Nuremberg-Linz or Karlsruhe-Munich axes'. It is not unlikely that this message from his revered chief had a catalysing effect on Eisenhower's mind. In any event, during the afternoon and evening of 28 March he dispatched three crucial signals.

The first was extraordinary. It was a personal communication to Stalin, sent to the Allied Military Mission in Moscow with a request that it should be forwarded and a full reply obtained, since 'it is essential I should know the Russians' plans in order to achieve the most rapid success'. Never before had he been in direct touch with Stalin, and on this first occasion he nakedly revealed to the Marshal his own immediate intentions. These were to encircle the Ruhr; then to effect a junction with the Russians in the Erfurt-Leipzig-Dresden area and, possibly, further south near Regensburg-Linz, ('thereby preventing the consolidation of German resistance in the Redoubt in Southern Germany'); and, to avoid any complications, to concert these moves with the Russians', about which he requested information. The second was to General Marshall, reporting his action and his decisions. The third was to Montgomery. No signal was sent to London.

Montgomery's instructions began: 'I agree generally with your plan up to the point of gaining contact with Bradley to the east of the Ruhr. . . . As soon as you and Bradley have joined hands in the Kassel-Paderborn area Ninth Army will revert to Bradley's command.' In this and a later signal Eisenhower elaborated the new concept about which he had informed Stalin and Marshall, and in the second signal he added: 'You will see that in none of this do I mention Berlin. So far as I am concerned, that place has become nothing but a geographical location; I have never been interested in those. My purpose is to destroy the enemy forces and his powers to resist.' As a final sop to Montgomery he concluded: 'When the time comes, we must manifestly do everything possible to cross the Elbe without delay, drive to the Baltic coast at Lübeck and seal off the Danish peninsula.' In other words, as the Americans would say, Montgomery and the British were to be firmly and explicitly excluded from the end run.

The Field Marshal was stunned. Apart from the fact that Berlin had so often been referred to in Eisenhower's statements of intent, he had gone ahead in good faith, and his troops were already on the move. But in view of Eisenhower's instructions there was nothing he could do other than to return a dignified reply: 'I note from FWD 18272 that you intend to change the command set up. If you feel this is necessary I pray you do not do so until we reach the Elbe as such action would not help the great movement which is now beginning to develop.' (It was this signal which elicited from Eisenhower the second and fuller account of his aims, mentioned above.) At the same time Montgomery informed London that 9 U.S. Army was to be removed from his command and given back to Bradley, who would thrust for the final kill towards Leipzig and Dresden. 'I consider,' he said, 'we are about to make a terrible mistake.'

This news only added fuel to the flames already blazing in Whitehall, for a copy of Eisenhower's signal to Stalin was in Churchill's hands. It had got there by a secondary route, passed 'for information'. Now he had received fresh facts which also should have come directly from the Supreme Commander. Much was awry. Alan Brooke was at his most trenchant in recording the British reaction. 'To start with, Eisenhower has no business to address Stalin direct, his communications should be through the Combined Chiefs of Staff; secondly, he produced a telegram which was unintelligible; and finally, what was implied in it appeared to be adrift and a change from all that had been agreed on.' From Montgomery's point of view, the main fact which

THE END IN EUROPE

→ British and Commonwealth forces
→ United States forces
← Soviet forces

NORTH
SEA

Wilhelmshaven
Emden
Bremerhaven
Groningen
Leeuwarden
Bremen
Oldenburg
Zwolle
Nienburg
AMSTERDAM
Deventer
Rheine
s'Gravenhage
Amersfoort
Osnabrück
Ha
ROTTERDAM
Arnhem
Münster
Bielefeld
Bocholt
Paderborn
Nijmegen
Wesel
Lippstadt
Duisburg
Dortmund
ESSEN
Ka
Dusseldorf
COLOGNE

BELGIUM
BRUSSELS

GERM

LUX

FRANKFURT
Mainz

FRANCE

STUTTG

0   100
Miles

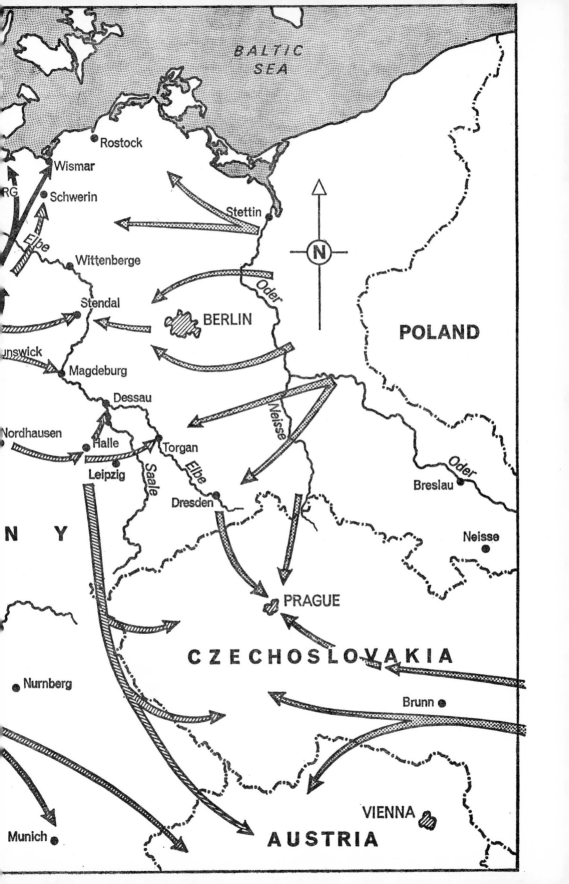

emerged from the ensuing three-cornered wrangle between London, Washington and Reims was that there was no change in Eisenhower's policy. On 31 March the American Joint Chiefs of Staff ratified it, stating that 'the battle of Germany is now at a point where the Commander in the Field is the best judge of the measures which offer the earliest prospect of destroying the German armies or their power to resist'. But the damage was grave. Eisenhower was left feeling puzzled and bitter, for he was convinced that even in his communication with Stalin he had been acting within his full rights. He savagely complained to Marshall about British criticism of his actions and instructions. 'I submit that these things are studied daily and hourly by me and my advisers and that we are animated by one single thought which is the early winning of this war.' A debate in which Montgomery, for once, was not a main protagonist had, unquestionably, the effect of worsening still further his relations with SHAEF and the Supreme Commander.

For him and for the Allies Eisenhower's actions had, however, another, an unpredictable, and an immensely significant effect. As soon as Stalin received Eisenhower's signal he decided it was a lie: this, he calculated, was simply a cover story to conceal the fact that the Americans and British were determined to take Berlin themselves. He immediately summoned Zhukov and Koniev back to Moscow for a conference at which they were ordered to produce plans, virtually over-night, for capturing the city at the *earliest possible moment*.

Stalin's instant reaction raises in a simple but acute form the question whether the Americans (personified by Eisenhower) or the British (personified by Montgomery) were correct in their thinking about Berlin. It is a point where one must pause, for Montgomery and Alan Brooke and the British in general have been supercilious about Eisenhower's decisions. A point, therefore, when one must ask whether Montgomery was capable, at the highest level, of thinking things through. I doubt this. When one says, as one must do, that he was our best general since Wellington, one has to add that he would not have been capable, as Wellington was, of dealing with Talleyrand at the Congress of Vienna. The wise Dutch historian Professor Geyl once observed that 'it is well known that demonstrating an error demands more time than committing it'. Not much time need be spent in suggesting that Montgomery, for both personal and political reasons, fell, when he was thinking about Berlin, into the trap which the subtle mind of Lloyd George defined: 'there is no greater fatuity than a political judgement dressed in military uniform'.

There can be little doubt, to begin with, that his military thinking was warped, wholly naturally, by personal ambition. He had come so far. There was Berlin, a glittering prize. It seemed only just that he and his troops should capture it. Like Mark Clark before Rome, his eyes were switched to a false objective. And like Churchill he was suffering from the romantic fallacy that capital cities matter. Yet, strictly speaking, it had been more important to cross the Seine than to capture Paris, and more important to breach the Gustav Line than to capture Rome.

Moreover, for the British the essential targets were elsewhere—the ports, Hamburg, Bremen, Emden; long-suffering Holland; Denmark and Norway. To have taken Berlin and to have cleared this vast area would have required a great American reinforcement. (Indeed, when Eisenhower suggested that Montgomery was being rather slow in the last phase of the campaign Montgomery sharply retorted that this was due to the detachment from 21 Army Group of the U.S. Ninth Army.) But in the spring of 1945, even more than was the case in earlier months when the issue was argued so urgently, it was a practical impossibility that great quantities of Americans should be provided to enable Montgomery to add to his laurels. Bradley and Patton, Marshall and the American public had quite different ideas: and with good reason.

Beyond all this lies a more important consideration. It can be summarised in one word: ECLIPSE. This was the name given to the Allied plan for the carve-up of Germany when victory had been achieved. It had a long history. C.O.S.S.A.C. had devoted much attention to the problem, and from November 1943 the European Advisory Commission—Sir William Strang for Britain, Winant (the U.S. Ambassador in London), and Gusev the Soviet Ambassador to the United Kingdom—teased out all the implications, ending up with a proposal that conquered Germany should be split into three zones, occupied respectively by the British, Americans and Russians. Many details were inevitably raised in these discussions which it is irrelevant to note here: the essence of the matter is that this was the basic plan which emerged, and was ratified at the Yalta Conference, with the important modification that a zone was also allocated to the French. The significant point is that the plan also made proposals, which were agreed by all parties, for the treatment of Berlin. Berlin, like Germany, was to be carved up into zones each occupied by one of the Allied powers: but the city itself would lie within the area to be controlled and dominated by the Russians.

Montgomery and his superiors certainly knew of this plan and this agreement. So, indeed, did Hitler and a small circle who had the privilege of inspecting an ECLIPSE map which came into German hands. The copy of the translation of the plan made at Jodl's H.Q. is reproduced in *The Last Battle* by Cornelius Ryan (Collins, 1966). It is signed by de Guingand and dated January 1945.

I find it strange that ECLIPSE rarely appears in the published assessments of

Montgomery's—or indeed Churchill's—thinking at this time. Yet granted the fact of the Yalta ratification on 11 February 1945, all that was implied by ECLIPSE bore fundamentally on both the military and political decisions which had now to be made by the Anglo-American *bloc*. And I find it very hard to understand how the short-term political benefit, as the Prime Minister and his Field Marshal saw it, of being first into Berlin could have compared with the indubitable fact that, according to an agreement which could not be denied and which the Russians would certainly have waved in the face of the world, the bulk of the troops entering Berlin from the west would soon have had to withdraw—ignominiously.

Was Eisenhower naive? Or was it Montgomery who was seduced by the *ignis fatuus* of Berlin? With hindsight it can be clearly seen that the Russians were determined to enter the city at all costs; that they had in their hands a contractual guarantee which assured their permanent presence; that they had the will and the force to establish and maintain, both at the time of the German collapse and subsequently, a rigorous domination of their portion of shattered Germany and their share of the sliced-up capital; and that when Unconditional Surrender had been achieved more Anglo-American troops would be demobilised than the Russians would wish to release: the old card game of 'I stick: you twist'. It is interesting to observe that in the final chapter of *Victory in the West*, a general assessment of the conduct of the campaign in N.W. Europe, the Official British Historian comes down, virtually without reservations, on the side of Eisenhower rather than Montgomery.

From the Rhine Montgomery moved fast and furiously to the east—if not so dramatically as the Americans. Into their military record must always be written the fact that when Bradley's 12 Army Group swung its arms around the Ruhr, and met in a clasp at Paderborn, more German prisoners fell into their hands than at any surrender during the Second World War—Stalingrad and Tunisia were not statistically comparable. One Field Marshal, Model, committed suicide: 30 other general officers and 320,000 prisoners were taken.

This advance of 21 Army Group to the Elbe was not easy. Here it paused, and its last-minute rush from its river-crossings to the Baltic (where 6 Airborne Division got to Wismar not more than a few hours before the Russians, and by so doing saved Denmark, Holland and much of northern Germany from a Russian penetration) was also a difficult enterprise. There were no great battles. But those in the divisions concerned discovered what the *Panzer Faust* (the German equivalent of the *Bazooka*), could achieve in the hands of young boys and the Training Battalions of N.C.O.s and officers which were whipped up to provide stopping points along the line of the Allies' progress. During these last days Dempsey deployed about 1,000 tanks along his 2 British Army front: of these at least 125 were destroyed or badly damaged by the Germans, while roughly 500 more were so maimed that they were incapable of action for a day. And many good men died. A study of the winning of the Victoria Cross during these last weeks is as informative as would be a comparable study of the British advance after the early days of August 1918: it was a moment in time when victory seemed imminent but death was still waiting round the next curve in the road. Montgomery maintained the morale of his armies to the end: and some among them were very tired. These last days showed how firmly he had penetrated the mentality of his men and persuaded them that, as Hitler said once they must not be prepared to die until five minutes past midnight.

The climacteric moment was not long delayed. It was at 1830 hrs. on 4 May 1945 that, in a tent on Luneburg Heath, Montgomery signed a document headed:

INSTRUMENT OF SURRENDER
OF
ALL GERMAN FORCES IN HOLLAND, IN
NORTHWEST GERMANY INCLUDING ALL ISLANDS,
AND IN DENMARK

The arrangements in the tent were simple. Montgomery has described them in his *Memoirs*: 'a trestle table covered with an army blanket, an inkpot, an ordinary army pen that you could buy in a shop for twopence'. Of the five German signatories Admiral von Friedeburg, the chief, shortly afterwards took poison, and another, General Kinzel, shot himself. *Consummatum est.*

> *In fifty years, when peace outshines*
> *Remembrance of the battle lines,*
> *Adventurous lads will sigh and cast*
> *Proud looks upon the plundered past.*
> *On summer morn or winter's night,*
> *Their hearts will kindle for the fight,*
> *Reading a snatch of soldier-song,*
> *Savage and jaunty, fierce and strong;*
> *And through the angry marching rhymes*
> *Of blind regret and haggard mirth,*
> *They'll envy us the dazzling times*
> *When sacrifice absolved our earth.*

But on this day of his personal triumph Montgomery knew, in his heart, that Siegfried Sassoon, the poet of his earlier Armageddon, was right to add:

> *Some ancient man with silver locks*
> *Will lift his weary face to say:*
> *'War was a fiend. . . .'*

14

'The most over-rated general'?

'Well-schooled, well-trained, experienced, Montgomery was competent, adequate. He was not great. . . . He is, I think, vastly over-rated, the most over-rated general of World War II.'

Martin Blumenson, in *Armor*

'The faults that people find in him arise entirely from overwhelming self-centredness which makes him entirely impervious to other people's feelings.'

Lord Halifax's *Diary*, à propos Churchill

'Why is it that whenever I mention the name of Montgomery there is always a cold hush?'

P. J. Grigg, Secretary of State for War, to Harold Nicolson: quoted in the latter's *Diaries*

'Under your command I have never been asked to do anything but advance.'

General Sir Miles Graham to Field Marshal Montgomery

Karl Marx said of John Stuart Mill that his eminence was due to the flatness of the surrounding country. In no sense is this true of Montgomery. Modern war has the effect of those prolonged and seismic movements of the earth which convert common-or-garden carbon into incidental diamonds: from the *bons généraux ordinaires* the exceptions emerge. Total war, long in its time-span and ravenous in its consumption of ground, provides for a good commander breathing-space, years in which to mature, and also *Lebensraum* within which to perfect his art. Certainly this was the case between 1939 and 1945. Few of the engaged countries failed, in the end, to throw up extremely effective generals. Some, indeed, did so very early. Montgomery was not, in fact, surrounded by a Sahara of inefficiency but by what might be called a Himalayan range of peaks of achievement among which his qualities appear salient because they were indeed pre-eminent. He must be judged in relationship to his peers. These were, among others, Wavell, Alexander, Auchinleck and Slim; Manstein, Model, Manteuffel, Guderian, Rommel; MacArthur, Eisenhower, Bradley and Patton; from a long Russian list, at least Zhukov and Koniev: and there was more than one good general among the Japanese. So when those to whom I have talked who had most reason to be resentful of how Montgomery had treated them nevertheless always finished by saying '*but* you must be sure to indicate that he was our best general since Wellington', they were posing a problem which must be faced in this final chapter: what, by almost universal consent, made him stand out among his peers in the Second World War—and, a telling point, was this a subjective judgement born from the conditions of the time or is it one which can sustain a delayed and rigorous assessment?

One thing is certain. When the time came for him to do what he had to do he slid into his place as a completely qualified soldier. By experience of action, by reading and deep thought, by that important process of teaching intelligent juniors which forces one to clear one's mind, by the devoted concern of a lifetime to make the Army a weapon rather than a gesture, Montgomery when he took over Eighth Army was a complete professional, and when he came back to England was a professional hardened by fighting Germans from Alamein to the Sangro. This in itself was a novelty in British history. When John Terraine added, as a sub-title to his biography of Haig, 'the educated soldier', of course in a sense he was right: in 1914 there were few if any who could match Haig, with his practical Boer War experience and his technical *expertise* as Haldane's right-hand man in the re-making of the British Army. But this education was as nothing compared with the sheer professional elegance of Montgomery, tried and tested in the First World War, an outstanding trainer of officers between the wars, a brooding and outspoken realist about the war that was to come, a commander under whom, as Sir Miles Graham puts it, his troops would never (except locally) be asked to do anything but advance. When Montgomery went to Normandy I suppose he did so as the most completely equipped general that Great Britain has ever sent to war. The German staff system squeezed out, at the top, a type of hard, expert, self-assured man: Montgomery was one of the few British who could look these professionals in the face. In this sense he was certainly *not* overrated. Brilliantly though a Bradley or a Patton might pick up a skill, like some of their own generals in their own Civil War, no American could match him in technique and in all that a prepared mind can bring to the battlefield.

Sometimes inept in his control of his public relations, Montgomery allowed the idea to proliferate that he was a kind of Blimp—a man from the backwoods of '14–'18. This was misleading. A detached view reveals that within the armies under his command during the Second World War there was as much originality expressed in thought and action as in any of the armies engaged—on both sides. He ran his show, it might seem, like a self-appointed God: yet he had enough acumen to find a place for men and ideas which others found heretical. There was a large liberality in Montgomery's conduct of war, in spite of the fact that he always exercised a tight control;

a flexibility and open-mindedness which is easily overlooked. His quick understanding and immediate application of the capacities of Hobart's 79 Armoured Division is a case in point: the Americans missed a trick here . . . but not Montgomery. It was under Montgomery, too, that the inventive Simonds and his Canadians were able to evolve the ingenious techniques they applied in the battle of the Falaise Gap (and later, in other ways, during the battle for the Reichswald Forest). Moreover, while the need for his mammoth operation at the time of the crossing of the Rhine may be called into question, what cannot be disputed is his stage-management of a massive technological achievement embodying many original ideas. From the days of the deception scheme before Alamein this was the pattern: here, it must be affirmed, was a general who was not a Upas Tree: under his shadow the brilliant and the unconventional, far from withering, were presented with opportunities. Arnhem may have been ill-judged: but it was under Montgomery that the most daring enterprise of the whole campaign was launched. Montgomery knew he was taking the devil of a risk. (When Dempsey came to him with the detailed plan for MARKET GARDEN he said 'What! Are you asking me to drop cowpats all over Europe?') There is nothing novel about this. All good British commanders in the Second World War took risks: Wavell against the Italians in 40/41, Slim in Burma. To win a battle without enough strength you had to do so. I simply wish to establish the fact that, though for many good reasons the cast of his mind and the conduct of his campaigns were cautious, Montgomery was not a man of absolutely fixed ideas. His thoughts did not run on tram-lines. He was neither a bigot nor hide-bound, and he was not incapable of chancing his arm. Had he served with Monash in the last victorious months of 1918 I think they would have seen eye to eye.

His great gift was to be able to take the large view. What divides the first-class fighting general from the true commander is just this, and it may be well expressed by saying that what Freyberg was incapable of Montgomery could do. Freyberg, Churchill's 'salamander', could drive himself and his New Zealanders to death, but he lacked the intellectual poise which might have enabled him to see the war in full scope: this Montgomery had and used. How many of the Allied commanders took as broad a view as he did? Of course he was, on occasion, wildly wrong in terms both of personal judgement and military realism: but he thought *big*, and those who could think big during the Second World War were rare. There was always a man who could win a battle—but campaigns?

He could also take a dispassionate view of people. Through this book there has been a running theme: Montgomery's interest in and support of the young and aspiring officer. It cannot be doubted that in all he did for the training of the Army between the two World Wars, in all he did in the way of picking and choosing and encouraging men who would later matter, he 'did the State some service'. It was a concern which persisted when the war came to life. He was a keen assessor of the special capacities of individual divisions—51 Highland for this job, the New Zealanders for that, the rugged 50 Division for another. And he assessed men, as he assessed formations, shrewdly. I have made the point earlier that he surrounded himself with an exceptionally qualified staff, and that he selected prudently his subordinate generals: Britain was splendidly served by the men Montgomery put in charge of his corps and divisions, men like Dempsey, O'Connor, Hobart, Horrocks, Gale, Roberts, Rennie, Lyne. Careful and critical in this matter of senior appointments, he was also discriminating, not only as an Army Commander but as a person, in his choice of the young men who, on his behalf, established their authority as his liaison officers—one of the most difficult tasks on the battlefield. At Montgomery's behest they had to go up to the front, talk to the battalion, brigade and divisional commanders, and come back and tell him what was actually happening. It was an invaluable intelligence network. There is a classic account of the system in Churchill's *Memoirs*, the passage in which Winston describes how he attended the Rhine crossing and how, that night, Montgomery's homing pigeons came back to build up for him a true picture of what was happening. They were handpicked—by him. One is now the High Master of Montgomery's old school, St. Paul's. Others have found a top place in industry. There was one, nearest to him, John Poston, a young officer in the 11th Hussars, who began his personal association with Montgomery as his A.D.C. when Montgomery took over Eighth Army: transferred to this dangerous business of liaison, he used, as his friends in the war-scarred 11th Hussars have told me, to go, right up to the end, into their forward positions (and the armoured cars were as forward as you could be), to obtain information for his master. He was killed at the front shortly before the German collapse. What Montgomery has written about John Poston tells one much both about himself and his eye for a man. Like Wellington, he knew a good one when he saw one. This was an inestimable gift. In a total war an army tends to be diverse: Montgomery's flair was to be able, at all levels, to pick the right man within the diversity. It is not—as his predecessors in the desert, Wavell and Auchinleck, discovered to their cost—an automatic endowment.

As to his capacity as a trainer of troops, little need be said because it is indisputable. Whether as a teacher at Staff Colleges, as a Divisional Commander in the doldrums of France in 1939/40, as the man in charge of that section of Britain which was most nakedly exposed to the threat of a German invasion, or in his subsequent and more dramatic appointments, Montgomery displayed an eminent ability to quicken the interest of the men under him in the realities of war, and, in spite of what some considered then and some still consider to be a way of expressing himself like a latterday Prophet, to infuse them not only with a fighting spirit but also with a professional willingness to master their required techniques. It is a good general who can not only make a bored soldier want to fight, but also make him want to fight well. This was an art Montgomery acquired and carefully perfected: for this alone he deserves a place in the annals of British military history—he and Sir John Moore would find no discomfort in sitting side by side.

And here we approach something extremely curious about Montgomery. On the one hand, he was certainly a man capable of causing Grigg's 'cold hush'. On the other, probably no senior British commander proved himself so capable of drawing to his side both the men he led into action and the nation they represented. Montgomery was the people's—if not the club-men's—general.* It was an extraordinary and improbable achievement on the part of a lonely, difficult, introverted and widowed soldier. How, therefore, when Montgomery went to France in 1944, did he carry the nation and the army with him?

The answer is that he cared about and understood both the army and the people, and that this was abundantly evident. When he addressed the dockers or railwaymen who had to handle his infrastructure, just as when he addressed his British or American assault divisions, they tasted the tang of truth. This, they realised, was a man who could stand up and be counted. He generated confidence when to be confident was essential. This was particularly true of his military command. He had the art of communicating to the simple soldier the sense that he was a wonderful part of a wonderful army.

To do this is a form of genius rarely attained by a field commander. Montgomery could twist the Eighth Army round his little finger, and though the intimacy of the desert was dissipated in N.W. Europe, the spell remained strong. And while there are cases, of course, of staffs and subordinates staying steadily beside their Supremo—Napoleon's Marshals, Wolseley's 'ring'— there are few more exemplary instances than that of Montgomery, whose brilliant staff stuck to him like leeches and whose troops would have followed him to the end of the world. The men in the military clubs who scoffed at the popularity-mongering upstart had no conception of the true meaning of this gift: but I remember *my* men, in an obscure artillery unit of the Eighth Army, being very cross with Montgomery because he had told us that, over a

---

* An interesting phenomenon was the effect on their families of the men who at one time or another returned from the Eighth Army. They broadcast an impression among the weary and sceptical civilian population that here, at least, was a man they had served under in whose army a common soldier had a decent chance. Such effects are hard to assess: but this was something that certainly happened, that certainly spread round the country, and that must certainly have assisted Montgomery in his drive to elevate civilian morale before D-Day.

long stretch, we would be in Tripoli on a certain day. We didn't quite make it. The point was that the men were angry because they had had supreme confidence in Montgomery's prediction, and were short on the date. This is the way to win a war.

The Good Fairy at his christening brought other gifts: calm and clarity. Montgomery could carry himself away from the battle, and think. At Alamein this was notable. It was notable also in Normandy. He was never muddled. Those who served with him were impressed by the way he could always break down the issue into the essentials. Sir Miles Dempsey told me, shortly before his death, that in his command of 2 British Army in Normandy he had the constant experience of going to see Montgomery when things were apparently not as they should be: always, he said, he arrived to face a man who was not disturbed, and who could offer that estimate of the situation which comes from keeping your brain on ice. Dempsey entered into a glow of confidence, and left the presence reassured. Sir Richard O'Connor made exactly the same point to me. (Those who enjoy sniping at Montgomery might note that these were two of the most distinguished officers in the British Army, deeply versed in combat in two World Wars, over whose eyes the wool was not easily pulled.) Montgomery, in fact, was like Wellington: he could retain poise amid fluster. Slim had this gift too, and Wavell, and Alexander and Auchinleck: but there were many commanders in the last war, of a more mercurial disposition, who lacked this supreme gift of absolute self-control. Montgomery was, of course, helped by a *régime* which irritated others but certainly helped to preserve his equanimity. His habit of retiring early during a battle, and his refusal to be woken up except for the most urgent reasons, have caused much caustic comment, but out of the routine a method emerged of tranquil consideration: his idiosyncrasy undoubtedly produced more gain than loss. And while Montgomery shared with Haig the ability to keep cool in an emergency, the Commander-in-Chief in the Second World War surpassed the Commander-in-Chief of the B.E.F. in two vital respects: he was able both to invigorate his immediate subordinates and to be articulate to his troops. So in Montgomery one can observe the rare combination of an introverted ability to withdraw and ponder, and a strong extroverted capacity to communicate and inspire.

Why, then, the undoubted 'cold hush'? Another Fairy was at his christening—with poisoned gifts. Too many of his best qualities were matched by folly or misjudgement. His life has always been conducted in counterpoint . . . the best and the worst of him strode side by side. Clarity of assessment: some said 'a simple mind'. A dynamic personal relationship with the armies in the field and the Home Front: some said 'vulgar self-presentation'. A shrewd concept of modern war: yet some said 'a charlatan'. Looking back over his career, one has the sense that Montgomery was a man doomed to seek self-destruction, as if he had a death wish: a man made to be misunderstood. He has therefore had to endure both injustice and misinterpretation. These could be any general's scars. For Eisenhower the knives have long been sharpened, as for Montgomery. Yet few soldiers of Montgomery's eminence have generated so ferocious an antipathy or seen their motives and actions so grossly and maliciously distorted. People may disapprove of Eisenhower's generalship, for example, but they don't hate or despise him. In Montgomery's case feelings have sometimes become frenetic. Why?

To place him in a proper perspective is to see that he was a man who got some things absolutely right and some things disastrously wrong. This is true both of his military decisions and his personal behaviour: on both counts he laid himself open to criticism, and on both he was and is stigmatised in terms which have often been bitter, contemptuous, savage. The unfortunate fact is that in several instances such criticism, though often ill-founded, has a certain rough justice in that Montgomery's own presentation of his case was sometimes so misleading (and usually so self-complacent) that it invited an inevitable counter-attack.

Critics of his military capacity have frequently been conditioned by a distaste for his personality. But it is not impossible to seek a detached view and to ask, objectively, what were the flaws in his generalship? One is immediately visible. In three of the great theatres, Russia, North Africa and N.W. Europe, it may be remarked that apart from the great sieges and set-piece assaults a high percentage of the fighting was a war of motion. The tank was the queen of the battlefield. Against this dramatic back-cloth Montgomery's own performance has seemed, to some, to have a diminished quality. The darting Rommel, the power drives of Patton, the immense scale of the armoured manoeuvres by both Russians and Germans on the Eastern Front appear to put Montgomery in the shade. And indeed he was no great manager of armour. His use of tanks at and after Alamein, and at GOODWOOD in Normandy, can be defended but is certainly open to question; and in the advances from the two great set battles which his genius turned into victories there is a strong case for believing that he might have fostered the forward movement more effectively. When Hannibal refused to exploit from Cannae, and move on Rome, that considerable cavalry leader Maharbal said to him 'Truly the gods have not bestowed all things upon the same person. You know how to conquer, Hannibal; but you do not know how to make use of your victory.' There were times when Montgomery's entourage must have had similar thoughts—Eisenhower's entourage uttered them! And indeed any just assessment of Montgomery must recognise that—even taking into account the left hook at Mareth, Guards Armoured Division's dash to

Brussels and II Armoured Division's dash to Antwerp, and the fact that it was, after all, Montgomery's master plan which set Patton free to race from Brittany to the Seine—even taking such evidence into account, the war of motion was not his *forte*. To play a war game, to put Montgomery in charge of either side in the greatest tank action ever fought, that at Kursk, is to make the point mercilessly.

But while it is right to develop this line of criticism, there is a danger that in pushing it too far a deeper truth may be obscured. For what was Montgomery's *essential* rôle as Commander-in-Chief of the British armies in Africa and N.W. Europe? It was to achieve guaranteed success with the steadily waning manpower of a relatively small nation. Before 1914 the inarticulate Foch once had to explain to a group of young officers the drill for the advance of a division. There was a prolonged silence: and then he uttered. '*Le perroquet*', he said, '*animal subtil*': and silence returned. But the point was there. The parrot climbs its cage by gripping firmly with one claw: next the other moves upward; then the lower claw rises—and so on. This, in principle, was Montgomery's technique from Alamein to the Baltic. If, in his insistence on proceeding via a sequence of certainties, he lost opportunities through sloth in exploitation* and an habitual carefulness in the preparation of his attacks, at least he never, in any important sense, lost a battle. Moreover, when he *had* to shed blood he got results, which was certainly more than could always be said of his American critics. It is instructive to compare the two actions in N.W. Europe which most closely resemble those fought on the Western Front in '14–'18. In the battle of the Reichswald Forest, Operation VERITABLE, Montgomery's British and Canadian divisions sustained 15,500 casualties in a month—but they achieved their purpose, by clearing the west bank of the Rhine. In the Hürtgen Forest battle (Ernest Hemingway called it 'Passchendaele with tree bursts') Hodges drove his American First Army divisions in frontal attack after frontal attack, amid appalling conditions, to an ultimate sacrifice of 24,000 casualties whose wastage achieved virtually nothing. The Americans—and the Russians—could afford such 'conspicuous expenditure' of lives: but for Montgomery (and for England) a death must pay a dividend.

His refusal to squander his soldiers was a by-product both of the compassion instilled in him by the Great War, and also of the hard facts—men were in short supply. His insistence on certain success was realistic—and valuable. Surely this was the mentality necessary for the man who had to fight Alamein and Normandy—those two battles where the commander,

---

* In his Wellington Bicentenary Lecture, Montgomery said of his predecessor: 'he sometimes lost part of the fruits of victory through an inability to soar from the known to seize the unknown'. This was autobiography.

like Jellicoe in '14–'18, carried the nation's fate in the palm of his hand. In these matters the greater should include the less: and while it must be admitted that in sundry smaller engagements Montgomery was 'sticky', went in for what the Americans called 'primping', and was maddeningly deliberate in ensuring a solid administrative base, nevertheless this was not too great a price to pay for a temperament capable of triumphantly taking the strain during those crucial days in Egypt and France.

There is a much more severe censure to be laid at his door. That absolute self-certainty which gave him such assurance in the planning and conduct of his battles, and upheld his spirits in dark moments, had another side. There is little doubt that from time to time his conviction about the right course of action was subtly, or even directly, affected by his deep-seated desire for prominence. A military plan tainted by an attempt to satisfy the commander's ego is unlikely to be the best plan: an irrelevant factor has been introduced into the calculation. Yet so it was at Enfidaville: it is impossible not to feel that Montgomery's initial idea of bursting past the mountain massif and down the narrow seaward plain (which Horrocks recognised as the death-knell of the Eighth Army), was not the result of a flamboyant urge to beat First Army into Tunis, an urge which destroyed his judgement. Still more was this the case in N.W. Europe—from the Seine onwards. However correct Montgomery may have been in ventilating the military virtues of a single thrust in the north (and these may be questioned) he behaved like a man not fully in control of himself as he continued (even after he said he would stop), to argue both for the single thrust and a single ground commander (implicitly himself), long after it had become clear beyond any measure of doubt that Eisenhower was adamant. It was not an entirely self-controlled man who drove a tolerant and long-suffering chief like Eisenhower as far as that terrible day at the end of December 1944, when Eisenhower sat in his office with a signal which, had he despatched it to Washington, would have meant Montgomery's ruin. What unseated his judgement was pique. For both the 'single thrust' and the 'single ground commander' concepts there were perfectly good supporting arguments—after all, the C.I.G.S. and the British Chiefs of Staff were with Montgomery on these issues. Where Montgomery erred was in pressing his case far beyond the point of no return. His impulsion came, I am sure, from the deep sense of frustration, and deprivation, and diminution of his ego which haunted him from the moment when, after Normandy, Eisenhower exercised his right and assumed the authority of Supreme Commander. Only Montgomery can know how consciously his strategical arguments were conditioned by a desire to recover the dominating status he had enjoyed before and after D-Day—a status now taken over by a man for whose capacity he sometimes displayed what verged on contempt. There was certainly a sub-conscious drive: and it is more likely that this was the operative factor—particularly if one studies de Guingand's account of his return to Montgomery's H.Q. after his dramatic dash to prevent Eisenhower from dispatching the fatal signal. 'It was one of the few times that I saw Montgomery really worried and disturbed, for I believe he was genuinely and completely taken by surprise and found it difficult to grasp what I was saying. . . . I felt terribly sorry for my Chief, for he now looked completely nonplussed—I don't think I had ever seen him so deflated. It was as if a cloak of loneliness had descended on him.'

The truth is that, in some respects, Montgomery lived inside a cocoon, and this accounts for much of the personal animosity he aroused, animosity of which he was simply not aware and of which he was incredulous when it struck him. So sharp, so observant, so constantly on the *qui vive*, his mind was nevertheless, in part of its functioning, curiously detached from reality. There were times when Montgomery could make an ass of himself and yet, like Bottom, be blithely unaware of his metamorphosis. The famous affair of the Flying Fortress in North Africa is a case in point: it is almost inconceivable, but it is true, that even when Eisenhower's anger was evident Montgomery could not understand why the whole thing was not being treated as a huge joke. The catastrophic Ardennes press conference is another instance. Ignoring the exacerbation caused by the German broadcast of a twisted version, one still has to admit, studying Montgomery's actual text, that it could hardly have been better calculated to wound a sensitive ally justly proud, at that moment, of a great feat of arms. Yet it is most questionable whether Montgomery had the remotest notion of the appalling consequences which must predictably follow when he had stopped blowing his own trumpet.

This self-absorption damaged him in two other respects. First, though he was supreme at communicating his aims to his subordinate officers and the soldiers of his armies, he was clumsy in conveying sideways and upwards, to his equals and seniors, the pith of his purpose. The master-simplifier,* he would reduce a military problem to its essentials, formulate the relevant plan, and that was that. Anyone else in high authority, he tended to assume, ought to spot the answer as easily as he did: it was *obvious*. Thus both Eisenhower and his staff, and even the C.I.G.S. and the Chiefs of Staff, were at times misled about his intentions and reasonably perturbed when

---

* The gift of simplification also, of course, paid huge dividends. He always told his troops exactly what they were going to do, in short lucid messages which they could comprehend. They knew where they were going. In his television lectures on 'Civilisation' Lord Clark observed: 'Mahomet, the prophet of Islam, preached the simplest doctrine that has ever gained acceptance; and it gave to his followers the invincible solidarity that had once directed the Roman legions. In a miraculously short time—about 50 years—the Classical world was over-run.' 'Invincible solidarity' is a good description of Eighth Army's ethos.

what they thought was going to happen failed to occur. The anxieties over Montgomery's re-grouping at Alamein are a shining example: it never struck him that news of divisions being withdrawn from the line might cause alarm and despondency. And all the complicated confusion and ill-feeling which followed the GOODWOOD operation in Normandy would have been considerably reduced if Montgomery had only been at pains to let his masters know, without any possibility of misunderstanding, exactly what was in his mind. This obscurantism was a weakness.

Secondly, his introversion gravely affected his personal relationships—not always, indeed, for with the chosen few he could be the most delightful and considerate of companions, and, on a larger plane, he was brilliant at establishing a rapport with soldiers and civilians *en masse*. But he had a dismissive temperament: if he decided a man was no good he was out, out into outer darkness. On such occasions Montgomery could be brutal. Few will forgive him his treatment of Ramsden in August 1942. And this intermittent failure in empathy, in sympathy, and in humanity had consequences of an incalculable magnitude when the time came for Montgomery to work alongside the Americans.

It is *just* possible that had, say, Alexander been in command of Eighth Army when it linked up with First Army a common understanding could have been struck between the British and Americans which might have provided a platform of mutual confidence from which to launch future operations: but that is a pipe dream. What is certain is that the possibility of erecting such a platform never arose. Montgomery's arrogant disdain and his mistaken glorification of *his* Army saw to that, and his attitude towards the Americans in Sicily widened the gulf. Bradley and Patton never forgot: and in N.W. Europe they took a sweet revenge. This was lunacy. I said earlier that Montgomery had the gift of thinking big: but the way he dealt with his American comrades-in-arms was so often small-minded. In the spring of 1943 the war still had far to run. There would be many more battles, and obviously the Americans would become increasingly the predominant partners. A simple calculation would have shown that mere enlightened self-interest required a well-oiled alliance. But Montgomery preferred to play the part of a saboteur. The result was that even though, in Normandy, he handled the Americans with exceptional tact and even though Bradley fully recognised this, nothing could prevent the old wounds opening. By the time the Allies reached Germany a chasm yawned, and even Eisenhower, who had patiently built so many bridges in the past, had now been driven into a state of uncontrollable rage.

This Cromwellian figure, as Churchill called him, was certainly not without warts! And yet, in a final analysis, the plea of those generals I talked to must be granted: he *is* our finest commander since Wellington. For who are the rivals? In the nineteenth century, nobody. In the First World War, Haig? Certainly nobody else. But in spite of the stature Haig attained in 1918, his generalship is marred by too much that is indefensible for him to be considered a competitor. We are reduced to Montgomery's contemporaries, of whom only three can be reasonably held to be in the same class, Wavell, Alexander and Slim.

Wavell did what Montgomery never could have done. His mastery with shoe-string forces of the vast area for which he was responsible from 1939 to 1941 was a model of well-calculated extemporisation which none of his fellow-generals could have equalled—certainly not Montgomery. Nor, under Montgomery, would O'Connor have been allowed to achieve his classic victory at Beda Fomm. In his A.B.D.A. command, again, hopeless though it was, Wavell acquitted himself in a style far beyond Montgomery's reach. All this is true. But what is also true is that these were tasks suited to Wavell. To put it bluntly, his aptitudes were for the 'colonial' war—on however large a scale. It is to be doubted whether he had the requisite ability or insight to master-mind those huge technological conflicts which total war entailed: in short, Wavell and D-Day do not look convincing companions. (I believe this to be so in full knowledge that Wavell was one of that small group of forward-looking officers who, in the 'thirties, were trying to modernise an antediluvian army.) Nor, indeed, can one be quite sure about his skill as a battle-commander as compared with his pre-eminent capacity as a Supremo. His record in the desert in the spring and summer of 1941 displays a disconcerting unsureness of touch. I do not think that Wavell stands in the lists.

Nor Alexander: and I suspect that he would be the first to agree. With a record of extreme gallantry and an ineffable grace of manner, cool, considerate and open-minded, he was superbly cast as the man to tidy up the mess in Tunisia and, holding the ring in Italy, to achieve final victory there with ever-diminishing forces. The successful plans for DIADEM (the breakthrough at Cassino leading to the fall of Rome), and the last great battle of encirclement on the Po were both characterised by elegance, imagination and ingenuity . . . but how much did his Chief of Staff, John Harding, contribute? Alexander was unquestionably outstanding. But I do not believe that he could have shaped the invasion plan, prepared the armies, and fought the bridgehead battle of Normandy with anything like the all-round competence and imaginative foresight displayed by Montgomery. (Nor, for that matter, do I believe that, admirable long-stop though he was, he could have gone up into the field at Alamein and beaten Rommel in battle.) Alexander is wreathed in laurels: let that suffice.

T

Of Slim it may be said that he was a supreme example of the right man in the right place, and that he led XIV Army to victory in a manner far beyond Montgomery's grasp. This was, in part, because his training and his inclinations ideally fitted him to his task. But in spite of his marvellous triumph over administrative impossibilities, his strategical ingenuity, his hold over his multi-racial army, and his maintenance of the objective in spite of an appalling terrain and an indomitable enemy, one wonders whether he would have been so successful in what for him was essentially alien territory, the main theatre of war, Europe. We can but speculate. Had Montgomery's career ended in Africa I would certainly have placed Slim, on his XIV Army record, above Montgomery. But magnificent though the reconquest of Burma may have been, the liberation of Europe made larger demands on the supreme military directorate. Slim's limitation was in experience and scale—not that this was the fault of a great man and a remarkable soldier. But that was how the dice fell. He never had the chance to learn how to orchestrate hundreds of guns. He had no opportunity to command tanks in their thousands. Able though he was at integrating air and army, he had never to come to terms with the vast air-fleets available in the west. Undoubtedly he would have been *persona grata* with the Americans—a man who could manage Stilwell could manage Bradley—but it is as difficult to imagine Slim as it is to imagine Wavell in charge on 6 June 1944. Yet this, surely, was the acid test of British generalship in the Second World War. Montgomery was exposed to the test and passed it: and it is this which to my mind establishes him, warts and all, as Wellington's true successor.

Manfred Rommel once told me that the one certainty to which his father adhered in planning was that the unexpected would certainly happen tomorrow. There was a large allowance for contingency in Rommel's thinking. Montgomery's method was precisely the opposite. Every possibility, every conceivable variant was so carefully analysed in advance that when the time came to draw up a final plan the unexpected and the contingent had usually been catered for. This was one of Montgomery's outstanding achievements—to restore to the British Army that respect for meticulous preparation which reached a high degree of *expertise* in the First World War but subsequently lapsed. One has only to compare the plan for CRUSADER with the plan for Alamein to mark the change in quality. CRUSADER was, by contrast, an amateur concept. Alamein was professional. Can one, for example, imagine Montgomery (as happened in CRUSADER) sending his armour out into the blue and leaving it there, halted, *to see what would happen?*

Careful planning—which involved the rigorous exercise of foresight—was one aspect of Montgomery's basic principle for waging war . . . the doctrine of 'balance'. One must never be caught on the wrong foot: never run short of reserves: never let one's freedom to fight and manoeuvre be hampered by lack of supplies. The trick, always, was to force one's opponent off balance while retaining, oneself, a perfect poise. This doctrine was preached by Montgomery so long and so loudly that it occasioned a good deal of ridicule: and yet . . . what a number of his subordinates, from generals to battalion commanders, have registered the sense they felt of comfortable security under Montgomery's command. In his armies men rarely looked over their shoulders: they confidently faced to the front. Only a great commander can have a comprehensive theory of warfare which, when put into practice, is so demonstrably and regularly successful that his soldiers habitually share his sense of certainty. This was Montgomery's achievement.

Too much is often made of the fact that he emerged as an operational commander just when the flow of troops and equipment was dramatically increasing, as the American arsenals began to pour out their wares. Of course this is true. But, in a relative way, earlier British commanders in the desert had been supplied with strong reinforcements of men and metal and had simply squandered them. The point about Montgomery is that he knew how to use what he got. I place him as the first British general in the Second World War to be mentally and technically equipped to tackle the *Materialenschlacht* which, increasingly and rapidly from the autumn of 1942 onwards, was the form that fighting took in the western world. His ability to organise and control (and understand) the immense variety of equipment produced for the forces was impeccably demonstrated on D-Day and, in a triumphant final fling, at the crossing of the Rhine. He was a modern general, completely at home amid the complexities of a technological age.

During the last century and a half, in fact, there has been no one in the British Army to surpass him for sheer professionalism or sustained success in the field: and that is why, in spite of all his weaknesses and limitations, he has every claim to be accepted, without cavil, as Wellington's heir.

Appendix

After the surrender of the Germans many strange things happened and many an odd fox ran for cover. This classic example was supplied to me by my friend Harold Harris, whose Intelligence Unit went swiftly into Hamburg:

'The story of Ribbentrop's arrest was as follows. He had arrived in Hamburg a few days before the town gave in. On arrival, he called on an old acquaintance from his days in the wine trade, and asked him to put him up. The wine merchant was too frightened to do so, but told Ribbentrop where he might find a room. And he promised not to betray him. In fact Ribbentrop was betrayed in the end by the wine merchant's son and the son's mistress. The two had a bitter row about something, which ended in the woman stamping out, late at night, saying that she was going to the British Town Major next morning to denounce the wine merchant and his son who knew where Ribbentrop was. It was well known that Ribbentrop was one of the war criminals for whom there was a hue and cry. Positive that she would carry out her threat, the son went to his father and begged him to reveal the address, so that he could get in first. Otherwise both would be in trouble.

'The father gave in, the son made inquiries about the right people to tell, and late that night turned up at the Area Security Office (the Gauhaus) with his story. Lieutenant Adams was the duty officer and, accompanied by a couple of N.C.O.s from his section, arrested Ribbentrop while he was still in bed.

'Ribbentrop claimed that he had originally come to Hamburg in furtherance of a mission, entrusted to him by the Führer, to work for a rapprochement with the British. He had been so appalled by the British hatred for the Germans revealed in the first days of the occupation (a hatred which, he insisted, was not reciprocated) that he had decided to lie low until the bad feeling died down. Then he would emerge and carry out the Führer's mission. It was not a likely tale and nobody paid much attention to it. On his arrest, he handed over a sealed letter to Jimmy Adams for the Prime Minister, and a curious covering open letter addressed to Field Marshal Montgommery [*sic*] in which he not only mis-spelt this name and Eden's, but even displayed ignorance of Churchill's Christian name—a remarkable feat for the German Foreign Minister.'

Bibliography

Agar-Hamilton, J. A. L., and Turner, L. C. F. *Crisis in the Desert, May–July 1942*, O.U.P., 1952.
Alexander, Field Marshal the Earl. *The Alexander Memoirs, 1940–1945*, Cassell, 1962.
Barnett, Corelli, *The Desert Generals*, Kimber, 1960.
Belfield, E., and Essame, H. *The Battle for Normandy*, Batsford, 1965.
Blumenson, Martin. *Kasserine Pass*, Houghton Mifflin, 1967.
Blumentritt, Maj.-Gen. Günther. *Von Rundstedt*, Odhams Press, 1952.
Bradley, General Omar N. *A Soldier's Story*, Eyre and Spottiswoode, 1951.
Bryant, Sir Arthur. *The Turn of the Tide*, Vols. I and II, Collins, 1957 and 1959.
Bullock, Alan. *Hitler*, Odhams Press, 1952.
Caccia-Dominioni, Paolo. *Alamein, 1933–1962*, Allen and Unwin, 1966.
Carver, Lieut.-Gen. Michael. *Tobruk*, Batsford, 1964.
Carver, Lieut.-Gen. Michael. *El Alamein*, Batsford, 1962.
Chaplin, Lieut.-Col. *The Queen's Own Royal West Kent Regiment*, Michael Joseph, 1954.
Chapman, Professor Guy. *Why France Collapsed*, Cassell, 1968.
Churchill, Winston. *The Second World War, passim*, Cassell.
Ciano, Count. *Diary, 1939–1943*, Heinemann, 1946.
Clarke, Brig. Dudley. *The Eleventh at War*, Michael Joseph, 1952.
Clifton, Brig. George. *The Happy Hunted*, Cassell, 1952.
Connell, John. *Auchinleck*, Cassell, 1959.
Connell, John. *Wavell*, Collins, 1964.
Cunningham, Admiral Lord. *A Sailor's Odyssey*, Hutchinson, 1951.
De Guingand, Maj.-Gen. Sir Francis. *Operation Victory* and *Generals at War*, Hodder and Stoughton.
Divine, David. *The Blunted Sword*, Hutchinson, 1964.
Douglas, Keith. *Alamein to Zem Zem*, Faber, 1946.
Douglas of Kirtleside, Marshal of the R.A.F. Lord. *Years of Command*, Collins, 1966.
Eisenhower, Gen. Dwight D. *Crusade in Europe*, Heinemann, 1949.
Eisenhower, Gen. Dwight D. *The Papers of Dwight Eisenhower: The War Years*, Johns Hopkins Press, 1970.
Eisenhower, John S. D. *The Bitter Woods*, Putman, 1969.
Elstob, Peter. *Hitler's Last Offensive*, Secker and Warburg, 1971.
Essame, Major-Gen. H. *The Battle for Germany*, Batsford, 1969.

Fergusson, Brig. Sir Bernard. *The Black Watch and the King's Enemies*, Collins, 1950.
Fergusson, Brig. Sir Bernard. *The Watery Maze*, Collins, 1961.
Fuller, Maj.-Gen. *The Decisive Battles of the World*, Vol. 3, Eyre and Spottiswoode, 1956.
Gale, Gen. Sir Richard. *With the 6th Airborne Division in Normandy*, Sampson Low, 1948.
Gale, Gen. Sir Richard. *Call to Arms*, Hutchinson, 1968.
Görlitz, Walter. *The German General Staff*, Hollis and Carter, 1953.
Guderian, Gen. Heinz. *Panzer Leader*, Michael Joseph, 1952.
Hibbert, Christopher. *The Battle of Arnhem*, Batsford, 1962.
Hibbert, Christopher. *Benito Mussolini*, Longmans, 1963.
Hitler, Adolf. *Hitler's Table Talk*, Weidenfeld and Nicolson, 1953.
Horne, Alistair. *To Lose a Battle*, Macmillan, 1969.
Horrocks, Lieut.-Gen. Sir Brian. *A Full Life*, Collins, 1960.
Howard, Michael. *The Mediterranean Strategy in the Second World War*, Weidenfeld and Nicolson, 1968.
Jacobson, H. A., and Rohwer, J. *Decisive Battles of World War II*, André Deutsch, 1965.
Jackson, Maj.-Gen. W. G. F. *The Battle For Italy*, Batsford, 1967.
Joly, Cyril. *Take These Men*, Constable, 1955.
Kahn, David. *The Codebreakers*, Weidenfeld and Nicolson, 1966.
Kennedy, Maj.-Gen. Sir John. *The Business of War*, Hutchinson, 1957.
Kennedy Shaw, W. B. *Long Range Desert Group*, Collins, 1945.
Kesselring, Field Marshal. *Memoirs*, Kimber, 1963.
Kippenberger, Maj.-Gen. *Infantry Brigadier*, O.U.P., 1949.
Lewin, Ronald. *Rommel as Military Commander*, Batsford, 1968.
Liddell Hart, Capt. Sir Basil. Many books, but in particular *The Tanks*, 2 vols., Cassell, 1959; *Memoirs*, 2 vols., Cassell, 1965; *History of the Second World War*, Cassel, 1970.
Lindsay, Lieut.-Col. Martin. *So Few Got Through*, Collins, 1946.
Macdonald, Charles B. *The Mighty Endeavour : American Armed Forces in the European Theater in World War II*, O.U.P., 1969.
Macintyre, Donald. *The Battle for the Mediterranean*, Batsford, 1964.
Macksey, Maj. Kenneth. *Crucible of Power*, Hutchinson, 1969.
Macksey, Maj. Kenneth. *The Shadow of Vimy Ridge*, Kimber, 1965.
Macksey, Maj. Kenneth. *Armoured Crusader*, Hutchinson, 1967.
Majdalany, Fred. *The Battle of El Alamein*, Weidenfeld and Nicolson, 1965.
Majdalany, Fred. *The Fall of Fortress Europe*, Hodder and Stoughton, 1969.
Martel, Lieut-Gen. Sir Giffard. *An Outspoken Soldier*, Sifton Praed, 1949.
Mellenthin, Maj.-Gen. von. *Panzer Battles*, 1939–1945, Cassell, 1955.
Montgomery, Field Marshal the Viscount of Alamein. *Memoirs*, Collins, 1958.
Montgomery, Field Marshal the Viscount of Alamein. *Normandy to the Baltic* (1946), and *El Alamein to the River Sangro* (1948), Hutchinson.
Montgomery, Field Marshal the Viscount of Alamein. *The Path to Leadership*, Collins, 1961.

Montgomery, Field Marshal the Viscount of Alamein. *A History of Warfare*, Collins, 1968.

Montgomery, Field Marshal the Viscount of Alamein. *Alamein and the Desert War*, Sphere Books and the Sunday Times, 1967 (Contributor).

Moorehead, Alan. *Mediterranean Front; A Year of Battle; The End in Africa; Eclipse;* and *Montgomery*, Hamish Hamilton.

Mordal, Jacques. *Dieppe, The Dawn of Decision*, Souvenir Press, 1963.

Morgan, Lieut.-Gen. Sir Frederick. *Overture to Overlord* (1950), and *Peace and War* (1961), Hodder and Stoughton.

Namier, Sir Lewis. *In the Nazi Era*, Macmillan, 1952.

Nobécourt, Jacques. *Hitler's Last Gamble*, Chatto and Windus, 1967.

Official Histories. I refer *passim* to the relevant volumes in the Military Series of the *United Kingdom History of the Second World War* (H.M.S.O.). Professor Postan's account of the development of weapons and M. R. D. Foot's history of *S.O.E. in France* have been instructive, as have, especially, Capt. Roskill's volumes on the war at sea.

Patton, General George S. *War as I Saw It*, W. H. Allen, 1950.

Peniakoff, Lieut.-Col. Vladimir. *Private Army*, Cape, 1950.

Phillips, Brig. C. E. Lucas. *Alamein*, Heinemann, 1962.

Rommel, Erwin. *The Rommel Papers* (ed. B. H. Liddell Hart), Collins, 1953.

Ryan, Cornelius. *The Last Battle*, Collins, 1966.

Ryan, Cornelius. *The Longest Day*, Gollancz, 1960.

Schmidt, Heinz Werner. *With Rommel in the Desert*, Harrap, 1951.

Shepperd, Col. G. A. *The Italian Campaign 1943–45*, Arthur Barker, 1968.

Slessor, Marshal of the R.A.F. Sir John. *The Central Blue*, Cassell, 1956.

Smyth, Brig. The Right Hon. Sir John. *Bolo Whistler*, Müller, 1967.

Stevens, W. G. *New Zealand in The Second World War : Bardia to Enfidaville*, N.Z. War History Branch, 1962.

Strawson, John. *The Battle for North Africa*, Batsford, 1969.

Sweet-Escott, Bickham. *Baker Street Irregular*, Methuen, 1965.

Tedder, Marshal of the R.A.F. Lord, *With Prejudice*, Cassell, 1966.

Thompson, R. W. *The Montgomery Legend* (1967) and *Montgomery The Field Marshal* (1969), Allen and Unwin.

Tugwell, Lieut.-Col. M. A. J. *Arnhem: The Ten Germs of Failure*, Royal United Service Institution Journal, December 1969.

Tuker, Lieut.-Gen. Sir Francis. *Approach to Battle*, Cassell, 1963.

Verney, Maj.-Gen. *The Desert Rats*, Hutchinson, 1954.

Wavell, Field Marshal the Earl. *Generals and Generalship*, The Times Publishing Company, 1941.

Westphal, Gen. Siegfried. *The German Army in the West*, Cassell, 1951.

Wheeler-Bennett, Sir John. *The Nemesis of Power*, Macmillan, 1953.

Wilmot, Chester. *The Struggle for Europe*, Collins, 1952.

Young, Brig. Desmond. *Rommel*, Collins, 1950.

Index